Development of Achievement Motivation

This is a volume in the Academic Press
EDUCATIONAL PSYCHOLOGY SERIES

Critical comprehensive reviews of research knowledge, theories, principles, and practices

Under the editorship of Gary D. Phye

Development of Achievement Motivation

EDITED BY

Allan Wigfield
Department of Human Development
University of Maryland

Jacquelynne S. Eccles
Department of Psychology
and
Institute for Research on Women and Gender
University of Michigan

ACADEMIC PRESS
An Elsevier Science Imprint

San Diego   San Francisco   New York   Boston   London   Sydney   Tokyo

The sponsoring editor for this book was Nikki Levy, the editorial coordinator was Barbara Makinster, the production manager was Paul Gottehrer, and the manufacturing manager was Molly Wofford. The cover was designed by Cathy Reynolds. Composition was done by Electronic Publishing Services, Inc., New York, and the book was printed and bound by Edward Brothers, Ann Arbor, Michigan.

Cover photo credit: © 2001 PhotoDisk

This book is printed on acid-free paper. ∞

Academic Press
An Elsevier Science Imprint
525 B Street, Suite 1900, San Diego, California 92101-4495, USA
http://www.academicpress.com

Academic Press
32 Jamestown Road, London NW1 7BY, UK
http://www.academicpress.com

Library of Congress Catalog Card Number: 2001092780

International Standard Book Number: 0-12-750053-7

PRINTED IN THE UNITED STATES OF AMERICA
01   02   03   04   05   06   EB   9   8   7   6   5   4   3   2   1

Contents

Can I Do This Activity?

2. THE DEVELOPMENTAL COURSE OF ACHIEVEMENT
MOTIVATION: A NEED-BASED APPROACH
Martin V. Covington and Elizabeth Dray

3. THE DEVELOPMENT OF ABILITY CONCEPTIONS
Carol S. Dweck

2

Do I Want to Do this Activity, and Why?

4. THE DEVELOPMENT OF COMPETENCE BELIEFS, EXPECTANCIES FOR SUCCESS, AND ACHIEVEMENT VALUES FROM CHILDHOOD THROUGH ADOLESCENCE
Allan Wigfield and Jacquelynne S. Eccles

5. ETHNICITY, GENDER, AND THE DEVELOPMENT OF ACHIEVEMENT VALUES

Sandra Graham and April Z. Taylor

6. THE DEVELOPMENT OF SELF-DETERMINATION IN MIDDLE CHILDHOOD AND ADOLESCENCE

Wendy S. Grolnick, Suzanne T. Gurland, Karen F. Jacob, and Wendy Decourcey

7. STUDENT INTEREST AND ACHIEVEMENT: DEVELOPMENTAL ISSUES RAISED BY A CASE STUDY

K. Ann Renninger and Suzanne Hidi

8. THE DEVELOPMENT OF GOAL ORIENTATION

Eric M. Anderman, Chammie C. Austin, and Dawn M. Johnson

9. THE CONTRIBUTION OF SOCIAL GOAL SETTING TO CHILDREN'S SCHOOL ADJUSTMENT
Kathryn R. Wentzel

$$\boxed{3}$$

What Do I Need to Do to Succeed?

10. THE DEVELOPMENT OF ACADEMIC SELF-REGULATION: THE ROLE OF COGNITIVE AND MOTIVATIONAL FACTORS
Paul R. Pintrich and Akane Zusho

11. WHAT DO I NEED TO DO TO SUCCEED . . .WHEN I DON'T UNDERSTAND WHAT I'M DOING!?: DEVELOPMENTAL INFLUENCES ON STUDENTS' ADAPTIVE HELP SEEKING
Richard S. Newman

$$\boxed{4}$$

Motivation and Instruction

12. GOOD INSTRUCTION IS MOTIVATING
Deborah Stipek

13. INSTRUCTIONAL PRACTICES AND MOTIVATION DURING MIDDLE SCHOOL (WITH SPECIAL ATTENTION TO SCIENCE)

Douglas J. Mac Iver, Estelle M. Young, and Benjamin Washburn

Contributors

Numbers in parentheses indicate the pages on which the authors' contribution begin.

Eric M. Anderman (197), Educational and Counseling Psychology, University of Kentucky, Lexington, Kentucky 40506-0017

Chammie C. Austin (197), Educational and Counseling Psychology, University of Kentucky, Lexington, Kentucky 40506-0017

Martin V. Covington (33), Department of Psychology, University of California, Berkeley, Berkeley, California 94720

Wendy Decourcey (147), Department of Psychology, Clark University, Worcester, Massachusetts 01610-1477

Elizabeth Dray (33), Department of Psychology, University of California, Berkeley, Berkeley, California 94720

Carol S. Dweck (57), Department of Psychology, Columbia University, New York, New York 10027

Jacquelynne S. Eccles (1, 91), Department of Psychology and Institute for Research on Women and Gender, University of Michigan, Ann Arbor, Michigan 48106

Sandra Graham (121), Department of Education, University of California, Los Angeles, Los Angeles, California 90095-1521

Wendy S. Grolnick (147), Department of Psychology, Clark University, Worcester, Massachusetts 01610-1477

Suzanne T. Gurland (147), Department of Psychology, Clark University, Worcester, Massachusetts 01610-1477

Suzanne Hidi (173), Ontario Institute for Studies in Education of the University of Toronto, Toronto M5S1V6, Canada

Karen F. Jacob (147), Department of Psychology, Clark University, Worcester, Massachusetts 01610-1477

Dawn M. Johnson (197), Educational and Counseling Psychology, University of Kentucky, Lexington, Kentucky 40506-0017

Douglas J. Mac Iver (333), CRESPAR, Johns Hopkins University, Baltimore, Maryland 21218-3888

Richard S. Newman (285), School of Education, University of California, Riverside, Riverside, California 95251-0128

Frank Pajares (15), Educational Studies Department, Emery University, Atlanta, Georgia 30322

Paul R. Pintrich (249), Combined Program in Education and Psychology, University of Michigan, Ann Arbor, Michigan 48109

K. Ann Renninger (173), Program in Education, Swarthmore College, Swarthmore, Pennsylvania 19081-1397

Dale H. Schunk (15), College of Education, University of North Carolina, Greensboro, Greensboro, North Carolina 27402

Deborah Stipek (309), School of Education, Stanford University, Stanford, California 94305-3096

April Z. Taylor (121), Department of Education, University of California, Los Angeles, Los Angeles, California 90095-1521

Benjamin Washburn (333), CRESPAR, Johns Hopkins University, Baltimore, Maryland 21218-3888

Kathryn R. Wentzel (221), Department of Human Development, University of Maryland, College Park, Maryland 20742

Allan Wigfield (1, 91), Department of Human Development, University of Maryland, College Park, Maryland 20742

Estelle M. Young (333), CRESPAR, Johns Hopkins University, Baltimore, Maryland 21218-3888

Akane Zusho (249), Combined Program in Education and Psychology, University of Michigan, Ann Arbor, Michigan 48109

Preface

Researchers who study achievement motivation are interested in why individuals engage in the variety of achievement-related behaviors they do. These researchers attempt to answer questions such as: Why do some children persist even when faced with very challenging tasks or activities? Why do other children give up quickly on such tasks, despite having the ability to do the task? How do children make choices about which activities to pursue? What kinds of goals do children have for their academic performance? How do different instructional practices influence children's motivation to engage in different academic tasks? How children's motivation change as they go through school?

Over the past 30 years researchers have done a great deal of important work that provides answers to these questions. These researchers have developed theoretical models of children's achievement motivation, and defined and assessed crucial constructs contained in those models. They have examined how children's motivation develops, and also how it relates to children's performance in school and choice of which activities to pursue. Other researchers have examined how various instructional practices influence children's motivation, and how such influences change (in both positive and negative ways) as children go through school. As contributors to this work, as well as consumers of it, we perceived a need for a book that would provide a comprehensive overview of current work on the development of motivation and how instructional practices influence children's motivation. Although there are a number of important edited volumes on motivation in the literature, no recent volume presents a comprehensive overview both of the development of achievement motivation and how it is influenced by school experiences. To fill this gap we invited prominent scholars to write chapters in which they described the development of the particular aspects of motivation they study in their own work. We invited other scholars to author chapters on how instructional practices influence motivation.

Why this focus on development and instruction? It is clear from our own work and that of many others that motivation changes in important ways during childhood and adolescence (see the introductory chapter for more details on the nature of these changes), and we wanted to capture these changes in a comprehensive way. Further, these changes occur due to changes within the child, as well as changes in the instructional environments they encounter. Thus, to understand the development of motivation a focus on the educational experiences children have is crucial.

The book has several other purposes. One is to provide an overview of current theoretical models of children's achievement motivation. We wanted the volume to provide an eclectic view of the field, rather than in-depth coverage of just one or two models. We accomplished this purpose by inviting authors from different theoretical perspectives to contribute to this volume. Although we were not able to include every theoretical perspective, most of the currently prominent theoretical models are represented in the volume.

Another purpose is to help provide definitional clarity to the field. As discussed in more detail in the introductory chapter, in the motivation field there are a number of different terms used to describe seemingly similar constructs. This is particularly true with respect to terms having to do with children's perceptions of ability and efficacy, and children's goal orientations. By having authors clearly define the construct they study along with reviewing the research they and others have done on the construct, we hope to arrive at better definitional clarity for the field. Some of the authors in this volume compared the construct they discussed to related constructs, which provided further definitional clarity. We think having clear definitions of different terms is crucial in order for the field to move ahead.

Yet another purpose is to present work on gender and ethnic differences in motivation. As our country becomes more diverse it is crucial to understand how factors such as gender and ethnicity influence children's motivation, and whether the theoretical models we have developed work well for different groups. That is, are these models general, or do they apply only to specific groups? Our approach to this issue was to have all authors write about this issue rather than having separate chapters on these topics. This approach means that these issues are integrated across the book, rather than being relegated to separate chapters. Some authors provide more detail on these topics than do others, but all did deal with these issues.

The book is organized into four sections. The first three sections present work coming from different theoretical perspectives on the development of motivation, and we organized the sections based on the particular focus of the theoretical perspectives represented in each section. The first section focuses primarily on theories and constructs having to do with children's competence-related beliefs and their development. Such constructs have received a great deal of attention in motivation research for the last several decades.

We include in this section chapters on self-efficacy, self-worth, and conceptions of ability.

The second section includes chapters which focus on theoretical models having to do with the reasons or purposes children have for doing achievement activities. These topics have been a strong focus of motivation researchers over the last several years. Included in this section are chapters on achievement values, self-determination, interest, goal orientation, and social goals and their relations to motivation.

The third section includes chapters that link motivation and behavior. This link is crucial because motivation alone is not enough to promote achievement; children must translate their motivation into effective action. The chapters in this section discuss motivation and self-regulation, and academic help seeking.

The final section of the book concerns instructional influences on motivation. As noted earlier, the kinds of instructional practices children and adolescents experience strongly influence their motivation, and so it is crucial to structure instructional practices so that they facilitate children's motivation. There are two chapters in this section, one on instructional practices during the preschool and elementary grades and their influence on motivation, and one focusing on instructional practices at middle school.

This book is aimed primarily at graduate students in the fields of developmental and educational psychology. The literatures in these fields have been somewhat distinct, as researchers in each field often publish in different journals and attend different conferences. Thus, students in each discipline likely receive different emphases as they learn about motivation. We invited authors from both fields to contribute to the volume in order to bridge the two fields. Along with graduate students, advanced undergraduate students interested in motivation should be interested in this volume. Faculty members as well as researchers outside the universities who study motivation should be interested in this volume, both for the overview of current theories that it provides and the many suggestions for future research that the authors give. Our strongest hope is that the volume helps provide the basis for the next generation of research on the development of motivation.

Allan Wigfield
University of Maryland

Jacquelynne S. Eccles
University of Michigan

Introduction

ALLAN WIGFIELD

University of Maryland, College Park, Maryland

JACQUELYNNE S. ECCLES

University of Michigan, Ann Arbor, Michigan

DEFINING MOTIVATION AND ITS DEVELOPMENT

Research on motivation, and achievement motivation in particular, has burgeoned over the last 30 years in both the educational psychology and developmental psychology literatures. Achievement motivation refers to motivation in situations in which individuals' competence is at issue (Nicholls, 1984). Achievement motivation theorists attempt to explain people's choice of achievement tasks, persistence on those tasks, vigor in carrying them out, and quality of task engagement (Eccles, Wigfield, & Schiefele, 1998). The kinds of motivational constructs and processes that theorists use to explain behaviors such as persistence, vigor, quality, and performance are quite different now than they were in earlier models of motivation. Currently, theorists who have proposed models of achievement motivation posit that individuals' achievement-related beliefs, values, and goals are among the most important determinants of these outcomes. These theoretical models stand in stark contrast to earlier motivational models that emphasized constructs such as drives, or processes such as reinforcement (see Weiner, 1990). Over the last 30 years we have learned much about these motivational beliefs, values, and goals and how they develop. Our major purpose in editing this book was to provide prominent motivation researchers from different theoretical perspectives the opportunity to present a current review of their own work and that of others on the development of motivational beliefs, values, and goals.

The word "development" is in the title of the book because of our abiding interest in how children's motivation changes across the school years. An important question to answer at the outset is what exactly do we mean by development? There are a number of important ways in which children's motivation changes as children go through their school years (see Wigfield, 1994). One fundamental way is that children's understanding of crucial motivational constructs (such as their concept of ability) changes as they mature (see Nicholls, 1978; 1990). Thus children of different ages are likely to have quite different understandings of motivation. Most of the relevant work has focused on children's views of ability and intelligence. This work has shown that children's conceptions of ability change in interesting ways as they go through childhood. For instance, younger children often see ability and effort as covarying positively; in contrast many older children see ability and effort as inversely related (Nicholls, 1990). Such differences have important implications for children's achievement behaviors.

Second, children's motivation becomes more differentiated and complex throughout the childhood years. This differentiation begins surprisingly early (see Eccles, Wigfield, Harold, & Blumenfeld, 1993; Harter, 1998; Marsh, Craven, & Debus, 1998). Many children begin school with a global sense of their competence and a general interest in learning about different things (Harter, 1983). Even as early as first grade, however, children begin to develop a differentiated set of beliefs, values, and goals about the specific activities they encounter. Thus a child may feel very confident about math and have a deep interest in doing it, but a weaker sense of competence for reading and less interest in it. This differentiation is likely to have important implications for children's achievement behavior, especially their choices regarding which to pursue and their responses to negative performance feedback.

Although this pattern of global to differentiated beliefs, values, and goals has been posited to characterize the development of children's motivation, some theorists take a somewhat different view. In the self-efficacy literature Bandura (1997) argued that children's self-efficacy initially is task-specific, and gradually becomes more generalized. Hidi and Harackiewicz (2000) discussed how children's interests often are quite situation specific and become generalized into deeper personal interests (see also Renninger & Hidi, Chapter 7, this volume). Thus these theorists argue that the development of these aspects of motivation go from specific to general. Taking these views together, perhaps very early on children's motivation is quite general and soon becomes differentiated to different areas. Within these areas, children's specific experiences could lead to a specific sense of efficacy and interest in specific activities (or lack of efficacy and interest). As children accumulate more experiences their specific sense of efficacy and interest can generalize, at least within specific areas. Thus the pattern of change in motivation may be more complex than once thought.

Third, the levels of children's motivation changes as they mature. Much has been written about how young children are optimistic about their abilities and thus are positively motivated for school learning (Eccles *et al.*, 1998; Stipek & Mac Iver, 1989). Over the school years many children's academic motivation decreases due to changes both in themselves and in the school environments they experience. For some children this change is not necessarily problematic. For others, however, such changes lead them to withdraw from achievement situations and avoid them whenever possible. Further, researchers recently have shown that even some preschool-age children are already at risk for developing negative motivational beliefs and goals (Dweck, 1998).

Fourth, children's beliefs, values, and goals relate more closely to their performance and choice as they get older. Thus motivation and behavior become more closely linked. Although researchers continue to study the exact nature of this relation, many researchers think that it becomes reciprocal over time with motivation influencing achievement and vice versa (Bandura, 1997; Eccles *et al.*, 1998; Marsh & Yeung, 1997; Wigfield, 1994). The question of "which causes which" thus has been replaced by a more nuanced view, emphasizing the mutual influences of motivation and achievement behaviors on each other.

Each of these kinds of changes occur due to changes in individual children, as well as changes in the educational contexts children experience (Eccles & Midgley, 1989; Wigfield, Eccles, & Rodriguez, 1998; Stipek, 1996). As they get older, children become better at understanding and using the evaluative information they receive. A personal example illustrates this developmental change. The first author and his family were out for dinner when his son Dennis, who was in first grade, brought his first report card home. One of Dennis' friends asked him how his report card was. After hearing Dennis' answer, the boy proudly told Dennis he had received "All Ss and N/As." N/A of course stands for not applicable! By the second reporting period N/As probably were no longer a source of pride for this boy, as he learned to distinguish between the self-relevant and self-irrelevant information on his report card. As they continue through school this more sophisticated understanding of evaluative feedback continues to grow (see Stipek & Mac Iver, 1989). At the same time, the kinds of evaluative information children receive, and the kinds of educational environments students encounter, change in important ways as well. Ss (and N/As) are replaced by letter grades. Testing and other forms of evaluation become more frequent. Students are separated into different groups for instruction. All of these experiences (and many others) influence children's motivation in important ways (see Eccles & Midgley, 1989; Stipek, 1996; Wigfield *et al.*, 1998). Thus the development of motivation is a complex interaction of change within the individual child and change in the environments they encounter. Both kinds of change are discussed by the authors in this book.

PURPOSE OF THE BOOK

With these ideas about how motivation changes in mind, we invited prominent scholars in the achievement motivation field to contribute chapters to this book, asking them to discuss how the motivational constructs upon which they focus change over childhood and adolescence. We asked other prominent scholars to provide chapters on instructional influences on motivation during elementary and secondary school. Thus analysis of individual-level development and systematic age-related changes in the contexts of different instructional practices form the core unifying theme of this book.

Given this theme, we invited scholars from both educational and developmental psychology to contribute to the volume. There is interesting and important work on motivation going on in both fields, as attested in part by the presence of chapters in recent major handbooks of both educational and developmental psychology. Despite this broad interest in motivation in both fields, researchers in each field have remained somewhat separate, attending different conferences and submitting their work to different journals. To further our understanding of the development of motivation we believe it is crucial to integrate the work across these two fields, and so included authors who are prominent in each.

We wanted this volume to present a comprehensive overview of the different theoretical models of motivation as well as the constructs associated with these models, in order to provide as complete a picture as possible of where the field is going. We thus wanted the book to be an eclectic collection, rather than an in-depth look at one particular motivation theory. Although not all current models are represented, most are, including: self-efficacy theory, self-worth theory, expectancy–value theory, entity vs. incremental intelligence theory, self-determination theory, interest theory, goal orientation theory, and social goal theory. The prevalence of the term "self" is not an accident; self-oriented theories dominate the field of motivation today.

A major concern we have about the motivation field is the proliferation of terms for constructs that on the surface are relatively similar. The clearest examples of this is the variety of related-to perceptions of ability and self-efficacy, and the variety of terms for different goal orientations (see the special issue of *Contemporary Educational Psychology* from 2000 edited by Murphy & Alexander, see also Eccles *et al.*, 1998). Thus clarifying similarities and differences among these terms was a major goal of this book. We addressed this goal by asking authors in each theoretical tradition to define the constructs they study and review the research on these constructs. We believe it is time to begin consolidating these constructs. One way to do this is to examine each individual construct very carefully, with comparisons to other similar constructs. We asked authors to do this comparative analysis. Many did! We hope such definitional clarity will move the field ahead.

Along with work on these seminal motivational constructs, we also were interested in links of motivation to the regulation of achievement behavior. Much has been written about how motivation on its own is not enough to produce achievement. Individuals can be highly motivated but not engage effectively in behavior because they lack effective strategies or are unable to guide and direct their own behavior (Boekaerts, Pintrich, & Zeidner, 2000; Zimmerman, 2000). We therefore solicited chapters on the development of motivation and self-regulation, and academic help seeking. Self-regulation is one of the main ways in which individuals translate motivation into achievement. Knowing when one needs help, and being willing to ask for it, is a crucial aspect of the ability to regulate one's own behavior. Unfortunately, many children choose not to seek academic help even when they need it.

As mentioned earlier, motivation is not just a characteristic of the individual but also a result of the home and school environmental contexts individuals encounter. We have had a long-standing interest in the socialization of motivation in home and at school, particularly in the influences of different instructional practices on motivation and on how these influences change over time (e.g., Eccles & Blumenfeld, 1985; Eccles & Midgley, 1989; Eccles *et al.*, 1998; Wigfield & Eccles, 1994, 1995; Wigfield *et al.*, 1998). We therefore solicited chapters on instructional influences, with one chapter focusing on instruction during the early school years and a second focusing on secondary school instruction.

We challenged each author to write about the role of gender and ethnicity in influencing children's motivation. As our society becomes more diverse it is becoming increasingly important to understand how the development of motivational processes may vary across different cultural groups. A critical question is whether the same constructs and theories work for these different groups. Many researchers studying motivation have examined the relations of gender to different aspects of motivation. There is less research on how children's racial and ethnic heritages influence their motivation, but work on this topic is increasing. Some of this work suggests that the strength of relations between certain motivational constructs and achievement is weaker in some cultural groups than in others (Graham, 1994). If this is true, then we need to question how universal different theoretical models of motivation are. Rather than having separate chapters on gender and ethnicity, we asked each author to discuss these topics. There is some variation across the chapters in the depth of coverage of these issues, but each author does discuss them in meaningful ways, setting the stage for new research on these important topics.

ORGANIZATION AND CONTENTS OF THE BOOK

We organized the presentation of motivational theories and constructs around three motivational questions: (1)"Can I do this task?", (2) "Do I want to do this task and why?", and (3) "What do I need to do to succeed at this activity?" These three questions each define a section of the book.

When answering the first question, "Can I do this activity?", children think about their perceived competence and confidence in being able to do different activities. Constructs pertaining to one's ability have held center stage in research on motivation for the last several decades. We include in this section chapters on self-efficacy, self-worth, and conceptions of ability.

The second question, "Do I want to do this activity and why?", focuses on the reasons and purposes children have for engaging or not engaging in different achievement activities. Even if they are quite competent at an activity, children may not engage in it if they do not have a purpose for doing. The constructs included in this section are central to this choice aspect of motivation. We include in this section chapters on achievement values, self-determination, interest, goal orientation, and social goals and their relations to motivation.

The third question, "What do I need to do to succeed?", links motivation, cognition, and behavior. As mentioned above, motivation on its own is not enough to successfully complete an activity; children and adolescents must manage their achievement behavior to accomplish their valued goals. Thus included in this section are chapters on motivation and self-regulation and academic help seeking.

The final section of the book concerns instructional influences on motivation. There are two chapters in this section, one on instructional practices during the preschool and elementary grades and one focusing on instructional practices at middle school.

OVERVIEW OF CHAPTERS FOCUSED ON COMPETENCE-RELATED BELIEFS

Chapter 1, written by Dale Schunk and Frank Pajares, concerns the development of self-efficacy. Schunk and Pajares compare the definition of self-efficacy with definitions of other related constructs like self-concept and competence beliefs, and then provide a review of family, peer, and school influences on the development of self-efficacy. They move to a discussion of self-efficacy's effects on learning and achievement, and also discuss how different instructional practices influence students' self-efficacy.

Covington and Dray discuss their research on successful undergraduate students' retrospective accounts of what motivated them to do well in school in Chapter 2. This work is grounded in Covington's self-worth theory of motivation, which has as its basic premise that students equate their sense of worth with their ability to achieve. Covington and Dray's findings illustrate the complex interplay of intrinsic and extrinsic motives in successful students' academic efforts. They conclude their chapter with some interesting ideas on how self-worth and self-determination theory may be integrated, and provide some suggestions for educational reform based on their work.

Dweck, in Chapter 3, discusses work on the development of children's conceptions of ability, arguing that these beliefs have a strong influence on children's achievement motivation. She presents work on the precursors of the development of these conceptions. Dweck discusses how many children develop a "mature" conception of ability as a relatively stable capacity; she terms this the "entity" view of ability. However, Dweck also notes that although children may develop this "mature" conception of ability, many children do not. Instead, these children believe that ability can be modified through learning. Dweck calls this the "incremental" view of ability. She discusses motivational consequences of each of these views.

OVERVIEW OF CHAPTERS FOCUSED ON REASONS FOR ENGAGING IN ACHIEVEMENT ACTIVITIES

The chapters in this section focus on children's purposes and reasons for engaging (or not engaging) in achievement activities and the extent to which children determine their own engagement, or are compelled to do so. As noted earlier, even when children believe they are competent at an activity they may not engage in it enthusiastically if they do not have a compelling purpose or reason to do so. Research on competence and efficacy beliefs dominated the motivation field for many years, but work on purposes and reasons for achievement has grown rapidly of late.

In this section Chapters 4 and 5 focus on children's valuing of achievement. In Chapter 4, Wigfield and Eccles review research on the development of children's competence-related beliefs and values, with a focus on children's valuing of achievement. Much of this research stems from Eccles, Wigfield, and colleagues' expectancy–value model of motivation (Eccles *et al.*, 1983; Eccles *et al.*, 1998). In discussing the development of competence beliefs and values, Wigfield and Eccles discuss how both the structure and level of children's beliefs and values change over time. They then discuss how these beliefs and values relate to achievement behaviors, achievement goals, and the ways in which children learn to regulate their achievement behavior. Because this chapter deals with competence beliefs and values, it could have been placed in section 1 or 2. We put it in this section because of the relative neglect of values in the motivation literature.

Graham and Taylor, in Chapter 5, also discuss children's achievement values, with a focus on gender and ethnic differences in achievement values. They are particularly interested in the question of whether African American children devalue the importance of school success. They review their work on middle school children's valuing of school, in which they use a new and fascinating peer nomination methodology to assess children's relative valuing of school. Their research demonstrates that there are complex gender by ethnicity interaction effects on children's valuing of achievement. They conclude with an interesting discussion of how stereotypes and perceived barriers to educational success may differentially influence children from different ethnic groups' valuing of achievement.

In Chapter 6, Grolnick, Gurland, Jacob, and Decourcey discuss the development of children's self-determination, or their sense of autonomy, regarding their schoolwork and other activities. They contrast self-determination with the feeling of being controlled by others. They discuss the relations of self-determination to intrinsic and extrinsic motivation, presenting a continuum of extrinsically motivated behaviors that move closer toward intrinsic motivation. They turn to a fascinating discussion of the development of self-determination and factors that influence it in the home and school environments. They focus in particular on the role of autonomy support in fostering self-determination, and how children come to internalize achievement behaviors.

Chapter 7, by Renninger and Hidi, concerns the development of children's interest. The literatures on interest and achievement motivation have been somewhat distinct, despite the fact that both influence outcomes such as performance and choice, and so we are pleased to have a chapter on interest in this volume. Renninger and Hidi begin by differentiating between personal and situational interest, a fundamentally important distinction in this literature. The heart of the chapter is the presentation of an illustrative case study of a middle school-aged child that that Renninger and Hidi use to contextualize research on the development of interest. From the perspective of the case study, they review research on how children's interests develop, and how interest influences children's learning and engagement in different activities.

Chapters 8 and 9 focus on children's goals for achievement, as goal orientations and other kinds of goals have received much research attention of late in the achievement motivation literature. Anderman, Austin, and Johnson discuss the development of children's goal orientations, focusing on the mastery and performance goal orientations that have been prominent in the literature and the recent distinction between performance approach and performance avoid goal orientations. Anderman and his colleagues begin Chapter 8 with a discussion of the different terms that have been used for these goal orientations in the literature, a crucial discussion because of debates about the meaning of these different terms. They then move to a discussion of the development of goal orientations during childhood and adolescence, discussing in particular how changes in the school and classroom environments as children move into middle school and influence children's goal orientations so that they become more focused on performance rather than mastery goals. They end their chapter by discussing a number of important new directions for research on goal orientations.

Wentzel reviews work on children's social goals and how these goals influence their adjustment to school in Chapter 9. She discusses three different perspectives on the nature of social goals, a social cognitive perspective focusing on knowledge of social goals, a perspective viewing the pursuit of social goals as a motivational process related to competence, and a perspective defining social goals as motivational orientations influencing children's responses to social situations. Wentzel reviews research pertaining to each of these perspectives. She then combines these three different perspectives into an integrated model of social goals. She ends with a discussion of the research on the development of social goals, focusing on how they are socialized in the home and school settings.

CHAPTERS FOCUSED ON STUDENTS' REGULATION OF THEIR ACHIEVEMENT BEHAVIORS

As noted earlier, for motivation to affect learning, children must engage effectively in achievement behaviors that lead to positive outcomes. Children's regulation of their behavior thus is an important link between motivation and achievement. The chapters in this section focus on different aspects of the self-regulation of achievement behavior. In Chapter 10 Pintrich and Zusho review work on the development of academic self-regulation. They describe different phases of self-regulation and different areas (cognitive, motivational, behavioral, contextual) that have to be regulated, discussing the development of self-regulation in these different phases and areas. They then discuss cognitive and motivational factors that influence self-regulated learning, again taking a developmental perspective on each set of factors. They note that students' cognitive capabilities to self-regulate increase at the same time their motivation to regulate sometimes is declining, influenced in part by the educational contexts in which they are in.

Richard Newman, in Chapter 11, discusses how children respond to academic difficulty, focusing in particular on adaptive help seeking, or knowing when one needs to solicit help and how to do it. He suggests that adaptive help seeking is one important strategy of self-regulated learning. He argues that sociocultural theory and self-determination theory provide insights regarding the socialization of adaptive help-seeking. He then discusses how teachers and peers can influence children's adaptive help-seeking in both positive and negative ways, discussing the thorny problem of some children's unwillingness to seek academic help when they need it.

CHAPTERS FOCUSED ON INSTRUCTIONAL PRACTICES AND STUDENT MOTIVATION

In this final section of the book the authors focus on how different instructional practices influence students' motivation and learning. Given the developmental focus of the book, one chapter focuses on instruction at the preschool and elementary levels, and the second focuses on instructional practices in middle school. Deborah Stipek begins Chapter 12 on instructional practices in preschool and elementary school by noting that instructional practices advocated by curriculum experts in mathematics and literacy overlap in important ways with instructional practices advocated by motivational researchers. She then turns to a review of she and her colleagues' research on how different instructional practices influence students' learning and motivation. Findings from her studies in elementary school suggest that the best practices foster both academic learning and motivation. However, in kindergarten her findings indicated that practices enhancing social and motivational development may not enhance academic achievement. Stipek discusses ways to resolve this dilemma.

Mac Iver, Young, and Washburn discuss instructional practices at middle school and how these practices influence students' motivation, with a special focus on instructional practices in science in Chapter 13. They note that middle school is a time when many students' motivation declines, and talk about reform efforts directed at alleviating these declines. They then turn to a fascinating description of their own research on changing instructional practices in inner-city schools to facilitate students' motivation and learning. They describe their instructional approach as both "minds-on," meaning providing time for reflection, and "hands-on," meaning providing opportunities for active learning. They found this approach to learning had positive effects on the different aspects of students' motivation that they measured. They conclude their chapter with a discussion of how an emphasis on minds-on and hands-on practices can influence learning and motivation in other subject areas.

We hope this book provides you the reader with a picture of where research is on the development of motivation and how children's motivation is influenced by different instructional practices they experience. As well, we hope your thinking about directions for future research is stimulated by this book, as the authors have provided excellent suggestions for future research. As evidenced by the chapters in this book research and theory in the area of motivation is maturing. There still is much to do and we look forward to the next generation of research on the development of motivation.

References

Bandura, A. (1997). *Self-efficacy: The exercise of control.* New York: W. H. Freeman.

Boekaerts, M., Pintrich, P. R., & Zeidner, M. (2000). Self-regulation: An introductory overview. In M. Boekaerts, P. R. Pintrich, & M. Zeidner (Eds.), *Handbook of self-regulation* (pp. 1–9). San Diego, CA: Academic Press.

Dweck, C. S., (1998). The development of early self-conceptions: Their relevance for motivational processes. In J. Heckhausen & C. S. Dweck (Eds.), *Motivation and self-regulation across the life span* (pp. 257–280). Cambridge, UK: Cambridge University Press.

Eccles, J. S., & Midgley, C. (1989). Stage/environment fit: Developmentally appropriate classrooms for early adolescents. In R. Ames & C. Ames (Eds.), *Research on motivation in education* (Vol. 3, pp. 139–181). New York: Academic Press.

Eccles, J., & Wigfield, A. (1985). Teacher expectations and student motivation. In J. B. Dusek (Ed.), *Teacher expectancies* (pp. 185–226.) Hillsdale, NJ: Lawrence Erlbaum Associates.

Eccles, J., Wigfield, A., Harold, R., & Blumenfeld, P. (1993). Age and gender differences in children's self and task perceptions during elementary school. *Child Development*, 64, 830–847.

Eccles, J. S., Wigfield, A., & Schiefele, U. (1998). Motivation to succeed In W. Damon (Series Ed.) & N. Eisenberg (Volume Ed.) *Handbook of child psychology* (5th ed., Vol. III, pp. 1017–1095). New York: Wiley.

Graham, S. (1994). Motivation in African Americans. *Review of Educational Research*, 64, 55–117.

Harter, S. (1983). Developmental perspectives on the self-system. In E. M. Hetherington (Vol. Ed.) P. H. Mussen (Series Ed.), *Handbook of child psychology* (4th Ed., Vol. 4, pp. 275–385). New York: Wiley.

Harter, S. (1998). The development of self representations. In N. Eisenberg (Vol. Ed.) and W. Damon (Series Ed.), *Handbook of child psychology* (5th Ed., Vol. 3). New York: Wiley.

Hidi, S., & Harackiewicz, J. M. (2000). Motivating the academically unmotivated: A critical issue for the 21st century. *Review of Educational Research*, 70, 151–180.

Marsh, H. W., Craven, R. & Debus, R. (1998). Structure, stability, and development of self-concepts: A multicohort-multioccasion study. *Child Development*, 69, 1030–1053.

Marsh, H. W., & Yeung, A. S. (1997). Causal effects of academic self-concept on academic achievement: Structural equation models of longitudinal data. *Journal of Educational Psychology*, 89, 41–54.

Nicholls, J. G. (1978). The development of the concepts of effort and ability, perceptions of academic attainment, and the understanding that difficult tasks require more ability. *Child Development*, 49, 800–814.

Nicholls, J. G. (1984). Achievement motivation: Conceptions of ability, subjective experience, task choice, and performance. *Psychological Review*, 91, 328–346.

Nicholls, J. G. (1990). What is ability and why are we mindful of it? A developmental perspective. In R. J. Sternberg & J. Kolligian (Eds.), *Competence considered*. New Haven, CT: Yale University Press.

Stipek, D. J. (1996). Motivation and instruction. In R. C. Calfee & D. C. Berliner (Eds.), *Handbook of educational psychology*. New York: Macmillan.

Stipek, D. J., & Mac Iver, D. (1989). Developmental change in children's assessment of intellectual competence. *Child Development*, 60, 521–538.

Weiner, B. (1990). History of motivation research in education. *Journal of Educational Psychology*, 82, 616–622.

Wigfield. A. (1994). Expectancy–value theory of achievement motivation: A developmental perspective. *Educational Psychology Review*, 6, 49–78.

Wigfield, A., Eccles, J. S., & Rodriguez, D. (1998). The development of children's motivation in school contexts. In. A. Iran-Nejad & P. D. Pearson (Eds.), *Review of research in education* (Vol. 23). Washington, DC: American Educational Research Association.

Wigfield, A., & Eccles, J. S. (1994). *Middle grades schooling and early adolescent development, Part I.* Special issue, *Journal of Early Adolescence*, 14, No. 2.

Wigfield, A., & Eccles, J. S. (1995). *Middle grades schooling and early adolescent development, Part II.* Special issue, *Journal of Early Adolescence*, 15, No. 1.

Zimmerman, B. J. (2000). Attaining self-regulation: A social cognitive perspective. In M. Boekaerts, P. R. Pintrich, & M. Zeidner (Eds.), *Handbook of self-regulation* (pp. 13–39). San Diego, CA: Academic Press.

PART
I

Can I Do This Activity?

CHAPTER

1

The Development of Academic Self-Efficacy

DALE H. SCHUNK

University of North Carolina at Greensboro, Greensboro, North Carolina

FRANK PAJARES

Emory University, Atlanta, Georgia

Current views of cognitive development stress that the construction of knowledge varies as a function of an individual's developmental level and experiences (Meece, 1997; Siegler, 1991). These views focus on changes in processing functions; for example, attention, encoding, retrieval, metacognition, use of strategies.

In similar fashion, contemporary motivation theories focus on the cognitive and affective processes that instigate, direct, and sustain human action. Researchers investigate the operation of such processes as goals, expectations, attributions, values, and emotions (Pintrich & Schunk, 1996).

In this chapter we focus on the development of one type of motivational process: perceived self-efficacy. *Self-efficacy* refers to beliefs about one's capabilities to learn or perform behaviors at designated levels (Bandura, 1986, 1997). Much research shows that self-efficacy influences academic motivation, learning, and achievement (Pajares, 1996; Schunk, 1995).

We initially provide theoretical background information on self-efficacy to show its relation to other similar motivation constructs. The bulk of the chapter is devoted to research on the development of self-efficacy in children and adolescents. The chapter concludes with suggested research directions.

THEORETICAL BACKGROUND

Social Cognitive Theory

Self-efficacy is grounded in a larger theoretical framework known as *social cognitive theory*, which postulates that human achievement depends on interactions between one's behaviors, personal factors (e.g., thoughts, beliefs), and environmental conditions (Bandura, 1986, 1997). In this view, self-efficacy affects one's behaviors and the environments with which one interacts, and is influenced by actions and conditions.

Self-efficacy is hypothesized to have effects on task choice, effort, persistence, and achievement (Bandura, 1986, 1997; Schunk, 1995). Compared with students who doubt their learning capabilities, those who feel efficacious for learning or performing a task participate more readily, work harder, persist longer when they encounter difficulties, and achieve at a higher level.

Learners obtain information to appraise their self-efficacy from their actual performances, vicarious (observational) experiences, forms of persuasion, and physiological reactions. Students' own performances offer the most reliable guides for gauging self-efficacy, whereas the effects of the other sources are more variable.

Although self-efficacy is an important determinant of achievement, it is not its only influence. No amount of self-efficacy will produce a competent performance when requisite skills and knowledge are lacking. *Outcome expectations*, or beliefs about the anticipated consequences of actions, are important because students do not engage in activities they believe will lead to negative outcomes. *Value* refers to students' beliefs about the importance of learning or what use will be made of what they learn. Value beliefs affect behavior because learners show little interest in nonvalued activities (Wigfield, 1994).

Relation to Other Constructs

There are other motivation constructs that seem conceptually similar to self-efficacy. Outcome expectations and self-efficacy often are related, but they are not synonymous. Self-efficacy refers to beliefs about what one can do; outcome expectations denote the expected consequences of what one does. Students who feel efficacious about performing well in a course may not expect to receive a good grade because they believe the instructor does not like them.

Another similar construct is *self-concept*, defined as one's collective self-perceptions that are formed through experiences with and interpretations of the environment, and are heavily influenced by reinforcements and evaluations by significant others (Shavelson & Bolus, 1982). These constructs differ both in specificity and content. Self-efficacy refers to beliefs that one is able to learn or perform specific tasks; self-concept comprises perceptions of one's competence in general or in a given domain (e.g., academic, social, motor skills) (Pajares & Schunk, in press). Further, whereas self-efficacy is concerned with judgments about capabilities, self-concept also includes feelings of self-worth that accompany competence beliefs.

A third similar construct is *effectance motivation*, defined as the motivation to interact effectively with one's environment and control critical aspects (White, 1959). In young children, effectance motivation is diffuse and affects many interactions. With development it becomes more specialized and manifests itself in achievement behaviors in various school subjects. Like self-efficacy, effectance motivation includes perceived capabilities for influencing important aspects of one's life. Unlike self-efficacy, however, effectance motivation is a global construct and lacks self-efficacy's specificity.

The notion *of perceived control* is also relevant to self-efficacy. People who believe they can control what they learn and perform are more apt to initiate and sustain behaviors directed toward those ends than are individuals who hold a low sense of control over their capabilities (Bandura, 1997). Perceived control is generic; thus, it is meaningful to speak of perceived control over learning or performing and over outcomes. Further, perceived control is only one aspect of self-efficacy. There are many factors that influence self-efficacy, including perceptions of ability, social comparisons, attributions (beliefs about the causes of outcomes), time available, and perceived importance. Students may believe they can control their effort, persistence, and use of learning strategies, yet still feel inefficacious about learning because they view the learning as unimportant and do not want to invest time.

Another similar construct is *self-competence*. Expectancy–value theorists assess judgments of competence in terms of students' *expectancy* and *ability beliefs* (Wigfield & Eccles, 2000). Expectancy beliefs consist of students' expectations for success; items ask students how well they will do in an academic area or how well they can learn new material. Ability beliefs consist of students' perceptions of their competence but also include comparisons of these abilities across different academic areas and to other students; items ask students how good they are in an academic subject, how they rate themselves in that subject compared with their classmates, and how good they are in that subject compared with another.

Self-competence and self-efficacy differ in level of specificity. Expectancy and ability beliefs are domain specific, whereas self-efficacy beliefs are typically task specific. It bears noting, however, that self-efficacy beliefs can be and sometimes are assessed at a domain-specific level. The second difference is that self-efficacy does not include a comparative component. Such comparisons—which include peer modeling—can be powerful influences on self-perceptions of competence (Schunk, 1995), but comparative information is not integral to one's self-efficacy judgments.

DEVELOPMENT OF SELF-EFFICACY

Familial Influence on Self-Efficacy

Beginning in infancy, parents and caregivers provide experiences that differentially influence children's self-efficacy. Home influences that help children interact effectively with the environment positively affect self-efficacy (Bandura, 1997; Meece, 1997). Initial sources of self-efficacy are centered in the family, but the influence is bidirectional. Parents who provide an environment that stimulates youngsters' curiosity and allows for mastery experiences help to build children's self-efficacy. In turn, children who display more curiosity and exploratory activities promote parental responsiveness.

Children are motivated to work on the activities, and thereby learn new information and skills, when environments are rich in interesting activities that arouse children's curiosity and offer challenges that can be met. There is much variability in home environments. Some contain materials such as computers, books, and puzzles that stimulate children's thinking. Parents who are heavily invested in their children's cognitive development may spend time with them on learning. Other homes do not have these resources, and adults may devote little time to children's education.

Parents who provide a warm, responsive, and supportive home environment, encourage exploration and stimulate curiosity, and provide play and learning materials accelerate their children's intellectual development (Belsky, 1981). Parents also are key providers of self-efficacy information when they arrange for varied mastery experiences (Bandura, 1997). Such experiences occur in homes enriched with activities and in which children have freedom to explore.

With respect to vicarious sources, parents who teach children ways to cope with difficulties and model persistence and effort strengthen children's self-efficacy. As children grow, peers become increasingly important (Steinberg, Brown, & Dornbusch, 1996). Parents who steer their children toward efficacious peers provide further vicarious boosts in self-efficacy.

Homes also are prime sources of persuasive information. Parents who encourage their youngsters to try different activities and support their efforts help to develop children who feel more capable of meeting challenges (Bandura, 1997).

Peer Influence

Peers influence children's self-efficacy through *model similarity*. Observing similar others succeed can raise children's self-efficacy and motivate them to perform the task if they believe that they, too, will be successful (Schunk, 1987). Observing others fail can lead students to believe that they lack the competence to succeed and dissuade them from attempting the task. Model similarity is most influential for students uncertain about their performance capabilities, such as those lacking task familiarity and information to use in judging self-efficacy or those who have experienced difficulties and hold doubts (Bandura, 1986; Schunk, 1987). Model similarity is potent among children and adolescents because peers are similar in many ways and students at these developmental levels are unfamiliar with many tasks.

Peer influence also operates through *peer networks*, or large groups of peers with whom students associate. Students in networks tend to be highly similar (Cairns, Cairns, & Neckerman, 1989), which enhances the likelihood of influence by modeling. Networks help define students' opportunities for interactions and observations of others' interactions, as well as their access to activities (Dweck & Goetz, 1978). Over time, network members become more similar to one another. Discussions between friends influence their choices of activities and friends often make similar choices (Berndt & Keefe, 1992).

Peer groups promote motivational socialization. Changes in children's motivational engagement across the school year are predicted accurately by their peer group membership at the start of the year (Kindermann, McCollam, & Gibson, 1996). Children affiliated with highly motivated groups change positively; those in less motivated groups change negatively. Peer group academic socialization may influence the group's academic self-efficacy and motivation.

Further support for these contentions comes from research by Steinberg et al. (1996), who tracked students from entrance into high school until their senior year and found developmental patterns in the influence of peer pressure in many areas, including academic motivation and performance. Peer pressure rises during childhood and peaks around grade 8 or 9 but then declines through high school. A key time of influence is roughly between ages 12 and 16, during which, interestingly, parental involvement in children's activities declines.

Steinberg et al. investigated whether students who began high school academically equivalent (i.e., with similar grades) but became affiliated with different peer crowds remained academically similar. Students in academically oriented crowds achieved better during high school than did students in less academically oriented crowds. It should be noted that although parental influence declines, it does not disappear. Parents can launch children onto a trajectory by establishing goals for them and by involving them in groups and activities.

Role of Schooling

Research often shows that students' perceptions of academic competence decline as they advance in school (Eccles, Wigfield, & Schiefele, 1998; Pintrich & Schunk, 1996). This decline has been attributed to various factors, including greater competition, more norm-referenced grading, less teacher attention to individual student progress, and stresses associated with school transitions.

A somewhat different trend emerges for self-efficacy. Given its subject specificity, we might expect that with development, children's self-efficacy would increase. The standard school curriculum includes skills (e.g., reading, mathematical computations) that are taught and reintroduced in later grades and serve as the building blocks for advanced skills. As children move through school they gain experience with these tasks, which should raise their self-efficacy. In support of this point, researchers have shown that older students judge self-efficacy higher than do younger ones (Shell, Colvin, & Bruning, 1995; Zimmerman & Martinez-Pons, 1990).

Nonetheless, the preceding negative school practices can retard the development of academic self-efficacy, especially among students who are less academically prepared to cope with increasingly challenging academic tasks. For example, lock-step sequences of instruction frustrate some students who fail to grasp skills and increasingly fall behind their peers (Bandura, 1997). Ability groupings can hurt self-efficacy among those relegated to lower groups. Classrooms that allow for much social comparison tend to lower the self-efficacy of students who find their performances inferior to those of their peers.

Another factor that is important is how well students experience a sense of relatedness to the school environment. Hymel, Comfort, Schonert-Reichl, and McDougall (1996) suggested that students' involvement and participation in school depend in part on how much the school environment contributes to their perceptions of autonomy and relatedness, which in turn influence self-efficacy and academic achievement. Although parents and teachers contribute to feelings of autonomy and relatedness, peers become highly significant during adolescence. The peer group context enhances or diminishes students' feelings of relatedness (i.e., belonging, affiliation).

Transitional Influences

Periods of transition in schooling bring additional factors into play that affect self-efficacy. Eccles and her colleagues (Eccles & Midgley, 1989; Eccles, Midgley, & Adler, 1984) have investigated the transition from elementary school to junior high. Elementary students remain with the same teacher and peers for most of the school day. Children receive much attention and individual progress is stressed.

The transition brings several changes. Because many elementary schools typically feed into the same junior high and because students change classes, they are exposed to many different peers whom they do not know. Most evaluation is normative, and there is less teacher attention to individual progress. The widely expanded social reference group, coupled with the shift in evaluation standards, requires that students reassess their academic capabilities. Perceptions of general academic competence typically begin to decline by grade 7 (Harter, 1996; Midgley, Feldlaufer, & Eccles, 1989), although some research shows that the decline begins earlier (Wigfield et al., 1997).

Developmental Changes in Self-Appraisal Skill

Like other cognitive capabilities, self-appraisal skill improves with development. Most children are optimistic about what they can do. In self-efficacy research it is not uncommon for children to feel highly efficacious about accomplishing difficult tasks; even providing them with feedback indicating low performance may not decrease self-efficacy (Pajares, 1996; Schunk, 1995). Less frequently, children underestimate their capabilities and believe that they cannot acquire basic skills.

The incongruence between children's self-efficacy beliefs and their actual performances may be due to various causes. Children often lack task familiarity and do not fully understand what is required to execute a task successfully. As they gain experience, their judgmental accuracy improves. Children may be unduly swayed by certain task features and decide based on these that they can or cannot perform the task while ignoring many other features. In subtraction, for example, children may focus on how many numbers the problems contain and judge longer problems to be more difficult than those with fewer numbers, even when the longer ones are conceptually simpler. As their cognitive capability to focus on multiple features improves, so does their accuracy.

Children also may have faulty knowledge about their performance capabilities. In writing, for example, it is difficult for children to know how clearly they can express themselves or whether their writing skills are improving (Schunk & Swartz, 1993). Teacher feedback—especially at the elementary level—is intended to encourage and stress what children do well. Children may believe they can write well when in fact their writing is below normal for their grade level. As children gain task experience and engage in peer social comparisons, their self-assessments of competence become more accurate.

The preceding discussion should not imply that younger children's self-appraisal skills cannot become more accurate. Instruction and opportunities to practice self-evaluation enhance judgmental accuracy (Schunk, 1995). Instructional interventions that convey clear information about children's skills or progress raise efficacy–performance correspondence (Schunk, 1981, 1995).

GENDER AND ETHNIC DIFFERENCES
IN SELF-EFFICACY

Gender Differences

Researchers typically report that boys and men tend to be more confident than girls and women in mathematics, science, and technology (Meece, 1991; Pajares & Miller, 1994; Wigfield, Eccles, & Pintrich, 1996) even though achievement differences in these areas either are diminishing or have disappeared (Eisenberg, Martin, & Fabes, 1996). Conversely, in areas related to language arts, male and female students exhibit similar confidence even though the achievement of girls typically is higher (Pajares & Valiante, 2001).

Gender differences in self-efficacy are confounded by a number of factors. First, they often are nullified when previous achievement is controlled (Pajares, 1996). Boys and girls also have a tendency to respond to self-efficacy instruments differently. Boys are more self-congratulatory, whereas girls are more modest (Wigfield et al., 1996).

A third confounding factor involves how gender differences are assessed and reported. Students usually are asked to provide confidence judgments that they possess certain academic skills or can accomplish academic tasks. Pajares and his colleagues asked students to provide self-efficacy judgments in the traditional manner (confidence in possessing writing skills) but also to make comparative judgments regarding their writing ability versus that of other boys and girls in their class and school (Pajares, Miller, & Johnson, 1999; Pajares & Valiante, 1999). Although girls outperformed boys, girls and boys reported equal writing self-efficacy. When students were asked whether they were better writers than their peers, girls judged themselves to be better writers than boys.

Another confounding factor deals with the nature of the self-belief that may be undergirding those differences. Some researchers contend that gender differences in social, personality, and academic variables may be due to gender orientation, or the stereotypic beliefs about gender that students hold (Eisenberg, Martin, & Fabes, 1996; Harter, Waters, & Whitesell, 1997). Eccles's (1987) model of educational and occupational choice posits that cultural milieu factors, such as students' gender role stereotypes, are partly responsible for differences in course and career selection and in confidence beliefs and perceived value of tasks and activities. Pajares & Valiante (2001) found that gender differences favoring middle school girls in writing self-efficacy were nullified when gender orientation beliefs were controlled.

Gender differences are related to developmental level. There is little evidence for differences in self-efficacy among elementary-aged children. Differences begin to emerge following children's transition to middle school (Eccles & Midgley, 1989; Wigfield et al., 1996), with girls typically showing lower self-efficacy.

Among adolescents, gender differences in self-efficacy should not be expected when students receive performance information about their capabilities or progress in learning. Schunk and Lilly (1984) found that although girls initially judged self-efficacy for learning a novel mathematical task lower than did boys, following an instructional program that included performance feedback girls and boys did not differ in achievement or self-efficacy for solving problems.

Social cognitive theory does not endow either gender or gender self-beliefs with agentic and motivating properties (Bussey & Bandura, 1999). Researchers have observed that students typically view such areas as mathematics, science, and technology as male domains (Eisenberg, Martin & Fabes, 1996). In these areas, a masculine orientation is associated with confidence and achievement because masculine self-perceptions are imbued with the notion that success is a masculine imperative (Eccles, 1987; Hackett, 1985). The language arts typically are associated with a feminine orientation because writing is viewed by most students as a female domain. A feminine orientation is associated with motivational beliefs related to success in writing. One possible approach to modifying these perceptions is to alter boys' and girls' views of academic subjects so they are perceived as relevant and valuable.

Ethnic Differences

Graham's (1994) summary of the literature on the competence beliefs of African-American students revealed that they maintain optimism and positive self-regard in the face of social and economic disadvantage. Graham also found evidence that the academic self-beliefs of African-Americans are strong even in the face of achievement failure. Moreover, the competence beliefs of African American students are as strong and often stronger than those of their white peers. Similar findings have been reported with Hispanic-American samples (Lay & Wakstein, 1985; Stevenson, Chen, & Uttal, 1990).

These are findings primarily from studies of generalized competence beliefs. When the belief assessed is task-specific self-efficacy, results can differ. Pajares and Kranzler (1995) found that the mathematics self-efficacy of African-American students was lower than that of their white peers, and Pajares and Johnson (1996) found that the writing self-efficacy of Hispanic high school students was lower than that of non-Hispanic white students. In each case, minority students reported positive math self-concepts. It may be that beliefs at differing levels of specificity perform different functions for minority students (Edelin & Paris, 1995).

Graham (1994) acknowledged that self-efficacy is an important component of academic motivation but noted that it has been too sparsely examined in studies of minority students. Self-efficacy beliefs assessed at differing levels of specificity might help explain the relationship between perceptions of competence and academic achievement, how these perceptions are related to other motivation constructs, and whether the origins of these beliefs differ for minority children and across socioeconomic levels.

There are conditions under which self-efficacy has little, if any, influence on human functioning (Bandura, 1986; Schunk, 1995). When social and economic systems are prejudicial, students may find that no amount of skillful effort will bring about desired outcomes. They may possess the confidence and skill required to achieve but may choose not to apply these advantages because they lack the incentives. Self-efficacy may also be unrelated to achievement in schools lacking the teachers, equipment, or resources required to help students perform academic tasks.

Bandura also suggested that when social constraints and inadequate resources impede academic performances, self-efficacy may exceed actual performance because students are unable to do what they know. This observation helps shed light on findings regarding the competence beliefs of minority students in some contexts. There is a need to explore the role that schools play as social systems in developing and cultivating self-efficacy as well as the effects of these systems' incentives on students' self-efficacy.

SELF-EFFICACY FOR LEARNING AND ACHIEVEMENT

Table 1 portrays a model of how self-efficacy operates in learning and achievement situations. At the outset of an activity, students differ in their self-efficacy for learning as a function of their prior experiences, personal qualities (e.g., abilities, attitudes), and social supports. The latter include the extent that parents and teachers encourage students to learn, facilitate their access to resources necessary for learning (e.g., materials, facilities), and teach them self-regulatory strategies that enhance skill acquisition and refinement. Ban-

TABLE I
Self-Efficacy for Learning and Achievement

	Pretask	Task Engagement	Posttask
Personal qualities		Personal influences	Motivation
Prior experience	Self-Efficacy		
Social support		Situational influences	Self-efficacy

dura, Barbaranelli, Caprara, and Pastorelli (1996) found that parents' academic aspirations for their children affected children's academic achievements directly and indirectly by influencing children's self-efficacy.

As students engage in activities, they are affected by personal (e.g., goal setting, information processing) and situational influences (e.g., rewards, teacher feedback). These factors provide students with cues about how well they are learning. Motivation and self-efficacy are enhanced when students perceive they are performing well or becoming more skillful. Lack of success or slow progress will not necessarily lower self-efficacy and motivation if learners believe they can perform better by adjusting their approach (e.g., expending more effort, using effective task strategies; Schunk, 1995).

RESEARCH ON SELF-EFFICACY

Educational Correlates of Self-Efficacy

A wealth of research indicates that self-efficacy correlates with several educational outcomes. Many studies have obtained significant and positive correlations between self-efficacy for learning or performing tasks and subsequent achievement on those tasks (Pajares, 1996; Schunk, 1995).

Self-efficacy also correlates with indexes of self-regulation, especially use of effective learning strategies. For example, Pintrich and De Groot (1990) found that self-efficacy, self-regulation, and cognitive strategy use by grade 7 students were positively intercorrelated and predicted achievement. Bouffard-Bouchard, Parent, and Larivee (1991) found that high school students with high self-efficacy for problem solving displayed greater performance monitoring and persisted longer than students with lower self-efficacy. Zimmerman and Bandura (1994) obtained evidence showing that self-efficacy for writing correlated positively with college students' goals for course achievement, self-evaluative standards (satisfaction with potential grades), and actual achievement.

Predictive Utility of Self-Efficacy

Several researchers have used casual models to test the predictive utility of self-efficacy. Schunk (1981) found with path analysis a direct effect of instructional treatment on achievement and an indirect effect through persistence and self-efficacy, an indirect effect of treatment on persistence through self-efficacy, and a direct effect of self-efficacy on achievement and persistence.

Pajares and Kranzler (1995) also used path analysis to determine that mathematics self-efficacy has as powerful a direct effect on mathematics performance as does mental ability, a variable often presumed to be the strongest predictor of academic achievement. Pajares and Miller (1994) showed that mathematics self-efficacy was a better predictor of the mathematics performance of college undergraduates than were mathematics self-concept, perceived usefulness of mathematics, prior experience with mathematics, and gender. Using path analysis, Zimmerman and Bandura (1994) showed that self-efficacy affected achievement directly and indirectly through its influence on goals.

Schunk and Gunn (1986) used path analysis and found that children's long division achievement was directly influenced by use of effective strategies and self-efficacy. The strongest influence on self-efficacy was ability attributions for success. Relich, Debus, and Walker (1986) also found that self-efficacy exerted a direct effect on division achievement and that instructional treatment had both a direct and an indirect effect on achievement through self-efficacy.

Schack (1989) found with path analysis that gifted children's self-efficacy at the end of the school year was strongly affected by previous participation in independent investigations and by self-efficacy assessed after such participation. The latter measure also predicted subsequent participation in independent investigations.

Effects of Instructional Practices on Self-Efficacy

Research in diverse settings has explored the effects of instructional and other classroom processes on self-efficacy. There is strong evidence in support of the hypothesized relations shown in Table 1 across grade levels (e.g., elementary, middle/junior high, secondary, postsecondary), content areas (e.g., mathematics, writing, reading, computer applications), and types of student (e.g., regular, remedial, gifted) (Pajares, 1996; Schunk, 1995). Some instructional and other processes that are beneficial for developing self-efficacy are proximal and specific learning goals, strategy instruction and strategy verbalization, social models, performance and attributional feedback, and performance-contingent rewards (Schunk, 1983, 1984, 1995; Schunk, Hanson, & Cox, 1987; Zimmerman, Bandura, & Martinez-Pons, 1992). What these different processes have in common is that they inform students of their capabilities and progress in learning. This information also motivates students to continue to perform well.

Much has been written about the deleterious effect on students' intrinsic interest of offering rewards for performing enjoyable tasks (Lepper, Sethi, Dialdin, & Drake, 1997). Less has been written about how students develop interest. The development of interest depends in part on enhanced self-efficacy. Bandura and Schunk (1981) found that proximal goals promoted children's self-efficacy and intrinsic interest. Instructional practices should raise interest when they inform children they are making progress in learning and raise their self-efficacy.

FUTURE RESEARCH DIRECTIONS

The preceding research makes it clear that self-efficacy is a key construct that affects motivation and achievement in children and adolescents; however, much research is still needed. Research in the following areas across developmental levels will provide valuable insights into the role of self-efficacy and how it changes with development.

Generality of Self-Efficacy

Research is needed to the extent of which self-efficacy beliefs generalize from one domain to another and whether such generalization varies as a function of development. Self-efficacy typically is defined as perceived capabilities within specific domains (Bandura, 1997; Pajares, 1996). Although most researchers have not investigated whether self-efficacy generalizes beyond specific domains, there is some evidence for a generalized sense of self-efficacy (Smith, 1989).

We might expect some cross-domain generality. Students' initial self-efficacy for learning is affected by their aptitudes, prior experiences, and social supports (Schunk, 1995; see Table 1). Children who generally perform well in mathematics should have higher self-efficacy for learning new content than those who have had learning difficulties. Self-efficacy might generalize to the extent that the new domain builds on prior skills (e.g., self-efficacy for subtracting and multiplying may transfer to long division).

There even could be generalization across dissimilar domains to the extent that students believe the two domains share skills. Thus, students who believe that writing term papers and preparing science projects involve planning and organizing and feel efficacious about planning and organizing may have high self-efficacy for performing well on their first science project. From a developmental perspective, we might predict that this tendency to generalize would increase with cognitive development and experience because older students could determine the prerequisites of the new domain and would draw on prior knowledge.

Self-Efficacy Outcomes

Future research needs to investigate how self-efficacy relates to its outcomes as a consequence of development. Bandura's (1986) point that self-efficacy influences choice of activities, effort, and persistence is seen most clearly in contexts in which behavior reflects performance of previously learned skills (e.g., engaging in feared activities). In academic settings, the influence of self-efficacy on these motivational indexes is complex.

The early school grades are skill oriented. Teachers assign tasks they expect all students to master. Children's self-efficacy generally is high, and they often overestimate their capabilities (Pajares, 1996). Choice of activities is not a good index because students often do not choose the learning activities in which they engage.

Persistence also presents problems. Students typically persist on activities not necessarily because of high self-efficacy but rather because the teacher keeps them on task. Educational research has yielded inconsistent results on the relation of self-efficacy to persistence (Schunk, 1995). A positive relation may be found in the early stages of learning, when greater persistence leads to better performance. As skills develop, students should require less time to complete a task, which means that self-efficacy will relate negatively to persistence. With development, children are better able to determine how much persistence may be necessary to succeed. Thus, self-efficacy may predict persistence better at the higher grades. This issue needs to be explored during academic learning.

Research during learning also is needed on effort. Although learning problems begin to appear in the early grades, most children master the basic skills. Effort should be a more reliable outcome of self-efficacy with development.

Technology Self-Efficacy

With the explosion of technology in schools, researchers should investigate how students develop self-efficacy for learning to use technology. Although children and adolescents are increasingly more technologically competent, there remains wide variability among students.

As with other skills, we should expect that performance attainments, vicarious experiences, and persuasive communications would influence self-efficacy in the context of sound instruction. Some questions that need to be addressed are: Do children benefit more from mastery experiences? Does exposure to technologically competent peer models enhance adolescents' self-efficacy? How can technology be integrated across the curriculum to promote self-efficacy at different developmental levels?

CONCLUSION

Self-efficacy has been shown to play an important role in achievement contexts, and much research supports the idea that it can influence the instigation, direction, persistence, and outcomes of achievement-related actions. In this chapter we have traced how self-efficacy changes with development and have elucidated variables that affect this change. We also have suggested profitable areas of future research. We are encouraged by the rapid increase in self-efficacy research. The future should provide greater clarification of the operation of self-efficacy in different domains and highlight ways that self-efficacy can be enhanced in learners across developmental levels.

References

Bandura, A. (1986). *Social foundations of thought and action: A social cognitive theory.* Englewood Cliffs, NJ: Prentice Hall.

Bandura, A. (1997). *Self-efficacy: The exercise of control.* New York: Freeman.

Bandura, A., Barbaranelli, C., Caprara, G. V., & Pastorelli, C. (1996). Multifacted impact of self-efficacy beliefs on academic functioning. *Child Development, 67,* 1206–1222.

Bandura, A., & Schunk, D. H. (1981). Cultivating competence, self-efficacy, and intrinsic interest through proximal self-motivation. *Journal of Personality and Social Psychology, 41,* 586–598.

Belsky, J. (1981). Early human experience: A family perspective. *Developmental Psychology, 17,* 2–23.

Berndt, T. J., & Keefe, K. (1992). Friends' influence on adolescents' perceptions of themselves at school. In D. H. Schunk & J. L. Meece (Eds.), *Student perceptions in the classroom* (pp. 51–73). Hillsdale, NJ: Lawrence Erlbaum Associates.

Bouffard-Bouchard, T., Parent, S., & Larivee, S. (1991). Influence of self-efficacy on self-regulation and performance among junior and senior high-school age students. *International Journal of Behavioral Development, 14,* 153–164.

Bussey, K., & Bandura, A. (1999). Social cognitive theory of gender development and differentiation. *Psychological Review, 106,* 676–713.

Cairns, R. B., Cairns, B. D., & Neckerman, J. J. (1989). Early school dropout: Configurations and determinants. *Child Development, 60,* 1437–1452.

Dweck, C. S., & Goetz, T. (1978). Attributions and learned helplessness. In J. Harvey, W. Ickes, & R. Kidd (Eds.), *New directions in attribution research* (pp. 157–179). Hillsdale, NJ: Lawrence Erlbaum Associates.

Eccles, J. S. (1987). Gender roles and women's achievement-related decisions. *Psychology of Women Quarterly, 11,* 135–172.

Eccles, J. S., & Midgley, C. (1989). Stage–environment fit: Developmentally appropriate classrooms for young adolescents. In C. Ames & R. Ames (Eds.), *Research on motivation in education* (Vol. 3, pp. 139–186). San Diego: Academic Press.

Eccles, J. S., Midgley, C., & Adler, T. (1984). Grade-related changes in the school environment: Effects on achievement motivation. In J. Nicholls (Ed.), *Advances in motivation and achievement: The development of achievement motivation* (Vol. 3, pp. 283–331). Greenwich, CT: JAI Press.

Eccles, J. S., Wigfield, A., & Schiefele, U. (1998). Motivation to succeed. In N. Eisenberg (Ed.), *Handbook of child psychology: Vol. 3. Social, emotional, and personality development* (pp. 1018–1095). New York: Wiley.

Edelin, K. C., & Paris, S. G. (1995, April). *African American students' efficacy beliefs and the match between beliefs and performance.* Paper presented at the annual meeting of the American Educational Research Association, San Francisco.

Eisenberg, N., Martin, C. L., & Fabes, R. A. (1996). Gender development and gender effects. In D. C. Berliner & R. C. Calfee (Eds.), *Handbook of educational psychology* (pp. 358–396). New York: Macmillan.

Graham, S. (1994). Motivation in African Americans. *Review of Educational Research, 64,* 55–117.

Hackett, G. (1985). The role of mathematics self-efficacy in the choice of math-related majors of college women and men: A path analysis. *Journal of Counseling Psychology, 32,* 47-56.

Harter, S. (1996). Teacher and classmate influences on scholastic motivation, self-esteem, and level of voice in adolescents. In J. Juvonen & K. R. Wentzel (Eds.), *Social motivation: Understanding children's school adjustment* (pp. 11–42). Cambridge, U.K.: Cambridge University Press.

Harter, S., Waters, P., & Whitesell, N. (1997). Lack of voice as a manifestation of false self-behavior among adolescents: The school setting as a stage upon which the drama of authenticity is enacted. *Educational Psychologist*, 32, 153–173.

Hymel, S., Comfort, C., Schonert-Reichl, K., & McDougall, P. (1996). Academic failure and school dropout: The influence of peers. In J. Juvonen & K. R. Wentzel (Eds.), *Social motivation: Understanding children's school adjustment* (pp. 313–345). Cambridge, U.K.: Cambridge University Press.

Kindermann, T. A., McCollam, T. L., & Gibson, E., Jr. (1996). Peer networks and students' classroom engagement during childhood and adolescence. In J. Juvonen & K. R. Wentzel (Eds.), *Social motivation: Understanding children's school adjustment* (pp. 279–312). Cambridge, U.K.: Cambridge University Press.

Lay, R., & Wakstein, J. (1985). Race, academic achievement, and self-concept of ability. *Research in Higher Education*, 22, 43–64.

Lepper, M. R., Sethi, S., Dialdin, D., & Drake, M. (1997). Intrinsic and extrinsic motivation: A developmental perspective. In S. S. Luthar, J. A. Burack, D. Cicchetti, & J. R. Weisz (Eds.), *Developmental psychopathology: Perspectives on adjustment, risk, and disorder* (pp. 23–50). New York: Cambridge University Press.

Meece, J. L. (1991). The classroom context and students' motivational goals. In M. L. Maehr & P. R. Pintrich (Eds.), *Advances in motivation and achievement* (Vol. 7, pp. 261–285). Greenwich, CT: JAI Press.

Meece, J. L. (1997). *Child and adolescent development for educators*. New York: McGraw-Hill.

Midgley, C., Feldlaufer, H., & Eccles, J. (1989). Change in teacher efficacy and student self- and task-related beliefs in mathematics during the transition to junior high school. *Journal of Educational Psychology*, 81, 247–258.

Pajares, F. (1996). Self-efficacy beliefs in achievement settings. *Review of Educational Research*, 66, 543–578.

Pajares, F., & Johnson, M. J. (1996). Self-efficacy beliefs in the writing of high school students: A path analysis. *Psychology in the Schools*, 33, 163–175.

Pajares, F., & Kranzler, J. (1995). Self-efficacy beliefs and general mental ability in mathematical problem-solving. *Contemporary Educational Psychology*, 20, 426–443.

Pajares, F., & Miller, M. D. (1994). The role of self-efficacy and self-concept beliefs in mathematical problem-solving: A path analysis. *Journal of Educational Psychology*, 86, 193–203.

Pajares, F., Miller, M. D., & Johnson, M. J. (1999). Gender differences in writing self-beliefs of elementary school students. *Journal of Educational Psychology*, 91, 50–61.

Pajares, F., & Schunk, D. H. (in press). Self-efficacy, self-concept, and academic achievement. In J. Aronson & D. Cordova (Eds.), *Psychology of education: Personal and interpersonal forces*. San Diego: Academic Press.

Pajares, F., & Valiante, G. (1999). Grade level and gender differences in the writing self-beliefs of middle school students. *Contemporary Educational Psychology*, 24, 390–405.

Pajares, F., & Valiante, G. (2001). Gender differences in writing motivation and achievement of middle school students: A function of gender orientation? *Contemporary Educational Psychology*, 20, 366–381.

Pintrich, P. R., & De Groot, E. V. (1990). Motivational and self-regulated learning components of classroom academic performance. *Journal of Educational Psychology*, 82, 33–40.

Pintrich, P. R., & Schunk D. H. (1996). *Motivation in education: Theory, research, and applications*. Englewood Cliffs, NJ: Merrill/Prentice Hall.

Relich, J. D., Debus, R. L., & Walker, R. (1986). The mediating role of attribution and self-efficacy variables for treatment effects on achievement outcomes. *Contemporary Educational Psychology*, 11, 195–216.

Schack, G. D. (1989). Self-efficacy as a mediator in the creative productivity of gifted children. *Journal for the Education of the Gifted*, 12, 231–249.

Schunk, D. H. (1981). Modeling and attributional effects on children's achievement: A self-efficacy analysis. *Journal of Educational Psychology*, 73, 93–105.

Schunk, D. H. (1983). Reward contingencies and the development of children's skills and self-efficacy. *Journal of Educational Psychology*, 75, 511–518.

Schunk, D. H. (1984). Enhancing self-efficacy and achievement through rewards and goals: Motivational and informational effects. *Journal of Educational Research*, 78, 29–34.

Schunk, D. H. (1987). Peer models and children's behavioral change. *Review of Educational Research*, 57, 149–174.

Schunk, D. H. (1995). Self-efficacy and education and instruction. In J. E. Maddux (Ed.), *Self-efficacy, adaptation, and adjustment: Theory, research, and application* (pp. 281–303). New York: Plenum Press.

Schunk, D. H., & Gunn, T. P. (1986). Self-efficacy and skill development: Influence of task strategies and attributions. *Journal of Educational Research*, 79, 238–244.

Schunk, D. H., Hanson, A. R., & Cox, P. D. (1987). Peer-model attributes and children's achievement behaviors. *Journal of Educational Psychology*, 79, 54–61.

Schunk, D. H., & Lilly, M. W. (1984). Sex differences in self-efficacy and attributions: Influence of performance feedback. *Journal of Early Adolescence*, 4, 203–213.

Schunk, D. H., & Swartz, C. W. (1993). Goals and progress feedback: Effects on self-efficacy and writing achievement. *Contemporary Educational Psychology*, 18, 337–354.

Shavelson, R. J., & Bolus, R. (1982). Self-concept: The interplay of theory and methods. *Journal of Educational Psychology*, 74, 3–17.

Shell, D. F., Colvin, C., & Bruning, R. H. (1995). Self-efficacy, attributions, and outcome expectancy mechanisms in reading and writing achievement: Grade-level and achievement-level differences. *Journal of Educational Psychology*, 87, 386–398.

Siegler, R. S. (1991). *Children's thinking* (2nd ed.). Upper Saddle River, NJ: Prentice Hall.

Smith, R. E. (1989). Effects of coping skills training on generalized self-efficacy and locus of control. *Journal of Personality and Social Psychology*, 56, 228–233.

Steinberg, L., Brown, B. B., & Dornbusch, S. M. (1996). *Beyond the classroom: Why school reform has failed and what parents need to do*. New York: Simon & Schuster.

Stevenson, H. W., Chen, C., & Uttal, D. H. (1990). Beliefs and achievement: A study of black, white, and Hispanic children. *Child Development*, 61, 508–523.

White, R. W. (1959). Motivation reconsidered: The concept of competence. *Psychological Review*, 66, 297–333.

Wigfield, A. (1994). The role of children's achievement values in the self-regulation of their learning outcomes. In D. H. Schunk & B. J. Zimmerman (Eds.), *Self-regulation of learning and performance: Issues and educational applications* (pp. 101–124). Hillsdale, NJ: Lawrence Erlbaum Associates.

Wigfield, A., & Eccles, J. S. (2000). Expectancy–value theory of achievement motivation. *Contemporary Educational Psychology*, 25, 68–81.

Wigfield, A., Eccles, J. S., & Pintrich, P. R. (1996). Development between the ages of 11 and 25. In D. C. Berliner & R. C. Calfee (Eds.), *Handbook of educational psychology* (pp. 148–185). New York: Macmillan.

Wigfield, A., Eccles, J. S., Yoon, K. S., Harold, R. D., Arbreton, A. J. A., Freedman-Doan, C., & Blumenfeld, P. C. (1997). Change in children's competence beliefs and subjective task values across the elementary school years: A 3-year study. *Journal of Educational Psychology*, 89, 451–469.

Zimmerman, B. J., & Bandura, A. (1994). Impact of self-regulatory influences on writing course attainment. *American Educational Research Journal*, 31, 845–862.

Zimmerman, B. J., Bandura, A., & Martinez-Pons, M. (1992). Self-motivation for academic attainment: The role of self-efficacy beliefs and personal goal-setting. *American Educational Research Journal*, 29, 663–676.

Zimmerman, B. J., & Martinez-Pons, M. (1990). Student differences in self-regulated learning: Relating grade, sex, and giftedness to self-efficacy and strategy use. *Journal of Educational Psychology*, 82, 51–59.

CHAPTER

2

The Developmental Course of Achievement Motivation: A Need-Based Approach

MARTIN V. COVINGTON

Department of Psychology, University of California at Berkeley, Berkeley, California

ELIZABETH DRAY

School of Education, University of California at Berkeley, Berkeley, California

INTRODUCTION

Various psychologists, most notably Erik Erikson (1968, 1980), have argued that individuals have dramatically different psychological needs at various times in their lives. In the case of education, research findings indicate that the failure of schools to meet students' needs can result in declines in academic motivation as well as in classroom achievement, and that these needs depend on one's developmental level (Eccles, Lord, & Midgley, 1991; Eccles, Midgley, et al., 1993; Eccles, Wigfield, Midgley, Reuman, MacIver, & Feldlaufer, 1993). Although a number of researchers have examined the underlying nature of achievement-related behaviors from a need-based perspective (e.g., Covington, 1984, 1992; Deci & Ryan, 1992; Deci, Vallerand, Pelletier, & Ryan, 1991; Eccles, Midgley, et al., 1993; Eccles, Wigfield, et al., 1993), few have placed their inquiries in a long-term, developmental context (for exceptions, see Midgley & Maehr, 2000; Wigfield, Eccles, & Pintrich, 1996).

The research reported here examines the development of achievement motivation from a protracted perspective, over time, and focuses in particular on the positive, affective elements of motivation—namely, the enjoyment of intellectual discovery, pride in a job well done, and an appreciation for what is being learned, apart from any grade—what has been commonly referred to as *intrinsic motivation* (Covington, 1999). In essence, we ask which factors, singly and in combination, influence the willingness to learn for its own sake, and whether these factors change in number and saliency as individuals move from one level of schooling to another throughout their educational careers. To achieve this developmental viewpoint, we employed a retrospective methodology in which college students recalled the events and experiences that, in hindsight, they judged to have significantly influenced their love of learning, beginning in the elementary years and progressing through high school.

This inquiry is part of a larger investigation conducted under the auspices of the Teaching/Learning Project at the University of California at Berkeley (Covington, 1992, 1998). The overall purpose of this project is to explore the nature of intrinsic motivation and especially its relationship to the various extrinsic rewards that dominate classroom life, including grades, praise, and gold stars. The present developmental inquiries are nested within a broader set of interlocking questions, all of which were triggered by a puzzling observation that formed the original impetus for this entire undertaking (Covington, 1999). On the one hand, many observers have feared that the will to learn for its own sake will be compromised by the excessive use of tangible rewards to motivate behavior (e.g., Kohn, 1993). Yet, on the other hand, this assumption of an antagonism between intrinsic motivation and extrinsic rewards is contradicted by the everyday observations of teachers that students often do, in fact, value what they are learning even when extrinsic rewards and punishments dominate in the form of good and poor grades, respectively.

What is the relationship between a grade focus and caring about what one is learning, and just how adversarial is this relationship anyway? To address this and related questions, we initiated inquiries employing successive yearly cohorts of Berkeley lower division undergraduates enrolled in an introductory psychology course offered by the senior author. The most important aspect of this inquiry was that the research was fully integrated into the ongoing life of these classes. Data collection became a continuous, natural part of the curriculum itself. For instance, in one study students were asked to report changes in their reasons for continuing work on assignments from week to week, as well as to provide information on various self-inducements used to sustain their involvement (e.g., "I looked for ways that my work might be getting better and better"). During these classes, students became candid, yet committed and involved informants—committed and involved because our inquiries were situated in an authentic context of great personal significance for students.

One final comment on the nature of this research. Obviously, the population from which this sample of students was drawn is unrepresentative of the vast majority of school-age youngsters in America. Not only were they older adolescent college students, but highly selected ones at that. Indeed, a near majority of our students were either high school valedictorians or class officers. In an important way, however, this is the perfect group to consult regarding the questions before us. Where else is an appreciation for what one is learning and for the personal, idiosyncratic rewards of learning more in jeopardy than among students whose very sense of self is, potentially, so completely and narrowly defined by a past history of extraordinary competitive accomplishments? In fact, we wondered, initially, if these accumulated successes, beginning in the earliest years of school, might have long ago compromised the capacity of our students to value what they were learning for its own sake.

Self-Worth Theory

The basic perspective taken by our inquiries is that all achievement dynamics, including the valuing of intrinsic rewards, depend on a central, pervasive, and ongoing developmental need that involves establishing and maintaining a sense of personal worth. According to self-worth theory (Covington, 1992, 1998; Covington & Beery, 1976), most students equate their sense of worth with the ability to achieve successfully. But the meaning and perceived role of ability in this equation can differ widely. For some students, intellectual ability is seen as a means to an end, that is, instrumental for achieving intrinsically oriented objectives including self-improvement, a greater understanding of people and events, and the satisfaction of one's curiosities. Researchers working in the tradition of achievement goal theory have referred to these objectives variously as learning goals or task and mastery goals (Ames, 1992; Anderman & Midgley, 1997; Covington, 2000; Midgley, Kaplan, Middleton, & Maehr, 1998). The rewards associated with these goals are typically absolute. They are plentiful and not dependent on the number of people striving to achieve them; rather, their achievement depends on whether the individual, or any number of individuals, has measured up to the prevailing standards. Individuals who prefer these goals have been characterized as *success oriented*; that is, they approach success for its inherent challenges, but the challenges are crafted within reasonable limits, with the possibility of failure closely balanced against the chances of success (Atkinson, 1957).

By contrast, other individuals tend to employ a relative yardstick for measuring their worth, that is, judging their adequacy in comparison to the performances of others and treating the pursuit of ability status as a goal in itself, as the mark of their worthiness. Such self-enhancing (Skaalvik, 1997) or ego-oriented goals (Thorkildsen & Nicholls, 1998) are typically translated into a rank order standing by grades. And, it is exceptionally high grades that are most valued because their scarcity (due to competition) implies outstanding ability, while low grades imply incompetence, hence worthlessness. Individuals who adopt such a competitive, grade-focused test of their worth risk a crisis of identity because only a few can win at such a game. As a result, these individuals are typically *failure avoidant*. Given the competitive scarcity of best grades as well as the ever-present likelihood of punishment in the form of disappointing grades, the goal of these students is to avoid failure or at least avoid the implication of failure—that they are incompetent (Covington & Omelich, 1991). Unfortunately, the self-protective strategies often chosen by these students, ironically, are likely to hasten the very failures they are seeking to avoid. But at least they are failures that deflect the implication of incompetency by, for instance, procrastinating or by taking an extraordinarily heavy course load. In the case of procrastination, failure will more likely be attributed by others to poor planning, not to a lack of ability, and overburdening one's self is attributed to ambitiousness.

This competitive mentality and the competitive grading systems that support it have a developmental history of their own. Schools become more ability focused and therefore more competitive as children move through the grade levels (Eccles, Midgley et al., 1993; Eccles, Wigfield et al., 1993; Midgely & Maehr, 2000). Consequently, worth becomes defined more and more by the struggle over an ever-shrinking supply of good grades. Faced with these mounting pressures, some students may drop out of school, at least psychologically, if not actually. Other students struggle marginally to maintain a sense of self-worth under siege, while yet others succeed in negotiating this gauntlet at least in terms of maintaining a credible GPA, but not without cost in the form of continuing self-doubts.

This vision of school life conjured up by self-worth theory is disturbing. It portrays classrooms as places where the rules often favor lackluster or misplaced effort and self-deception, with few apparent winners and many losers. However unfortunate, it is only in such a context as this that a realistic exploration of the nature of intrinsic valuing can take place. Two observations are especially relevant to our inquiries. First, there is the previously mentioned assumption, favored by many researchers, that the relationship between intrinsic and extrinsic motivation is basically antagonistic, such that the will to learn for its own sake is inhibited by the presence of tangible rewards such as school grades. This antagonism is thought to arise for several reasons. For one thing, providing tangible rewards as goads to achievement may divert attention from the true value of learning. From a self-worth perspective, learning may become a means to attain rewards in support of one's ability status, so that, for example, when rewards such as grades are no longer offered in exchange for doing an assignment, students will show little or no inclination to continue in their studies (Condry & Koslowski, 1979). Moreover, the withholding of rewards or the offering of insufficient rewards, as in the case of receiving only a passing grade, can amount to a punishment (Kohn, 1993). Students become preoccupied not with what they are learning, but with the fear-driven necessity to perform better the next time. Furthermore, there is the possibility that if teachers attempt to reward already existing intrinsic engagement, say, by praising a student's extracurricular interests, then para-doxically these activities may actually be discouraged. This phenomenon is referred to as the *overjustification effect* (Greene, Sternberg, & Lepper, 1976; Lep-per, Greene, & Nisbett, 1973). According to this interpretation, the value of an already justifiable activity becomes suspect by the promise of additional rewards—hence the term overjustification—so that the learner may come to assume that "if someone has to pay me to do this, it must not be worth doing for it's own sake." (See the Spring 1996 issue of *Review of Educational Research* for a recent debate on this topic.)

The second observation drawn from a self-worth perspective suggests that the degree to which students care about learning depends on the resolution of a conflict between approach tendencies that favor intrinsic reasons for learning and failure-avoidant tendencies that tend to undermine intrinsic motivation (Elliot & Harackiewicz, 1996). Recent research (Covington, 1998) suggests that students deal with this potential conflict in a variety of ways. For some students, the so-called *failure avoiders*, the conflict is minimal because for them the intrinsic valuing of what is learned has a low priority. Their over-whelming need is to maintain a sense of worth by avoiding failure, or at least the implications of failure. Clearly, these fear-inspired tactics are at odds with intrinsic reasons for learning. Learning is valued only to the extent in which it serves to aggrandize or protect one's ability status.

By contrast, for students described as *success oriented*, the potential approach–avoidant conflict is also minimal, but for the opposite reason. Suc-cess-oriented students count their worth in terms of approaching success and by the intrinsic payoffs inherent in this goal. Our research, like that of Elliot and his colleagues (Elliot & Harackiewicz, 1996; Elliot, McGregor, & Gable, 1999), indicates that approach- or success-oriented students are more task involved than are failure-prone students and employ superior study strate-gies. These students' accomplishments are more appreciated for their posi-tive properties, and grades are perceived not necessarily as threatening but rather as feedback, suggesting how to increase self-understanding and per-sonal skills. For success-oriented students, then, the relationship between intrinsic valuing and grades is best described as complementary and sup-portive, not antagonistic as is the case for *failure avoiders*.

Finally, for a third group of students, the conflict inherent in this approach–avoidant dichotomy is maximized because they are driven simul-taneously both by high hopes of success and by an excessive fear of failure. On the one hand, these so-called *overstrivers* (Covington & Omelich, 1987, 1991) share an approach orientation with success-oriented students result-ing in an enhanced taste for intrinsic valuing for both groups. Yet, on the other hand, overstrivers also pursue success as a way to avoid failure. Overstrivers share much in common with those individuals identified as approach–per-formance-oriented by Elliot and Harackiewicz (1996). This approach–avoid-ance combination makes striving for excellence a fear-provoking ordeal. But because overstrivers become so successful in this defensive pursuit, their GPA soars; yet self-doubts about the ability to succeed remain because the goal is perfection, not just mastery. It is our impression that in terms of absolute numbers, overstrivers become increasingly overrepresented as a given cohort of students moves through the grade levels. Because of their consistently outstanding accomplishments, overstrivers are disproportionately retained in the educational system until college where they likely represent a near majority of students.

This self-worth analysis suggests that the functional relationship between intrinsic valuing and extrinsic payoffs depends in part on the motivational disposition of students. For some students these processes appear to be antagonistic, as in the case of failure-avoiding students; for others conflicting, as in the case of overstrivers, and for yet others, like success-oriented students, complementary.

In addition to the conceptual starting point provided by self-worth theory, our thinking about the developmental course of intrinsic motivation owes a considerable debt to two other prominent theoretical perspectives: the self-determination theory and stage–environmental fit theory.

Self-Determination Theory

Self-determination theory is concerned with the nature and nurturing of those basic needs thought to support intrinsic task engagement, including a need for autonomy, a need for affiliation (relatedness), and a need for competency (for reviews, see Deci & Ryan, 1992; Deci, Vallerand, Pelletier, & Ryan, 1991; Ryan & Deci, 2000). Deci and his colleagues have convincingly demonstrated that when these needs are satisfactorily met, individuals transform the otherwise negative impact of extrinsically controlling rewards into personal, internally regulated events that reflect intrinsic engagement.

By contrast, when these needs are not met, feelings of self-determination fade, and this is followed by a reduction in creative expression. According to Deci and his colleagues, the key to whether instructional conditions favor intrinsic engagement resides in the subjective meaning attributed to the achievement feedback received by the learner. If, for example, teacher feedback is perceived as positive information regarding the learner's competency, then the intrinsic aspects of what is being learned will be enhanced. But to the extent that feedback carries with it the implication of being placed under surveillance and controlled by powerful others, valuing will be destroyed. It is the proposed linkage between feelings of autonomy, relatedness, and competency that forms an essential focus of our research. By employing a retrospective methodology, we hope to extend considerably the time frame within which these self-determination dynamics can be observed.

Stage–Environmental Fit Theory

Stage–environmental fit theory, applied to motivation (Eccles, Midgley, et al., 1993; Eccles, Wigfield, et al., 1993), argues that students have different combinations of psychological needs at each level of their development, and unless these needs are satisfied, academic achievement and an appreciation for learning will suffer. In this regard much attention has been devoted to the dynamics of school transition, especially the entry of students into middle school, for early adolescent development is characterized by a variety of lifestyle changes that can impact academic achievement negatively unless they are properly addressed by schools, including the stress of pubertal changes, increases in self-consciousness, and an accelerating search for self-identity. Eccles and her colleagues have identified various ways that the social and intellectual structure of middle schools likely fail to support these developmental demands (Eccles, Wigfield, et al., 1993). One potentially disruptive factor is the greater emphasis on teacher control at the middle school level compared with that occurring in the prior years of elementary school, and consequently fewer opportunities for students to make choices regarding their own learning. Thus, it is argued that at a time when early adolescents generally experience an increased desire for autonomy, the opportunities for independent thinking and self-initiated behavior in school are on the decline. The result is a reduction in interest in subject matter and an ebbing of the capacity for intrinsic engagement.

Other similar mismatches regarding interpersonal, emotional needs have also been put forward. For example, it has been widely documented that as young adolescents work to form their identities, others play an important referential role (e.g., Erickson, 1968, 1980), making these youngsters more sensitive to comparisons with others. With this in mind, the increasing prevalence of normative grading in many middle schools, increased feelings of competition, and greater social comparisons have been singled out as having an unduly negative influence on a commitment to doing well in school among early adolescents (Anderman, Maehr, & Midgley, 1999). In addition, as young adolescents become increasingly in need of support from others, these youngsters nonetheless report feeling less academic support and nurturance from their teachers due to large class sizes and the advent of multiple teachers in the middle school years (Eccles, Wigfield, et al., 1993).

We have argued that many students are placed at risk for ever valuing what they have learned. Not only are students thought to be discouraged from satisfying their curiosities when they are rewarded tangibly for these positive impulses, but also, because of the scarcity of these rewards, the majority of students must struggle to avoid failure rather than to approach success. Then there is the threat of punishment in the form of poor grades, which promises to diminish the individual's sense of worth. Finally, there is the ever-present possibility of the failure of schools to meet the legitimate developmental needs of students. Taken together, these dynamics would seem to allow little room for the growth of a capacity for intrinsic task engagement. Yet, despite these formidable circumstances, our inquiries provide clear evidence that much of what students learn is acquired out of personal interest and curiosity, not out of fear or from feeling obligated, or merely for the pursuit of high grades.

In a series of preliminary studies, each involving several hundred of our college students and featuring open-ended essays, we found that students spontaneously experienced many examples of what one informant called "surplus knowledge," that is, knowledge acquired above and beyond grade-driven considerations (Covington, 1999). Moreover, our informants also made it clear that these frequent experiences were highly regarded not only for their role in promoting valued personal perspectives, but also for their usefulness in enhancing the meaning of everyday events, and for their ability to transform an individual for the better. Furthermore, students often volunteered that such personally transforming knowledge promoted respect, even awe, for the process of knowledge creation itself, irrespective of the subject matter involved.

As we became increasingly convinced that this appreciation for learning was genuine, the more puzzled we became. How could students care about their lessons in the context of an overweaning grade focus and a brutalizing gauntlet of selective sorting in a world dominated by extrinsically oriented rewards (Covington & Mueller, 2001)? What are the mechanisms at work that sustain such caring, and do they follow a lawful developmental course over the academic career of these students? In many respects these questions, and certainly their eventual answers, became entwined—in fact, the answers fused to create a broader understanding of the dynamics of school life. The most helpful perspective on these questions, especially regarding developmental issues, was provided by the results of a large-scale study that is reported here in some detail.

CARING ABOUT LEARNING: A RETROSPECTIVE STUDY

The most recent cohort of Berkeley students, some 460 in number, were asked to track, retrospectively, the events in school they recalled as having been especially influential in shaping their motivation to achieve, and especially caring about what they were learning, apart from grade considerations. These memories were prompted through a series of self-report, Likert-type questions designed to elicit recollections regarding the extent to which basic needs were or were not met in school. Following the lead provided by self-determination theory, we inquired about the degree to which *autonomy* needs were satisfied (e.g., "How much choice did you have in your school assignments and how to do them?"), the degree to which *relatedness* needs were satisfied both by teachers (e.g., "How much did your teachers value and respect your ideas?") and by peers (e.g., "How much did you feel left out by your classmates?"), and about feelings of *competency* and in being in control of events (e.g., "How much did you feel you had the ability to do well academically?"). Additionally, as part of our central focus on a self-worth perspective, students were asked to recall the extent to which different reasons (or motives) for achieving prevailed for them, including working for good grades to prove one's ability, to avoid doing badly, and to please others by staying out of trouble.

Our participants were asked to rate this same panel of questions three different times, once with respect to their memories of the upper elementary school years, once for their recollections of the middle school years, and finally once for the high school years. In all three instances, the dependent variable of interest reflected the same affective, intrinsic aspects of academic life (e.g., "How much did you value and appreciate what you were learning?"). When it came time to recall the middle school and high school years, the entire sample was split equally and assigned on a random basis to report events and feelings associated either with English/social studies classes or math/science classes, respectively. To anticipate some of our findings, this subject matter manipulation amounted to a non significant variation across the entire data panel, suggesting that whatever the developmental dynamics of intrinsic motivation might prove to be, they are likely to operate in a highly similar manner across subject matter domains.

To benefit from a complementary analysis of the school transition dynamics described by stage–environmental fit theory, we also asked our informants to rate the degree of change on key variables experienced in their move from elementary to middle school and from middle school to high school, including changes in either positive or negative directions for teacher support, self-estimates of competency, and competitive pressure. All these self-report questions were accompanied by an extensive set of brief, open-ended essay questions that allowed randomly selected subsamples of students to elaborate in writing on their numerical ratings.

An initial examination of the numerical rating data served to extend our earlier reported findings of strong feelings of intrinsic engagement at the college level by confirming their presence back in time, insofar as memories served, to some of the earliest years of schooling. The mean scores for intrinsic engagement for the entire sample indicate an increasingly positive attitude toward learning over successive grade levels, except for a temporary dip during the middle school years; but with this otherwise positive progression eventually recovering to a maximum level in the high school years (Figure 1). We will return later to a more specific discussion of the dynamics responsible for this decline in the middle school years.

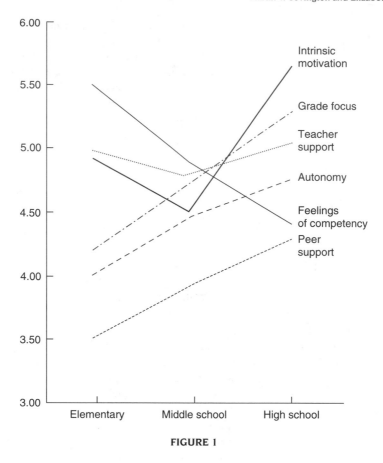

FIGURE I

The Role of Success

The findings regarding a growing capacity for valuing learning refocused our inquiries on the quintessential puzzle: If it is true that feelings of competition increase and a grade focus intensifies over the years, then should there not be a progressive decline, not an increase, in caring for learning? The answer to this apparent paradox came largely from insights gained by analyzing student essays. Basically, our informants were eloquent spokespersons for the benefits of success vis-à-vis intrinsic engagement, and in particular for the progressive accumulation of the kinds of *extraordinary* successes enjoyed by this highly selected group of students. While many other academically less successful students in the same age-mate cohort were doubtless losing interest in school partly as a result of the discouraging impact of mounting scholastic disappointments, our informants were enjoying the fruits of a highly satisfying process of academic self-sorting. Because they survived a rigorous course of successive academic elimination, beginning a decade or more earlier, these relatively few students now stand at the pinnacle of academic excellence as they begin college.

It was these successes, in turn, and the emerging recognition of their academic promise, that led our students to an increasing appreciation for the lessons being learned in school and for a valuing of the personal characteristics that set them apart from so many others—inquisitiveness, creativity, and a capacity for inventive thinking. This process is reflected in a bit of common sense wisdom: people enjoy doing those things at which they excel. Our students confirmed this proposition. For example, data collected from an earlier sample (McEvoy & Covington, 2000) indicated that for our students, subject matter appreciation depends primarily on whether they succeed in achieving their grade–goal aspirations, and to a far lesser extent on whether the material was personally meaningful or whether the instructional climate was supportive as when, for instance, an instructor is respectful of student ideas.

Incidentally, in retrospect, it seems self-evident that success and failure experiences would profoundly influence one's appreciation for what is being learned. Yet little prior research has considered the degree to which students feel successful (or not) in learning the material it was hoped they would come to value (for an exception, see Harter, Whitesell, & Junkin, 1998).

These valuing–performance dynamics are almost certainly reciprocal, with reciprocity expressing itself in either upward or downward spirals of appreciation depending on the quality of one's work. As to the uplifting side of these dynamics, time spent studying appears to be a key factor. According to our essay data, a growing appreciation caused by prior successes acts to increase subsequent achievement even more because valuing triggers more time studying, and more studying leads to better grades. Our research also suggests other ways that personal interest and appreciation may influence the process of upward-striving academic performances (Covington & Wiedenhaupt, 1997). We found that when students are task interested, they believe that grades are awarded by teachers to inspire class members to do their best work, a judgment that stands in considerable contrast to the reactions of the same students when they have little or no personal interest in an assignment. In this latter case, they tend to perceive grades as a method employed by teachers to guarantee a minimum amount of effort. The differential impact on subject matter appreciation of these two perceived functions of grades—one positive and the other manipulative—is obvious.

In summary, then, a picture emerges of a dynamic interplay, on the one hand, between accumulating successes and the pride and recognition that superior achievement brings and, on the other hand, a growing sense of appreciation for the processes of learning by which these successes are achieved. The net effect of this cyclical process is to spur individuals to greater achievements, success after success.

But what about failure? No one can succeed indefinitely. Will failure experiences along the way temporarily interrupt, or even derail, this upward-striving, self-reinforcing progression? Research conducted some years ago on a similar Berkeley sample provides an answer (Covington & Omelich, 1982). As long as students continued to learn and improve—improvement being the key—then isolated failure experiences along the way, although temporarily upsetting, had little lasting influence on the will to learn. These successful students, similar to those in the present sample, attributed their successes to their own efforts, and because the assignments were seen by them as challenging but not impossible, they also believed themselves sufficiently capable in the bargain.

Clearly, however, there is more involved in the development of a capacity for intrinsic engagement than a history of accumulated academic successes. Success does not operate in a vacuum. For instance, according to self-worth theory, it is the reasons for pursuing success, not merely the event of success itself, that also influence the extent to which students value learning. Moreover, success helps satisfy those developmental needs which, according to self-determination theory, are important to the growth and maintenance of intrinsic task engagement. We explored these additional sources of influence via a series of multiple regression analyses of our numerical self-report data. Several developmental needs as well as reasons for learning proved critical to the sustained growth of intrinsic valuing over the academic life span of our students, from elementary through high school years.

Grade-Focused Reasons for Learning

Striving for good grades as a way to prove one's ability contributed significantly to variations in the degree to which learning was valued in its own right across all three grade levels. These results find support in the self-worth proposition that many students equate their worth with a reputation for being able and, as a consequence, strive to secure such a reputation. Moreover, this ego-oriented reason for achieving was recalled by our informants as having increased significantly in degree as they moved first from the elementary to the middle school level, and then on into the high school years. The mean scores for the scale reflecting a need to prove one's self for the entire sample at each of the three school levels are displayed in Figure 1, along with the mean values for the other significant predictors of intrinsic motivation to be discussed shortly. Incidentally, displaying several predictors in a single figure is done only for simplicity's sake; it is not meant to imply an identity of scale values among the measures.

Finding that a blatantly self-serving motive such as the desire to prove one's superiority is implicated positively in a capacity for intrinsic valuing may appear counterintuitive. However, it makes a perverse kind of sense, given the competitive context in which many schools operate. Being ambitious, aggressive, and opportunistic augurs well for achieving the record of successes enjoyed by our students, and as we argued earlier, success in turn enhances an appreciation for the material being learned and renews one's dedication to continue learning. However, the impact of this self-aggrandizing motive on the development of intrinsic processes varies by student type.

First, consider success-oriented students. Although this group manifested the same pattern of an increasing need to prove one's self as was found for the two failure-oriented groups (i.e., *failure avoiders* and *overstrivers*), success-oriented students recalled a comparatively reduced presence of these ego-focused motives at each school level. This differential recollection makes sense in the case of success-oriented students who, as we noted earlier, derive their sense of worth more from intrinsic pursuits than from the need to win over others. Nonetheless, the presence of self-aggrandizing tendencies, even in trace amounts, affirms the obvious point that no one is immune from the dynamics set in motion by the pervasive societal assumption that individuals are only as worthy as their ability to achieve competitively.

By contrast—not surprisingly—overstrivers were by far the most grade focused of students across all three school levels, given their preoccupation with ability status as a core definition of self, and their dominant strategy of avoiding failure by succeeding. At the same time, overstrivers recalled valuing learning as much as did success-oriented students, doubtless because overstrivers also share an approach orientation. It is this competing presence of approach and avoidance tendencies that likely accounts for the singular emotional reaction of overstrivers when describing the subjective content of their success experiences. It is our impression that enjoyment for these students is defined largely in terms of the absence of failure, with consequent feelings of relief rather than the feelings of joy and genuine pride in accomplishment associated with the reactions of success-oriented students.

Competency

Our multiple regression analyses indicated that in addition to self-serving, grade-focused motives, feelings of competency recalled by our subjects also made a substantial, independent contribution to variations in the degree to which learning was valued at both the elementary and middle school levels. In effect, the more one feels equal to a task, intellectually speaking, the more task engaged one becomes—a point repeatedly confirmed by our informants' essays. Given the potential importance of this competency–engaged linkage, it is instructive to note that for all students, irrespective of their approach–avoidance status, mean levels of competency were recalled as steadily declining from a maximum in the elementary years to a low point in the high school years (see Figure 1). Similar declines are reported by other investigators and often are attributed to the advent of competitive grading and intensifying social comparisons, beginning in the middle school years. The present data corroborate this interpretation. As our informants reflected on each school level, one at a time, they recalled experiencing increasing feelings of being in competition with others, feelings that reached their maximum in the middle school years. These progressive declines in self-confidence are likely marginal in comparison to the increasing self-doubts of most students outside an elite college track. Nonetheless, they were particularly threatening to the failure-oriented students in our sample, especially for overstrivers who reported a particularly precipitous drop in their self-perceptions of ability over time. At some point in their academic careers these students likely came to a cruel realization: They believed themselves to possess in decreasing amounts that very quality of mind—ability—that was becoming increasingly important to their sense of worth via noteworthy successes.

Autonomy

Variations in the opportunities to exercise freedom of choice and to act autonomously in school also made significant positive contributions to variations in intrinsic motivation at both the elementary and middle school levels, independent of the variance already explained by grade-focused reasons for achieving and the need to feel competent. The recalled frequency of autonomous opportunities increased steadily over the grade levels (see Figure 1). Once again, like the competency variable, differences in autonomy ratings were found across student types. Success-oriented students recalled far greater opportunities to exercise autonomy than did either of the two failure-oriented groups, and this recollection was found at each of the three school levels. These data corroborate the consensus among researchers of the important benefits of freedom of choice to the nurturing of intrinsic values (Deci, Vallerand, Pelletier, & Ryan, 1991; Grolnick & Ryan, 1987; Pintrich, Roeser, & DeGroot, 1994; Vallerand, Fortier, & Guay, 1997).

Relatedness

Our results also indicate that both teacher and peer support are crucial to the development of a capacity for intrinsic valuing, if we are to judge by the significant degree of explained variance accounted for by these two factors across all school levels. However, recollections of the degree to which these positive factors were present varied over time (see Figure 1). Most notably, mean value for recalled teacher support declined substantially during the middle school years for all our informants, but rebounded during the high school years. Although everyone exhibited essentially the same pattern for recalled teacher support, differences by student type also emerged. The two student groups that shared an approach orientation (success-oriented students and over-strivers) remembered receiving considerably more support from teachers for their studies than did failure-avoiding students at all school levels.

While recalled teacher support declined during the middle school years, before rebounding during high school, perceptions of peer support increased steadily through time. With respect to individual differences, success-oriented students perceived higher levels of peer support than did failure-oriented students at all three school levels, with the differences favoring an approach orientation becoming quite pronounced in the high school years.

DISCUSSION

Overview

Taken as a whole, our findings present a picture of developmental dynamics that largely confirm earlier research and provides several notable qualifications that are likely a reflection on the unique characteristics of our sample. Our findings broadly confirm the central tenet of self-determination theory, namely, that satisfaction of the basic psychological needs for affiliation, autonomy, and competency is an essential ingredient in the process of coming to care about learning. Likewise, our evidence also substantiates an important role in this process for ego-focused reasons for learning, namely, striving to outperform others. This is consistent with the basic premise of self-worth theory, that is, students often come to equate their personal worth with the ability to compete successfully. In this connection, perhaps one of the most instructive aspect of our research is that it reminds us of the darker side of achievement dynamics as manifested in many schools today. This ego-focused mentality likely emerges as necessary for survival in school environments that feature competitive rivalry and the need to avoid failure rather than to approach success. Ironically enough, for all its defensive, self-aggrandizing characteristics, a grade–ability focus likely activates those qualities of mind and personality that in a competitive circumstance favor being highly successful in one's studies. And, as we have argued, being successful is in the vanguard of factors that promote a capacity for intrinsic engagement.

The fact that the pursuit of academic excellence is so fully dependent on less than worthy impulses, at least among the most promising of students, is regrettable—regrettable because even among academic winners, the psychological casualty rate can be prohibitive. This cost is reflected in the over-striver who amasses an enviable academic record as a way to offset persistent self-doubts, doubts that linger anyway, and in the upward-striving entrepreneur who sacrifices the joy of discovery for the sake of conformity. The cost is also reflected in what passes, emotionally, as the joy and excitement of learning, which on closer inspection is seen to be only thinly disguised relief at having not failed. In addition, the rewards of competitive success are often tarnished by the realization that one's pride depends on the ignoble sentiment of being better or more deserving than others.

Our findings also underscore the importance of the high school years as a time of relative abundance for those ingredients of intrinsic engagement identified by others and corroborated by us, including expanded opportunities for choice, teacher and peer support, and a determined focus to work for the highest grade possible. The high school years were recalled by our informants as a time of great encouragement regarding intrinsic task engagement. The sole exception to this positive picture was the pronounced deterioration of self-estimates of ability culminating in the high school years, which doubtless is the product of increasingly intense competitive rivalry as students moved through school.

By contrast, the move from the elementary to middle school years represented the low ebb for intrinsic engagement, as indicated both by our findings and by those of others (e.g., Eccles, Wigfield, et al., 1993; Harter, Whitesell, & Kowalski, 1992). Our findings regarding the causes of this hiatus during the period of transition from the elementary to the middle school years are additive to what is already known or suspected. As will be recalled, we ask our students to make specific comparisons on key variables regarding their transition from elementary to middle school and then from middle school to high school. Our informants indicated the extent to which, for example, feelings of close teacher support either increased, decreased, or remained the same in their move from the elementary to the middle school years. These change score data closely tracked our previously reported findings in which comparisons between elementary and middle school recollections were based on separate, independent ratings at each educational level. Like the earlier data, students reported an intensified need to prove themselves via an ability status as they moved into middle school, as well as increased feelings of competition and an increased resolve to pursue the highest grade possible.

Consistent with predictions of stage–environmental fit theory (Eccles, Midgley, et al., 1993; Eccles, Wigfield, et al., 1993), we also found increases in the degree to which students felt they were left out socially due to the demise of prior friendship networks in the elementary years. There was, however, no confirmation of the decline in self-perceived ability during the transition. Although this additional finding in no way invalidates the overall phenomenon of declines in self-confidence reported by us and by others (e.g., Simmons & Blyth, 1987), it does suggest that such declines may not necessarily be the property of transitions per se, but may represent a more general phenomenon caused by gradually increasing social comparisons as youngsters grow older, year by year. Also, contrary to some predictions of stage–environmental fit theory, our students recalled a slight increase, not the expected decreased, in opportunities for autonomous decision making in the transition to middle school. These perceptions of newly found freedoms probably are the result of a highly dedicated group of youngsters being empowered by teachers to work more on their own, trusting that these promising students will take responsibility for their own learning.

Overall, we gained the impression that while the middle school transition is potentially adverse, for our sample of youngsters at least, the move was not as perilous as had been previously thought. Several explanations for this impression come to mind. First, the climate of many middle schools has changed dramatically for the better in the decades following much of the earlier research on this issue. Interestingly enough, it was the widespread findings of inadequacy documented by these particular studies that triggered much of the reform efforts at the middle school level (see the Carnegie Report: Carnegie Council on Adolescent Development, 1989). Another possible explanation for the relatively benign recollections of our sample regarding their middle school experiences implicates the highly selective nature of our sample. Academically successful students are likely to weather changes involving school-to-school transitions more easily than are less well-prepared, academically average or below-average students who comprised many of the samples drawn for the earlier research.

Uniqueness of the Study

We have already interpreted several of our findings as possibly being the product of our highly selected sample. Two other findings, one occurring despite this selectivity, and the other emerging because of Berkeley's special demographics, warrant our attention.

The first finding concerns gender differences in the development of achievement motivation. Initially, we assumed that the highly selective nature of the college admission process, especially for entry into prestigious institutions, would obscure achievement-related gender differences typically found in unselected samples. However, although likely muted, some systematic gender differences did nonetheless emerge in our sample. Generally, females reported experiencing feelings of intrinsic task engagement to a greater degree than did males across each of the three levels of schooling investigated. Likewise our women recalled experiencing greater autonomy and peer and teacher support at all levels, as well as a more focused intensity regarding grades and the need to prove themselves. By contrast, our males recalled feeling more confident in their ability to achieve, a finding reported earlier by numerous investigators and frequently interpreted as the product of male defensiveness brought about by societal pressures to maintain an image of assertiveness, power and competency (Covington & Omelich, 1978; Snyder, Stephan, & Rosenfeld, 1976; Zuckerman, 1979).

Second, largely owing to the unique demographics of the San Francisco Bay area, one-third of our sample was of Asian descent of which Chinese–Americans comprised the largest subgroup. These relatively large numbers provided a special opportunity to extend our ongoing study of the ethnic factors involved in achievement dynamics. Basically, we found no differences in a disposition for intrinsic motivation between our Chinese–American students and their Caucasian counterparts at any of the three levels of schooling. Nor were there differences in feelings of autonomy, peer support, or teacher support at any of the levels. However, our Caucasian students did indicate being substantially more confident in their academic ability at all educational levels, while our Chinese–American students expressed a greater grade focus. One interpretation of this joint pattern—that many of our Chinese–Americans youngsters are striving to overcome feelings of inadequacy by succeeding—is strengthened by the findings of some of our previous retrospective research. Kumiko Tomiki and I (Covington & Tomiki, 1996; Tomiki, 1997) asked another sample of our students to recall the quality of the achievement climate in their homes. Chinese–American youngsters indicated that their parents stressed performance goals more than learning goals (e.g., "In my home getting good grades was more important than how much I was learning") to a greater degree than did Caucasian students. The former group also recalled more parental punishments (e.g., cutting allowances; being grounded) whenever they failed to meet parental standards, which they were afraid they might never satisfy (e.g., "I feel my family demanded more of me academically than I could ever achieve."). This combination of any disappointing performances being perceived by parents as violations of adult expectations in the face of overweening demands was closely associated with the presence of failure-prone behavior. Little wonder, then, that our Chinese–American students in the present sample were categorized as failure avoiders over Caucasian students by a margin of 2 to 1.

In addition to our sampling from a highly selected population, another unusual aspect of our research involved the use of a retrospective methodology. We believe this method provides a promising perspective for the study of developmental phenomena in general. It allows individuals to recapture and evaluate events from the perspective provided by the passage of time—a selective casting up of past accounts, so to speak, and the weighing of the ultimate importance of various prior life experiences against one another. This perspective is largely missing from traditional longitudinal studies when measurements taken repeatedly over time are treated as independent events for purposes of comparison. Other more practical advantages also accrue. For one thing, retrospective analyses are enormously cost-effective of time and research resources, and for another thing, they are essentially immune to the biasing effects of subject attrition once the sample is drawn.

Yet for all these potential benefits, there is the obvious concern that recalled events are not necessarily as they actually occurred, and that data like those reported here are in part a testimony to the power of selective attention, motivated forgetting, and other inaccuracies and distortions that mask true events. For instance, we might ask: Were our failure-avoiding students really systematically subjected to less supportive school environments over the years, or were these judgments merely the product of the lens through which they saw events? Almost certainly the latter interpretation is correct. But is not identifying and understanding the lens through which individuals perceive events and how these views change over time the proper pursuit of psychology? As long as educational planners are concerned with perceptions of reality as well as reality itself, retrospective methodology should provide an important complement to mainstream research techniques. Indeed, the fact that our data identify lawful relationships among variables and confirm much of what had been discovered by other means is reassuring and additive.

Integrating Theory and Practice

Our study invites a conceptual reapproachment between self-determination theory and self-worth theory, both of which derive their meaning from a need-based perspective. The closest point of theoretical contact is the importance accorded the concept of competency by both theories. For self-worth theory, feelings of competency are the defining ingredient of personal value—or as stated elsewhere "... people [in our society] are held to be only as good as their achievements" (Covington & Beery, 1976, p.6). For self-determination theory, feelings of competency represent a necessary precursor to creative expression and intrinsic task engagement. Research in this tradition has focused on identifying those instructional conditions that enhance feelings of being competent. Thus, for these theories, competency represents two sides of the same conceptual coin: in effect, competency resides both in the *person* and in the *situation*, respectively. When it comes to matters of educational reform, self-worth theory alerts us to the dangers of linking one's sense of personal value to competency defined competitively. Competition becomes a threat because it undercuts feelings of competency even when individuals may be performing satisfactorily. At the same time, self-determination theory underscores the dangers inherent in any teaching strategy that promotes feelings of being scrutinized, coerced, or under the control of others.

These two interlocking, need-based perspectives suggest some broad guidelines for educational reform when it comes to fostering a capacity for intrinsic task engagement. First and foremost, our research has demonstrated that being successful academically is the central motive force that drives feelings of competency, which in turn promote task engagement. But it is not just high grades that are the key; rather it is the subjective purpose ascribed to being competent that counts. When newly won competencies are seen as instrumental for meeting personally valued challenges or for satisfying one's curiosity, they promote intrinsic engagement. However, when competency is defined in terms of doing better than others or of aggrandizing one's ability status, then the application of one's competencies threatens the will to learn. Consider overstrivers, who may continue to harbor self-doubts about their worth despite outstanding academic records.

In effect, any efforts at educational reform must address the need for changing the reasons for achievement from negative and ultimately self-defeating to positive and self-empowering. The urgency of this point is well illustrated in our data. Recall that feelings of subject matter appreciation and task engagement are heavily dependent on the goal of proving one's ability, and this relationship held across the entire developmental range sampled. As already mentioned, we believe this dynamic to be the property of the competitive, institutional context in which our students found themselves. Fortunately, these talented students succeeded on both counts—coming to value what they had learned exceedingly well. But what of the vast majority of other less well-endowed or simply less well-prepared students in the American educational system? These countless youngsters are unlikely to fare as well as those in our sample. For many of them, success, when it does occur, is an unexpected event that is likely to be attributed to chance or to the good intentions of teachers, rather than caused by one's own ability or hard work. Such a conclusion cannot promote the growth of self-confidence. As a result, many of these youngsters deliberately misjudge their capacities, aspire after irrational goals for defensive purposes, and are crippled in their problem-solving efforts by anxiety and doubt. The progressive deterioration of self-perceived competency found in our study appears to be the product of an increasingly scarce supply of rewards as students move through the grade levels. For our high-achieving students, the impact of these self-doubts is offset in large part by their successes. But for many other less well-positioned students, no such compensatory mechanisms are available.

One promising approach to discouraging negative reasons for learning and encouraging meaningful and sufficient successes for all students involves the use of grading policies using absolute, or merit-based, criteria, that is, holding students to specific, clearly defined requirements so that any number of pupils can achieve a given grade as long as they live up to the quality of workmanship demanded by the teacher. Such procedures have been shown to enhance scholarly performance as well as to offset the reasons for learning associated with competitive pressure both at the college (Covington & Omelich, 1984) and the middle school levels (Covington & Teel, 1996). Merit-based successes also are likely to encourage feelings of competency without the stigma of surveillance or control. Basically, feedback generated in the context of absolute standards tends to empower students; that is, it suggests ways to improve and expand one's capabilities. This message is especially important in the event of failure. Encouragement conveys the impression that failure need not be perceived as a personal shortcoming, but rather as a short-fall of proper effort.

Our findings that the capacity for intrinsic engagement depends closely on feelings of autonomy underscores another benefit of absolute standards. Absolute standards encourage a greater sense of grading fairness and of personal control (Covington & Omelich, 1984) by reducing ambiguities regarding grading policy in the first instance and by strengthening the perceived linkage between degree of effort expended and achievement level in the second. Intrinsic engagement is best served when students are challenged incrementally, with the prospects for success maximized when students are allowed within some limits to set learning goals for themselves and to modify them as required so that if failure does occur, it acts to renew their efforts, not demoralize them.

All this having been said, it must be pointed out that—like all research, no matter how inclusive its intentions—our retrospective study has been highly selective of the factors chosen for investigation. We have focused primarily on the role of grade-oriented successes and on the satisfaction of various psychological needs to provide a developmental perspective on the nature and growth of intrinsic motivation. These decisions were made in part on practical and logistical grounds, since only so much can be accomplished in a given study; they in no way imply that other factors are either irrelevant or unnecessary to a fuller understanding of intrinsic motivation. Among these under-represented factors we can mention a few, by example, including the role that teacher instructional style plays in promoting task engagement, apart from the support dimension per se (Perry & Magnusson, 1987), the influence of the home environment on intellectual curiosity and independence, (Tomiki, 1996), and the impact of task variables on intrinsic engagement including the role as well as the quality of the curriculum itself, including the important task characteristics of novelty (Covington & Wiedenhaupt, 1997) and personal relevance (Stipek, 1996).

Clearly, adding more factors to an already complicated motivational, need-based equation increases exponentially the challenge to reform-minded educators. Effective school change is never easy; there are so many crosscutting issues. Nonetheless, there emerges from our findings and from those complementary views offered by others, one overarching proposition regarding the promotion of a love of learning and the willingness to continue learning over a lifetime. This goal is best served when teachers and students become allies, not adversaries, with teachers acting as mentors and resources for students as they prepare for the future.

References

Ames, C. (1992). Achievement goals and the classroom climate. In D. H. Schunk & J. L. Meece (Eds.), *Student perceptions in the classroom* (pp. 327–348). Hillsdale, NJ: Lawrence Erlbaum Associates.

Anderman, E. M., Maehr, M. L., & Midgley, C. (1999). Declining motivation after the transition to middle school: Schools can make a difference. *Journal of Research in Development in Education*, 32(3), 131–147.

Anderman, E. M., & Midgley, C. (1997). Changes in achievement goal orientations, perceived academic competence, and grades across the transition to middle-level schools. *Contemporary Educational Psychology*, 22 (3), 269–298.

Atkinson, J. W. (1957). Motivational determinants of risk-taking behavior. *Psychology Review*, 64, 359–372.

Carnegie Council on Adolescent Development (1989). *Turning points: Preparing American youth for the 21st century*. New York: Carnegie Corporation of New York.

Condry, J., & Koslowski, B. (1979). Can education be made "intrinsically interesting" to children? In D. Katz (Ed.), *Current topics in early childhood education*, Vol. II. Greenwich, CT: Ablex Publishing Corp.

Covington, M. V. (1984). The self-worth theory of achievement motivation: Findings and implications. *The Elementary School Journal*, 85(1), 5–20.

Covington, M. V. (1992). *Making the Grade: A Self-Worth Perspective on Motivation and School Reform*. Cambridge, U.K.: Cambridge University Press.

Covington, M. V. (1998). *The will to learn: A guide for motivating young people*. New York: Cambridge University Press.

Covington, M. V. (1999). Caring about learning: The nature and nurturing of subject matter appreciation. *Educational Psychologist*, 34(2), 127–136.

Covington, M. V. (2000) Goal theory, motivation, and school achievement: An integrative review. *Annual Review of Psychology*, 51, 171–200.

Covington, M. V., & Beery, R. G. (1976). *Self-worth and school learning*. New York: Holt, Rinehart & Winston.

Covington, M. V. & Mueller, K. J. (2001). Intrinsic versus extrinsic motivation: An approach avoidance reformulation. *Educational Psychology Review*. New York: Plenum Press.

Covington, M. V., & Omelich, C. L. (1978). *Sex differences in self-aggrandizing tendencies*. Unpublished manuscript, University of California at Berkeley.

Covington, M. V. & Omelich, C. L. (1982). Achievement anxiety, performance and behavioral instruction: A cost/benefits analysis. In R. Schwarzer, H. M. van der Ploeg, & C. D. Spielberger (Eds.), *Advances on test anxiety research* (Vol. 1, pp. 139–154). Hillsdale, NJ: Lawrence Erlbaum Associates.

Covington, M. V. & Omelich, C. L. (1984). Task-oriented versus competitive learning structures: Motivational and performance consequences. *Journal of Educational Psychology*, 76(6), 1038–1050.

Covington, M. V., & Omelich, C. L. (1987). "I knew it cold before the exam": A test of the anxiety blockage hypothesis. *Journal of Educational Psychology*, 79(4), 393–400.

Covington, M. V., & Omelich, C. L. (1991). Need achievement revisited: Verification of Atkinson's original 2 x 2 model. In C. D. Spielberger, I. G. Sarason, Z. Kulcsar, & G. L. Van Heck (Eds.), *Stress and emotion: Anxiety, anger and curiosity* (Vol. 14, pp. 85–105). Washington DC: Hemisphere.

Covington, M. V., & Teel, K. M. (1996). *Overcoming student failure: Changing motives and incentives for learning*. Washington, DC: American Psychological Association.

Covington, M. V., & Tomiki, K. (1996). *Achievement motivation: Child-rearing antecedents, culture and ethnicity*. Unpublished manuscript, University of California at Berkeley.

Covington, M. V., & Wiedenhaupt, S. (1997). Turning work into play: The nature and nurturing of intrinsic task engagement. In R. Perry & J. C. Smart (Eds.), *Effective teaching in higher education: Research and practice, special edition* (pp. 101–114). New York: Agathon Press.

Deci, E. L., & Ryan, R. M. (1992). The initiation and regulation of intrinsically motivated learning and achievement. In A. K. Boggiano & T. S. Pittman (Eds.), *Achievement and motivation: A social–developmental perspective* (pp. 9–36). New York: Cambridge University Press.

Deci, E. L., Vallerand, R. J., Pelletier, L. G., & Ryan, R. M. (1991). Motivation and education: The self-determination perspective. *Educational Psychologist*, 26(3 & 4), 325–346.

Eccles, J. S., Lord, S., & Midgley, C. (1991). What are we doing to early adolescents? The impact of educational contexts on early adolescents. *American Journal of Education*, 99(4), 521–542.

Eccles, J. S., Midgley, C., Wigfield, A., Buchanan, C. M, Reuman, D., Flanagan, C., & MacIver, D. (1993). Development during adolescence: The impact of stage–environment fit on young adolescents' experiences in schools and families, *American Psychologist*, 48(2), 90–101.

Eccles, J. S., Wigfield, A., Midgley, C., Reuman, D., MacIver, D., & Feldlaufer, H. (1993). Negative effects of traditional middle schools on students' motivation, *The Elementary School Journal*, 93(5), 553–574.

Elliot, A. J., & Harackiewicz, J. M. (1996). Approach and avoidance goals and intrinsic motivation; A mediational analysis. *Journal of Personality and Social Psychology*, 70(3), 461–475.

Elliot, A. J., McGregor, H. A., & Gable, S. (1999). Achievement goals, study strategies, and exam performance: A mediational analysis. *Journal of Educational Psychology*, 91(3), 549–563.

Erikson, E. H. (1968). *Identity: Youth and crisis.* New York: Norton.

Erikson, E. H. (1980). *Identity and the life cycle.* New York: Norton.

Greene, D., Sternberg, B., & Lepper, M. R. (1976) Overjustification in a token economy. *Journal of Personality & Social Psychology*, 34(6), 1219–1234.

Grolnick, W. S., & Ryan, R. M. (1987). Autonomy in children's learning: An experimental and individual difference investigation. *Journal of Personality & Social Psychology*, 52(5), 890–898

Harter, S., Whitesell, N. R., & Junkin, L. J. (1998). Similarities and differences in domain-specific and global self-evaluations of learning-disabled, behaviorally disordered and normally achieving adolescents. *American Educational Research Journal*, 35(4), 653–680.

Harter, S., Whitesell, N. R., & Kowalski, P. S. (1992). Individual differences in the effects of educational transitions on young adolescents' perceptions of competence and motivational orientation. *American Educational Research Journal*, 29(4), 777–808.

Kohn, A. (1993). *Punished by rewards.* Boston: Houghton-Mifflin.

Lepper, M. R., Greene, D., & Nisbett, R. E. (1973). Undermining children's intrinsic interest with extrinsic reward: A test of the "overjustification" hypothesis. *Journal of Personality & Social Psychology*, 28(1) 129–137.

McEvoy, A., & Covington, M. V. (2000). *Appreciation for learning: The effects of grades, personal interest and intellectual climate.* Unpublished manuscript, University of California at Berkeley.

Midgley, C., Kaplan, A., Middleton, M., & Maehr, M. L. (1998). The development and validation of scales assessing students' achievement goal orientations. *Contemporary Educational Psychology*, 23(2), 113–131.

Midgley, C., & Maehr, M. L. (2000). *The transition to high school study. Report to participating schools and districts.* Unpublished manuscript, University of Michigan, Ann Arbor.

Perry, R. P., & Magnusson, J. L. (1987). Effective instruction and students' perceptions of control in the college classroom: Multiple-lectures effect. *Journal of Educational Psychology*, 79(4), 453–460.

Pintrich, P. R., Roeser, R. W., & DeGroot, E. A. (1994). Classroom and individual differences in early adolescents' motivation and self-regulated learning. *Journal of Early Adolescence*, 14(2), 139–161.

Ryan, R. M., & Deci, E. L. (2000). Self-determination theory and the facilitation of intrinsic motivation, social development, and well-being. *American Psychologist*, 55(1), 68–78.

Simmons, R. G., & Blyth, D. A. (1987). *Moving into adolescence: The impact of pubertal change and school context.* New York: Aldine de Gruyter.

Skaalvik, E. (1997). Self-enhancing and self-defeating ego orientation: Relations with task and avoidance orientation, achievement, self-perceptions and anxiety. *Journal of Educational Psychology*, 89(1), 71–81.

Snyder, M. L., Stephan, W. G., & Rosenfeld, C. (1976). Egotism and attribution. *Journal of Personality and Social Psychology*, 33(4), 435–441.

Stipek, D. J. (1996). Motivation and instruction. In D. C. Berliner & R. C. Calfee (Eds.), *Handbook of Educational Psychology* (pp. 85–112). New York: Simon & Schuster Macmillan.

Thorkildsen, T. A., & Nicholls, J. G. (1998). Fifth graders' achievement orientations and beliefs: Individual and classroom differences. *Journal of Educational Psychology*, 90(2), 179–201.

Tomiki, K. (1997). *Influences of cultural values and perceived family environments on achievement motivation among college students.* Unpublished master's thesis, University of California at Berkeley.

Vallerand, R. J., Fortier, M. S., & Guay, F. (1997). Self-determination and persistence in a real life setting: Toward a motivational model of high school dropout. *Journal of Personality and Social Psychology*, 72(5), 1161–1176.

Wigfield, A., Eccles, J. S., & Pintrich, P. (1996). Development between the ages of 11 and 25. In D. C. Berlinger R. C. Calfee, (Eds.), *The handbook of educational psychology* (pp. 148–185). New York: Prentice Hall International.

Zuckerman, M. (1979). Attribution of success and failure revisited, or: The motivational bias is alive and well in attribution theory. *Journal of Personality*, 47(2), 245–287.

CHAPTER

3

The Development of Ability Conceptions

CAROL S. DWECK

Columbia University, New York, New York

INTRODUCTION

Children's conceptions of ability play a pivotal role in their achievement motivation. During grade school and middle school, critical changes take place in these conceptions and their influence on achievement motivation. It is during this time that children come to fully understand the idea of ability as a potentially stable trait of the self; to reason fluently about the relations among intellectual ability, effort, and performance; and, perhaps most important, to show a coherent relation both among their achievement beliefs and between their ability beliefs and their motivation.

As these conceptions develop, children become more concerned about their ability and more sensitive to evaluation, especially negative evaluation. Moreover, once they have developed a clear and coherent understanding of ability, the *particular* conception of ability they adopt will determine a great deal about their motivational patterns. It will influence such things as whether they seek and enjoy challenges and how resilient they are in the face of setbacks.

To understand these changes, I will review research on developmental changes in children's ability conceptions—their definitions of ability, self-perceptions of ability, and reasoning about ability—and research on how these

The Development of Achievement Motivation

developmental changes in ability conceptions alter children's achievement motivation.[1]

I will show that there are notable changes between kindergartners and 7–8 year olds, and between 7–8 and 10–12 year olds—that during each period, qualitative changes take place in children's thinking about ability and in their motivation.

Ability Conceptions in Perspective

Although I will devote most of the chapter to understanding the important and often dramatic changes that take as children develop their conceptions of ability, I will argue that a focus on these changes has misled researchers in some major respects:

1. It has led us to underestimate young children's motivational vulnerability by suggesting, erroneously, that until children understood intelligence as a stable capacity (that could be measured by their performance), they would not be vulnerable to motivational deficits in the face of failure. I will review research showing clear vulnerability on the part of a sizable number of children as young as preschool age. Moreover, their motivational systems (beliefs about self, goals, attributions, expectancies following failure, and behavior following failure) are in some ways remarkably similar to those of older children who are vulnerable.

I will show that early on there are already two types of motivational system in place: one built around *traits* of the self (characterized by a concern with qualities of the self and judgments about those qualities) and one built around *process* (characterized by a focus on effort and strategies that bring about success and that surmount failure). Moreover, these two systems are already associated with vulnerability and hardiness, respectively. However, the issue for these young children seems to be the goodness and badness of the self, rather than anything about ability.

Indeed, years pass between the time that this early system seems to be in place and the time that a similarly coherent trait vs. process system arises with respect to intellectual ability. Why is this? What happens in the meantime? For me, this is one of the mysteries (and challenges) of the development of ability conceptions, and one that I will grapple with in this chapter.

2. A focus on the development of conceptions of ability has also led us to overestimate the degree to which viewing abilities (and traits in general) as stable internal capacities that are unaffected by effort is the mature and correct view. I will review research showing that there are large individual differences

---

[1]Although there are meaningful differences between the terms "intelligence" and "ability," I will use them more or less interchangeably here because the phenomena I am examining most typically apply to both.

in the way mature individuals view intelligence and ability—in how they define it (e.g., as solely capacity based or as including effort and knowledge), in how malleable they view it to be (e.g., as largely fixed or as subject to growth), in how they view the relation between effort and ability (e.g., as an inverse relation vs. a more positive, synergistic one), and in how they judge ability.

Ironically, many of the beliefs held by the hardiest individuals look like the "immature" beliefs of the younger children—for example, the belief that effort is *part of* intelligence, that effort increases intelligence, and that the person who tries harder is the smarter one. I will argue, with others, that because intelligence is in many ways a social construction, there is more than one mature and correct view. Although development leads children to understand the alternative views, it does not lead them all to adopt the same one. Moreover, as I have noted, the one they adopt has important implications for their motivation.

In summary, I will focus on the changes that take place in children's conceptions of ability as they move through grade school and middle school. But I will place these changes in the context of younger children's motivational patterns (before clear conceptions of ability are established) and older students' motivational patterns (that can be based on varying conceptions of ability, after an understanding of ability is in place).

A Preliminary Note on the Nature of Development

Before I begin, it is critical to emphasize one more thing: The age at which abilities seem to appear often depends on the task. For example, Butler (1998) has shown that with a simplified task, even 4- and 5-year-olds can use social comparison information to assess their performance. Yet they do not show much spontaneous social comparison in natural settings for purposes of performance assessment for several more years. Similarly, with simpler tasks second and third graders show more sophisticated reasoning about effort and ability than they are usually thought to be capable of (Schuster, Ruble, & Weinert, 1999). Yet it is several more years before they can reason fluently and consistently about these variables.[2] The age at which something appears also depends on the setting. For example, Stipek & Daniels (1988) have shown that even kindergartners can have an accurate view of their class standing when the classroom emphasizes evaluation and comparisons. Yet it is several years before these assesssments start having real meaning for children, in the sense that they begin to have impact on their view of their general ability and their predictions of their future performance.

---

[2]It is interesting to note that with complex tasks even adults' reasoning breaks down (Surber, 1980).

Thus, to understand the development of ability conceptions, it is important to understand (1) when children are first capable of doing things, (2) when they typically start to do these things spontaneously and across a wide variety of tasks and settings, and (3) when these things begin to have impact on their motivation. In depicting age changes and patterns of development, I have tried, where possible, to take all three into account. However, my bolder generalizations typically refer not to when children first become capable of something, but to when they do it easily, spontaneously, and often, and to when it begins to have impact on their motivation.

"BEFORE" CONCEPTIONS OF ABILITY

Young children (preschoolers and kindergartners) do not seem to have a clear conception of ability as an internal quality that failure can call into question. Because of this, it was widely believed that they were immune to any harmful effects of failure (Dweck & Elliott, 1983; Nicholls, 1984; Stipek & Daniels, 1988). After all, if failure doesn't reflect on ability, then it should not be experienced as undermining. However, recent research with preschool and kindergarten children has shown that a sizable proportion of these young children show clear signs of impairment when they encounter a series of salient, visible failures (such as jigsaw puzzles they cannot complete) or when they meet with criticism for their performance (Hebert & Dweck, 1985; Heyman, Dweck, & Cain, 1992; Lewis, Allessandri, & Sullivan, 1992; Smiley & Dweck, 1994; cf. Kamins & Dweck, 1999). As I noted above, in reaction to these failures, they show many of the same reactions that we see when older vulnerable children encounter failure: negative affect, negative self-evaluations, plummeting expectations, lowered persistence, and impaired deployment of problem-solving strategies.

Stipek, Recchia, and McClintic (1992) have shown that even children as young as 2-1/2 years old show clear negative affect and gaze avoidance after a failure. Although they understand little about ability as yet, obviously something is going on. There is good evidence that this early motivational system is built around children's concerns about *goodness and badness* and their conceptions of goodness and badness. First, there is ample evidence that young children are highly concerned with issues of goodness and badness (Frey & Ruble, 1985; Paley, 1988; Smetana, 1985; Stipek & Daniels, 1990; Stipek & Tannatt, 1984; see also Ruble & Dweck, 1995). For example, Frey and Ruble (1985) found that when kindergarten children engage in social comparison, they often do so to examine other children's social conduct and to learn about classroom rules.

When young children describe people, it is often in terms of goodness and badness, and this is in striking contrast to the absence of other types of trait descriptions (Smetana, 1985). Even when young children are asked to explain how they know that someone is smart, they often make reference to a child's niceness or exemplary conduct (Stipek & Daniels, 1990; Stipek & Tannatt, 1984).

Next, in several studies (Hebert & Dweck, 1985; Heyman, Dweck, & Cain, 1992), preschool or kindergarten children were asked to role-play parents' and teachers' reactions to their incomplete or flawed work. Vulnerable children (those who displayed plummeting self-evaluations, expectations, affect, and persistence) role-played personal criticism relating to goodness and badness. Remarkably, virtually none ever mentioned anything about ability (see also Smiley & Dweck, 1994). The hardy, resilient children, too, revealed a heightened concern with issues of goodness. In their role playing, they enacted their parents waxing enthusiastic about what good children they are (while also in many cases suggesting the effort and strategies that the children might wish to deploy to remedy their performance). Virtually none of these children mentioned ability either.[3]

Finally, young children's conceptions of goodness predict their vulnerability to impairment in the face of failure. As will be seen later, work with older students has shown that holding the conception that ability is a fixed trait predicts impairment in the face of failure (see Dweck, 1999; Pomerantz & Ruble, 1997; Stipek & Gralinski, 1996). Interestingly, in young children, the belief that goodness–badness is a stable trait predicts vulnerability to impairment when they encounter failure or criticism (Heyman, Dweck, & Cain, 1992; see also Heyman & Dweck, 1998).

Children's interest in goodness and badness in the early years should come as no surprise, since adults use these years to socialize children into the rules and habits—the rights and wrongs—of civilized life. The early school years continue this socialization process, with conduct and rule-following still receiving ample instructional attention.

Although young children's self-concerns seem to revolve around issues of goodness and badness, not ability, they show two distinct motivational patterns that are highly reminiscent of the patterns shown by considerably older students vis-à-vis ability. One, the vulnerable one, we can call a "trait-oriented system" because it revolves around judging traits of the self (or the self in its entirety). Thus the vulnerable children believe in the stable trait of goodness–badness, they judge themselves to be deficient on this trait when they fail, and fall into negative affect and impaired behavior (Hebert & Dweck, 1985; Heyman, Dweck, & Cain, 1992; see also Kamins & Dweck. 1999). The other system, the more hardy one, can be called a "process-oriented system" because it revolves around effort and strategies. Thus the hardy children

---

[3]This greater emphasis on goodness–badness than on ability fits nicely with Stipek and MacIver's (1989) observation that young children seem to be more responsive to social reinforcement than to success–failure feedback.

believe that children can improve themselves, they role-play effort and strategy suggestions for improving performance, and in general talk extensively about the importance of practice and effort (Hebert & Dweck, 1985; Heyman, Dweck, & Cain,. 1992; see also, Heyman & Dweck, 1998). Moreover, they practice what they preach in that they remain persistent and effective.

Even though these two rather coherent motivational systems seem to be present, and, even though clear vulnerability is evident in a number of children, these young children still may be less vulnerable than older children. For example, it looks as though young children need a pretty powerful or obvious failure experience (cf. Butler, 1998) or one that involves criticism from an adult (see Stipek & MacIver, 1989) to reveal their vulnerability . Otherwise they seem quite mastery oriented. In addition, it may be that young children's vulnerability is a *reaction* to a salient failure, but unlike older vulnerable children, they may not behave in a pessimistic, risk-avoidant, or defensive way *before* a failure occurs (e.g., Benenson & Dweck, 1986). Finally, it is possible that these young children, even the vulnerable ones, are more resilient than older children in that they may more quickly and easily regain their optimism after a failure.

DEVELOPING ABILITY CONCEPTIONS

After these early years, in which ability concerns seem relatively mild, two rather dramatic sets of changes appear to take place in children's conceptions of ability—one at about 7–8 years old, when children begin to look very different from kindergartners, and one at about 10–12 years olds. Table 1 presents an overview of these changes. Let's look at each age in turn.

The Early Phase of Ability Conceptions (7- and 8-Year-Olds)

Interest in Ability

Although some evidence of ability awareness can be found in younger children (see Butler, 1998; Marsh, Craven, & Debus, 1991; Stipek & Daniels, 1988), it is at 7–8 years old that children suddenly become far more interested in ability—their social comparison changes sharply to reflect their growing concern with relative performance and relative ability. Frey and Ruble (1985) report that most of kindergarten children's classroom social comparisons are related to social concerns (friendship formation) or behavioral concerns (classroom norms). However, 7–8 year olds show enhanced interest in every type of peer behavior that is relevant to achievement comparisons and academic self-evaluation.

TABLE 1
Major Changes in Ability Conceptions

Kindergarten	7–8 Years	10–12 Years
Defintions and nature of ability		
Mixed domains $\longrightarrow$	Domain-specific $\longrightarrow$	Can isolate ability from other variables
Skills and knowledge, mastery standard	More internal quality, more normative standard	Possibly capacity, mastery or normative standard
Not seen as predicting future performance	More stable, predictive	Seen as potentially highly stable and predictive
Impact of academic outcomes		
Do not affect ability estimates	Affect ability estimates but not motivation	Affect ability estimates and motivation
Social comparison		
Low interest and impact	High interest, some impact on ability evaluation	Strong impact on self-evaluation and motivation
Self-evaluations of ability		
High and inaccurate	Lower and more accurate; begin to affect expectations	Accurate, but some underestimatation, and more impact on motivation
Relation to other beliefs and to motivation		
Not related to other motivational beliefs and low impact on motivation	$\longrightarrow$	Coalesce with other motivational beliefs to have high impact on motivation

Definitions of Ability: Differentiation of Academic Ability

At 7–8 years of age, there are also important changes in children's definitions of ability. First, ability becomes clearly demarcated as its own domain. Younger children are often found to mix domains, mixing smartness with conduct, social behavior/likability, or other skill domains (Heyman, Dweck, & Cain, 1992; Stipek & Daniels 1990; Stipek & Tannatt 1984; Yussen & Kane, 1985). For example, Stipek and Daniels (1990) found that many kindergartners predicted that good readers would share more and would be able to jump more hurdles. This is not entirely surprising, since in the first school years much of the school day is still devoted to socializing children and to playing games, and the different domains may not be clearly demarcated by teachers.

By 7–8 years of age, different domains seem to be fairly well understood. Not only is ability more clearly distinguished from social–moral qualities (Bempechat, London, & Dweck, 1991; Droege & Stipek, 1993; Frey & Ruble, 1985; Heyman, Dweck, & Cain, 1992; Stipek & Daniels, 1990), but different skill domains also become differentiated. For example, as Wigfield et al. (1997) have shown, children now demonstrate clear distinctions between math, reading, and physical skills in their self-perceptions of competence and in the value they attach to each of these domains.

Normative Definitions of Ability

Even when conceptions of ability are "purified" to contain only intellectual ability, what is the nature of this ability? For younger children, ability seems to be more related to concrete, observable things they know and can do (Cain & Dweck, 1989; Nicholls, Patashnick, & Mettetal, 1986; Yussen & Kane, 1985), and they have more individual, mastery standards for judging this kind of ability (Blumenfeld, Pintrich, & Hamilton, 1986). In contrast, at about 7–8 years of age, children are developing an awareness of ability as a more internal, less observable quality that is defined more normatively (i.e., being smart can mean outperforming others) (Butler, 1998 1999; Ruble, Boggiano, Feldman, & Loebl, 1980). For example, Ruble et al. (1980) found that unlike first graders, second graders now explain their level of smartness in normative, social comparison terms.

Not only do children at this time display a marked upsurge in social comparison with peers to determine relative ability, but this social comparison starts having an impact on children's self-evaluation of their general ability (Ruble, 1987; Ruble, Boggiano, Feldman, & Loebl, 1980).

Ability and Other Traits as More Stable Qualities

Indeed, about 7–8 years old is also the time that children are beginning to understand ability as a potentially stable personal quality. In younger children, there seems to be less sense of ability as having potentially long-term stability—and no consistent tendency to use ability information (or information about other traits) to make predictions about future behavior (e.g., Droege & Stipek, 1993; Rholes & Ruble, 1984; Stipek & Daniels, 1990). By 7–8 years of age, however, there is some increase in the belief that people will tend to have the same ability/traits over time and in the use of ability/trait information for making predictions about future performance/behavior (Rholes & Ruble, 1984; see also, Rotenberg, 1982). Even when younger children seem able to make appropriate trait inferences from past behavior, unlike those who are 7–8 years old, they still do not expect stability in future performance or behavior (Rholes & Ruble, 1984; see also Ferguson, Van Roosendale, & Rule, 1986). [In a similar vein, even when young children have accurate (rather than overly positive) perceptions of their ability—as they seem to when kindergartens make clear public normative evaluations—they are still more optimistic about the future than are older kids with similarly realistic perceptions of their present ability (Stipek & Dainels, 1988).] Thus although young children may draw ability inferences, they do not see future outcomes as being constrained by them, whereas at 7–8 years, they begin to do so.

As a side note, there is suggestive evidence that young children may find certain kinds of traits easier to grasp. For example, Yuill and Pearson (1998) show that even children 4–5 years old understand traits based on preferences or desires and can use them to make predictions (see also Heyman & Gelman, 1998). This raises the important question of whether effort is more like a motive trait and whether this is why effort inferences seem easier for children than ability inferences. Karabenick and Heller (1976), Kun (1977), and Surber (1980, 1984) all found that children have a far easier time making effort inferences than ability inferences. As these researchers have pointed out, effort (like motives and preferences) is more directly accessible to children from their experiences than are traits like ability (see also Stipek & MacIver, 1989).

Accuracy of Self-Perceptions

To return to the topic at hand, children 7–8 years old also seem to become more accurate in their self-perceptions of ability, and this typically means perceptions that are less positive and optimistic (e.g., Benenson & Dweck, 1986; Nicholls, 1978, 1979; Eccles, Wigfield, Harold, & Blumenfeld, 1993; Wigfield & Eccles, 2000; Wigfield, Eccles, & Pintrich, 1996; see Stipek & MacIver, 1989). A striking feature of most younger children is that they are highly optimistic about their class standing and future performance despite any actual deficiencies (although see Stipek & Daniels, 1988). Indeed the great majority place themselves at the top of their class (e.g., Benenson & Dweck, 1986). At about 7–8 years old, children's self-perceptions start moving into line with teachers' ratings of ability (Benenson & Dweck, 1996; Wigfield et al., 1997; Nicholls, 1978 1979; see Stipek & MacIver, 1989). And, their spontaneous self-evaluations, once largely self-praise, start to reveal more self-criticism (Frey & Ruble, 1987). Not surprisingly, these changes are ones that have prompted concern.

Why does this happen? What is responsible for the change from unrealistic optimism in younger children to a more realistic view? There are several, interrelated factors that are likely to play a role.

1. *General responsiveness to performance feedback.* First, it is important to note that this change is part of a more general change in children's tendency to tune into feedback and to use it to judge themselves. Before 7–8 years of age, success and failure feedback and normative information often have little impact. Now we see children starting to use success–failure feedback—both absolute and comparative—to judge their ability (Frey & Ruble, 1985, Ruble, 1987) and to predict their future performance (Entwistle & Hayduk, 1978; Parson & Ruble, 1977; Stipek & Hoffman, 1980). Thus this emergence from the happy haze of optimism represents a general trend for children to be more in touch with the performance feedback they receive.

2. *Definitions of ability.* I have already alluded to the change in definition of ability from more personal, mastery definitions to more normative definitions. This too may play a role in deflating children's optimism, for everyone can be smart when they focus only on their own task mastery, but, as many have pointed out, only some can be smart in a normative context (Butler, 1999; Nicholls, 1984).

3. *Beliefs about the stability of ability.* I have also mentioned the beginning belief in the stability of ability. When traits are believed to be *unstable*, one's present behaviors and outcomes (e.g., failures) do not have implications for future ones. Older children, who are starting to believe in more stable traits that have predictive value (Droege & Stipek, 1993; Rholes & Ruble, 1984), may no longer be as able to cast off unfavorable feedback as irrelevant to the self and to future performance.

4. *Reasoning skills.* During the period that children become more interested in ability and more likely to see it as more normatively defined and stable, we see a change in their reasoning skills, that is, their ability to use information to make inferences about ability. This change may be reciprocal: Greater reasoning skills may allow them to isolate ability more clearly and understand it better, but greater understanding of ability may enhance their ability to reason about it in relation to other variables.

What is the change in reasoning skills? Whereas younger children show highly limited ability to use covariation information (say, information about effort, the task, or other people's performance) in making inferences about ability, by 7–8 years old there is a clear increase in the ability to use this information (e.g., Schuster, Ruble, & Weinert, 1999). Moreover, Schuster et al. have shown precisely how young children's failure to use covariation information can lead directly to their unrealistic ability inferences.

5. *Changes in wishful thinking.* Young children seem happy to give rein to their self-interest—both on experimental tasks and in estimating their class standing—even when this conflicts with the facts (Schuster, Ruble, & Weinert, 1999; Stipek & Tannatt, 1984). For example, when they are given a judgment or reasoning task in which either they or another child are to be judged, they judge themselves significantly more favorably than they judge other children even though the information they are given is identical in both cases (e.g., Schuster, Ruble, & Weinert, 1999). Indeed, a tendency to indulge self-interest in the face of the facts (even when they are aware of these facts and able to use them when instructed to) has been found in young children across a variety of tasks (see, e.g., Nelson & Dweck, 1977). Older children no longer allow themselves this indulgence. By 7–8 years of age, children may feel compelled to give greater weight to data than to personal desire.

6. *Changes in educational contexts.* As children go on in school, academic work occupies a larger share of the day, grades and normative evaluation increase in frequency, and negative evaluations from teachers increase as well (Blumenfeld, Hamilton, Bossert, Wessels, & Meece, 1983; Stipek & MacIver, 1989;

Wigfield, Eccles, & Pintrich, 1996; Eccles, Wigfield, & Schiefele, 1998). All such changes can have impact on children's sense of their ability, and are detailed in Chapters 12 and 13 of this book. As an example here, MacIver (1987) has shown that frequency of evaluation can have a clear impact on students' self-perceptions of ability: In fifth grade math classrooms with lower levels of evaluation (and more differentiated task structures) even the poorer students could maintain relatively high perceptions of their ability. Thus although the typical finding is that perceptions of ability decline over the grade school years, there are environments that make this decline less likely.

Although this is quite a hefty list of changes that take place between kindergarten and second or third grade, more changes are yet to come. And although the earlier changes most certainly set the stage for these later ones, the later changes (that take place at about 10–12 years old) seem to have even more striking consequences for children's motivation. I will argue that not only do particular conceptions continue to develop, but, perhaps more important, these conceptions appear to come together into a "meaning system" to affect motivation and achievement.

Ability Conceptions Coalesce and Gain Impact (10–12 Year-Olds)

Reasoning About Ability and Effort

As children reach 10–12 years of age, some of the earlier trends continue. For example, reasoning skills continue to burgeon, and children become fluent in reasoning about the relations between ability, effort, and performance—especially in making inferences about ability from effort and performance information (Karabenick & Heller, 1976; Kun, 1977; Schuster, Ruble, & Weinert, 1999; Surber, 1980; see also Skinner, 1990). For example, they are more likely than younger children to say that given equal performance, the student who tries harder is the less able one (Nicholls & Miller, 1984).

It is at this time that "ability" as a factor that is potentially separable from effort comes into sharp focus. (Nicholls & Miller, 1984) Indeed, Skinner, in a study of children's causal beliefs, reports that it is only at 11–12 years old that effort and ability fall into clearly separate factors. Before then they both fall into a single "internal causes" factor. Although, as we will see, many students do not choose to view ability as something that is in fact separate from effort, they can now understand this view (Miller, 1985; Nicholls & Miller, 1984; Rholes, Blackwell, Jordan, & Walters, 1980; Rholes, Jones, & Wade, 1988). Similarly, although many will not choose to see high effort as readily implying low ability, they can now better understand this kind of inference (Surber, 1980, 1984).

Finally, at this time, more students begin to view ability/intelligence as a capacity rather than as a set of skills and knowledge (see Cain & Dweck, 1989;

Nicholls & Miller, 1984) and to view ability as a more fixed or stable trait (Droege & Stipek, 1993; Ruble & Flett, 1988; Stipek & Daniels, 1990)— although, as will be seen, there are still many students who appreciate this view but do not adopt it as their own.

New Definition of Ability: Consequences

As this view of ability begins to loom large, several things begin to happen. Self-ratings of ability become even lower (Marsh, 1989; Nicholls, 1979; Pintrich & Blumenfeld, 1985), and although the ratings tend to become more accurate (e.g., Blumenfeld, Pintrich, & Hamilton, 1986; Nicholls, 1979; Nicholls, Patashnick, & Mettetal, 1986), some children begin to *underestimate* their ability and class standing (Benenson & Dweck, 1986).

Not only do students' self-ratings become even more sensitive to academic outcomes (e.g., Butler, 1990, 1999), but many begin to equate smartness with their grades (Blumenfeld, Pintrich, & Hamilton, 1986) and to spontaneously use ability traits (like smartness) as an explanation for grades (Benenson & Dweck, 1986; Ruble, Boggiano, Feldman, & Loebl, 1980). For children who now view their intelligence as a stable capacity that predicts their future performance, such conclusions can be disheartening (cf. Butler, 1990 1999).

Moreover, as students come to believe more in the fixedness of ability, they seem to believe less in the effectiveness of effort to increase ability, to compensate for ability, or to aid performance (Butler, 1999 Chapman & Skinner, 1990; Droege & Stipek, 1993; Xiang, 1996; see also Dweck & Sorich, 1999).

It is soon after this time that students start interpreting praise and blame in new ways. For younger children, praise and blame are taken pretty much at face value, with praise being seen as indicating high ability and blame or anger as indicating low ability (Barker & Graham, 1987; Meyer et al., 1979). Now that ability can easily be isolated from effort and viewed in relation to task difficulty, praise for success can be taken as a sign of low ability if the task is easy (Barker & Graham, 1987; Meyer et al., 1979), and an angry response to failure can be taken as a sign of high ability (Barker & Graham, 1987).

Perhaps most interesting is the evidence that at this age children's ability conceptions and other achievement beliefs gain greater coherence, that is, they start to hang together as a "meaning system," as opposed to being a series of more isolated beliefs. And they also begin to have a more pronounced efffect on children's motivation and performance.

Beliefs Gain Greater Coherence

Many studies find that for the first time at ages 10–12, perceptions of ability start forming a network with other beliefs, as well as with values and goals. For example, younger children might say they are poor at something, but this does not mean they will devalue that activity or skill. Now competence pecep- tions in a domain start forming a tighter link with how much a child values that domain (Wigfield et al., 1997; see also Butler, 1990, 1999, for a demon- stration of how competence perceptions and interest now go hand and hand, particularly under competitive conditions).

(Low) perceptions of ability now predict a desire to avoid that domain. Stipek and Gralinski (1991) questioned third graders and junior high school students who thought they did poorly on their math test: "Do you wish you could stop taking math? If you had a choice, would you try to get out of tak- ing the next math test?" Only for the older students did perception of poor performance predict a desire to avoid math in the future (as well as their expected grade on the next math test).

Further, perceptions of ability now predict students' attributions for their success and failure. For example, Nicholls (1979) found that, by age 12, the more students perceived themselves as having high ability, the more they were attributing their successes to high ability (rather than to luck or effort), and the more they were attributing their failures to luck (rather than to abil- ity). Clearly this relation could well be reciprocal, with students' perceptions of ability influencing their attributions, but their attributions also influenc- ing their perceptions of their ability.

Beliefs in stable or fixed ability also begin predicting a network of other beliefs. Our studies with late grade school and junior high school children show that a belief in the non malleability of intelligence now predicts a valu- ing of performance goals (which will validate intelligence) over learning goals (that can increase intelligence) when the two are pitted against each other (Dweck & Leggett, 1988; Dweck & Sorich, 1999; Stone, 1998). It also predicts a more negative view of effort—specifically, the beliefs that effort implies low ability and that effort is ineffective given low ability, as well as a greater desire to avoid effort (i.e., greater endorsement of effort–avoidance goals) (Dweck & Sorich, 1999). Finally, it predicts a greater emphasis on ability vs. effort attri- butions for failure (Henderson & Dweck, 1990; Dweck & Sorich, 1999; see also Hong, Chiu, Dweck, Lin, & Wan, 1999), and it is not just the low achieving stu- dents who report that setbacks would tell them that they had low ability.

Another of our studies (Bempechat, London, & Dweck, 1991, Study 1) revealed a striking instance of beliefs suddenly coalescing at fifth grade. In this study, students in each grade from kindergarten to fifth grade were asked to think of someone they know who is smart in schoolwork, and to tell why they think he or she is smart. Their answers were coded as outcome oriented ("because she gets As") or action oriented ("because he does all his home- work"). Students' beliefs about intelligence as a fixed vs. malleable quality were also assessed. In kindergarten through fourth grade, children with fixed and malleable views of intelligence did not differ at all in their tendency to gener- ate outcome or action answers. However, at fifth grade there was, for the first time, a significant relation, with those favoring a fixed view also favoring outcome answers, and those favoring a malleable view giving more action answers. Interestingly, a nearly identical pattern was obtained for physical skills (being "good at games and sports"), with fifth graders who endorsed a fixed view of physical skills citing almost exclusively outcomes, and fifth graders endorsing a malleable view citing predominantly actions.

Thus, students who believe in fixed ability seem to develop a trait-focused belief system, seeking to validate their ability, devaluing effort relative to ability, and interpreting outcomes as reflecting on ability. Later, I will compare this trait-focused meaning system to the process-focused system of students who understand the idea of stable ability but continue to believe in intelligence as a personal quality that can be developed.

In short, students are developing more coherent systems of beliefs and values that revolve around their perceptions of their ability and their beliefs about the nature of ability.

Beliefs Affect Intrinsic Motivation and Performance

As beliefs about ability crystallize, there is a clear increase in the power of failure to sap students' intrinsic motivation and impair their performance; however this appears to occur mainly among students who view ability as a stable capacity (Miller, 1985; Pomerantz & Ruble, 1997; Rholes, Blackwell, Jordan, & Walters, 1980; Rholes, Jones, & Wade, 1988; see also, Henderson & Dweck, 1990; Dweck & Sorich, 1999). Butler (1999) provides a beautiful demonstration of how, earlier children can be wildly competitive, but losing does not seem to dampen their enthusiasm for continued social comparison, and losing does not seem to undermine either their interest or their performance. Now it can.

While it has not always been clear from the literature whether this increasing sensitivity to failure is a cognitive achievement or the adoption of a belief about ability, it seems to be some of both. Although younger children may endorse a view of intelligence as a fixed trait, such a view does not seem to predict impairment in the face of failure until about 10–12 years of age (Cain & Dweck, 1995; Henderlong & Lepper, 1997). Thus, some fuller understanding of what "ability as a fixed trait" means must be achieved. However, it cannot be all a matter of cognitive advancement, for this would mean that at some age, everyone would start being noticeably impaired after failure, and this is not the case. It would appear, then, that for older students, impairment in the face of failure might require both an understanding of ability or intelligence as a potentially stable trait *and* the adoption of the view of ability as unmalleable. This is exactly what Pomerantz and Ruble (1997) have found: Failure is disruptive to performance chiefly for these older children who *both* understand that ability can be a stable capacity *and* believe that it is a trait that cannot be developed through their efforts.

AFTER CONCEPTIONS OF ABILITY: INDIVIDUAL DIFFERENCES THAT PARALLEL DEVELOPMENTAL DIFFERENCES

Although achievement motivation researchers often refer to the view of intellectual ability as a stable capacity that is separate from effort as the "mature conception of ability," there is abundant evidence, as I have noted, that mature reasoners may understand that this is one perspective on intelligence or ability, but they need not adopt it. Many modern theorists of intelligence acknowledge that intelligence is a personal and social construction that can vary from person to person and from culture to culture (Carugati, 1990; Cornelius, Kenny, & Caspi, 1989; Rosenholz & Simpson, 1984; Wagner & Sternberg, 1994).

It can vary in its definition, and there are many adult definitions of intelligence that include personality and motivational components as an inherent part of intelligence (see, e.g., Yang & Sternberg, 1984). This begins to sound very much like the young children who fail to differentiate between effort and ability or between intellectual skills and personality or social characteristics. Yet even researchers now note the strong overlap between intelligence, personality, and interests (Ackerman & Heggestad, 1997).

People and cultures can also vary in whether they think intelligence can be influenced by effort and learning, with many experts—including Alfred Binet (1909, 1973), the inventor of the IQ test—strongly believing that children's basic capacities can be transformed through learning (see also Perkins & Grotzer, 1997). A number of creativity experts (e.g., Howe, 1990) even argue that creative genius arises from lengthy periods of dedication and not simply from large amounts of inherent ability.

Much of my own work has revolved around individual differences in the belief that intelligence can or cannot be developed through one's efforts (see Dweck, 1999). Interestingly, the view that intelligence can be developed (an "incremental" theory of intelligence) is often associated with many of the beliefs we saw in young children, along with with optimism and hardiness in the face of setbacks. In contrast, the view that intelligence cannot be developed (an "entity" theory) is associated with many of the beliefs that are said to characterize the more mature view of ability, and it is often associated with greater loss of confidence and with helplessness in the face of setbacks.[4]

As I suggested earlier, both views are available to the mature reasoner. Let us look more closely at the consequences of these different conceptions of ability. It is important to note that in most cases the association in question

---

[4]An entity theory refers to the belief that intelligence cannot be developed and is not under personal control. I will sometimes refer to it as a belief in "fixed" intelligence, but this is simply a convenient shorthand.

has been found not only when students' theories of intelligence have been measured, but also when they have been manipulated, thus supporting the idea that students' intelligence beliefs play a causal role in their goals, attributions, and effort beliefs, as well as their affect, intrinsic motivation, self-regulation, and performance in the face of difficulty. The fact that theories of intelligence can be manipulated also means that these beliefs are themselves sensitive to context and experience.[5]

I should also note that I will bring in studies with older (college) students where they are relevant, particularly since work with these older students rules out the possibility that differences stem from immature reasoning skills on the part of some of the participants. This work also can show that the patterns that emerge at 10–12 years of age are not simply a temporary result of coming to understand ability. That is, they are not a reflection of a temporary ability-mania, like the gender-mania children show when they first come to understand gender.

Finally, I would like to emphasize that there is an important distinction to be made between beliefs that can be motivating under favorable circumstances and beliefs that create hardiness in the face of failure. The belief that one's intelligence is on the line in an achievement situation can certainly light a fire under someone, but that same belief may be highly debilitating in the face of failure, particularly prolonged failure. I will take up this important point again later.

Entity vs. Incremental Theories of Intelligence

Definitions of Intelligence

What does intelligence consist of? Here I will simply mention a study with college students (Mueller & Dweck, reported in Dweck, 1999) showing that students holding an incremental theory were significantly more likely than those holding an entity theory to include knowledge and motivation in their definitions of intelligence (like young children). In contrast, students with an entity theory were significantly more likely to include references to broad abilities or capacity. Also when asked to complete the equation, Intelligence =__% ability + __% effort,

---

[5]When we measure theories of intelligence as an individual difference, 80–85% of students (later grade school through college) tend to agree consistently with an entity theory or with an incremental theory on our questionnaire, and they tend to be pretty evenly split among the two theories. Thus, most older students hold a clear theory, and both theories are quite popular. It should also be mentioned that it is possible to have an entity theory in one domain and an incremental theory in another. These domains could be different intellectual areas (reading vs. math), or they could be athletic ability vs. intellectual ability vs. musical ability, etc. In these cases, students would show different motivational patterns in the different domains.

incremental students (like young children) gave more weight to effort than ability, whereas entity students gave more weight to ability than effort.

Goal Choice

What is more important, looking smart or learning something new? When performance goals (a chance to prove an ability or avoid an invalidation of ability) are pitted against learning/mastery goals (a chance to increase ability), students with different conceptions of intelligence show different preferences. Those holding an entity theory of their intelligence tend to choose the performance goals compared to students holding an incremental theory, who tend to choose the learning goal to pursue (Aylor, 2000; Dweck & Sorich, 1999; Dweck & Leggett, 1988;Stone, 1998; see also Elliot & McGregor, 2000; Robins & Pals, 1998; Rhodewalt, 1994; Roedel & Schraw, 1995, for studies with older students). This is true both in American and Korean cultures (Kim, Grant, & Dweck, 2000). This means that students who believe in fixed intelligence will sacrifice learning in favor of a chance to look smart or avoid looking dumb.[6]

Attributions

What does failure mean? In line with their focus on ability and concerns about ability, students with an entity theory are more likely than those with an incremental theory to attribute their failures to a lack of ability rather than to effort, while incremental students key on effort (Dweck & Sorich, 1999; Henderson & Dweck, 1990; see also Hong, Chiu, Dweck, Lin, & Wan, 1999; Robins & Pals, 1998). This, too, is true for students in both the United States and Korea (Kim, Grant, & Dweck, 2000).

What are ability ascriptions based on? Butler (2000), in studies that both measured theories of intelligence and manipulated them, has shown that entity and incremental students use different bases for ascribing ability. First, for students with an entity theory, self-appraisals of ability were affected more by *normative* performance information than by temporal performance information. The oppposite was true for students with an incremental theory. Thus, for one group of students, relative standing is what counts, while for the other, changes in skills and knowledge over time are what count.

Second, when asked to judge ability from improving or declining performance, students with an entity theory weighed the initial outcome most heavily, and judged the *declining* performance as indicating higher ability than

---

[6]It is important to note that when performance and learning/mastery goals are *not* pitted against each other (and the value of each is assessed separately), students with different theories of intelligence often look quite similar in their endorsement of these goals. This was true in several of the studies cited above, such as Dweck & Sorich (1999) and Stone (1998). This means that although both classes of goals are considered valuable to most children, a direct confrontation between the two may be necessary to reveal underlying preferences.

the improving performance (both for themselves and others). In contrast, students with an incremental theory, in keeping with their focus on learning, weighed the last outcome most heavily, ascribing more ability to a student who had improved than to one who had deteriorated. Thus, one conception of intelligence puts the emphasis on mastery over time, whereas the other seems to put the emphasis on diagnosing underlying ability via normative information or initial performance.

Effort Beliefs

Does effort signify the presence or absence of ability? In many studies, a hallmark of younger children's thinking is their belief that the student who works harder is the smarter one. Of course, this is the wrong answer to a simultaneous equation in which two students work on the same task, exert different amounts of effort, and attain the same level of performance. But in many circumstances in real life, effort need not imply low ability and indeed effort in the incremental view can bring about higher ability (Stipek & Gralinski, 1996; see also Jagacinski & Nicholls, 1984).

In a study by Dweck and Sorich (1999), junior high school students holding to an incremental theory saw effort as enhancing ability, as an effective way to achieve even when ability was not high, and as a way to overcome obstacles (see also Stipek & Gralinski, 1996). Given a hypothetical failure, they said they would study harder the next time (whereas entity theorists more than incremental theorists said they would probably put in *less* effort the next time—and would consider cheating instead!).

In contrast, students holding an entity theory were more likely than those with an incremental theory to believe that high effort in school indeed implies low ability and that effort is ineffective anyway when ability is low (cf. Stipek & Gralinski, 1996). Not surprisingly, they were also more likely to have strong effort–avoidance goals. Thus for entity students, effort is more dangerous (it can show you're dumb), less effective, and more aversive.

Intrinsic Motivation

Several studies have suggested that holding an incremental theory of intelligence can foster intrinsic motivation [Aylor, 2000, Linehan, 1999; for studies with older students, see Aronson, Fried, & Good (in press); Jourden, Bandura, & Banfield, 1991 (physical skills); Robins & Pals, 1998] and also can foster its maintenance in the face of failure [Dweck, 1999; Golumbia, 1990; Kim, Grant, & Dweck, 2000; Kasimatis, Miller, & Marcussen, 1996 (college)]. Aronson, Fried, & Good (in press), for example, showed that African-American college students who were taught an incremental theory of intelligence showed higher enjoyment and valuing of academics (and earned higher grade point averages).

Self-Efficacy

Several studies with college students suggest that when students are given an incremental vs. entity theory, they are better able to maintain their level of self-efficacy in the face of challenge (Jourden, Bandura, & Banfield, 1991; Kasimatis, Miller, & Marcussen, 1996 (physical skills); Rohrback, 1993; Robins & Pals, 1998) or increase their self-efficacy over time as learning proceeds (Jourden, Bandura, & Banfield, 1991; Martocchio, 1994; Tabernero & Wood, 1999). The impact of students' theories, however, appears to go beyond the impact of self-efficacy (Braten & Olaussen, 1998; Tabernero & Wood, 1989; Wood & Bandura, 1989; see also Henderson & Dweck, 1990).

Defensive or Self-Defeating Behavior

In line with the greater focus on validating their ability and not invalidating it, a few studies have found that students with an entity theory engage in more defensive behavior that may be designed to protect perceived ability but is also self-defeating. Rhodewalt (1994), in a study of college students, found greater self-handicapping among entity theorists, that is, greater use of low effort, illness, or procrastination as advance excuses for potentially poor performance in the future. Hong et al. (1999), also in studies with college students, showed that entity theorists who had deficiencies that could strongly hinder their future performance (such as a language deficiency in the language in which their classes were conducted) rejected opportunies for remedial action, presumably because remedial action requires both effort and admission of deficiency. (This was true whether theories of intelligence were measured or manipulated.) Indeed, as noted above under "Effort Beliefs," students with entity views were more likely to say that if they did poorly in an area they would expend less effort on it in the future. (Dweck & Sorich, 1999; Kim, Grant, & Dweck, 2000) which is clearly self-defeating, especially if the area is an important one.

Performance

Several studies suggest that an incremental theory can aid performance both on challenging laboratory tasks (Pomerantz & Ruble, 1997; for studies with older students, see Jourden, Bandura, & Banfield, 1991; Tabernero & Wood, 1999; Wood & Bandura, 1989) and in school (Stipek & Gralinski, 1996), especially during a difficult school transition (Henderson & Dweck, 1990; Dweck & Sorich, 1999; for older students see Aronson, Fried, & Good, in press; Robins & Pals, 1998).

In these studies, prior ability and performance were equated across theory of intelligence groups (either because no prior difference existed, because any prior differences were controlled for statistically, or because participants were randomly assigned to experimental condition), so the effects of theories of intelligence were not a result of differences in prior performance. There is, however, some evidence that performance in school can sometimes influence the adoption of a theory of intelligence. For example, both Pomerantz & Saxon (2000) and Faria (1996) found that poorer performance in school could predict the adoption of an entity theory later on. This suggests that poor performance in evaluative contexts may lead some students to decide they have permanently inferior abilties.

Is an entity theory ever motivating? Just as it has been found that performance goals can be predictive of high grades when students are not facing challenge or failure (Grant, 2000), so too can an entity theory sometimes be predictive of high grades under these circumstances (Arshavsky, 1999; Eaton & Dembo, 1996). As noted earlier, perhaps by making students feel that their outcomes reflect on their permanent ability (Stone, 1998) an entity theory raises the stakes and stokes motivation, provided major setbacks are not encountered.

INFLUENCES ON CHILDREN'S CONCEPTIONS OF INTELLIGENCE

What practices might promote these different conceptions of intelligence in students? First, as experiments that manipulate students' theories about their intelligence show, these beliefs can be directly taught (see Aronson & Fried, & Good, in press; Dweck & Leggett, 1988; Hong, Chiu, Dweck, Lin, & Wan, 1999). Second, several experimental studies in which adults' feedback (criticism or praise) put the emphasis on trait judgment vs. process evaluation showed that trait judgment fosters an entity theory relative to process evaluation, which fosters a more incremental theory (Kamins & Dweck, 1999; Mueller & Dweck, 1998). For example, in studies by Mueller and Dweck, students received praise for their intelligence or praise for their effort after a successful first trial on a task. In two of these studies, it was found that students who were praised for their intelligence favored an entity theory compared to students who were praised for their effort. This was true not only when their theories were assessed after the success (when students might well buy into the idea that their high ability is fixed), but also when they were assessed after a subsequent failure.

In a preliminary field analog of these studies (Dweck & Lennon, 2001), we have assessed students' perceptions of their parents' practices, finding that students who perceived their parents to be conveying a process (learning, effort, strategies) message through their feedback were more likely to have incremental theories about their intelligence than were students who saw their parents as sending a trait (e.g., smart–dumb) message through their feedback.

Clearly much remains to be learned about how children's ability beliefs are shaped through their experiences at home and in school (and with their peers), but there are a number of avenues of research that look promising. In the next section, I look at studies on the how adults with different theories of intelligence think about and act toward children, and these too can provide clues about how children's ability beliefs might be shaped.

TEACHERS', PARENTS', AND EVALUATORS' CONCEPTIONS OF ABILITY

A variety of recent work suggests that adults who hold different theories of intelligence judge and treat children differently. For example, teachers or other adults with an entity theory appear to render judgments of students more quickly, often on the basis of initial performance (Butler, 2000) or preliminary information (Plaks, Stroessner, Dweck, & Sherman, 2001). Moreover, the judgments they make appear to be more rigid, that is, less open to revision. In fact, Plaks, et al. found that the more a student's performance went counter to intial expectations, the *less* attention entity theorists who were evaluating the student paid to it. Lee (1996), too, found that teachers with entity theories were more influenced by their initial expectations when they later evaluated and made placement decisions for a target child. Indeed Graziano, Jensen-Campbell, and Sullivan-Logan (1998) have shown how a great deal of the stability that might exist in children's temperament or personality can stem from adults' expectations of stability— and there is ample evidence that adults with an entity theory, in line with their theory of nonmalleability, have much higher expectations for stability in ability and other traits (see Chiu, Hong, & Dweck, 1997) and lower belief in their ability to infuence their child's learning (Wentzel, 1998).

Moreover, Smiley, Coulson, and Van Ocker (2000) have recently shown in a study of 4-year-olds and their parents that parents' theories of intelligence already predict the achievement tasks they prefer for their children, with incremental parents much more strongly than entity parents preferring challenging tasks for their children even if it means the child might not succeed. Next, incremental parents are already emphasizing effort in that they think effort is the reason children succeed, whereas entity parents are already emphasizing ability, in that they attribute children's success to talent. Reminiscent of Butler's (2000) findings that teachers with entity theories give more weight to normative information in judging ability, entity mothers in the study of Smiley et al. are more interested in comparative feedback from teachers. And, finally, fathers' implicit theories are already predicting children's task persistence, with incremental fathers having more persistent children.

GENDER, RACE, AND CULTURE

I have delineated two ability-related meaning systems, one organized around the trait of ability and one organized around processes like effort that use and feed ability. Do groups differ in the system they tend to adopt?

Gender

There is some suggestion that girls, especially bright girls, may more often than boys operate in the trait-focused system. They have been shown in some studies to hold more of an entity theory of intelligence (Xiang, 1996; see also Dweck, 1999) and to attribute failures more to lack of ability (Licht & Dweck, 1984; Stipek & Gralinski, 1991). Along with this, they have also been widely shown to have lower estimates of their ability and lower expectations of success in many areas (e.g., Stipek & Gralinski, 1991).[7] Most interestingly, much of this starts in grade school considerably before girls show any lag in achievement and when, in fact, girls are still earning higher grades than boys. Thus although the late grade school years are sometimes depicted as idyllic ones for girls before the upheaval of adolescence, these findings suggest that some of the roots of girls' later problems with achievement (especially math achievement) and depression may already be in place. It may be only with the greater challenges and conflicts of adolescence (as well as the more impersonal instruction and more stringent grading of junior high school) that these existing vulnerabilites express themselves.

Race

Although African-American students are often shown to earn lower grades than their European-American peers, several studies with college students have shown that they actually endorse a more incremental theory than do European-American students (Aronson, Fried, & Good, in press; Lewis, 1999). Nonetheless, Aronson, Fried, and Good have demonstrated that an intervention that emphasizes an incremental theory was successful in increasing school engagement and grade point averages for African-American students

---

[7]It must be mentioned, however, that girls' ability perceptions in English/reading and in music have been found to be appreciably higher than boys' (Wigfield et al. 1997). It is an interesting question whether, given their high ability perceptions, their confidence in these areas is more hardy and resilient in the face of challenge.

(as well as further increasing their endorsement of an incremental theory). It is possible that with the obstacles that African-American students face, an even greater belief in the utility of effort in increasing ability is needed. For example, it is possible that although they hold an incremental theory, situations that create "stereotype threat" (Steele & Aronson, 1997) can catapult students into a framework in which they feel their fixed intelligence is being tested. This is an area in which future research would be highly interesting.

Culture

There is abundant evidence that Asian cultures tend to be more effort oriented than American culture in that they see effort the key to achievement (Stevenson et al., 1990), but this does not mean that they adopt all of the process-focused system I have described. For example, they may not have more of an incremental of intelligence than Westerners and they may sometimes be less oriented toward learning goals and more toward performance goals than Westerners (e.g., Kim, Grant, & Dweck, 2000; see also Chiu, Hong, & Dweck, 1997). It may simply be that whatever theory or goal they adopt, they believe more in the efficacy of effort for reaching that goal. For example, in the study by Kim et al. Korean students were more likely than American students to say that a failure would make them doubt their ability, but they still said, more than the Americans, that they would apply more effort in the future. This, too, would be fascinating to pursue.

SOME BROAD QUESTIONS
FOR FUTURE RESEARCH

A picture of development has emerged, with a network of beliefs about goodness and badness dominating young children's motivation, and a network of beliefs about ability dominating achievement motivation from preadolescence on. What, however, rules motivation in the period between early childhood, when issues of goodness and badness rule, and preadolescence, when a coherent framework of ability beliefs emerges? We have seen that in these years, ability beliefs are forming and seem to control social comparison behavior, but do not yet have a consistent influence on children's attitudes, values, or coping. Do beliefs about goodness and badness continue to affect motivation until the ability system is in place? Or is this a period during which children tend to have no coherent system and so are in a way protected from setbacks and discouragement?

Some hint of what may be controlling motivation in this in-between period comes from new work by Butler and Baumer (2001). They found, first, that in the early school years, before social comparison has set in, most children tended to treat tasks as mastery/learning tasks rather than as performance (competence assessment) tasks, regardless of how the tasks were presented. Later, but before students had mature conceptions of ability, their achievement orientations seemed to reflect the orientation of the educational setting that they typically tended to be in. If they were typically in cooperative, nonevaluative settings, they tended to treat tasks as mastery/learning tasks, whereas if they were typically in competitive, evaluative educational settings, they tended to treat all tasks as competence assessments, again regardless of what the task instructions stressed.[8] (Only later, when children understood ability, could they more flexibly respond to whether the task instructions portrayed the task as a mastery/learning one or as a competence evaluation task.) This interesting study, then, suggests that perhaps in the in-between period children are guided most by what they find in their everyday learning environment.

Another question relates to how the early good–bad belief system may affect the emerging ability belief system. Do children tend to adopt the same meaning system for ability that they held for goodness, or is this a new domain affected by different experiences in different settings?

What happens to the early good–bad system once the ability system is in place? New research by Kamins and Dweck (2000) suggests that the early good–bad system is related to children's sense of contingent self-worth. Specifically, young children who believe that goodness–badness is a stable trait and show vulnerability to setbacks and criticism also believe that they are worthy only when they are behaving well, not when they are behaving poorly. In a related study with college students, a similar relation was found: Students who endorsed a belief in fixed intelligence also reported that their sense of worth rested on their academic success. Is this sense of contingent self-worth a very basic sense that is carried from early childhood into the later years? Or again, are these things that are constructed anew for different domains? (See Lawrence & Crocker, 1999, for a discussion of domain-specific contingencies of self-esteem.)

LESSONS FROM THE LITERATURE
(AND MORE QUESTIONS FOR THE FUTURE)

Reviewing this thriving literature has brought home a number of important points, and I would like to conclude by underscoring them.

- The importance of understanding when ability beliefs coalesce and come to have *motivational value*. As motivational psychologists and educators, we are interested not only in what children think but also in how this thinking affects

---

[8]It is interesting to note, however, that even the children at this age who treated tasks as competence assessments did not take failures as hard as older students confronting competence assessment tasks.

their actions—their important choices in school, their engagement with academic tasks, their ability to persist effectively in the face of setbacks. Thus it is important for us to understand when children's beliefs begin to affect important aspects of their motivation.

For example, in the early grade school years, children's beliefs about their class standing start becoming more realistic (instead of overly optimistic). Is this good or bad? The answer depends on what motivational impact this has. In the early grade school years it does not seem to predict much of anything, but later on it begins to, and apparently leads some children to become discouraged and to devalue their studies.

In a related vein, some children hold an entity theory of ability long before it hooks up with its network of other motivationally relevant beliefs (such as effort beliefs and attributions) and with persistence and performance.

Many fascinating questions emerge. What are these earlier nonmotivational versions of the beliefs doing? Are they stable? If so, are they sitting there "attracting" compatible beliefs over time that then coalesce to affect motivation? And, as I asked earlier, what is ruling motivation during the period in which the more inert, isolated beliefs do not seem to be doing so?

• The importance of understanding *when* a given belief might create vulnerability and when it might not. Some beliefs and goals can be highly motivating when things are going well, but may predict discouragement and poor performance when they are not, thus accounting for discrepant findings across studies. Here I stress the importance of studying how children deal with challenge or cope with failure as a way of understanding the full motivational value of ability beliefs.

Much lively research now surrounds the question of the adaptiveness of performance goals. In a recent study, Grant (2000) tracked students as they entered college and pursued a challenging pre-med curriculum. She found that several kinds of performance goals (including a desire to validate one's ability and a desire to validate it relative to others) look very motivating when students are not encountering difficulty. However, these same goals predict a strong loss of intrinsic motivation, as well as a failure to recover performance, after disappointing exam grades.

In the example of girls, given above, the same analysis can be applied : Bright girls' ability-focused belief systems may not pose a problem, and in fact could be motivating, until the adolescent environment creates the challenges and setbacks that reveal the vulnerability.

In summary, the adaptive value of ability beliefs (and goals) must be assessed under conditions of success *and* failure to understand their motivational value.

• The importance of *individual differences* as a tool for illuminating development. Developmental research that looks at change over age has revealed important overall trends in motivational variables and their relations. It has also shown how these trends might differ for certain gender or ethnic groups.

However, attention to individual differences has revealed other important things. For example, it has shown that motivational vulnerability can appear far younger than was thought. It has shown that similar trait vs. process meaning systems—that distinguish vulnerable from less vulnerable children—appear in younger children (around issues of goodness and badness) and in older children (around issues of ability). And it has revealed how process-oriented older students look in many ways like developmentally younger children in such things as their ability and effort beliefs.

Thus although there may be overall age differences in ability beliefs, looking only at age-wide differences may obscure within-age differences that have important implications for understanding motivation and development.

• The importance of *multiple methods* in the understanding of ability beliefs and their impact on achievement motivation. In the above example of girls' vulnerability, longitudinal correlational studies might show the emergence of such things as girls' greater depression or math-avoidant course choices after grade school, but experimental studies that expose girls to challenging tasks can reveal the earlier vulnerability before it expresses itself in their lives. Similarly, correlational studies can reveal environmental correlates of differences in ability conceptions (e.g., teacher or parent practices), but experimental studies can more precisely tease apart the components of these practices and their separate effects.

• The importance of distinguishing between *knowledge* and *beliefs*. A typical developmental question asks about the acquisition of knowledge: When do children come to understand something or build a more accurate picture of reality? This assumes that development inevitably leads children toward truth. But some of the most interesting motivational variables are constructions that may map poorly onto a known reality, yet may have enormous effects on behavior. For example, the students who retain confidence in their ability in the face of failure are not necessarily those who have the most ability (see Dweck, 1999). Moreover, when we think about conceptions of intelligence, even the experts aren't quite sure what intelligence is—so students' constructions of intelligence may differ in their impact but may not differ in their accuracy. Thus an important task for us is to understand more about how children construct their motivation-related "meaning systems," about the nature of these meaning systems, and about the motivational cost and benefits of different meaning systems.

Perhaps, as I noted earlier, we might best think of developmental changes in reasoning and knowledge as leading children *to be able to* understand and adopt frameworks of beliefs, but, as I have noted, they do not tell us which they *will* adopt.

In conclusion, ability conceptions lie at the heart of achievement motivation, and the literature on how these conceptions develop is a thriving one. Although important questions have been answered, there are enough fascinating ones left to keep us busy for a long time to come.

References

Ackerman, P. L., & Heggestad, E. D. (1997). Intelligence, personality, and interests: Evidence for overlapping traits. *Psychological Bulletin*, 121, 219–245.

Aronson, J., Fried, C. B., & Good, C. (in press). Reducing the effects of stereotype threat on African-American college students by shaping theories of intelligence. *Journal of Experimental Social Psychology*.

Arshavsky, N. (1999). *Goals and beliefs about school achievement among adolescents of three ethnic groups and their relation to these students' academic grades*. Unpublished doctoral dissertation, University of Wisconsin Madison.

Aylor, B. (2000). *Relationship between incremental thinking, instrinsic motivation and creativity*. Unpublished manuscript, Austin College, Sherman, TX.

Barker, G. P., & Graham, S. (1987). Developmental study of praise and blame as attributional cues. *Journal of Educational Psychology*, 79, 62–66.

Bempechat, J., London, P., & Dweck, C. S. (1991). Children's conceptions of ability in major domains: An interview and experimental study. *Child Study Journal*, 21, 11–36.

Benenson, J. & Dweck, C. S. (1986) The development of trait explanations and self-evaluations in the academic and social domains. *Child Development*, 57, 1179–1189.

Binet, A. (1909/1973). *Les idees modernes sur les enfants* [Modern ideas on children]. Paris: Flamarion.

Blumenfeld, P., Pintrich, P., & Hamilton, V. (1986). Children's concepts of ability, effort, and conduct. *American Educational Research Journal*, 23, 95–104.

Blumenfield, P. Wigfield, A., Pintrich, P., & Mecce, J. C. (1981).

Blumenfeld. P. C., Hamilton, V. L., Bossert, S., Wessels, K., & Meece, J. (1983). Teacher talk and student thought: Socialization into the student role. In J. Levine & M. Wang (Eds.), *Teacher and student perceptions: Implications for learning*. (pp. 143–192). Hillsdale, N. J.: Lawrence Erlbaum Associates.

Braten,. I., & Olaussen, B. S. (1998). The relationship between motivational beliefs and learning strategy use among Norwegian college students. *Contemporary Educational Psychology*, 182–194.

Burhans, K., and Dweck, C. S. (1995). Helplessness in early childhood: The role of contingent worth. *Child Development*, 66, 1719–1738.

Butler, R. (1990). The effects of mastery and competitive conditions on self-assessment at different ages. *Child Development*, 61, 201–210.

Butler, R. (1998). Age trends in the use of social and temporal comparison for self-evaluation: Examination of a novel developmental hypothesis. *Child Development*, 69, 1054–1073.

Butler, R. (1999). Information seeking and achievement motivation in middle childhood and adolescence: The role of conceptions of ability. *Developmental Psychology*, 35, 146–163.

Butler, R. (2000). Making judgments about ability: The role of implicit theories of ability in moderating inferences from temporal and social comparison information. *Journal of Personality and Social Psychology*, 78, 965–978.

Butler, R., & Baumer, S. (2001). *The role of context and development in children's constructions of motivational purposes and self-regulation*. Paper presented at the April meeting of the Society for Research in Child Development. Minneapolis, MN.

Cain, K., & Dweck, C. S. (1989). Children's theories of intelligence: A developmental model. In R. Sternberg (Ed.), *Advances in the study of intelligence*. Hillsdale, NJ: Lawrence Erlbaum Associates.

Cain, K., & Dweck, C. S. (1995). The development of children's achievement motivation patterns and conceptions of intelligence. *Merrill-Palmer Quarterly*, 41, 25–52.

Carugati, F. (1990). From social cognition to social representations in the study of intelligence. In G. Duveen & B. Lloyd (Eds.) *Social representations and the development of knowledge* (pp. 126–143). Cambridge, UK: Cambridge University Press.

Chapman, M., & Skinner, E. A. (1989) Children's agency beliefs, cognitive performance, and conceptions of effort and ability: Individual and developmental differences. *Child Development*, 60, 1229–1238.

Chiu, C., Hong, Y., & Dweck, C. S. (1997). Lay dispositionism and implicit theories of personality. *Journal of Personality and Social Psychology*, 73, 19–30.

Cornelius, S. W., Kenny, S., & Caspi, A. (1989). Academic and everyday intelligence in adulthood: Conceptions of self and ability tests. In J. D. Sinnott (Ed.), *Everyday problem solving: Theory and applications* (pp. 191–210). New York: Praeger.

Droege, K. L., & Stipek, D. J. (1993). Children's use of dispositions to predict classmates' behavior. *Developmental Psychology, 29*, 646–654.

Dweck, C. S. (1999). *Self-Theories: Their role in motivation, personality and development.* Philadelphia: Taylor & Francis.

Dweck, C. S., & Elliott, E. S. (1983). Achievement motivation. In P. Mussen and E. M. Hetherington (Eds.), *Handbook of child psychology.* New York: Wiley.

Dweck, C. S., & Leggett, E. L. (1988) A social-cognitive approach to motivation and personality. *Psychological Review, 95*, 256–273.

Dweck, C. S., & Lennon, C. (2001). *Person vs. process focused parenting: Impact on achievement motivation.* Paper presented at the April meeting of the Society for Research in Child Development, Minneapolis, MN.

Dweck, C. S., & Sorich, L. (1999). Mastery-oriented thinking. In C. R. Snyder (Ed.), *Coping.* New York: Oxford University Press.

Eaton, M. J., & Dembo, M. H. (1996). *Differences in the motivational beliefs of Asian and non-Asian students.* Paper presented at the April meeting of the American Educational Research Association, New York.

Eccles, J. S., Wigfield, A., & Schiefele, U. (1998). Motivation to succeed. In W. Damon and N. Eisenberg (Eds.), *Handbook of Child Psychology* (Vol. 3-pp. 1017–1095). New York: Wiley.

Eccles, J. S., Wigfield, A., Harold, R., & Blumenfeld, P. (1993). Age and gender differences in children's self- and task-perceptions during elementary school. *Child Development, 64*, 830–847.

Elliot, A. J., & McGregor, H. A. (2000). *A 2 x 2 achievement goal framework.* Unpublished paper, University of Rochester, Rochester, NY.

Entwistle, D., & Hayduk, L. (1978). *Too great expectations: Young children's academic outlook.* Baltimore, MD: Johns Hopkins University Press.

Faria, L. (1996). Personal conceptions of intelligence: A developmental study in Portugal. *Psychological Reports, 79*, 1299–11305.

Ferguson, T. J., van Roosendaal, J., & Rule, B. G. (1986). Informational basis for children's impressions of others. *Developmental Psychology, 22*, 335–341.

Frey, K. S. & Ruble, D. N. (1985). What children say when the teacher is not around: Conflicting goals in social comparison and performance assessment in the classroom. *Journal of Personality and Social Psychology, 48*, 550–562.

Frey, K. S., & Ruble, D. N. (1987). What children say about classroom performance: Sex and grade differences in perceived competence. *Child Development, 58*, 1066–1078.

Golumbia, L. R. (1990). *Motivational processes in adolescence: An experimental analysis of learning-disabled and nondisabled cognitions, affect, and behavior.* Doctoral dissertation, Wayne State University, Detroit.

Grant, H. (2000). *Achievement goals and their impact: Intrinsic motivation and achievement across the college transition.* Unpublished doctoral dissertation, Columbia University, New York.

Grant, Heidi, & Dweck, C. S. (2001) Cross-cultural response to failure: Considering outcome attributions with different goals. In F. Salili, C. Chiu, & Y. Hong (Eds.). (2001). *Student motivation: The culture and context of learning* (pp. 203–219). New York, NY: Plenum.

Graziano, W. G., Jensen-Campbell, L. A., & Sullivan-Logan, G. M. (1998). Temperament, activity, and expectations for later personality development. *Journal of Personality and Social Psychology, 74*, 1266–1277.

Harter, S. (1982). The Perceived Competence Scale for Children. *Child Development, 53*, 87–97.

Hebert, C., & Dweck, C. S. (1985). *Mediators of persistence in preschoolers.* Unpublished manuscript, Harvard University, Cambridge, MA.

Henderlong, J., & Lepper, M. R. (1997). *Conceptions of intelligence and children's motivational orientations: A developmental perspective.* Paper presented at the April meeting of the Society for Research in Child Development, Washington, DC.

Henderson, V., & Dweck, C.S. (1990). Achievement and motivation in adolescence: A new model and data. In S. Feldman and G. Elliott (Eds.), *At the threshold: The developing adolescent.* Cambridge, MA: Harvard University Press.

Heyman, G. D., & Dweck, C. S. (1998). Children's thinking about traits: Implications for judgments of the self and others. *Child Development.* 64, 391–403.

Heyman, G. D., Dweck, C. S., & Cain, K. (1992). Young children's vulnerability to self-blame and helplessness. *Child Development,* 63, 401–415.

Heyman, G. D., & Gelman, S. A. (1998). The use of trait labels in making psychological inferences. *Child Development,* 70, 604–619.

Hong, Y. Y., Chiu, C., Dweck, C. S., Lin, D., & Wan, W. (1999). Implicit theories, attributions, and coping: A meaning system approach. *Journal of Personality and Social Psychology,* 77, 588–599.

Howe, M. J. (1990). Children's gifts, talents, and natural abilities: An explanatory mythology? *Educational and Child Psychology,* 7, 52–54.

Jagacinski, C. M. & Nicholls, J. G. (1984). Conceptions of ability and related affects in task involvement and ego-involvement. *Journal of Educational Psychology,* 76, 909–919.

Jourden, F. J., Bandura, A., & Banfield, J. T. (1991). The impact of conceptions of ability on self-regulatory factors and motor skill acquisition. *Journal of Sport and Exercise Psychology,* 13, 213–226.

Kamins, M., & Dweck, C. S. (1999). Person vs. process praise and criticism: Implications for contingent self-worth and coping. *Developmental Psychology,* 35, 835–847.

Kamins, M., & Dweck, C. S. (2000). *Implicit theories, contingent self-worth, and motivation.* Unpublished data, Columbia University, New York.

Karabenick, J. D., & Heller, K. A. (1976). A developmental study of effort and ability attributions. *Developmental Psychology,* 12, 559–560.

Kasimatis, M., Miller, M., & Marcussen, L. (1996). The effects of implicit theories on exercise motivation. *Journal of Research in Personality,* 30, 510–516.

Kim, N. M., Grant, H., & Dweck, C. S. (2000). *Views of intelligence: A comparative study of effort and ability beliefs in Korean and American students.* Unpublished manuscript, Columbia University, New York.

Kun, A. (1977). Development of the magnitude–covariation principle and compensation schemata in ability and effort attributions of performance. *Child Development,* 48, 862–873.

Lawrence, J. S., & Crocker, J. (1999). Social stigma and self-esteem: The role of contingencies or worth. In D.A. Prentice & D. T. Miller (Eds.), *Cultural divides: Understanding and overcoming group conflict* (pp. 364–392). New York: Russell Sage.

Lee, K. (1996). A study of teacher responses based on their conceptions of intelligence. *Journal of Classroom Interaction,* 31, 1–12.

Levy, S. R., Plaks, J. E., Hong, Y., Chiu, C., & Dweck, C. S. (2001). Static versus dynamic theories and the perception of groups: Different routes to different destinations. *Personality & Social Psychology Review,* 5, 156–168.

Lewis, P. B. (1999). *Stereotype threat, implicit theories of intelligence, and racial differences in standardized test performance.* Unpublished dissertation, Kent State University, Kent, OH.

Lewis, M., Alessandri, S. M., & Sullivan, M. W. (1992). Differences in shame and pride as a function of children's gender and task difficulty. *Child Development,* 63, 630–638.

Licht, B. G., & Dweck, C. S. (1984). Determinants of academic achievement: The interaction of children's achievement orientations with skill area. *Developmental Psychology,* 20, 628–636.

Linehan, P. L. (1999). *Conceptions of ability: Nature and impact across content areas.* Unpublished dissertation, Purdue University, West Lafayette, IN..

MacIver, D. (1987). Classroom factors and student characteristics predicting students' use of achievement standards during ability self-assessment. *Child Development,* 58, 1258–1271.

Marsh, H. W. (1989). Age and sex effects in multiple dimensions of self-concept: Preadolescence to early adulthood. *Journal of Educational Psychology,* 81, 417–430.

Marsh, H. W., Craven, R.G., & Debus, R. (1991). Self-concepts of young children 5 to 8 years of age: Measurement and multidimensional structure. *Journal of Educational Psychology,* 83, 377–392.

Martocchio, J. J. (1994). Effects of concepts of ability on anxiety, self-efficacy, and learning in training. *Journal of Applied Psychology,* 79, 819–825.

Meyer, W. U., Bachman, M., Bermann, U., Hempelmann, M., & Ploeger, F. D. (1979). The informational value of evaluative behavior: Influences of praise and blame on perceptions and ability. *Journal of Educational Psychology*, 71, 259–268.

Miller, A. (1985). A developmental study of the cognitive basis of performance impairment after failure. *Journal of Personality and Social Psychology*, 49, 529–538.

Mueller, C. M., & Dweck, C. S. (1998). Intelligence praise can undermine motivation and performance. *Journal of Personality and Social Psychology*, 75, 33–52.

Nelson, S., & Dweck, C. S. (1977). Motivation and competence as determinants of young children's reward allocation. *Developmental Psychology*, 13, 192–197.

Nicholls, J. G. (1978). The development of the concepts of effort and ability, perceptions of academic attainments, and the understanding that difficult tasks require more ability. *Child Development*, 49, 800–814.

Nicholls, J. G. (1979). Development of perception of own attainment and causal attributions for success and failure in reading. *Journal of Educational Psychology*, 71, 94–99.

Nicholls, J. G. (1984). Achievement motivation: Conceptions of ability, subjective experience, task choice, and performance. *Psychological Review*, 91, 328–346.

Nicholls, J. G., & Miller, A. (1984). Conceptions of ability and achievement motivation. In R. Ames & C. Ames (Eds.), *Research on motivation in education* (Vol. 1-pp. 39–73). New York: Academic Press.

Nicholls, J.G., Patashnick, M., & Mettetal, G. (1986). Conceptions of ability and intelligence. *Child Development*, 57, 636–645.

Paley, V. G. (1988). *Bad guys don't have birthdays*. Chicago: University of Chicago Press.

Parsons, J. E., & Ruble, D. N. (1977). The development of achievement-related expectancies. *Child Development*, 48, 1075–1079.

Perkins, D. N., & Grotzer, T. A. (1997). Teaching intelligence. *American Psychologist*, 52, 1125–1133.

Pintrich, P., & Blumenfeld, P. (1985). Classroom experience and children's self-perception of ability, effort, and conduct. *Journal of Educational Psychology*, 77, 646–657.

Plaks, J. E., Stroessner, S. J., Dweck, C. S., & Sherman, J.W. (2001). Person theories and attention allocation: Preference for stereotypic vs. counterstereotypic information. *Journal of Personality and Social Psychology*, 80, 876–893.

Pomerantz, E. M., & Ruble, D. N. (1997). Distinguishing multiple dimensions of conceptions of ability: Implications for self-evaluation. *Child Development*, 68, 1165–1180.

Pomerantz, E. M., & Saxon, J. L. (2001). Conceptions of ability as stable and self-evaluative processes: A longitudinal examination. *Child Development*, 72, 152–173.

Rhodewalt, F. (1994). Conceptions of ability, achievement goals, and individual differences in self-handicapping behavior: On the application of implicit theories. *Journal of Personality*, 62, 67–85.

Rholes, W. S., Blackwell, J., Jordan, C. & Walters, C., (1980). A developmental study of learned helplessness. *Developmental Psychology*, 16, 616–624.

Rholes, W. S., Jones, M., & Wade, C. (1988) Children's understanding of personal dispositions and its relationship to behavior. *Journal of Experimental Child Psychology*, 45, 1–17.

Rholes, W. S., & Ruble, D. N. (1984). Children's understanding of dispositional characteristics of others. *Child Development*, 55, 550–560.

Robins, R. W., & Pals, J. (1998). *Implicit self-theories of ability in the academic domain: A test of Dweck's model*. Unpublished manuscript, University of California at Davis.

Roedel. T. D., & Schraw, G. (1995). Beliefs about intelligence and academic goals. *Comtemporary Educational Psychology*, 20, 464–468.

Rohrback, M. R. (1993). *Path analytic extension of control theory using individual differences*. Doctoral dissertation, University of Akron, Akron, OH.

Rosenholtz, S., & Simpson, C. (1984). The formation of ability conceptions: Developmental trend or social construction? *Review of Educational Research*, 54, 31–63.

Rotenberg, K. (1982). Development of character constancy of self and others. *Child Development*, 53, 505–515.

Ruble, D. N. (1987). The acquisition of self-knowledge: A self-socialization approach. In N. Eisenberg (Ed.), *Contemporary topics in developmental psychology* (pp. 243–270). New York: Wiley.

Ruble, D. N., Boggiano, A., Feldman, N. S., & Loebl, J. H. (1980). A developmental analysis of the role of social comparison in self-evaluation. *Developmental Psychology*, 16, 105–115.

Ruble, D. N., and Dweck, C. S. (1995). The development of self-conceptions and person conceptions. In N. Eisenberg (Ed.), *Review of Personality and Social Psychology, Vol 15: Social Development.* Thousand Oaks, CA: Sage.

Ruble, D. N., and Flett, (1988). Conflicting goals in self-evaluative information seeking: Developmental and ability level analyses. *Child Development*, 59, 97–106.

Schuster, B., Ruble, D. N., & Weinert, F. E. (1998). Causal inferences and the positivity bias in children: The role of the covariation principle. *Child Development*, 69, 1577–1596.

Skinner, E. S. (1990). Age differences in the dimensions of perceived control during middle childhood: Implications for developmental conceptualizations and research. *Child Development*, 61, 1882–1890.

Smetana, J. (1985). Children's impressions in of moral and conventional transgressions. *Developmental Psychology*, 21, 715–724.

Smiley, P. A., & Dweck, C. S. (1994). Individual differences in achievement goals among young children. *Child Development*, 65, 1723–1743.

Smiley, P. A., Coulson, S. L., & Van Ocker, J. C. (2000). *Beliefs about learning in mothers and fathers of preschoolers.* Paper presented at the April meeting of the American Educational Research Association, New Orleans.

Steele, C. M., & Aronson. J. (1997). Stereotype threat and the intellectual test performance of African Americans. *Journal of Personality and Social Psychology*, 69, 797–811.

Stevenson, H. W., Lee, S., Chen, C., Stigler, J. W., Hsu, C. C., & Kitamura, S. (1990). Contexts of achievement: A study of American, Chinese, and Japanese children. *Monographs of the Society for Research in Child Development*, 55, (Serial No. 221.).

Stipek, D. J., (1996). Motivation and instruction. In D. Berliner and R. Calfee (Eds.), *Handbook of educational psychology* (pp. 85–113). New York: Macmillan.

Stipek, D. J., & Daniels, D. (1988), Declining perceptions of competence: A consequence of changes in the child or the educational environment? *Journal of Educational Psychology*, 80, 352–356.

Stipek, D. J., & Daniels, D. H. (1990). Children's use of dispositional attributions in predicting the performance and behavior of classmates. *Journal of Applied Developmental Psychology*, 11, 13–28.

Stipek, D. J., & Gralinski, J. H. (1991). Gender differences in children's achievement-related beliefs and emotional responses to success and failure in mathematics. *Journal of Educational Psychology*, 83, 362–371.

Stipek, D. J., & Gralinski, J. H. (1996). Children's beliefs about intelligence and school performance. *Journal of Educational Psychology*, 88, 397–407.

Stipek, D. J., & Hoffman, J. (1980). Development of children's performance-related judgments. *Child Development*, 51, 912–914.

Stipek, D. J., & MacIver, D. (1989). Developmental change in children's assessment of intellectual competence. *Child Development*, 60, 521–538.

Stipek, D. J., Recchia, S., & McClintic, S. (1992). Self-evaluation in young children. *Monographs of the Society for Research in Child Development*, 56, (Serial No. 226).

Stipek, D. J., & Tannatt, L. (1984). Children's judgments of their own and peers' academic competence. *Journal of Educational Psychology*, 76, 75–84.

Stone, J. (1998). *Theories of intelligence and the meaning of achievement goals.* Doctoral dissertation, New York University, New York.

Surber, C. F. (1980). The development of reversible operations in judgments of ability, effort, and performance. *Child Development*, 51, 1018–1029.

Surber, C. F. (1984). The development of achievement-related judgment processes. In J. Nicholls (Ed.), *Advances in motivation and achievement*, (Vol. 3: pp. 137–184). Greenwich, CT: JAI Press.

Tabernero, C., & Wood, R. (1999). Implicit theories versus the social construal of ability in self-regulation and performance on a complex task. *Organizational Behavior and Human Decision Processes*, 78, 104–127.

Wagner, R. K., & Sternberg, R. J. (1984). Alternative conceptions of intelligence and their implications for education. *Review of Educational Research*, 54, 179–223.

Wenzel, K. (1998). Parents' aspirations for children's educational attainments: Relations to parental beliefs and social address variables. *Merrill-Palmer Quarterly*, 44, 20–37.

Wigfield, A., & Eccles, J.S. (2000). Expectancy–value theory of achievement motivation. *Contemporary Educational Psychology*, 25, 68–81.

Wigfield, A., Eccles, J. S., Yoon, K. S., Harold, R. D., Arbreton, A., Freedman-Doan, K., & Blumenfeld, P. C. (1997). Changes in children's competence beliefs and subjective task values across the elementary school years. *Journal of Educational Psychology*, 89, 451–469.

Wigfield, A., Eccles, J. S., & Pintrich, P. R. (1996). Development between the ages of 11 and 25. In D. C. Berliner and R.C. Calfee (Eds), *Handbook of educational psychology* (pp. 145–185).Englewood Cliffs, NJ; Prentice Hall.

Wood, R., & Bandura, A. (1989). Impact of conceptions of ability on self-regulatory mechanisms and complex decision making. *Journal of Personality and Social Psychology*, 56, 407–415.

Xiang, P. (1996). *Achievement goals and self-perceptions of ability in physical education: A cross-cultural perspective*. Doctoral dissertation, Louisiana State University, Shreveport.

Yang, S., & Sternberg, R.J. (1997). Taiwanese Chinese people's conceptions of intelligence. *Intelligence*, 25, 21–36.

Yull, N. & Pearson, A. (1998). The development of bases for trait attributions: Children's understanding of traits as causal mechanisms based on desire. *Developmental Psychology*, 34, 574–586.

Yussen, S., & Kane, P. (1985). Children's conceptions of intelligence. In S. R. Yussen (Ed.), *The growth of reflection in children* (pp. 207–241). New York: Academic Press.

PART

II

Do I Want to Do this Activity, and Why?

The Development of Competence Beliefs, Expectancies for Success, and Achievement Values from Childhood through Adolescence

ALLAN WIGFIELD

University of Maryland, College Park, Maryland

JACQUELYNNE S. ECCLES

University of Michigan, Ann Arbor, Michigan

In this chapter we review research on the development of children's competence–expectancy beliefs and achievement values. The research is based on an expectancy–value model of achievement motivation and behavior developed by Eccles and her colleagues (e.g., Eccles, 1993; Eccles et al., 1983; Wigfield, 1994; Wigfield & Eccles, 1992, 2000). Expectancy–value theory has been one of the most important views on the nature of achievement motivation, beginning with Atkinson's (1957) seminal work and continuing through the work of Battle (1965, 1966), the Crandalls (e.g., V. C. Crandall, 1969; V. J. Crandall, Dewey, Katkovsky, & Preston, 1964), and more recently Feather (1982, 1988, 1992) and Eccles, Wigfield, and their colleagues (e.g., Eccles, 1993; Eccles et al., 1983; Eccles, Adler, & Meece, 1984; Eccles, Wigfield, Harold, & Blumenfeld, 1993; Wigfield, 1994; Wigfield & Eccles, 1992, 2000; Wigfield et al., 1997). To characterize the theory very broadly, theorists adopting this perspective posit that individuals' expectancies for success and the value they have for succeeding are important determinants of their motivation to perform different achievement tasks, and their choices of which tasks to pursue.

The Development of Achievement Motivation

Atkinson (1957), who originally defined expectancies as individuals' antici-
pations that their performance will be followed by either success or failure,
defined value as the relative attractiveness of succeeding or failing on a task.

In previous theoretical and review articles on this work, we have presented
an expectancy–value model of achievement choice and behavior that expands
Atkinson's (1957) original defintions of expectancy for success and task value
(Eccles, 1993; Eccles et al., 1983), discussed the nature of achievement values (Parsons & Goff, 1980; Wigfield & Eccles, 1992), focused on how expectancies and values develop during childhood (Wigfield, 1994), and compared the
expectancy and value constructs to related constructs in the motivation literature (Wigfield & Eccles, 2000). In this chapter, we review recent work on
the development of children's expectancy beliefs and values, with a special
focus on gender and ethnic differences in expectancies and values. We present information on how competence–expectancy beliefs and values relate to
each other over time. We also discuss relations of competence beliefs,
achievement values, and achievement goals. Finally, we discuss how children's expectancies and values relate to their achievement behaviors and
activity choices. In this discussion we relate our work to recent work on the
self-regulation of behavior and action control, discussing the roles that
expectancies and values may play in the regulation of behavior.

ECCLES, WIGFIELD, AND COLLEAGUES'
EXPECTANCY–VALUE MODEL

Eccles et al. (1983) developed an expectancy–value model of achievement
choice as a framework for understanding early adolescents' and adolescents'
performance and choice in the mathematics achievement domain. Figure 1
presents a recent version of the model. Eccles et al. (1983) proposed that children's achievement performance, persistence, and choice of achievement tasks
are most directly predicted by their expectancies for success on those tasks
and the subjective value they attach to success on those tasks. Children's
expectancies and values themselves are most directly determined by other
achievement-related beliefs, including children's achievement goals and self-
schemata, and their task-specific beliefs (defined as beliefs about ability or
competence and task difficulty beliefs). Children's interpretations of their past
performance, and their perceptions of socializers' attitudes and expectations,

FIGURE 1 (RIGHT)
Eccles, Wigfield, and colleagues' expectancy–value model of achievement
motivation. (From Wigfield, A., and Eccles, J. S. (2000). Expectancy–value
theory of achievement motivation. *Contemporary Educational Psychology*, 25(1), 69.)

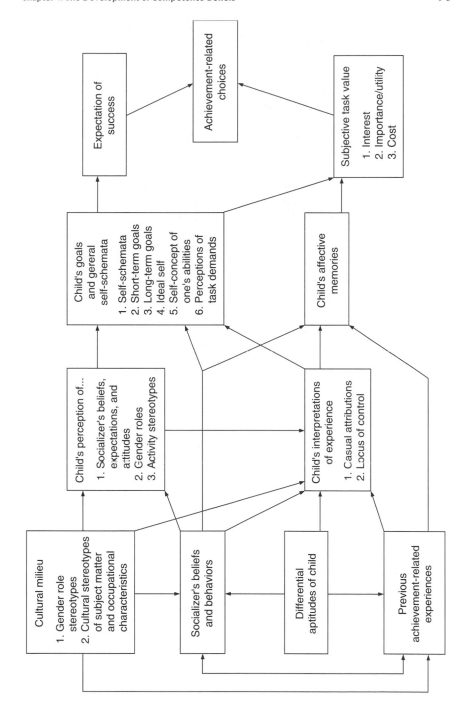

influence their goals and task-specific beliefs. Other influences are children's previous performance on different tasks, important socializers' beliefs, values, and behaviors, and various contextual and cultural influences.

For theoretical clarity it is crucial to define the expectancy and value constructs in the model (see also Wigfield & Eccles, 2000). Expectancies for success are defined as children's beliefs about how well they will do on an upcoming task. Beliefs about ability refer to children's evaluations of their competence in different areas. Related constructs also are prominent in other motivation models, in particular Bandura's (1997) self-efficacy theory, Covington's (1992) self-worth approach, Dweck and her colleagues' work on perceptions of intelligence (Dweck & Leggett, 1988), Ryan and Deci's (2000) self-determination perspective, and Weiner's (1979, 1985) attribution theory; these related constructs are discussed in Chapters 1, 2, 3, and 6 in this volume.

Wigfield and Eccles (2000) discussed how the definitions of the expectancy and ability belief constructs in our expectancy–value model differ from these other constructs (see also Pajares, 1996). Crucial differences include the level of specifity at which the constructs are defined and measured, and whether the focus primarily is on individuals' sense of their own competence, or their competence in comparison to others. For instance, Bandura and Schunk's construct of self-efficacy usually is measured quite specifically, and emphasizes the individual's own sense of whether they can accomplish a task. Theorists such as Covington, Dweck, and Ryan and Deci tend to take a more general approach to the definition and measurement of these constructs. We tend to measure these constructs at the domain-specific level, and to include individuals' comparative sense of competence along with their beliefs about their own ability. These are important differences, but a crucial similarity is that the individual's sense of competence is a key part of many models of motivation.

Values have both broad and more specific definitions. Rokeach (1973, 1979) broadly construed values as beliefs about desired end states. He identified a set of values that he believed were fundamental to human experience; some of these values concerned achievement. Schwartz (1992) also theorized about broad human values, listing 10 such values with achievement included as one of these values (see Rohan, 2000, for review of these theories). In the achievement motivation literature, subjective task values have been defined more specifically as how a task meets different needs of individuals (Eccles et al., 1983; Wigfield & Eccles, 1992). As discussed in more detail later, task values are a crucial part of the model because they impact individuals' choice. Individuals who feel competent at a given activity may not engage in it because it has no value for them.

Eccles et al. (1983) proposed four major components of subjective values: attainment value or importance, intrinsic value, utility value or usefulness of the task, and cost (see Eccles et al., 1983, and Wigfield & Eccles, 1992, for more detailed discussion of these components). Building on Battle's (1965, 1966) work, Eccles et al. defined attainment value as the importance of doing well on a given task. More broadly, attainment value also deals with identity issues; tasks are important when individuals view them as central to their own sense of themselves. Intrinsic value is the enjoyment one gains from doing the task; this component is similar in certain respects to notions of intrinsic motivation (see Ryan & Deci, 2000; Harter, 1981). Utility value or usefulness refers to how a task fits into an individual's future plans, for instance, taking a math class to fulfill a requirement for a science degree. Cost refers to what the individual has to give up to do a task (e.g., do I do my math homework or call my friend?), as well as the anticipated effort one will need to put into task completion. Sample items measuring these constructs can be found in Wigfield and Eccles (2000).

DEVELOPMENT OF CHILDREN'S COMPETENCE BELIEFS, EXPECTANCIES FOR SUCCESS, AND ACHIEVEMENT TASK VALUES

We and others have done extensive work on the development of children's competence beliefs, expectancies for success, and achievement values. Because this work has been reviewed in detail elsewhere (e.g., Eccles, Wigfield, & Schiefele, 1998; Wigfield, 1994; Wigfield & Eccles, 1992), we present just a brief summary here. One kind of change addressed is the extent to which children's beliefs and values are differentiated or distinct. A second kind of change considered is mean level change.[1]

The Structure of Children's Competence Beliefs and Values

Various researchers have examined the structure of children's beliefs about competence, and some have examined children's subjective task values, to assess how the structure of these constructs becomes differentiated (e.g., Eccles & Wigfield, 1995; Eccles, Wigfield, Harold, & Blumenfeld, 1993; Harter, 1982; Harter & Pike, 1984; Marsh, Barnes, Cairns, & Tidman, 1984; Marsh, Craven, & Debus, 1991, 1998). These researchers have factor-analyzed children's responses to various questionnaire measures of these constructs, and have found that even during the early elementary school years children dis-

---

[1]A third kind of change in children's beliefs and values concerns change in the meaning of these constructs across development. Children of different ages appear to have different conceptions of what ability is, with consequent influences on their motivation. Nicholls (1990) and Wigfield (1994) discuss these changes in depth.

tinguish different domains of competence, including math, reading, general school, physical ability, physical appearance, peer relations, parent relations, and general self-concept.

Eccles and Wigfield (1995) and Eccles et al. (1993) looked at whether children's competence beliefs and expectancies for success are distinct constructs, as is proposed in the model of Eccles et al. (1983). Children in their studies ranged in age from first through twelfth grade. Results of confirmatory factor analyses showed that children's competence beliefs and expectancies for success load on the same factor; hence these components are not empirically distinct. Therefore, two of the constructs proposed as separate in the model (competence beliefs, expectancies for success) are not empirically distinguishable.

By contrast, both children and adolescents do distinguish between their competence beliefs and subjective values. This finding is crucial for the expectancy–value model. Even during the very early elementary grades children appear to have distinct beliefs about what they are *good at* and what they *value* in different domains. The different components of task value are less differentiated during the elementary school years, becoming differentiated during early adolescence (Eccles & Wigfield, 1995; Eccles et al., 1993).

In summary, even young children's competence beliefs are differentiated clearly across various activities, although their competence beliefs and expectancies for success are less clearly differentiated. Different components of subjective values also have been identified, especially in children in fifth grade and above. These results generally are consistent with the notion that children's beliefs become more differentiated as they get older (Harter, 1998), although some of this differentiation occurs very early on, earlier than once thought.

Changes in the Mean Level of Children's Achievement Beliefs and Values

Several researchers have found that children's competence beliefs and expectancies for success for different tasks decline across the elementary school years and into the middle school years (see Dweck & Elliott, 1983; Eccles et al., 1998; Stipek & MacIver, 1989). To illustrate, in the findings of Nicholls (1979a) most first graders ranked themselves near the top of the class in reading ability, and there was no correlation between their ability ratings and their performance level. In contrast, the 12-year-olds' ratings were more dispersed and correlated highly with school grades (0.70 or higher).

Similar results have emerged in cross-sectional and longitudinal studies of children's competence beliefs in a variety of academic and nonacademic domains by Eccles and her colleagues (e.g., Eccles et al. 1993; Wigfield et al. 1997) and Marsh (1989). These declines, particularly for math, often continue into and through secondary school (Eccles et al., 1983, Eccles, et al., 1989; Wigfield, Eccles, MacIver, Reuman, & Midgley, 1991). Across the elementary school years, children's expectancies for success become more sensitive to both suc-cess and failure experiences and more accurate or realistic in terms of their relation to actual performance history (see Assor & Connell, 1992; Eccles et al., 1998; Parsons & Ruble, 1977; Stipek, 1984).

In contrast to these early studies using self-report measures, researchers using different methodologies (either asking different kinds of question or observing young children's reactions to their performance on different tasks) have shown that not all young children are optimistic about their abilities. Heyman, Dweck, and Cain (1993) observed that some preschool children already reacted negatively to failure, reporting that their failures mean they are not good people. Similarly, Stipek, Recchia, & McClintic (1992) reported that preschool children as young as 2 reacted both behaviorally and emo-tionally to failure experiences.

As with competence beliefs and expectancies for success, studies looking at changes in the mean level of children's values generally show that children value certain academic tasks less as they get older (see Eccles et al., 1998; Wigfield & Eccles, 1992, for complete reviews). The negative changes in chil-dren's competence-related beliefs and achievement values have been explained in two ways:

1. Because children become much better at understanding, interpreting, and integrating the evaluative feedback they receive, and engage in more social comparison with their peers, children become more accurate or real-istic in their self-assessments, leading some to become relatively more neg-ative (see Dweck & Elliott, 1983; Nicholls, 1984; Parsons & Ruble, 1977; Ruble, 1983; Shaklee & Tucker, 1979; Stipek & MacIver, 1989).

2. Because school environments change in ways that make evaluation more salient and competition between students more likely, some children's self-assessments will decline as they get older (e.g., see Blumenfeld, Pin-trich, Meece, & Wessels, 1982; Eccles & Midgley, 1989; Wigfield, Eccles, & Pintrich, 1996).

GENDER AND ETHNIC DIFFERENCES
IN COMPETENCE-RELATED BELIEFS
AND EXPECTANCIES FOR SUCCESS

Before discussing gender and ethnic differences, some words of caution are in order. As other authors have pointed out, drawing conclusions about sex, racial, and ethnic differences must be done carefully (see Eisenberg, Mar-tin, & Fabes, 1996; Graham, 1994; Ruble & Martin, 1998) . Although such dif-ferences often are observed, in general they tend to be relatively small in terms of the amount of variance explained (e.g., Marsh, 1989). Thus there often is substantial overlap between different groups in the many different variables measured in studies of sex and ethnic differences. Individual differences *within* groups typically are stronger than mean differences *between* groups; indeed, researchers have called for more study of these within-group variations rather than between-group comparisons, particularly in the case of ethnic differences (Graham, 1994). A major concern in interpreting racial and ethnic differences is that many researchers fail to consider the socioeconomic effects that often are confounded with racial and ethnic differences (see Graham, 1994). Even with these cautions in mind, there are reliable differences between various groups, and these differences are discussed in this section.

Gender Differences in Beliefs About Competence

Gender differences in competence-related beliefs during childhood and adolescence often are reported, particularly in gender-role stereotyped domains and on novel tasks (see Wigfield, Battle, Solomon, & Eccles, in press). For example, boys hold higher competence beliefs than girls for math and sports, even after all relevant skill-level differences are controlled. By contrast, girls have higher competence beliefs than boys for reading, English, and social activities (Eccles et al., 1989, Huston, 1983; Marsh, 1989; Marsh, et al., 1998; Wigfield, et al., 1991; Wigfield et al., 1997). These differences emerge remarkably early. Wigfield et al. (1997) conducted a longitudinal study of children's competence beliefs and valuing of different activities, including math, reading, and sports. They began when the children were in first, second, and fourth grade, and followed them for three years. The results showed that boys had higher competence beliefs for math and sports, and girls for English, even among the first graders. The age differences in beliefs did not change over time. Marsh, Craven, and Dubus' (1998) study of self-concepts included kindergarteners, and results were similar to those of Wigfield et al.

Few studies have looked at long-term change in children's competence beliefs. Jacobs, Lanza, Osgood, Eccles, & Wigfield (in press) followed the children in the study by Wigfield et al. (1997) through the end of high school, found that gender differences in math competence beliefs narrow by the end of high school. Gender differences in English competence beliefs favoring girls remain at the end of high school, but also are smaller than during the earlier school years.

The extent to which children endorse the cultural stereotypes regarding which sex is likely to be more talented in each domain predicts the extent to which girls and boys distort their ability self-concepts and expectations in the gender stereotypic direction (Early, Belansky, & Eccles, 1992; Eccles & Harold, 1991). That is, boys who believe that in general boys are better in math are more likely to have more positive competence beliefs in math. However, these sex differences are not always found (e.g., Dauber & Benbow, 1990; Schunk &

Lilly, 1982) and, when found, are generally quite small (Marsh, 1989, Marsh, et al., 1998).[2]

In summary, reliable sex differences in beliefs about competence for different activities have been found. One reason these differences are important is that competence-related beliefs are strong predictors of performance and task choice (Bandura, 1997; Eccles et al., 1983; Meece, Wigfield, & Eccles, 1990). Researchers looking at relations of competence beliefs to performance do not find sex differences in these relations; the links are as strong for girls as for boys (Meece, et al., 1990). But given that the sexes differ in their level of competence beliefs for different activities, performance differences may in part reflect these beliefs. For instance, on average girls doubt their competence in math more than boys do, and this likely influences their performance in math as well as their decisions about whether to continue doing math activities. Boys doubt their competence more in reading, again likely influencing their performance and choice.

Gender Differences in Achievement Task Values

Eccles, Wigfield and their colleagues have found gender-role stereotypic differences in both children's and adolescents' valuing of mathematics, music, sports, social activities, and English/reading (e.g. Eccles et al., 1989; Eccles, et al., 1993; Wigfield, et al., 1991, Wigfield et al., 1997). Across these studies, boys value sports activities more than girls do, although girls also value them highly. Relative to boys, girls value reading, English, and instrumental music more. Interestingly, recent work indicates that boys and girls value math equally (Eccles et al., 1993; Wigfield et al., 1997); in earlier work gender differences in the value of math emerged in high school (Eccles, et al., 1983). Recently we found that high school girls and boys reported valuing math equally (Jacobs et al., 2000). However, there are sex differences in interest in math and science-related fields during adolescence (see Gardner, 1998, and Wigfield, Battle, Solomon, & Eccles, in press, for review). By adolescence, girls report less interest in science than do boys and are much less likely to enroll in science and technically oriented classes, or pursue these areas for their careers.

---

[2]Work on children's attributions for success and failure is for the most part outside the scope of this chapter. However, because ability is a central attribution, work on sex differences in attributions to ability is germane to this section of the chapter. Sex differences in attributions to one's ability have been observed in some studies, but not in others. Some researchers (e.g., Dweck & Goetz, 1978) find that girls are less likely than boys to attribute success to ability and more likely to attribute failure to lack of ability. Others have found that this pattern depends on the kind of task used, occurring more with unfamiliar tasks or stereotypically masculine achievement task and sometimes does not occur at all (see Eccles et al., 1998, for further review).

Values also can be conceived more broadly to include things such as notions of what are appropriate activities for males and females to do. Sometimes such values can influence engagement in achievement-related activities. The role of conflict between gender roles and achievement in gifted girls' lives is well illustrated by results of an ethnographic study of a group of gifted elementary school girls. Bell (1989) interviewed a multiethnic group of third to sixth grade gifted girls in an urban elementary school regarding the barriers they perceived to their achievement in school. Five gender-role-related themes emerged with great regularity: (a) concern about hurting someone else's feelings by winning in achievement contests (b) concern about seeming to be a braggart if one expressed pride in one's accomplishments (c) over-reaction to nonsuccess experiences (apparently not being the very best is very painful to these girls) (d) concern over their physical appearance and what it takes to be beautiful and (e) concern with being overly aggressive in terms of getting the teacher's attention. In each case the gifted girls felt caught between doing their best and either appearing feminine or caring (see Eccles et al., 1998 for more details on gifted girls).

In summary, as with competence beliefs there are gender differences in children's and adolescents' valuing of different activities. These differences are important for understanding the development of gender differences in achievement, particularly as exemplified in choices of which activities to pursue. Although overall it appears that sex differences in achievement in different areas have declined over the last quarter century (see Eisenberg, Martin, & Fabes, 1996; Ruble & Martin, 1998), sex differences in choice of which activities and careers to pursue remain strong (see Wigfield, Battle, Solomon, & Eccles, in press). These differences are tied to the gender differences in valuing of various activities just reviewed.

Ethnic Differences in Competence Beliefs and Values

As is the case in many areas of psychology, less is known about the motivation of children from different racial and ethnic groups (see Graham, 1992). However, work in this area is growing quickly, with much of it focusing on the academic achievement difficulties of many African-American children (see Berry & Asamen, 1989; Hare, 1985; Slaughter-Defoe, Nakagawa, Takanishi, & Johnson, 1990). Recent work has also focused on other minority groups within the United States and on recent immigrant populations, some of whom are doing much better in school than both white middle class children and third-and-fourth generation members of the same national heritage (e.g., Slaughter-Defoe, Nakagawa, Takanishi, & Johnson, 1990; Chen & Stevenson, 1995, Kao & Tienda, 1995).

Graham (1994) reviewed the literature on differences between African-American and European-American students on such motivational constructs as need for achievement, locus of control, achievement attributions, and ability beliefs and expectancies. She concluded that, in general, the differences are not very large. Further, she argued that many existing studies have not adequately distinguished between race and socioeconomic status, making it very difficult to interpret any differences that emerge. Cooper and Dorr (1995) did a meta-analysis of many of the same studies reviewed by Graham in order to compare more narrative and more quantitative types of reviews. Although there were some important points of agreement across the two reviews, Cooper and Dorr concluded that there is evidence suggesting race differences in need for achievement favoring Whites, especially in lower socioeconomic status (SES) and younger samples.

Research on competence beliefs and expectancies has revealed more optimism among African-American children than among European-American children, even when the European-American children are achieving higher marks (e.g., Stevenson, Chen, & Uttal, 1990). But more importantly, Stevenson et al. found that the European-American children's ratings of their ability related significantly to their performance, whereas the African-American children's did not. Graham (1994) suggested the following explanations: (1) African-American and European- American children may use different social comparison groups to help judge their own abilities and (2) African-American children may say they are doing well to protect their general self-esteem, and may also devalue or disidentify academic activities at which they do poorly in order to protect their self-esteem. However, neither of these explanations has been adequately tested. If African-American children's competence-related beliefs indeed do not predict their school performance, then questions must be raised about how relevant theories focusing primarily on competence-related beliefs are for understanding these children's motivation.

Initially, researchers studying minority children's achievement values focused on the broader valuing of school by minority children and their parents. In general, these researchers find that minority children and parents highly value school (particularly during the elementary school years) and have high educational aspirations for their children (e.g., Stevenson, Chen, & Uttal, 1990). However, the many difficulties associated with poverty (see Duncan, Brooks-Gunn, & Klebanov, 1994; Huston, McLoyd, & Coll, 1994; McLoyd, 1990) make achievement of these educational aspirations problematic. It is important for researchers to extend this work to more specific value-related constructs. Graham and her colleagues have begun very important work in this area, and it is in Chapter 5 of this volume.

Researchers interested in ethnic and racial differences in achievement have proposed models linking social roles, stereotyping of groups, and individuals' competence-related beliefs and values (see Chapter 5 in this volume for further discussion). For example, Steele (1992) proposed stereotype vulnerability and disidentification to help explain the underachievement of African-American students. Confronted throughout their school career with mixed messages about their competence and potential and with the widespread negative cultural stereotypes about their academic potential and motivation, African-American students are likely to find it difficult to concentrate fully on their school work as a result of the anxiety induced by their stereotype vulnerability (see Steele & Aronson, 1995). In turn, to protect their self-esteem, they are likely to disidentify with academic achievement, leading to both a lowering of the value they attach to academic achievement and a detachment of their self-esteem from positive and the negative academic experiences alike. In support, researchers have found that academic self-concept of ability is less predictive of general self-esteem for some African-American children (Winston, Eccles, Senior, & Vida, 1997).

Fordham and Ogbu (1986) made a similar argument linking African-American students' perception of limited future job opportunities to lowered academic motivation: Since society and schools give African-American youth the dual message that academic achievement is unlikely to lead to positive adult outcomes for them and that they are not valued by the system, some African-American youth may create an oppositional culture that rejects the value of academic achievement. Ogbu (1992) discussed how this dynamic will be stronger for involuntary minorities who continue to be discriminated against by mainstream American culture (e.g., African-Americans, Native Americans) than for voluntary minority immigrant groups (e.g., recent immigrants from Southeast Asia). Although voluntary minorities have initial barriers to overcome due to language and cultural differences, these barriers can be overcome somewhat more easily than the racism faced by involuntary minorities, giving voluntary minorities greater access to mainstream culture and its benefits.

Contrary to this view, several investigators found no evidence of greater disidentification with school among African-American students (e.g., Steinberg et al., 1992; Taylor et al., 1994). But several studies show that disidentification, particularly as a result of inequitable treatment and failure experiences at school, undermines achievement and academic motivation (e.g., see Finn, 1989; Taylor et al., 1994). It is likely that some students, particularly members of involuntary minority groups, will have these experiences as they pass through the secondary school system.

Indeed, Osborn (1997) studied disidentification longitudinally from eighth through twelfth grade in a nationally representative sample of White, Hispanic, and African-American students, using data from the National Educational Longitudinal Study (NELS). He found that the self-reported grades of White students stayed stable over time, those of the Hispanic-American students decreased somewhat, and those of African-American students decreased the most. At all three time points the African-American students reported the high-est self-esteem. Relations of grades and self-esteem were significant but rel-atively modest for all groups in eighth grade. All groups showed some decrease over time in the relations of their self-esteem to their grades, but this decrease was most pronounced for African-American males. At both tenth and twelfth grades the correlations were not significant for this group; in all other groups they remained significant. This is important evidence for disidentification with school in African-American males. The sex differences in these correlations are particularly important to note; Steele's and Ogbu's analyses seem more applic-able to African-American males than to African-American females (see Gra-ham, and Taylor, Chapter 5, this volume, for further discussion of race by gender interactions).

Any discussion of motivational differences across different ethnic groups must take into account larger contextual issues. For example, Spencer and Markstrom-Adams (1990) argued that many minority children, particularly those living in poverty, have to deal with several difficult issues not faced by majority adolescents such as racist prejudicial attitudes, conflict between the values of their group and those of larger society, and scarcity of high-achiev-ing adults in their group to serve as role models. These difficulties can impede identity formation in these adolescents, leading to identity diffusion or inad-cquatc exploration of different possible identities (Taylor et al., 1994). Simi-larly, Cross (1990) argued that one must consider the development of both personal identities and racial group identity. Some African-American adoles-cents who have positive personal identities may be less positive about their racial group as a whole, whereas others may have negative personal identi-ties but positive orientations toward their group. Cross argued that many researchers have confounded these two constructs, leading to confusion in our understanding of identity development in, and its motivational implica tions for, African-Americans.

Finally it is critical to consider the quality of the educational institutions that serve many of these youth: 37% of African-American youth and 32% of Hispanic youth, compared to 5% of European-American and 22% of Asian youth, are enrolled in the 47 largest city school districts in this country. In addition, African-American and Hispanic youth live in some of the poorest school districts in this country: 28% of the youth enrolled in city schools live in poverty and 55% are eligible for free or reduced cost lunch, suggesting that class may be as important (or more important) as race in the differences that emerge. Teachers in these schools report feeling less safe than teachers in other school districts, dropout rates are highest, and achievement levels at all grades are the lowest (Council of the Great City Schools, 1992). Finally, schools that serve these populations are less likely than schools serving more advantaged populations to offer either high-quality remedial services or advanced courses and courses that facilitate the acquisition of higher order thinking skills and active learning strategies. Even children who are extremely motivated may find it difficult to perform well under these educational circumstances.

Graham (1994) made several important recommendations for future work on African-American children's motivation. We think these recommendations can be applied more broadly to work on different racial and ethnic groups. Two particularly important recommendations are (1) the need to separate out effects of race and social class, and (2) the need to move beyond race comparative studies to studies that look at individual differences within different racial and ethnic groups (e.g., McClendon & Wigfield, 1998), and at the antecedents and processes underlying variations in achievement outcomes among minority youth (e.g., Connell, Spencer, & Aber, 1994; Luster & McAdoo, 1994; Schneider & Coleman, 1993; Tienda & Kao, 1995). Studies of recent immigrant populations and comparative studies of different generations of immigrant populations move in these directions. For example, work by Stevenson and his colleagues, by Tienda and her colleagues, and by Fuligni demonstrates the power of the types of motivational construct discussed thus far in explaining both within- and between-group variation in academic achievement (e.g., Chen & Stevenson, 1995; Lummis & Stevenson, 1990).

EXPECTANCIES, VALUES, GOALS, AND ACHIEVEMENT BEHAVIORS

The work reviewed in the preceding sections provides a picture of our current knowledge about the development of competence-related beliefs and achievement task values in different groups. For the most part in the preceding discussion we treated these constructs separately. In our model these constructs are said to interrelate, to relate to other constructs, and to relate to different achievement outcomes. We turn to these interrelations in the sections that follow and describe some of our recent empirical efforts designed to address them.

Relations Among Competence-Related Beliefs and Subjective Task Values

In original statements of the expectancy–value model, competence beliefs were posited to predict both expectancies for success and achievement values. Relations between expectancies and values themselves were not specified. Researchers have found that children's' competence and expectancy beliefs relate positively to their subjective values (e.g., Battle, 1966; Eccles & Wigfield, 1995), with the relations apparent as early as first grade (Wigfield et al., 1997). These findings contrast with Atkinson's (1957) assertion that the most valued tasks are the ones that are difficult for individuals to do (i.e., tasks on which individuals have low expectancies for success). It appears that for real-world achievement, individuals value the tasks at which they think they can succeed.

Eccles and Wigfield (1995) and Wigfield et al. (1997) looked at how the different components of task value related to competence and expectancy beliefs. Wigfield et al. (1997) found that children's competence-related beliefs related more strongly to their interest in academic activities than to the perceived usefulness of the activities. In nonacademic domains (sport, music) these relations were similar in size. Eccles and Wigfield (1995) in their study of fifth through twelfth graders' math self-perceptions and values found that relations between competence–expectancy beliefs and both interest and perceived importance were stronger than relations of competence–expectancy beliefs and perceived usefulness of math. Thus the more intrinsic aspects of value (interest and importance) relate more closely to children's competence-related beliefs.

Much has been written in the motivation field about relations of competence beliefs and interest; for instance, both Harter (1978) in her effectance motivation model and Ryan and Deci (2000) in their self-determination perspective propose that competence beliefs and intrinsic motivation relate positively. Our work provides further support for these relations. We have begun to examine relations over time between children's competence-related beliefs and values, focusing on the interest component of value. This work addresses the crucial question of causal relations between competence beliefs and value. In this work we used data from the Michigan Childhood and Beyond Study (see Eccles et al., 1993; Wigfield et al., 1997) to examine the relations over a three year period in three different cohorts of children ranging in age from second through sixth grades. We looked at these relations in the achievement domains of math, reading, and sport. Interesting cohort and domain differences emerged in the structural equation modeling analyses. For the youngest cohort (second through fourth graders), competence-related beliefs were linked over time, as were children's ratings of interest, but there were few direct links over time between competence beliefs and interest. In the older cohorts relations over time among the constructs generally were stronger. When cross-construct relations over time emerged, they tended to be from competence-related beliefs to interest rather than the reverse. This pattern was most likely to occur in the domains of reading and sport; in math few of the cross-construct relations were significant.

Our work is the first study to look at these relations over time, and the results indicate that competence beliefs appear to take some causal precedence, as predicted in our earlier model (Eccles et al., 1983). For the achievement domains we studied, a sense of competence appears to influence the level of interest of children of elementary school age in the activity, especially reading and sport. These results have important implications for motivational intervention, notably that it may be better to focus initially on competence beliefs when working with children with motivational problems.

Relations of Competence-Related Beliefs, Achievement Values, and Achievement Goals

With the emphasis in motivation theory on cognitive aspects of motivation, many motivation researchers have begun to study the goals children have for achievement. Researchers studying children's goals have focused on the content of these goals, relations between academic and social goals, and goal orientations children have toward achievement (see Chapter 8 by Anderman, Austin, and Johnson and Chapter 9 by Wentzel for review).

Because goals and values both have to do with the purposes individuals have for engaging in different activities, we have been interested in exploring possible relations between children's achievement values and achievement goals, focusing on children's goal orientations (see Wigfield, 1994; Wigfield & Eccles, 1992). As discussed in greater detail in Chapter 8, for a number of years two kinds of goal orientations were the major focus of researchers. The first emphasizes individuals' attempts to master tasks and increase their competence. This orientation is labeled task involved by Nicholls and his colleagues (e.g., Nicholls, 1979b; Nicholls, Cobb, Yackel, Wood, & Wheatley, 1990) and Maehr, Midgley, and their colleagues (e.g., Maehr & Midgley, 1996; Midgley et al, 1998); it is classified as learning by Dweck and her colleagues (e.g, Dweck & Leggett, 1988), and as mastery oriented by Ames (1992). The second kind of goal orientation concerns individuals' attempts to maximize favorable evaluations of their competence and minimize negative evaluations of competence. This orientation labeled ego involved by Nicholls and his colleagues, and performance by Dweck and colleages and Ames, Maehr, Midgely, and their colleagues. Although there are some differences in the conceptualizations of these goal orientations by different researchers (see Thorkildsen & Nicholls, 1998), many motivation researchers believe they overlap in substantial ways. Goal theorists generally posit that a task or mastery orientation has important motivational benefits.

Researchers have now made further distinctions between different kinds of performance goals. Performance–approach goals lead individuals to do achievement tasks to get better grades than others and to demonstrate their good performance. By contrast, performance–avoidance goals involve attempts to avoid failure or the appearance of incompetence. Such goals can inhibit achievement strivings (see Elliott & Harackiewiz, 1996). This distinction is reminiscent of the approach–avoid distinction contained in the classic Atkinson (1957) expectancy–value model of achievement motivation. This distinction is discussed in more detail in Chapter 8.

Wigfield (1994) and Wigfield and Eccles (1992) discussed ways in which children's achievement values might relate to their goal orientation. They suggested that when an individual values a task primarily for intrinsic reasons, they would be likely to approach the task with a mastery goal orientation. If the individual valued the task primarily for utilitarian reasons then perhaps they would approach it with a performance orientation, attempting the task if they know they can succeed, and avoiding it if it seemed too difficult.

Wigfield, Anderman, and Eccles (2000) used data from the Michigan Childhood and Beyond study in an empirical assessment of relations between third through sixth grade children's competence beliefs, achievement values, and goal orientations. They had two fundamental purposes in this work: to assess whether the constructs were empirically distinct, and to look at relations among them. The questionnaires children completed included items assessing competence-related beliefs, achievement values, and goal orientations; to date no study has addressed all three constructs together. The items assessing goal orientations tapped mastery goals, performance–approach goals, and extrinsic goals, which have to do with accomplishing schoolwork because parents or teachers want the child to. Confirmatory factor analyses indicated a six-factor solution best fit the data; one competence belief factor, two task values factors (interest and usefulness–importance), and three goal factors (mastery, performance–approach, and extrinsic). Children's competence-related beliefs related significantly to both their mastery and performance–approach goals, but not to extrinsic goals. Children's achievement values related significantly to all three kinds of goals, but the relations were strongest for task mastery goals.

The most intriguing results of this study are that children's achievement values and goal orientations formed distinct factors. Although both constructs deal broadly with the purposes children have for engaging in different activities, they appear to be distinct. These results lend support to both expectancy–value theory and goal theory. Given the distinctiveness of each construct, an interesting task for future research is to examine further the relations between them. Our results indicate that values and goals are positively related. How might these relations unfold over time? Does the way in which children value different activities influence the kinds of goal orientations they have? Or do their goal orientations lead them to value tasks in different ways (see Wigfield, 1994; Wigfield & Eccles, 1992, for further discussion)? Such questions await further research.

Competence Beliefs, Achievement Values, and the Self-Regulation of Achievement Behavior

In various presentations of the model, we have posited that individuals' expectancies for success and achievement values predict their achievement outcomes, including their performance, persistence, and choices of which activites to do (e.g. Eccles, 1993; Eccles et al., 1983; Eccles et al., 1998). We have obtained empirical support for these proposed links in longitudinal studies of children ranging in age from 6–18. The major findings from these studies are that even when the level of previous performance is controlled, students' competence beliefs strongly predict their performance in different domains, including math, reading, and sport. Students' achievement task values predict both intentions and actual decisions to keep taking mathematics and English and to engage in sports. The relations are evident in children as young as first grade, although the relations strengthen across age (Eccles, 1984a, 1984b; Eccles et al., 1983; Eccles & Harold, 1991; Meece,Wigfield, & Eccles, 1990; Wigfield, 1997; see Wigfield, 1994; Wigfield & Eccles, 1992 for more detailed review of these studies). Note one important difference between these findings and the links predicted in the model: In the model, competence-related beliefs and values were posited to predict the same outcomes. In the empirical work, children's competence-related beliefs have their strongest direct effects on performance, while achievement values have their strongest direct effects on choice. Because of the positive relations of competence-related beliefs and values, it is important to note that each does have indirect effects on the other achievement outcomes.

Most of our empirical work to date has examined how children's competence beliefs and values relate to these rather general achievement outcomes like course grades and course enrollment decisions. Wigfield (1994) provided a more micro-level analysis of the relations of children's achievement values, and their achievement behaviors. He suggested that students who value different academic activities likely will study harder and more effectively. They also should continue to pursue goals they have set even if they encounter difficulties. Wigfield also discussed the issue of the synchrony of the components of achievement values. Some children may find certain achievement activities interesting, important to them, and useful. Others may see utility in some tasks, but have little interest in doing them. Children whose values are in synchrony may be more positively motivated to engage in an activity than those whose values are not in synchrony. Our empirical work shows that the components of task value do relate positively to one another, particularly the interest and importance components. Thus many children's values may be synchronous, but given that the relations among the value components are not at unity, this is not always the case.

The previous discussion concerns how children's expectancies and values help to regulate their achievement behaviors. The question of how people regulate their behavior in different areas has been a focus of a great deal of research over the past two decades (see Pintrich & Zusho, Chapter 10, this volume, and Boekaerts, Pintrich, & Zeidner, 2000, for review). Researchers have developed various models of self-regulatory and volitional processes having to do with the control of action (see Wigfield, 1994, for discussion of how achievement values and volitional processes may relate). These models are relevant to this section of our chapter because they go beyond documentation of relations of beliefs and behavior to a consideration of processes involved in these relations. Some of these processes could be incorporated into expectancy–value models to clarify the links between beliefs, values, and achievement behaviors. At the same time, expectancy–value models have relevance for models of self-regulation, in as much as the particular beliefs and values included in the models likely influence the ways in which individuals regulate their behavior. We consider next some of the ways in which these two bodies of work can be connected.

As is the case in studies of motivation, researchers proposing models of self-regulation have attended more to competence-related beliefs than to values. For instance, Schunk and Ertmer (2000) and Zimmerman (2000) take a social–cognitive approach to self-regulation. These researchers discuss phases of self-regulation, including forethought/planning, performance, and reflections on performance. Self-efficacy plays a prominent role in each of these phases; Zimmerman highlights efficacy's role in goal setting, to give one example. When individuals believe they can accomplish different activities, they set loftier goals for themselves. Efficacy beliefs also help guide performance and play a part in the self-regulation of that performance. Rheinberg, Vollmeyer, and Rollett (2000) also posit that expectancies are important determinants of individuals' goals and the strength of their motivation in different learning situations.

Carver and Scheier (2000) have developed an intriguing model of self-regulation dealing with how intentions are translated into actions and then assessed. The assessments involve elaborate feedback processes that help the individual determine whether the goal has been achieved, particularly by the use of standards in judging one's behavior. Decisions about whether to continue to pursue the activity, or withdraw from it, are an important part of the model. Individuals' expectations play a key role in how confident they are about whether they can attain a goal, and also figure in decisions about whether to maintain engagement or to disengage. When expectancies are high, continued engagement is more likely. From the perspective of this model, processes involved in the relations of competence beliefs to performance thus include how individuals set goals for themselves, their confidence while they are doing different activities, and how they interpret feedback they receive about their performance.

In contrast to competence-related beliefs, achievement values have played a less central role in many models of self-regulation, although they have received some attention. Schunk and Ertmer (2000) noted that the value of an activity is an important part of the forethought or preengagement phase of self-regulation; when activities are valued, students will devote more time both to planning for them and doing them. Rheinberg et al. (2000) also incorporated values into their model. They specified different questions individuals pose to themselves concerning potential links of their actions to desired outcomes. One of the questions is a "values" question: Are the consequences of the action important enough to me? If the answer is yes, the individual more likely will undertake the action. If no, then engagement is less likely.

Generally, however, those posing models of self-regulation emphasize goals rather than values; goals are given a prominent role in leading people to action (e.g., Boekaerts & Niemivirta, 2000; Carver & Scheier, 2000; Pintrich, 2000; Schunk & Ertmer, 2000; Zimmerman, 2000). Some of these researchers emphasize goal orientations (Boekaerts & Niemivirta; Pintrich), whereas others discuss specific goals for different tasks or activities (Carver & Scheier, Schunk & Ertmer, Zimmerman). There may be an intersection of these constructs in the notion of a goals hierarchy. Both Carver and Scheier and Shah and Kruglanski (2000) posit that some goals are organized in hierarchies. For Carver and Scheier the *importance* of the goal is a basis for the goal hierarchy; goals at higher levels of the hierarchy are thought to be more important to the individual. From the perspective of expectancy–value theory, goal hierarchies also may be organized around the other aspects of task value. Different goals may be more or less useful to the individual, or more or less interesting. We have predicted that the relative value attached to the goal should influence its placement in a goal hierarchy, as well as the likelihood that the individual will try to attain the goal.

Shah and Kruglanski (2000) also stressed that goals are related laterally as well as hierarchically. They stated that goals are more likely to be attained when they are in synchrony with other goals. When goals conflict, however, they are harder to fulfill. The person's achievement values again could play a role in determining how much goals are in synchrony with one another, or in conflict. The cost aspect of values defined by Eccles et al. (1983) could be particularly relevant in these relations. As discussed earlier, cost concerns are important for task choice: Individuals understand that doing one activity (studying) precludes doing another activity (going outside to play). Thus the relative cost of different activities could have an impact on the kinds of goals one sets: If an activity is perceived as too costly, then goals to attain it might be changed.

One essential part of behavioral regulation is choice of whether or not to continue to do different activities; such choices often can be complex in real-world achievement situations where there are many uncertainties about probable outcomes (see Busemyer & Townsend, 1993; Byrnes, 1998 for discussion of complex decision making under uncertainty). The decision about whether to continue or discontinue an activity often comes as individuals reflect back on their performance (see Schunk & Ertmer, 2000; Zimmerman, 2000). Scheier and Carver (2000) provide a fascinating discussion of how information processing through feedback loops, affective reactions, and expectancies for success provides the basis for deciding whether or not to continue doing an activity. As discussed earlier, we have found that children's valuing of different activities predicts their choices about which activities to pursue, often more strongly than expectancies for success. Thus we would argue that the role of values in such decision making needs to be considered more carefully in models of self-regulation.

How might the self-regulatory models influence expectancy–value models? Certain of the processes we have discussed, such as Carver and Scheier's (2000) feedback notions, and the different phases of behavioral regulation discussed by Schunk and Ertmer (2000) and Zimmerman (2000), seem particularly useful in conceptualizing more clearly relations of expectancies, values, performance, and choice. The incorporation of such processes from recent models of self-regulation into expectancy–value models would allow them to address the nuances of performance and choice more clearly.

This chapter (and book) focuses on the development of various motivational processes, and we conclude this section with a brief consideration of developmental issues regarding expectancies, values, and self-regulation. The kinds of self-evaluative process involved in the regulation of behavior require sophisticated cognitive processing of performance and other information, something young children have difficulty with, as discussed earlier. Although the regulation of achievement behavior is an important educational goal, many children only gradually learn how to regulate their own behavior. Zimmerman (2000) discussed developmental levels of self-regulation, beginning with the observation of someone who already is skilled at self-regulation. Next is emulation, in which the individual can model his or her behavior after the expert. The third level is self-control, where learners can regulate behavior on their own in relatively simple, structured settings. Individuals are said to be self-regulated when they can adapt and control their own behavior under a range of conditions and circumstances. Zimmerman does not assume these phases form an invariant sequence. It also is possible that in very new learning situations some of the levels may need to be revisited. However, Zimmerman notes that once learners have reached level 4, it often is their own choice that determines whether they act in self-regulated ways.

The processes by which expectancies and values influence (and are influenced by) self-regulation are also likely to change over time. As discussed earlier, children's competence-related beliefs and values initially are optimistic and not accurate in terms of their relations to performance. Their influence on self-regulatory processes likely is limited at this time. As children's beliefs and values reflect their performance more closely, they can have a stronger impact on self-regulation, and decisions about whether to continue to engage in activities. The specific ways these complex relations change over time await further study.

FUTURE RESEARCH DIRECTIONS

Suggestions for future research have been made throughout the chapter. In this final section we discuss some additional topics we think are deserving of future research.

Research on Competence Beliefs

As a result of the focus in the motivation literature on competence-related beliefs, we have learned a great deal about them. There still is important work to do on the development of competence-related beliefs, however (see also Chapter 1 by Schunk and Pajares, this volume). One important issue is to continue to examine how similar or different the various constructs in this area (self-efficacy, competence beliefs, expectancies) are. Theoretically, distinctions among them can be drawn; but as discussed earlier, empirically they often are strongly related. For instance, Skaalvik and Rankin (1998) factor-analyzed children's responses to a self-efficacy measure and to a broader measure of self-concept of ability. They found that the two sets of items loaded on the same factor. In our work, competence beliefs and expectancies also load together. Yet there are some compelling theoretical reasons for distinguishing among these constructs.

The issue of domain specificity vs generality of competence beliefs also is an important one to consider (see also Schunk & Ertmer, Chapter 1, this volume; Wigfield, 1997). In our work different areas of academic and nonacademic competence can be clearly distinguished even in young children; children have a differentiated view of their abilities (Eccles et al., 1993). Yet as children accumulate more experience in a domain, perhaps they also develop a general sense of competence (or incompetence) in that domain. Marsh's (1990) work on the structure of academic self-concept showing higher order factors explaining relations among first-order factors exemplifies this idea. This generalized sense would be much more sophisticated than the earlier undifferentiated sense of competence Harter (1983) discussed, since it is based on extensive experience in a given domain. The developmental progression of such more generalized belief structures still is not completely understood.

Research on Achievement Values

As mentioned earlier there has been less work on the development of children's achievement values than on their competence-related beliefs. This situation is changing in important ways, however. We now have charted the course of development from childhood through adolescence of the different components of task value specified in our model (e.g., Eccles et al., 1993;

Jacobs et al., 2000; Wigfield, et al., 1991; Wigfield et al., 1997). Graham (Chapter 5 in this volume) is doing some very interesting work on valuing of achievement in different groups of students, using a peer nomination methodolgy.

Other researchers are contributing important work on achievement values. In the lead article in a special issue of *Educational Psychologist* devoted to achievement values, Brophy (1999) made the point that we still do not understand how learners come to value different learning activities. He discussed how children's valuing of activities is facilitated when the activities are meaningful to them, are connected to other things they do, and are authentic; these points are similar to those made by cognitive researchers on how to foster learning. Brophy emphasized teachers' roles in scaffolding children's valuing of learning, helping them to appreciate and recognize as authentic different activities that they do. He also proposed that there may be a motivational zone of proximal development (ZPD) along with a cognitive ZPD, and argued that learning occurs best when students are in both their cognitive and motivational ZPDs.

In particular, students may appreciate learning activities when they see that the activity relates to their future goals. Raynor (1969) and Raynor and Entin (1982) expanded Atkinson's (1957) classic expectancy–value theory to include future orientation as an important motivational characteristic. Markus and Nurius's (1976) notion of "possible selves" also deals with individuals' sense of themselves in the future. In our model, concerns about the future are best exemplified in the attainment value notion, which deals with how tasks and activity relate to the individuals' sense of themselves.

Husman and Lens (1999) recently reintroduced a concern for the future into expectancy–value theory with their notion of future time perspective (FTP); see also Lens (1986). They stated that FTP can be characterized by its extensivity, or how long into the future the individual is looking, and by realism, or how likely the future goal is. Lens and his colleagues have shown that valuing of the future has important motivational implications; students with stronger FTPs are more motivated to succeed in school (see Husman & Lens, 1999, for review). Thus although researchers have argued for the importance of proximal goals (e.g., Schunk, 1991), this work suggests that more distal goals seem crucial too. Husman and Lens also discussed how FTP can relate to students' goal orientations. Students with stronger FTPs seem to be more mastery oriented in their approach to learning, though the relations are complex.

These interesting new directions in work on the valuing of achievement need further exploration, in order that our understanding of children's achievement values continue to grow. There are fascinating developmental questions that can come out of the work just reviewed. For instance, how is the motivational ZPD best characterized, and how might it change over time? Young children often have FTPs, but when do these become realistic enough to influence their motivation? What exactly are the relations of students' current motivations to their FTP, and to their achievement outcomes?

We close this section on values with one last suggestion. Earlier we mentioned that there has been some interesting work on how children's notions or understanding of what "ability" means change over time. Such work has not been done on children's achievement values, and it could prove to be quite informative. How do younger children as compared to older children think about the "usefulness" of a given activity? How might their sense of interest change over time (see Wigfield, 1994, for further discussion)? Such work also would inform work on children's sense of the future, particularly the issue of when children's FTPs become more realistic. Interview methods such as those used by Nicholls (1978) to probe children's understanding of ability possibly could be adapted to study children's developing understanding of different components of achievement values.

Influence of Context on Children's Competence Beliefs and Values

Contextual influences on motivation have taken center stage in work on motivation, as researchers move beyond an individual difference approach to motivation (see Eccles et al., 1998; Turner & Meyer, 1999; Urdan, 1999). Turner and Meyer discussed how attention to contextual influences can alter some general conclusions coming from work on motivation. For instance, researchers have discussed how "optimal challenge" often is motivating for students. Turner and Meyer discussed how the school's norms and values can have a strong impact on the level of challenge students prefer; in some situations many students may find optimal challenge too risky, and so seek to avoid challenge. It is difficult to make conclusions about students' motivation without considering closely the classroom contexts in which they find themselves.

We have long been interested in contextual influences on competence and values, focusing in particular on how changes in school and classroom contexts as children move from elementary to middle school influence their motivation (e.g., Eccles et al., 1993; Wigfield, Eccles, & Pintrich, 1996). We also have been interested in how various teaching practices influence students' motivation. Although researchers have learned much about how different educational contexts influence motivation, much more remains to be done in this area. Tests of models like the expectancy–value model discussed in this chapter must be done in a variety of educational contexts.

To conclude, we have learned much about the development of competence beliefs and values over the past decade and a half. Much remains to be done, and we look forward to continuing research in this area.

Acknowledgments

Much of the research on the development of children's competence beliefs and values discussed in this chapter was supported by grant HD-17553 from the National Institute of Child Health and Human Development (NICHD). Other research discussed in this chapter was supported by grant MH-31724 from the National Institute for Mental Health, HD-17296 from NICHD, grant BNS-8510504 from the National Science Foundation, and grants from the Spencer Foundation.

References

Ames, C. (1992). Classrooms: Goals, structures, and student motivation. *Journal of Educational Psychology*, 84, 261–271.

Assor, A., & Connell, J. P. (1992). The validity of students' self-reports as measures of performance affecting self-appraisals. In D. H. Schunk & J. L. Meece (Eds.) *Student self-perceptions in the classroom* (pp. 25–47). Hillsdale, NJ: Lawrence Erlbaum Associates.

Atkinson, J. W. (1957). Motivational determinants of risk taking behavior. *Psychological Review*, 64, 359–372.

Bandura, A. (1997). *Self-efficacy: The exercise of control*. New York: W. H. Freeman.

Bell, L. A. (1989). Something's wrong here and it's not me: Challenging the dilemmas that block girls success. *Journal for the Education of the Gifted*, 12, 118–130.

Berry, G. L., & Asamen. J. K. (Eds.).(1989) *Black students: Psychosocial issues and academic achievement* (pp. 40–68). Newbury Park, CA: Sage.

Blumenfeld, P., Pintrich, P. R., Meece, J., & Wessels, K. (1982). The formation and role of self-perceptions of ability in elementary school classrooms. *Elementary School Journal*, 82, 401–420.

Boekaerts, M., & Niemivirta, M. (2000). Self-regulated learning: Finding a balance between learning goals and ego-protective goals. In M. Boekaerts, P. R, Pintrich, & M. Zeidner (Eds.), *Handook of self-regulation* (pp. 417–450). San Diego: Academic Press.

Boekaerts, M., Pintrich, P. R., & Zeidner, M. (2000). Self-regulation: An introductory overview. In M. Boekaerts, P. R, Pintrich, & M. Zeidner (Eds.), *Handook of self-regulation* (pp. 1–9). San Diego: Academic Press.

Brophy, J. E. (1999). Toward a model of the value aspects of motivation for education: Developing appreciation for particular learning domains and activities. *Educational Psychologist*, 34, 75–86.

Busemeyer, J. R., & Townsend, J. T. (1993). Decision field theory: A dynamic-cognitive approach to decision making in an uncertain environment. *Psychological Review*, 100, 432–459.

Byrnes, J. B. (1998). *The nature and development of self-regulated decision making*. Hillsdale, NJ: Lawrence Erlbaum Associates.

Carver, C. S., & Scheier, M. F. (2000). On the structural of behavioral self-regulation. In M. Boekaerts, P. R, Pintrich, & M. Zeidner (Eds.), *Handook of self-regulation* (pp. 41–84). San Diego: Academic Press.

Chen, C., & Stevenson, H. W. (1995). Motivation and mathematics achievement: A comparative study of Asian-American, Caucasian-American, and East Asian high school students. *Child Development*, 66, 1215–1234.

Connell, J. P., Spencer, M. B., & Aber, J. L. (1994). Educational risk and resilience in African American Youth: Context, self, and action outcomes in school. *Child Development*, 65, 493–506.

Cooper, H., & Dorr, N. (1995). Race comparisons on need for achievement: A meta-analytic alternative to Graham's narrative review. *Review of Educational Research*, 65, 483–508

Council of the Great City Schools, (1992). *National urban education goals: Baseline indicators*, 1990–91. Washington, DC: Council of the Great City Schools.

Covington, M. V. (1992). *Making the grade: A self-worth perspective on motivation and school reform.* New York: Cambridge University Press.

Crandall, V. C. (1969). Sex differences in expectancy of intellectual and academic reinforcement. In C. P. Smith (Ed.), *Achievement-related motives in children* (pp. 11–45). New York: Russell Sage Foundation.

Crandall, V. J., Dewey, R., Katkovsky, W., & Preston, A. (1964). Parents' attitudes and behaviors and grade school children's academic achievements. *Journal of Genetic Psychology*, 104, 53–66.

Cross, W. E., Jr. (1990). Race and ethnicity: Effects on social networks. In M. Cochran, M. Larner, D. Riley, Gunnarsson, & C. Henderson (Eds.), *Extending families: The social networks of parents and their children.* New York: Cambridge University Press.

Dauber, S. L., & Benbow, C. P. (1990). Aspects of personality and peer relations of extremely talented adolescents. *Gifted Child Quarterly*, 34, 10–15.

Duncan, G. J., Brooks-Gunn, J., & Klevbanov, P. K. (1994). Economic deprivation and early childhood development. *Child Development*, 65, 296–318.

Dweck, C. S., & Elliott, E. S. (1983). Achievement motivation. In P. H. Mussen (Ed.), *Handbook of child psychology* (3rd ed., Vol. IV, pp. 643–691). New York: John Wiley & Sons.

Dweck, C. S., & Goetz, T. E. (1978). Attributions and learned helplessness. In J. H. Harvey, W. Ickes, & R. F. Kidd (Eds.), *New directions in attribution research* (Vol. 2). Hillsdale, NJ: Lawrence Erlbaum Associates.

Dweck, C. S., & Leggett, E. (1988). A social-cognitive approach to motivation and personality. *Psychological Review*, 95, 256–273.

Early, D. M., Belansky, E., & Eccles, J. S. (March, 1992). *The impact of gender stereotypes on perceived ability and attributions for success.* Poster presented at the Biennial Meeting of the Society for Research on Adolescence, Washington DC

Eccles, J. S., (1993). School and family effects on the ontogeny of children's interests, self-perceptions, and activity choice. In J. Jacobs (Ed.), *Nebraska Symposium on Motivation, 1992: Developmental perspectives on motivation.* (pp. 145–208) Lincoln: University of Nebraska Press.

Eccles, J. S. (1994). Understanding women's educational and occupational choices: Applying the Eccles et al. model of achievement-related choices. *Psychology of Women Quarterly*, 18, 585–609.

Eccles, J. S., Adler, T. F., & Meece, J. L. (1984). Sex differences in achievement: A test of alternate theories. *Journal of Personality and Social Psychology*, 46, 26–43.

Eccles, J. S. & Harold, R. D. (1991). Gender differences in sport involvement: Applying the Eccles' expectancy–value model. *Journal of Applied Sport Psychology*, 3, 7–35.

Eccles, J. S., & Midgley, C. (1989). Stage/environment fit: Developmentally appropriate classrooms for early adolescents. In R. Ames & C. Ames (Eds.), *Research on motivation in education* (Vol. 3, pp. 139–181). New York: Academic Press.

Eccles, J. S., & Wigfield, A. (1985). Teacher expectations and student motivation. In J. B. Dusek (Ed.), *Teacher expectations* (pp. 185–217). Hillsdale, NJ: Lawrence Erlbaum Associates.

Eccles, J. S., & Wigfield, A. (1995). In the mind of the achiever: The structure of adolescents' academic achievement-related beliefs and self-perceptions. *Personality and Social Psychology Bulletin*, 21, 215–225.

Eccles, J. S., Wigfield, A., Flanagan, C., Miller, C., Reuman, D., & Yee, D. (1989). Self-concepts, domain values, and self-esteem: Relations and changes at early adolescence. *Journal of Personality*, 57, 283–310.

Eccles, J. S., Wigfield, A., Harold, R., & Blumenfeld, P. B. (1993). Age and gender differences in children's self- and task perceptions during elementary school. *Child Development*, 64, 830–847.

Eccles, J. S., Wigfield, A., & Schiefele, U. (1998). Motivation to succeed. In N. Eisenberg (Vol. Ed.) & W. Damon (Series Ed.), *Handbook of child psychology* (5th ed., Vol. 3, pp. 1017–1095). New York: John Wiley & Sons.

Eccles (Parsons), J., Adler, T. F., Futterman, R., Goff, S. B., Kaczala, C. M., Meece, J. L., & Midgley, C. (1983). Expectancies, values, and academic behaviors. In J. T. Spence (Ed.), *Achievement and achievement motivation* (pp. 75–146). San Francisco: W. H. Freeman.

Eisenberg, N., Marin, C. L., & Fabes, R. A. (1996). Gender development and gender effects. In D. C. Berliner & R. C. Calfee (Eds.), *Handbook of educational psychology* (pp. 358–396). New York: Macmillan.

Elliott, A. J., & Harackiewicz, J. M. (1996). Approach and avoidance goals and intrinsic motivation: A mediational analysis. *Journal of Personality and Social Psychology, 54*, 5–12.

Feather, N. T. (1982a). Expectancy–value approaches: Present status and future directions. In N. T. Feather (Ed.), *Expectations and actions: Expectancy–value models in psychology* (pp. 395–420). Hillsdale, NJ: Lawrence Erlbaum Associates.

Feather, N. T. (1982b). *Expectations and actions: Expectancy–value models in psychology* . Hillsdale, NJ: Lawrence Erlbaum Associates.

Feather, N. T. (1988). Values, valences, and course enrollment: Testing the role of personal values within an expectancy–value framework. *Journal of Educational Psychology, 80*, 381–391.

Feather, N. T. (1992). Values, valences, expectations, and actions. *Journal of Social Issues, 48*, 109–124.

Finn, J. D. (1989). Withdrawing from school. *Review of Educational Research, 59*, 117–142.

Fordham, S., & Ogbu, J. U. (1986). Black students' school success: Coping with "the burden of 'acting white'". *The Urban Review, 18*, 176–206.

Gardner, P. L. (1998). The development of males' and females' interests in science and technology. In L. Hoffmann, A. Krapp, K. A. Renninger, & J. Baumert (Eds.), *Interest and learning* (pp. 41–57). Kiel, Germany: Institute for Science Education.

Graham, S. (1992). Most of the subjects were European American and middle class: Trends in published research on African Americans in selected APA journals 1970–1989. *American Psychologist, 47*, 629–639.

Graham, S. (1994). Motivation in African Americans. *Review of Educational Research, 64*, 55–117.

Hare, B. R. (1985). Stability and change in self-perceptions and achievement among African American adolescents: A longitudinal study. *Journal of African American Psychology, 11*, 29–42.

Harter, S. (1978). Effectance motivation reconsidered: Toward a developmental model. *Human Development, 1*, 34–64.

Harter, S. (1982). The perceived competence scale for children. *Child Development, 53*, 87–97.

Harter, S. (1983). Developmental perspectives on the self-system. In P. H. Mussen (Ed.), *Handbook of child psychology* (Vol. 4, pp. 275–385). New York: John Wiley & Sons.

Harter, S. (1998). The development of self-representations. In N. Eisenberg (Vol. Ed.) & W. Damon (Series Ed.), *Handbook of child psychology* (5th ed., Vol. 3, pp. 553–617). New York: John Wiley & Sons.

Harter, S., & Pike, R. (1984). The Pictorial Scale of Perceived competence and Social Acceptance for Young Children. *Child Development, 55*, 1969–1982.

Heyman, G. D., Dweck, C. S., & Cain, K. M. (1993). Young children's vulnerability to self-blame and helplessness: Relationships to beliefs about goodness. *Child Development, 63*, 401–415.

Husman, J., & Lens, W. (1999). The role of the future in student motivation. *Educational Psychologist, 34*, 113–125.

Huston, A. C., McLoyd, V., & Coll, C. G. (1994). Children and poverty: Issues in contemporary research. *Child Development, 65*, 275–282.

Jacobs, J. E., Lanza, S., Osgood, D. W., Eccles, J. S., & Wigfield, A. (in press). Changes in children's self-competence and values: Gender and domain differences across grades one through twelve. *Child Development*.

Kao, G., & Tienda, M. (1995). Optimism and achievement: The educational performance of immigrant youth. *Social Science Quarterly, 76*, 1–19.

Lens, W. (1986) Future time perspective: A cognitive-motivational concept. In D. R. Brown & J. Veroff (Eds.), *Frontiers of motivational psychology* (pp. 173–190). New York: Springer-Verlag.

Lummis, M., & Stevenson, H. W. (1990). Gender differences in beliefs and achievement: A cross-cultural study. *Developmental Psychology, 26*, 254–263.

Luster, T., & McAdoo, H. P. (1994). Factors related to the achievement and adjustment of young African American children. *Child Development*, 65, 1080–1094.

Maehr, M. L., & Midgley, C. (1996). *Transforming school cultures*. Boulder, CO: Westview Press.

Markus, H., & Nurius, P. (1976). Possible selves. *American Psychologist*, 1, 954–969.

Marsh, H. W. (1990). A multidimensional, hierarchical self-concept: Theoretical and empirical justification. *Educational Psychology Review*, 2, 77–171.

Marsh, H. W. (1989). Age and sex effects in multiple dimensions of self-concept: Preadolescence to early adulthood. *Journal of Educational Psychology*, 81, 417–430.

Marsh, H. W., Craven, R. G., & Debus, R. (1991). Self-concepts of young children 5 to 8 years of age: Measurement and multidimensional structure. *Journal of Educational Psychology*, 83, 377–392.

Marsh, H. W., Craven, R. G., & Debus, R. (1998). Structure, stability, and development of young children's self-concepts: A multicohort–multioccasion study. *Child Development*, 69, 1030–1053.

McClendon, C., & Wigfield, A. (1998). Group differences in African-American adolescents' achievement-related beliefs about math and science. *Journal of Black Psychology*, 24, 28–43.

McLoyd, V. C. (1990). The impact of economic hardship on African American families and children: Psychological distress, parenting, and socioemotional development. *Child Development*, 61, 311–346.

Meece, J. L., Wigfield, A., & Eccles, J. S. (1990). Predictors of math anxiety and its consequences for young adolescents' course enrollment intentions and performances in mathematics. *Journal of Educational Psychology*, 82, 60–70.

Midgley, C. M., Kaplan, A., Middleton, M., Maehr, M. L., Urdan, T., Anderman, L., Anderman, E., & Roeser, R. (1998). The development and validation of scales assessing students' achievement goal orientations. *Contemporary Educational Psychology*, 23, 113–131.

Nicholls, J. G. (1978). The development of the concepts of effort and ability, perceptions of academic attainment, and the understanding that difficult tasks require more ability. *Child Development*, 49, 800–814.

Nicholls, J. G. (1979a). Development of perception of own attainment and causal attributions for success and failure in reading. *Journal of Educational Psychology*, 71, 94–99.

Nicholls, J. G. (1979b). Quality and equality in intellectual development: The role of motivation in education. *American Psychologist*, 34, 1071–1084.

Nicholls, J. G. (1984). Achievement motivation: Conceptions of ability, subjective experience, task choice, and performance. *Psychological Review*, 91, 328–346.

Nicholls, J. G. (1989). *The competitive ethos and democratic education*. Cambridge MA: Havard University Press.

Nicholls, J. G. (1990). What is ability and why are we mindful of it? A developmental perspective. In R. J. Sternberg & J. Kolligian (Eds.), *Competence considered*. New Haven, CT: Yale University Press.

Nicholls, J. G. (1992). Students as educational theorists. In D. H. Schunk & J. L. Meece (Eds.), *Student self-perceptions in the classroom* (pp. 267–286). Hillsdale, NJ: Lawrence Erlbaum Associates.

Nicholls, J. G., Cobb, P., Yackel, E., Wood, T., & Wheatley, G. (1990). Students' theories of mathematics and their mathematical knowledge: Multiple dimensions of assessment. In G. Kulm (Ed.), *Assessing higher order thinking in mathematics* (pp. 137–154). Washington, DC: American Association for the Advancement of Science.

Ogbu, J. G. (1992). Understanding cultural diversity and learning. *Educational Researcher*, 21, 5–14.

Osborn, J. W. (1997). Race and academic disidentification. *Journal of Educational Psychology*, 89, 728–735.

Pajares, F. (1996). Self-efficacy beliefs in academic settings. *Review of Educational Research*, 66, 543–578.

Parsons, J. E., & Goff, S. B. (1980). Achievement motivation and values: An alternative perspective. In L. J. Fyans (Ed.), *Achievement motivation* (pp. 349–373). New York: Plenum.

Parsons, J. E., & Ruble, D. N. (1977). The development of achievement-related expectancies. *Child Development*, 48, 1075–1079.

Pintrich, P. R. (2000). The role of goal orientation in self-regulated learning. In M. Boekaerts, P. R. Pintrich, & M. Zeidner (Eds.), *Handook of self-regulation* (pp. 451–502). San Diego: Academic Press.

Raynor, J. O. (1969). Future orientation and motivation of immediate activity: An elaboration of the theory of achievement motivation. *Psychological Review, 76.*

Raynor, J. O., & Entin, E. E. (1982). *Motivation, career striving, and aging.* Washington, DC: Hemisphere.

Rohan, M. J. (2000). A rose by any name? The values construct. *Personality and Social Psychology Review, 4,* 255–277.

Rokeach, M. (1973). *The nature of human values.* New York: Free Press.

Rokeach, M. (1979). From individual to institutional values with special reference to the values of science. In M. Rokeach (Ed.), *Understanding human values* (pp. 47–70). New York: Free Press.

Rheinberg, F., Vollmeyer, T., & Rollet, W. (2000). Motivation and action in self-regulated learning. In M. Boekaerts, P. R, Pintrich, & M. Zeidner (Eds.), *Handook of self-regulation* (pp. 503–529). San Diego: Academic Press.

Ruble, D. (1983). The development of social comparison processes and their role in achievement-related self-socialization. In E. T. Higgins, D. N. Ruble, and W. W. Hartup (Eds.), *Social cognition and social development: A sociocultural perspective* (pp. 134–157). New York: Cambridge University Press.

Ruble, D. N., & Martin, C. L. (1998). Gender development. In W. Damon (Series Ed.) and N. Eisenberg (Vol. Ed.), *Handbook of child psychology* (5th Ed., Vol. 3, pp. 933–1016). New York: John Wiley & Sons.

Ryan, R. M., & Deci, E. L. (2000). Intrinsic and extrinsic motivators: Classic definitions and new directions. *Contemporary Educational Psychology, 25,* 54–67.

Scheier, C. S., & Carver, M. F. (2000). On the structure of behavioral self-regulation. In M. Boekaerts, P. R, Pintrich, & M. Zeidner (Eds.), *Handook of self-regulation* (pp. 41–84). San Diego: Academic Press.

Schneider, B. & Coleman, J. S. (1993). *Parents, their children, and schools.* Boulder, CO: Westview Press.

Schunk, D. H. (1991) Self-efficacy and academic motivation. *Educational Psychologist, 26,* 207–231.

Schunk, D. H. (1994). Self-regulation of self-efficacy and attributions in academic settings. In D. H. Schunk & B. J. Zimmerman (Eds.), *Self-regulation of learning and performance.* Hillsdale, NJ: Lawrence Erlbaum Associates.

Schunk, D. H., & Ertmer, P. A. (2000). Self-regulation and academic learning: Self-efficacy enhancing interventions. In M. Boekaerts, P. R, Pintrich, & M. Zeidner (Eds.), *Handook of self-regulation* (pp. 631–649). San Diego: Academic Press.

Schunk, D. H., & Lilly, M. V. (1982). *Attributional and expectancy change in gifted adolescents.* Paper presented at the annual meeting of the American Educational Research Association. New York.

Schwartz, S. H. (1992). Universals in the content and structure of values: Theoretical advances in empirical tests in 20 countries. In M. P. Zanna (Ed.), *Advances in experimental social psychology* (Vol. 24, pp. 1–65). San Diego: Academic Press.

Shah, J. V., & Kruglanski, A. W. (2000). Aspects of goal networks: Implications for self-regulation. In M. Boekaerts, P. R, Pintrich, & M. Zeidner (Eds.), *Handook of self-regulation* (pp. 85–110). San Diego: Academic Press.

Shaklee, H., & Tucker, D. (1979). Cognitive bases of development in inferences of ability. *Child Development, 50,* 904–907.

Skaalvik, E. M., & Rankin, R. J. (1998, April). *Self-concept, self-efficacy, and achievement in mathematics: A test of casual relations.* Paper presented at the annual meeting of the American Educational Research Association, San Diego.

Slaughter-Defoe, D. T., Nakagawa, K., Takanishi, R., & Johnson, D. J. (1990). Toward cultural/ecological perspectives on schooling and achievement in African- and Asian-American children. *Child Development, 61,* 363–383.

Spencer, M. B., & Markstrom-Adams, C. (1990). Identity processes among racial and ethnic minority children in America. *Child Development, 61,* 290–310.

Steele, C. M. (1992, April). Race and the schooling of black Americans. *The Atlantic Monthly.*

Steele, C. M., & Aronson, J. (1995). Stereotype threat and the intellectual test performance of African-Americans. *Journal of Personality and Social Psychology, 69,* 797–811.

Steinberg, L., Dornbusch, S., & Brown, B. (1992). Ethnic differences in adolescents achievements: An ecological perspective. *American Psychologist, 47,* 723–729.

Stevenson, H. W., Chen, C., & Uttal, D. H. (1990). Beliefs and achievement: A study of black, white, and Hispanic children. *Child Development*, 61, 508–523.

Stipek, D. J. (1984). The development of achievement motivation. In R. Ames & C. Ames (Eds.), *Research on motivation in education* (Vol. 1, p. 145–174). New York: Academic Press.

Stipek, D. J., & MacIver, D. (1989). Developmental change in children's assessment of intellectual competence. *Child Development*, 60, 521–538.

Stipek, D. J., Recchia, S., & McClintic, S. M. (1992). Self-evaluation in young children. *Monographs of the Society for Research in Child Development*, 57 (2, Serial No. 226).

Taylor, R. D., Casten, R., Flickinger, S., Roberts, D., & Fulmore, C. D. (1994). Explaining the school performance of African-American adolescents. *Journal of Research on Adolescence*, 4, 21–44.

Thorkildsen, T. A., & Nicholls, J. G. (1998). Fifth graders' achievement orientations and beliefs: Individual and classroom differences. *Journal of Educational Psychology*, 90, 179–201.

Turner, J. C., & Meyer, D. K. (1999). Integrating classroom context into motivation theory and research: Rationale, methods, and implications. In T. Urdan (Ed.), *Advances in motivation and achievement* (Vol. 11: The role of context, pp. 87–121. Creenwich CT: JAI Press.

Urdan, T. C. (1999). Forward. In T. C. Urdan (Ed.), *Advances in motivation and achievement* (Vol. 11, The Role of Context, pp. ix–xi). Greenwich, CT: JAI Press.

Weiner, B. (1979). A theory of motivation for some classroom experiences. *Journal of Education Psychology*, 71, 3–25.

Weiner, B. (1985). An attributional theory of achievement motivation and emotion. *Psychological Review*, 92, 548–573.

Wigfield, A. (1994). Expectancy-value theory of achievement motivation: A developmental perspective. *Educational Psychology Review*, 6, 49–78.

Wigfield, A. (1997). Reading motivation: A domain specific approach to motivation. *Educational Psychologist*, 32, 59–68.

Wigfield, A., Anderman, E., & Eccles, J. S. (2000, April). *Relations among children's ability-related beliefs, achievement values, and achievement goals.* Paper presented at the annual meeting of the American Educational Research Association, New Orleans.

Wigfield, A., Battle, A., Solomon, L., & Eccles, J. S. (in press). Sex differences in motivation, self-concept, career aspirations, and career choice: Implications for cognitive development. In A. McGillicuddy-DelLisi & R. DeLisi (Eds.), *Biology, sociology, and behavior: The development of sex differences in cognition.* Greenwich, CT: Ablex.

Wigfield, A., & Eccles, J. (1992). The development of achievement task values: A theoretical analysis. *Developmental Review*, 12, 265–310.

Wigfield, A., & Eccles, J. S. (2000). Expectancy–value theory of motivation. *Contemporary Educational Psychology*, 25, 68–81.

Wigfield, A., Eccles, J., Mac Iver, D., Reuman, D., & Midgley, C. (1991). Transitions at early adolescence: Changes in children's domain-specific self-perceptions and general self-esteem across the transition to junior high school. *Developmental Psychology*, 27, 552–565.

Wigfield, A., Eccles, J. S., Pintrich, P. R.. (1996). Development between the ages of eleven and twenty-five. In D. C. Berliner and R. C. Calfee (Eds.), *The handbook of educational psychology*, New York: MacMillan Publishing.

Wigfield, A., Eccles, J. S., Yoon, K. S., Harold, R. D., Arbreton, A., Freedman-Doan, C., Blumenfeld, P. C. (1997). Changes in children's competence beliefs and subjective task values across the elementary school years: A three-year study. *Journal of Educational Psychology*, 89, 451–469.

Winston, C., Eccles, J. S., Senior, A. M., & Vida, M. (1997). The utility of and expectancy–value model of achievement for understanding academic performance and self-esteem in African American and European American adolescents. *Zeitschrift fur Padagogische Psychologie (German Journal of Educational Psychology)*, 11, 17–186.

Zimmerman, B. J. (2000). Attaining self-regulation: A social cognitive perspective. In M. Boekaerts, P. R, Pintrich, & M. Zeidner (Eds.), *Handook of self-regulation* (pp. 13–39). San Diego: Academic Press.

Zimmerman, B. J., & Bonner, S. (in press).

CHAPTER

5

Ethnicity, Gender, and the Development of Achievement Values

SANDRA GRAHAM AND APRIL Z. TAYLOR

University of California, Los Angeles, California

For the psychologist concerned with academic achievement, the study of motivation provides a rich framework for addressing some of the most pressing issues facing our educational system today. These issues often revolve around problem areas—low test scores, grade retention, early withdrawal, and various disciplinary practices associated with antisocial behavior, like suspension and expulsion. By all indicators, such problems have been disproportionately observed in ethnic minority children, particularly African-American youth. One might therefore hope that a motivational approach, which focuses on the *why* of achievement-related behavior rather than behavior itself, might offer fresh insights into the educational challenges faced by many African-American students, who by some accounts appear to be losing ground in the academic footrace (e.g., Phillips, Crouse, & Ralph, 1998).

Many approaches to motivation can broadly be cast within an expectancy–value framework, although the chapters in this volume highlight several contemporary models that enlist other core constructs, such as achievement goals and self-regulatory processes. From an expectancy–value perspective, motivation is determined by some combination of the perceived likelihood that a goal will be attained (the expectancy component) and how much that goal is desired or wanted (the value component). Much of what we know about the motivational patterns of African Americans has focused on the expectancy component of expectancy–value theory. It has been argued that a pattern of school failure can be linked to (predicted by) Black children's low expectations for future success and the perception of themselves as relatively incompetent.

Low expectations and low self-concept are often precursors to failure; several chapters in the present volume corroborate this empirical fact. Yet the relations between maladaptive expectancy-related beliefs and school achievement among African-American youth are far from certain. A few years ago one of us reviewed the empirical literature on motivation in Black students (Graham, 1994). That review found very little evidence that African Americans suffered from either low expectancy for future success or low academic self-concept, even when they were doing poorly in school according to the standard indicators. If anything, the opposite—some would argue counterintuitive—pattern emerged. Compared with their higher achieving White classmates, African-American students were found to be remarkably optimistic and to endorse positive self-views. There is much corroborating empirical evidence, both preceding and following the Graham (1994) review, for high self-esteem among African Americans and for weak relations between self-esteem and performance (see, e.g., Crocker & Major, 1989; Gray-Little & Hafdahl, 2000).

In this chapter we want to make the case for a different motivational approach to the study of the academic challenges of some African-American youth, one that focuses on the values component of expectancy–value theory. Unlike achievement-related expectancies, which largely center on beliefs about ability (Can I do it?), values have to do with desires and preferences (Do I want it?) and are more concerned with the perceived importance, attractiveness, or usefulness of achievement activities (e.g., Feather, 1992; Wigfield & Eccles, Chapter 4, this volume). Like expectancies, values have motivational significance because they guide thoughts, feelings, and behavior. For example, what we judge to be important, attractive, or useful influences the activities we choose, how we evaluate other people and events, and our worldviews (see Rohan, 2000). Values also are rooted in the moral constructs of "ought" and "should" (Rokeach, 1973), as illustrated by the belief that one should try hard in school regardless of perceived abilities.

Because values have such motivational properties, it might be argued that many Black students do poorly in school because they deny the importance, attractiveness, and utility of academic success, or because their own life experiences are discrepant with the notion that students ought to feel morally obligated to exert effort in school. In our work with urban teachers, we are struck with how often an implicit focus on values emerges in the teachers' lay theories about why so many Black adolescents are underachieving in school. For example, we hear comments such as (1) "They can do the work but they just don't seem to *care*;" (2)"The kids have not come to terms with the reality that you have to work hard in school to guarantee success in life;" and (3) "In the peer culture, one risks rejection by exerting effort in school."

As motivation researchers there is little we can say to either support or refute these teachers' laments, for at present there is very little research that directly examines achievement values among African-American youth from a motivational perspective. Values, in fact, have been relatively neglected in motivation research (see Brophy, 1999). The one notable exception is research by Eccles, Wigfield, and their colleagues on task-specific beliefs (e.g., Eccles & Wigfield, 1995; Wigfield & Eccles, Chapter 4, this volume). Because that research has not been directly concerned with issues of race, ethnicity, and task value, or the broader sociocultural context in which achievement values emerge, it does not shed light on the question of whether or why African-American students devalue effort and whether this devaluing is related to disengagement from school. This is not a criticism of our colleagues' important theoretical and empirical contributions, but rather a recognition that ethnicity and culture have not been their prime focus.

In the remainder of this chapter, we elaborate our approach to studying achievement values in the context of ethnicity and development. We begin with a brief historical overview of early motivation research on the achievement syndrome that tried to tackle some of the complex issues related to race and achievement values. Next we turn to perspectives from the disciplines of sociology, anthropology, and social psychology that offer explanations for the presumed devaluing of achievement among African Americans. Then we present some of our own empirical research that addresses these issues. Although our focus remains on African-American youth, we have broadened our perspective to include multiethnic samples who share some of the same motivational beliefs and school achievement patterns as their African-American counterparts. The chapter concludes with recommendations for future motivation theory and research.

HISTORICAL PERSPECTIVE

We have to go back nearly half a century to find research guided by motivation theory that addresses race and achievement values. In the 1950s and 1960s the dominant theme in motivation research was the achievement motive (Nach), a personality trait that distinguished individuals according to their tendency or desire to do things well and to compete against a standard of excellence. David McClelland and his colleagues were the first psychologists to study Nach experimentally, and this work culminated in the publication of The Achievement Motive in 1953 (McClelland, Atkinson, Clark, & Lowell, 1953). John Atkinson (1964) furthered this experimental tradition with a theory of motivation incorporating the achievement motive that dominated motivation research throughout the 1960s.

Building on the McClelland and Atkinson theoretical foundation, Bernard Rosen introduced the concept of the achievement syndrome, a set of interrelated factors that consisted of the achievement motive, achievement aspirations, and achievement values (Rosen, 1959). This third component in Rosen's model was comprised of values related to being active (i.e., self-actualizing) rather than passive, individualistic rather than collectivist, and future rather than present oriented. Rosen was interested in whether the three components of the achievement syndrome were indeed related to one another, and whether there might be ethnic and social class differences in motives, aspirations, and values. An underlying assumption guiding this work was that the endorsement of particular achievement values resulted from specific child-rearing practices and that differences between ethnic groups in these practices would be related to different value orientations. The child-rearing correlates of high achievement values were thought to be training in mastery, particularly from the mother; fostering of early independence and self-reliance, especially from the father; and high parental nurturance (e.g, Rosen & d'Andrade, 1959). Such patterns of family life stood in stark contrast to the portrayal of African-American families that began to emerge in the 1950s and 1960s. Black families during that era were characterized as disorganized, unstable, largely father absent, and harshly authoritarian (e.g., Rainwater, 1966). The social climate of the times therefore supported the belief among motivation researchers that differences between African Americans and Whites in family structure would be predictive of disparate achievement values.

Thereafter followed a number of studies that compared mean differences between ethnic groups (mainly African-American and White respondents) on the components of the achievement syndrome, the relations between components, and their child-rearing antecedents (see Graham, 1994). In retrospect, this comparative racial literature was largely disappointing. It was never clearly documented that the components of the achievement syndrome were interrelated in any racial group; mean differences between racial groups were not reliable; and studies of the presumed linkage between child-rearing patterns and the achievement syndrome yielded unexpected and at times counterintuitive findings. For example, in some studies the reported achievement values of African-American samples were higher than those of their more economically advantaged White counterparts (Turner, 1972) and in other studies, higher achievement values were associated with the *absence* of parental training for mastery and independence in Black children (Rosen, 1959). Rather than attempting to address such unexpected findings, studies on race and the achievement syndrome, including achievement values, merely faded from view by the 1970s.

PERSPECTIVES FROM OTHER DISCIPLINES

It was probably good for the field that a socialization approach to race differences in achievement values suffered an early demise. Our appraisal of the socialization literature is that there has never been strong empirical support for the belief that particular child-rearing practices are systematically related to specific motivation variables. Confirming our view, we surveyed the tables of contents and subject indexes of five popular motivation textbooks, including two with an educational focus (Pintrich & Schunk, 1996; Stipek, 1998). In each we found only scattered references to parenting variables.

With the waning of interest by 1980 in a socialization approach and the achievement motive in general, motivation researchers concerned about relations between race and achievement values were forced to look beyond their own disciplinary boundaries. And indeed, several analyses emerging from the disciplines of sociology, anthropology, and social psychology were found to offer new insights, each providing an explanation for the presumed devaluing of achievement strivings among African-American youth.

Sociologists point to the opportunity structure in American society as they argue that economic and social disadvantage have led many Black students to believe that their efforts in school will have relatively little payoff in terms of economic and social mobility (e.g., Mickelson, 1990). That is, the perceived barriers imposed by a society that perpetuates inequality along race and class lines communicate to minority youngsters that there is little relationship between their efforts and eventual outcomes. The perception of barriers is likely to manifest itself as low educational and occupational aspirations (e.g., Cook, et al.), or perceived discrimination by members of higher status groups (e.g., van Laar, 2000). It is too early to tell whether the economic prosperity of the 1990s has meaningfully altered minority students' perceptions of barriers to opportunity.

Anthropologists offer a related but different perspective on achievement values with their focus on the historical circumstances and cultural forces that have shaped the experiences of African Americans. American Blacks are what John Ogbu calls an involuntary minority—that is, a group whose members have become part of the American fabric not by choice, but as a result of slavery, conquest, or colonization (Fordham & Ogbu, 1986; Ogbu, 1997). One consequence of this history is that acceptance of mainstream values about working hard and trying to succeed in school may be perceived as threatening to one's social identity. Particularly during adolescence, African-American youngsters may adopt oppositional identities whereby they show relative indifference or even disdain toward achievement behaviors that are valued by the larger society. Fordham and Ogbu (1986) coined the term "acting white" to describe African-American high school students' perceptions of their same-race peers who work hard to do well in school. While scholars disagree about the level of empirical support for the "acting white" construct (e.g., Cook & Ludwig, 1998; Foley, 1991), there is more consensus among researchers that many ethnic minority adolescents experience a particular kind of conflict between achievement strivings and their desire to be accepted by the general peer group (e.g., Arroyo & Zigler, 1995; Steinberg, Dornbusch, & Brown, 1992). This conflict is well captured in an ethnographic study by Hemmings (1996), who quotes the lament of one academically successful African American male in an inner city high school: "You're a nerd if you're sittin' up and doing homework all the time and don't help out other people. You don't want to be a nerd in this school because other kids will ruin your life" (p. 42).

Yet a third disciplinary perspective is represented by social psychologists who focus on the relations between self-esteem and school achievement. Because these linkages have not been well documented in African Americans (e.g., Graham, 1994), social psychologists have argued that Black students often seek outlets other than achievement success to feel good about themselves or to avoid feeling bad. This esteem-protecting mechanism has been described with various labels, including disidentification with academic achievement (Osborne, 1997; Steele, 1997) disengagement (Major, Spencer, Schmader, Wolfe, & Crocker, 1997) and selectively devaluing performance dimensions on which the self or one's group is perceived to do poorly (e.g., Crocker, Major, & Steele, 1998). The general idea underlying the social psychological analysis is that achievement values function as a moderator of the relations between self-esteem and performance. If one attaches little value or psychological importance to a particular domain such as academic achievement, then failure in that domain will not jeopardize self-views.

In summary, three processes reflective of three disciplinary perspectives can be enlisted as explanations for why African-American students might devalue effort and high achievement in school. Sociologists focus on the perceived barriers to success, anthropologists highlight identity conflict, and social psychologists emphasize self-esteem maintenance. The relevant literatures remain distinct, although they clearly capture interrelated processes. It is also worth noting that there are particular methodologies associated with these different disciplinary perspectives on race and achievement values. Sociologists primarily rely on survey methods, anthropologists tend to prefer ethnographic approaches, and social psychologists whose work is relevant employ laboratory experimental paradigms as their primary research tools.

A NEW EMPIRICAL APPROACH TO THE STUDY OF ACHIEVEMENT VALUES

In light of the historical and cross-disciplinary literatures that shaped our thinking as motivation psychologists, we set out to examine achievement values in African-American adolescents. Given their position in the opportunity structure, their unique cultural and historical circumstances, and the possible disassociation of positive self-regard from achievement strivings, is there evidence that African-American middle school students do indeed devalue the importance of trying hard and doing well in school? We focused on early adolescence because this is the developmental period during which attitudes toward school, including achievement values, take on heightened significance and may be particularly salient determinants of academic performance.

Choosing a methodology for our research posed several challenges. Because there is little agreement in the literature about the definition of values (Rohan, 2000), the question of the best method for studying this elusive construct is open to debate. We wanted an approach that was broader than targeting task-specific beliefs as in the Eccles and Wigfield research, yet one that was less daunting than the broad constructs and associated methodologies that emerged from the other disciplines discussed earlier. We also wanted to avoid the kind of direct probing that might be biased by social desirability and self-presentational concerns. For example, studies that directly ask adolescents whether they value schoolwork, put forth effort, or think that getting a good education has long term benefits generally reveal that all respondents, including African Americans, readily endorse these beliefs (e.g., Steinberg, Dornbusch, & Brown, 1992).

Our alternative was to use peer nomination procedures in which participants select classmates who fit various behavioral descriptions. Such procedures have a long history in the peer relations literature, where they have been successfully employed with studies of children's social status, such as being popular vs. rejected or aggressive vs. victimized (see Coie, Dodge, & Copotelli, 1982). In the present studies, we asked participants to nominate the classmates they most admired, respected, and wanted to be like. Our rationale for these questions was that if we can identify the characteristics of individuals whom an adolescent admires, respects, and wants to be like, this tells us something about the characteristics that the adolescent values.

Our method is not entirely unprecedented in motivation research. In early training studies to enhance the achievement motive (*Nach*), one popular technique was to have adolescents construct an "admiration ladder" on which they listed the names of individuals they most and least wanted to be like (Alschuler, Tabor, & McIntyre, 1971). This exercise then became the focus of discussions about "the qualities the students value in the people they most admire" (Alschuler, Tabor, & McIntyre, 1971, p. 142). Our peer nomination procedures can therefore be thought of as an adaptation of the admiration ladder.

Participants also nominated classmates who fit the descriptions of trying hard and getting good grades, not trying and receiving poor grades, following or not following school rules, dressing well, and being good at sports. Asking these additional questions permitted us to investigate relations between being "valued" (i.e ., nominated as admired, respected, etc.) and other characteristics that are salient during adolescence. Finally, data were gathered on students' academic achievement level. This allowed us to examine whether classmates nominated as admired, respected, and someone others wanted to be like were those who were high or low in achievement as defined by more objective criteria.

We used this procedure in two studies (see Graham, Taylor, & Hudley, 1998, for further details about the method). The first study was conducted with about 300 low SES African-American sixth to eighth graders selected from 10 classrooms of a predominantly Black (99%) middle school in metropolitan Los Angeles. Located in an economically depressed community, the school qualified for Title I compensatory education funds and a majority of the student body was eligible for the district free lunch program.

Nominations for "who do you (1) admire, (2) respect, and (3) want to be like" were highly correlated. That is, students who were nominated as admired also tended to be nominated as respected and as someone the nominator wanted to be like. Each student's number of nominations on the three questions was therefore summed to create a single index that was labeled "value" nominations. Our main goal in the analysis was to examine the choice patterns of male and female nominators as a function of gender and achievement level (high, average, or low) of the nominated student. In this way we were able to determine whether boys and girls preferentially valued same- or other-gender classmates and high vs. average vs. low achievers. Figure 1 displays these value nominations for girls (top half) and boys (bottom half).

It is evident here that females overwhelmingly reported that they valued other girls rather than boys (92 vs. 8% of the nominations). Female respondents also nominated high achieving girls (48%) more than average achieving (28%) or low achieving girls (16%). Boys on the other hand were more likely to value male than female classmates (69 vs. 31%). As the bottom half of Figure 1 shows, boys tended to overnominate their low achieving male classmates (25%) and undernominate their high achieving peers (16%) (these percentages were significantly different from chance). That is, when nominating other males, boys were *least* likely to select their high achieving same-gender classmates as those they admired, respected, and wanted to be like.

Using the same analysis strategy, we next examined girls' and boys' nomination patterns in response to four of the remaining questions: who tries hard, follows school rules, does not try hard, and does not follow school rules. The pattern was quite clear for female and male nominators. Girls were overwhelmingly nominated for the positive characteristics of trying hard and following school rules, particularly high achieving girls. Hardly any boys—not even high achieving boys—were nominated. For the more negative characteristics of not trying hard and not following school rules, the opposite pattern of nominations prevailed for both female and male nominators. Boys were greatly overnominated as not trying and not following school rules, particularly low achieving boys. Hardly any girls—not even low achieving girls—were selected for these more negative characteristics.

Let us now summarize these findings. Our methodology combined sociometric procedures from the peer relations literature and techniques first used by achievement-motive theorists to study values. We were guided by the belief that asking students to nominate classmates whom they admire, respect, and want to be like tells something about the characteristics these students value. The findings therefore suggest that African-American girls do indeed value academic effort and success. Girls consistently chose their high achieving, same-gender classmates as those they admire, respect, and want

FEMALE NOMINATORS

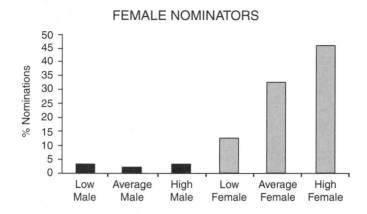

MALE NOMINATORS

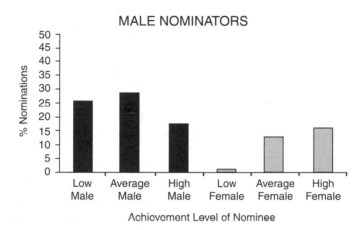

Achievement Level of Nominee

FIGURE 1

Percentage of classmates nominated as valued by African American females (top panel) and males (bottom panel) as a function of gender and achievement level of nominee. (From Graham, S., Taylor, A., & Hudley, C. (1998). *Journal of Educational Psychology, 90*, 606–620. Study 1. With permission.)

to be like. These same high achievers were also consistently nominated as classmates who worked hard in school and followed school rules. Thus, girls' value nominations indicated preference for their female classmates who were not only high achieving by objective criteria (i.e., teacher ratings) but also were perceived to be hardworking and socially responsible.

In contrast, the data portray a more complex picture of achievement values among African-American early adolescent boys. The majority of boys' nominations went to other boys, and the least valued among these nominees were high achieving boys. The findings therefore suggest less valuing of academic achievement among African-American boys than girls.

Although we emphasize differences between African-American boys and girls in what we conceptualize as achievement values, there were two reasons why we felt the need to replicate the findings with a multiethnic sample. First, one cannot be certain that the gender patterns we describe are unique to this particular population. Other studies with multiethnic samples and different assessment tools also report that adolescent boys seem to value academic success and hard work less than do girls (e.g., Berndt & Miller, 1990). Thus, the valuing of low achievers by male respondents may reflect more generalized gender preferences during adolescence rather than patterns that are unique to African-American boys.

Second, there could be gender X ethnicity interactions in value preferences if there are other ethnic groups of adolescent males whose experiences are similar to those of African Americans. Latinos, for example, are the fastest growing ethnic group in the United States, yet as a group they experience much of the same kind of social and economic marginality as African Americans and similarly high rates of school failure (e.g., Suarez-Orozco & Suarez-Orozco, 1995). Furthermore, there is evidence that Latino male adolescents also endorse beliefs about barriers to social mobility, experience identity conflict, and display the same kinds of oppositional behaviors that Ogbu and others have attributed to African-Americans (e.g., Matute-Bianchi, 1991). Thus as members of ethnic minority groups with marginalized status, it could be that Black and Latino male adolescents would tend to devalue academic achievement and trying hard more than their White male counterparts from the dominant group.

In the replication study (Graham et al., 1998, Experiment 2), participants were 400 low SES African-American, Latino, and White sixth to eighth graders recruited from an ethnically diverse middle school in metropolitan Los Angeles. The student body was approximately 50% Latino and 30% African-American; the remaining 20% were primarily White, but there were also small numbers of Asians, Persians, and biracial youngsters. These percentages are typical of the ethnic composition of public schools in urban Los Angeles that have a racial mix of students.

As in the first study, nominations for being admired, respected, and someone others wanted to be like were highly intercorrelated and were summed to create a single value index. The analyses were more complex than in the first study because ethnicity of nominator and nominee were also relevant factors. Initial analyses showed that girls across all three ethnic groups overwhelmingly preferred other girls (90%) as someone they admired, respected, and wanted to be like, and boys across all ethnic groups strongly preferred other boys (71%) on these same questions. We therefore focused on within-gender analyses of the nomination data . That is, we examined girls' nominations of other girls and boys' nominations of other boys as a function of achievement level (high, average, low) and ethnicity (African American, Latino, White) of the nominee.

Figure 2 shows the data for the three groups of female nominators (African-American, Latina, and White). The pattern to the nominations is quite similar across the three ethnic groups and conceptually replicates the results for African-American females reported in the first study. All three groups showed within-ethnicity preference in nominating other girls as someone they admired, respected, and wanted to be like. All three groups were also least likely to select low achievers (white bars) compared with their nominations for average (diagonals) and high achievers (black bars).

When we turn to the nomination data for male respondents in the three ethnic groups, the pattern of findings is quite different. Figure 3 depicts the data for males nominating other males as a function of ethnicity and achievement level of nominee. The first trend to note is that all three groups of boys also showed within-ethnicity preferences in identifying persons they valued. For African-American and Latino boys, the most highly valued peers within their ethnic group were low achievers. But notice the pattern for White male nominators. It is more similar to that for all groups of girls, in that White males were least likely to value low achievers over average and high achievers.

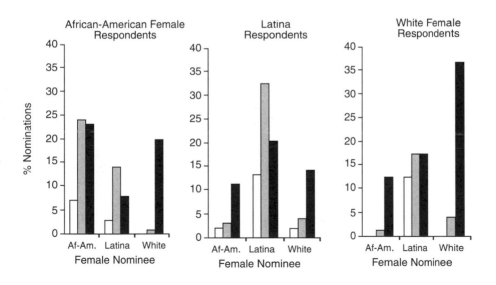

□ Low Ach.   ▨ Avg Ach.   ■ High Ach.

FIGURE 2

Percentage of female classmates nominated as valued by female nominators in three ethnic groups, as a function of ethnicity and achievement level of nominee. (From Graham, S., Taylor, A., & Hudley, C. (1998). *Journal of Educational Psychology*, 90, 606–620. Study 2. With permission.)

Sandra Graham and April Z. Taylor

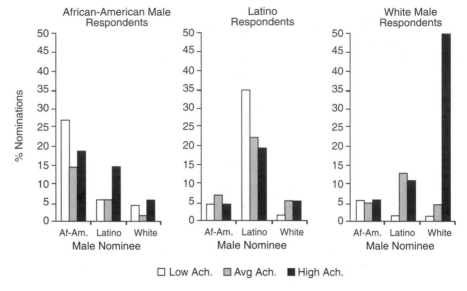

FIGURE 3

Percentage of male classmates nominated as valued by male nominators in three ethnic groups, as a function of ethnicity and achievement level of nominee. (From Graham, S., Taylor, A., & Hudley, C. (1998). *Journal of Educational Psychology*, 90, 606–620. Study 2. With permission.)

The remaining four questions asked respondents to nominate classmates who try hard, follow school rules, do not try hard, and do not follow school rules. For the positive characteristics of trying hard and following school rules, mostly girls of all three ethnic groups were nominated. For the two negative characteristics of not trying hard and not following school rules, male and female nominators were quite in agreement that these characteristics described male rather than female classmates (86 vs. 14% for not trying and 81 vs. 19% for not following school rules). The nomination patterns also varied by ethnicity and achievement level of male nominee. These data are displayed in Figure 4 for female and male nominators separately, but averaged across ethnicity of nominator. Two clear patterns are evident in Figure 4. First, both boys and girls nominated low achieving over average and high achieving boys as not trying and not following school rules. And second, these low achievers were predominantly African American and Latino rather than White male classmates. Thus, as in the first study, being male and a low achiever was associated with negative characteristics, and this was particularly true for ethnic minority male nominees.

Taken together, the data from these two studies clearly describe a relationship between achievement values, gender, and ethnicity. In the first

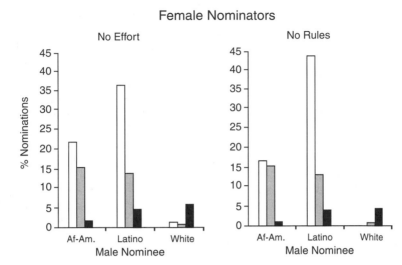

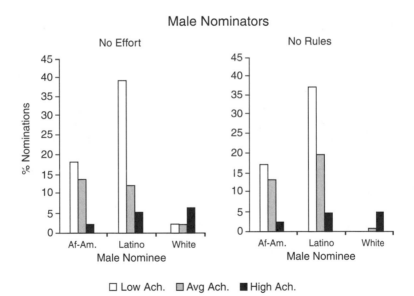

FIGURE 4

Percentage of male classmates nominated as not trying hard and not following school rules, as a function of ethnicity and achievement level of nominee. (From Graham, S., Taylor, A., & Hudley, C. (1998). *Journal of Educational Psychology*, 90, 606–620. Study 2. With permission.)

study, a strong gender effect suggested more devaluing of academic achievement among African-American males than females. However, this observed gender effect was moderated by ethnicity in the second study, where devaluing academic achievement was evident only among African-American and Latino boys. White males were just as likely as girls in all three ethnic groups to value high achievers within their own ethnic group. Male and female nominators across the two studies also were remarkably consistent in nominating low achieving ethnic males as not trying hard and disobeying school rules, suggesting that most of the adolescent respondents associated being male, a low achiever, *and an ethnic minority* with academic disengagement and social noncompliance.

We believe these results underscore some of the problems faced by ethnic minority adolescent males when viewed from a values perspective. Minority males perform more poorly than their female counterparts on most indicators of school success. It is therefore not surprising that they might devalue behavioral domains in which they anticipate poor outcomes. But poor school performance as a possible antecedent to devaluing achievement is only part of the ethnic male's dilemma. In both studies, it was low achieving minority males who were overwhelmingly nominated as not trying hard and not following school rules, suggesting that stereotypes, or shared beliefs, about Black and Latino males are largely negative. We suspect that the African-American and Latino boys in our research are well aware of how they are seen by others and that this awareness may have influenced what appeared to be their relative indifference to those who display achievement behaviors that are valued by the larger society. Claude Steele has written poignantly about how coping with negative stereotypes about their academic competence has led many African-American students to academically disengage and discount the importance of school success (Steele, 1997). Negative stereotypes can promote self-doubt and loss of confidence in one's environment, both of which foreshadow motivational decline.

A Further Exploration of Stereotypes

This issue of negative stereotypes about adolescent minority boys both intrigued and encouraged us to pursue the topic further, using nomination procedures in a different experimental manipulation that more closely followed the stereotyping literature (Hudley & Graham, 2000). The procedure, introduced as a study of "First Impressions," presented sixth to eighth grade participants with large picture boards that contained 12 pictures randomly arranged. The pictures were high-quality color photographs of unknown middle school students who varied systematically by gender and ethnicity (Black, Latino, White). Thus there were two pictures of African-American girls, two

African-American boys, two Latina girls, etc. The color photos were arranged to resemble a yearbook page.

Respondents had to pick one photo to match each of several descriptions. Two of the descriptions portrayed students who studied hard and did well in school, and two described students who did poorly and/or did not care much about school. For each question, the respondent had a different set of 12 photos to choose from, but the photos always systematically varied the ethnicity and gender of the pictured student. Although still relying on nominations, notice how this procedure differs from that of our earlier studies. In the earlier research, respondents nominated actual classmates from their homeroom, people who they knew and interacted with regularly. Thus one could argue that the nominations for positive or negative characteristics were unbiased (i.e., nonstereotypical) judgments of observed behavior. In the present studies, participants nominated unknown peers, and their preferences were based only on information about gender and ethnicity of the stimulus person. Any systematic pattern to the data based on such cues could then be more revealing of bias, or stereotypes about particular groups.

We used the "First Impressions" methodology in two studies: one with a population of African-American sixth to eighth graders who attended an all-Black middle school, and the other with a multiethnic sample (African Americans, Latinos, and Whites) selected from two ethnically diverse middle schools. (See Hudley & Graham, 2000, for details about the method.) The findings in the two studies were virtually identical, and here we present the pattern of results for the multiethnic second study.

Figure 5 shows which pictures were selected for each question type as a function of the gender and ethnicity of the adolescent in the photo. We display the data collapsed across gender and ethnicity of respondent (nominator) because all the participants were quite in agreement about which picture cues were associated with particular achievement descriptions. If no stereotypes or biases were operating, we would not expect any of the photo types to be selected at greater than chance levels. However, it is evident in the top two panels of Figure 5 that photos of unknown girls of all three ethnic groups were selected for the two high-achievement descriptions and that hardly any male photos were chosen. In contrast, for descriptions of low achievement strivings (bottom half of Figure 5), the choices were mostly boys. But note that it was ethnic minority males, more so than White males, whose pictures were selected.

We think that these data corroborate the argument we are advancing about negative stereotypes and being an ethnically minority male, and how these two factors together relate to achievement values. We believe that minority males, more than other adolescents, must cope with the dual stressors of academic challenge and negative stereotypes about their group, and that these stressors can undermine the endorsement of achievement values.

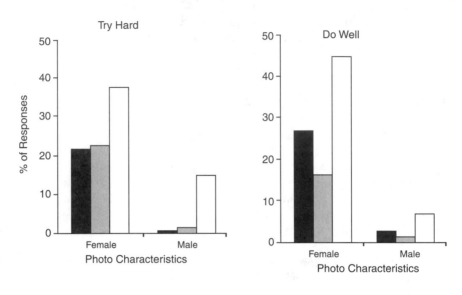

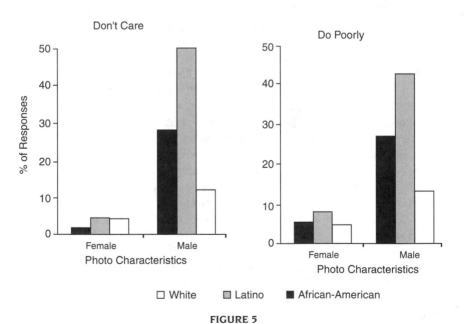

FIGURE 5

Percentage choice as a function of gender and ethnicity of photo cue in each of four achievement scenarios.

Developmental Concerns

Thus far all our analyses have focused on adolescence. Yet an important theme of this volume is the development of motivational processes. At what age or developmental period do we begin to see the kind of gender- and ethnicity-related patterns of achievement values that have been examined in our adolescent studies?

The relatively small literature on achievement task values that includes developmental analyses indicates that children value school subjects less as they increase in age, particularly as they approach the transition from elementary to middle school (Wigfield & Eccles, 1992; Wigfield et al., 1994). Changes in classroom reward structure over these years, such as increasing public evaluation, competition, and ability grouping, are known contributors to many students' declining interest in academic activities as they approach adolescence. At the same time, children are developing a more "mature" understanding of the characteristics of low ability (i.e., that it may be stable and uncontrollable) and more realistic (performance-based) expectations for future success (see review in Stipek & MacIver, 1989). It has also been documented that lower expectancies can depress achievement values (MacIver, Stipek, & Daniels, 1991).

The hypothesized correlates of achievement (de)valuing that have guided our thinking are also likely to become more significant as children enter adolescence. For example, media portrayals are among the most effective transmitters of social stereotypes, and it is known that adolescents are the most frequent consumers of popular media (e.g., Blosser, 1988). In addition, identity conflict is one of the hallmarks of adolescence (e.g., Erikson, 1968), and there is evidence that perceptions of barriers to opportunity increase from the early elementary to middle school years (Cook et al., 1996). All this related developmental research might therefore lead us to predict less valuing of high achievers and more valuing of low achievers among boys as they increase in grade level.

In the next study, we set out to replicate our methods for studying values using peer nomination procedures with a sample of second, fourth, and seventh graders . The children were selected from a low income urban middle school and a feeder elementary school, both of which were over 90% African American. We used the same peer nomination questions employed in the adolescent studies, but with appropriate word changes where necessary. We also had objective measures of children's achievement level based on teacher ratings.

The nominations for who do you admire, respect, and want to be like were again combined to create a single values index. As in the adolescent studies, girls across all grade levels nominated other girls rather than boys (75 vs. 25%), whereas boys were more likely to nominate other boys rather than girls (70 vs. 30%). Figure 6 shows the value nominations for African-American girls

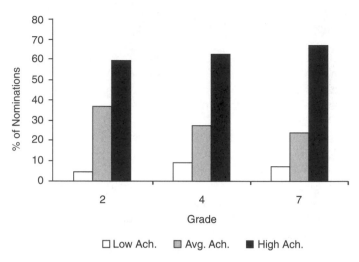

FIGURE 6
Percentage of African-American female classmates nominated as valued
by female nominators as a function of grade level of nominator and
achievement level of nominee.

nominating other girls as a function of grade level of nominator and achievement level of the female nominee. These data are entirely consistent with the adolescent studies. Across all three grade levels, girls were more likely to nominate their high achieving female classmates as those they admire, respect, and want to be like.

Figure 7 shows the data for males nominating other males across the three grade levels. Here the critical comparison is the changing pattern of nominations that went to high achieving male classmates from elementary to middle school. It is evident in Figure 7 that high achievers received the majority of value nominations from second graders (51%) and fourth graders (52%). By seventh grade, however, the pattern reverts back to what we documented in the middle school studies. High achieving male classmates were least likely to be nominated (21%) as someone the seventh grade male nominator admired, respected, and wanted to be like. There is also a steady but nonsignificant increase across grade level in value nominations that went to low achievers.

In addition to the peer nomination procedures, we included a series of questions adapted from Cook et al. (1996) to measure perceptions of educational and occupational barriers. For example, respondents were asked to think about why they might not be able to continue going to school or get the job they wanted. They then rated on 4-point scales their agreement with a number of perceived barriers. Among the environmental barriers to education were *bad teachers* and *no good schools in my neighborhood*. Among the occupational barriers were *no good jobs in my community* and *hiring discrimination* (i.e., "They don't hire

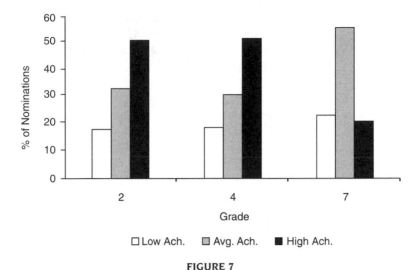

FIGURE 7

Percentage of African-American male classmates nominated as valued by male nominators as a function of grade level of nominator and achievement level of nominee.

people like me"). Each barrier was accompanied by an illustration that was discussed with the second and fourth graders to ensure understanding.

We found gender and grade level effects for both barrier types. African-American boys perceived greater educational and occupational barriers than did African-American girls, and the perceived obstacles increased across grade level for both boys and girls. Then we turned to the relationship between endorsement of barriers and value preferences. Our hypothesis was that high perceived barriers would be related to preference (more nominations) for low achievers. All respondents were divided into high vs. low barrier groups based on a median split of their ratings on the educational barrier questions. We then calculated the number of value nominations that went to low achievers in each barrier group.

At each grade level and for both male and female nominators, the percent of nominations for low achievers was related to perception of educational barriers in a manner consistent with our hypothesis. It was the high barrier group in each grade who most valued the low achievers: 65 vs. 35% in second grade, 79 vs. 21% in fourth grade, and 73 vs. 27% in seventh grade. Thus, even though there were mean differences in perceptions of barriers across gender and developmental level, the relationship between this variable and value preference remained constant. To the degree that children and young adolescents anticipate that factors outside their control can negatively influence educational and occupational outcomes, they may be less likely to value effort and success in school.

These analyses remain exploratory at this point, and there is much that we do not yet know about our high barrier group, particularly the youngest respondents. Are these children doing more poorly in school than their classmates who perceive more educational and occupational opportunity? Are they judged by their teachers as more socially deviant, possibly reinforcing the perception of oneself as marginalized? Are the relations between perceived barriers and value preferences the same in ethnic groups other than African Americans? We are gathering data on these and other such questions that hopefully will shed new light on the social context of developing achievement values.

SUMMARY: ETHNICITY, GENDER, AND DEVELOPING (DECLINING?) ACHIEVEMENT VALUES

We devised a new methodology for studying achievement values that yielded replicable findings across several studies. Based on our results, we believe that it would be a mistake to suggest that African-American or Latino youngsters *as a group* devalue effort. Ethnic minority girls in all age groups that we studied showed a consistent pattern of admiring, respecting, and wanting to be like high achievers. Ethnic minority (African-American) boys in the elementary grades also displayed this same pattern of value preferences.

These data tell us two things. First, there are complex ethnicity by gender by age interactions which appear when one is studying achievement values. And second, these interactions highlight some of the problems faced by many adolescent minority males. In comparative educational research that examines gender as well as ethnic differences between groups, it is clear that ethnic minority males (i.e., African American and Latino) are faring more poorly than females (e.g., Davis, 1994; Matutei-Bianchi, 1991; Osborne, 1997; Simmons, Black, & Zhou, 1991). The ethnicity by gender differences increase across the school years and are particularly apparent when the measures are so-called markers of adolescent success (i.e., high school graduation) and young adult mobility (i.e., enrollment in and completion of college) (see review in Sidanius & Pratto, 1999). In addition to these academic challenges are the negative stereotypes about their group that adolescent males confront. We found in our adolescent studies with multiethnic minority respondents that being a male and an ethnic minority was associated with academic disengagement and social deviance. This is entirely consistent with the larger stereotype literature, where it has often been shown that the shared cultural beliefs about ethnic minorities are largely negative. The most prevalent stereotype about African-American males, for example, is that they are unintelligent, unmotivated, and violent (e.g., Devine & Elliott, 1995; Niemann, Jennings, Rozelle, Baxter, & Sullivan, 1994).

As ethnic minority males enter adolescence, their academic difficulties escalate and the negative images of their groups become more salient. It is not surprising that the perception of barriers to educational and occupational opportunity increased from elementary to middle school for boys in our research, which would be consistent with a heightened awareness of how one's group is viewed in the larger social context. Thus we argue that the multiple stressors of academic challenge, coping with negative stereotypes, and perceived barriers to opportunity can erode the endorsement of achievement values in some ethnic minority adolescent males. The developmental analyses of Eccles, Wigfield, and their colleagues have already captured how changing perceptions about the self (Can I do it?) may be at odds with a school structure across the elementary and middle school years that promotes public evaluation and social comparison (Eccles, Wigfield, & Schiefele, 1998). This person–environment mismatch contributes to declining perceptions of task value from middle childhood to early adolescence. We believe that a fuller understanding of developmental shifts in achievement values will need to better incorporate gender and ethnicity on the "person" variable side, and increasing experiences with stereotype-driven prejudice and discrimination on the "environment" variable side. Longitudinal research rather than (in addition to) the cross-sectional approach used in our studies also will be needed.

We have been emphasizing declining achievement values, but the methodology we used might also be helpful in uncovering the characteristics that adolescent males *do* value in their male peers. Although not reported here, we found that minority boys in our adolescent studies admired, respected, and wanted to be like their male peers who were perceived to be good at sports. Like academics, sports is an achievement domain in which persistence and hard work are the hallmark of a good athlete, just as they are the markers of a good student. It could therefore be that adolescent minority boys do value achievement—but in an arena other than academics. What may be needed is attention to ethnicity by gender by *context* interactions in the study of achievement values.

FIVE RECOMMENDATIONS FOR MOTIVATION THEORY AND RESEARCH

We conclude with a set of recommendations for motivation theory and research that evolves from our approach. None of these suggestions is discussed in detail. Rather, they should be thought of as general guidelines and, in some cases, cautionary notes.

1. *More attention to the social context.* Theories of achievement motivation, including traditional expectancy–value approaches, have been intrapersonal in nature. The focus has been on individual needs, beliefs (e.g., expectancies),

goals, task values, and self-regulatory mechanisms. Even the achievement-related emotions that have been most studied (e.g., pride, shame, anxiety) are intrapsychic feeling states. Yet the contexts for achievement strivings, be they classrooms or playing fields, are inherently interpersonal. Self-directed thoughts and feelings are in part shaped by interactions with others, including teachers, parents, and peers. Furthermore, the appraisals and evaluations of these significant others are important topics in the study of motivation. Weiner (2000) has offered a rich conceptual analysis of motivation as a complex interplay between self- and other-perception when viewed from an attributional perspective. There are many other excellent examples in the field of motivation research that place the study of individual achievement strivings within a social context (see Juvonen & Wentzel, 1996). We think that our approach to achievement values as a function of ethnicity and gender highlights an important and understudied feature of this larger social context.

2. *Attend to gender by ethnicity interactions.* Individual differences have played a prominent role in motivation theory and research, whether conceptualized as motivational traits like the achievement motive, or as moderating influences like gender and age. Regarding gender, there is an empirical literature (albeit mixed) supporting the belief that girls are more vulnerable to motivational deficits than boys. For example, it has been argued that gender-role socialization and stereotypes lead girls to question their academic competence more, particularly in math; to display more maladaptive reactions to failure, including low ability attributions; to perceive more barriers to success; and experience more conflict between individual achievement strivings and social conformity (see reviews in Eccles, Wigfield, & Schiefele, 1998; Ruble & Martin, 1998). We would argue that taking ethnicity into account may require rethinking the gender analyses showing motivational patterns that typically favor boys. In our own and related comparative research, it is ethnic minority boys who appear to be most at risk for motivational deficits. Particularly during adolescence and with motivation research conducted in urban settings, it is probably too limiting to study gender in the absence of gender by ethnicity interactions.

3. *Be open to multidisciplinary perspectives.* As ethnicity assumes a more important role in motivation research, so too will there be a need for multidisciplinary perspectives. Because ethnicity is integrally linked to social status, the motivation researcher will be compelled to go beyond the individual-focused boundaries of the discipline. In our efforts to better understand race and achievement values, we turned to the disciplines of sociology, anthropology, and social psychology. Analyses from those disciplines suggested that perceiving barriers to opportunity (the sociological perspective), adopting an oppositional identity (the anthropological perspective), and protecting one's self-esteem (the social psychological perspective) might be important mechanisms that mediate the relation between ethnicity and achievement values.

We have already begun to explore the developing links between perception of barriers and the characteristics of peers that an individual values. As in the study of achievement values, the time seems right for other topics in motivation research to draw on the contributions of other disciplines.

4. *There is a role for comparative ethnic research.* Like other scholars who study minority child development, we are sensitive to the drawbacks of comparative racial/ethnic research (see Garcia Coll et al., 1996). In reviewing motivation research on African Americans, one of us (Graham, 1994) concluded that the comparative racial approach that so dominated the field had done little to advance our understanding of motivational processes in ethnic minority populations. This was because racial comparisons had little basis in theory and tended to ignore within-ethnic-group variability (including gender).

We believe there is a role for comparative ethnic analyses in motivation research if they are carried out with methodological rigor and if they can shed light on psychological processes. In our adolescent studies, we wanted to know whether the devaluing of achievement by boys was a phenomenon more unique to African Americans and their own particular social, cultural, and historical circumstances, or whether there might be a more general process that was characteristic of ethnic minorities with marginalized status. We found evidence for the latter possibility by including Latinos and Whites in a comparative framework. Whether the same pattern of gender differences would appear in other ethnic groups with different circumstances (e.g., Asian Americans) is an intriguing question that could offer fresh insights into the relationship between motivation and social status.

But we must be guarded in our encouragement of cross-ethnic group research, for there are complexities in studying ethnic groups with different immigrant histories that one does not encounter when the comparisons focus on African Americans and Whites. For example, it is clear that the adjustment outcomes of some immigrant (voluntary) minority groups differ across generations, with better outcomes occurring for recent immigrants in comparison to those with second-generation status or beyond (e.g., Fuligni, 1997; Zhou, 1997). As generational status influences social and economic mobility, it will play an increasing role in shaping beliefs about performance, including achievement values.

5. *Encourage intervention research.* Our methodology was adapted from procedures first used in the 1960s by David McClelland and colleagues in studies designed to enhance the achievement motive (Alschuler, Tabor, & McIntyre, 1971). These researchers created the "admiration ladder" to stimulate discussion among children and adolescents about the characteristics they valued in others. There is no reason for not incorporating similar techniques into contemporary motivation enhancement programs. Furthermore, if our goal is preventive intervention, then change efforts based on endorsing achievement values would need to be implemented before the critical

transition to early adolescence, when motivation begins to decline among all youth and identity issues and negative stereotypes become so salient for ethnic minorities.

The burden for motivational change to enhance achievement values should not remain solely with the individual student. For example, there is much that teachers can do in the way they provide performance feedback to minimize unintended behavior that might convey low expectations of students (e.g., Graham, 1991) or enhance stereotype threat (Cohen, Steele, & Ross, 1999). And school administrators should become more sensitized to how policies related to discipline, such as suspension and expulsion, can promote perception of discrimination and barriers to opportunity among ethnic minority adolescents.

It is evident to us that the study of achievement values and how they are expressed in the broader context of social and cultural influences might provide important clues for understanding the academic challenges faced by many ethnic minority youth. We hope that our approach will stimulate new and creative ways of conceptualizing values within a motivational framework, as well as more awareness of the complex forces associated with ethnic minority status. We see these as useful steps to both promote the field of motivation in educational psychology and assure its continued vitality.

References

Alschuler, A., Tabor, D., & McIntyre, J. (1971). *Teaching achievement motivation*. Middletown, CT.: Education Ventures.

Arroyo, C., & Zigler, E. (1995). Racial identity, academic achievement, and the psychological well-being of economically disadvantaged adolescents. *Journal of Personality and Social Psychology, 69*, 903–914.

Atkinson, J. (1964). *An introduction to motivation*. Princeton, NJ: Van Nostrand.

Berndt, T., & Miller, K. (1990). Expectancies, values, and achievement in junior high school. *Journal of Educational Psychology, 82*, 319–326.

Blosser, B. (1988). Ethnic differences in children's media use. *Journal of Broadcasting & Electronic Media, 32*, 453–470.

Brophy, J. (1999). Toward a model of the value aspects of motivation in education: Developing appreciation for particular learning domains and activities. *Educational Psychologist, 34*, 75–85.

Cohen, G., Steele, C., & Ross, L. (1999). The mentor's dilemma: Providing critical feedback across the racial divide. *Personality and Social Psychology Bulletin, 25*, 1302–1318.

Coie, J., Dodge, K., & Coppotelli, H. (1982). Dimensions and types of social status: A cross-age perspective. *Developmental Psychology, 18*, 557–570..

Cook, P., & Ludwig, J. (1998). The burden of "acting white": Do black adolescents disparage academic achievement? In C. Jencks & M. Phillips (Eds.), *The Black–White test score gap* (pp. 375–400). Washington, DC: The Brookings Institution.

Cook, T., Church, M., Ajanaku, S., Shadish, W., Kim, J., & Cohen, R. (1996). The development of occupational aspirations and expectations among inner-city boys. *Child Development, 67*, 3368–3385.

Crocker, J., & Major, B. (1989). Social stigma and self-esteem: The self-protective properties of stigma. *Psychological Review, 96*, 608–630.

Crocker, J., Major, B., & Steele, C. (1998). Social stigma. In D. Gilbert, S. Fiske, & G. Lindzey (Eds.), *Handbook of social psychology* (4th ed., Vol. 2, pp. 504–533). New York: McGraw-Hill.

Davis, J. (1994). The effects of school context, structure, and experiences on African American males in middle and high school. *Journal of Negro Education, 63*, 570–587.

Devine, P., & Elliott, A. (1995). Are racial stereotypes really fading? The Princeton trilogy revisited. *Personality and Social Psychology Bulletin, 21*, 1139–1150.

Eccles, J., & Wigfield, A. (1995). In the mind of the actor: The structure of adolescents' achievement task values and expectancy-related beliefs. *Personality and Social Psychology Bulletin, 21*, 215–225.

Eccles, J., Wigfield, A., & Schiefele, U. (1998). Motivation to succeed. In N. Eisenberg (Ed.), *Handbook of child psychology* (5th ed., Vol. 3, pp. 1017–1095). New York: John Wiley.

Erikson, E. (1968). *Identity: Youth and crisis.* New York: Norton.

Feather, N. (1992). Values, valences, expectations, and actions. *Journal of Social Issues, 48*, 109–124.

Foley, D. (1991). Reconsidering anthropological explanations of ethnic school failure. *Anthropology & Education Quarterly, 22*, 61–86.

Fordham, S., & Ogbu, J. (1986). Black students' school success: Coping with the burden of acting white. *Urban Review, 18*, 176–206.

Fuligni, A. (1997). The academic achievement of adolescents from immigrant families: The roles of family background, attitudes, and behavior. *Child Development, 68*, 351–363.

Garcia Coll, C., Lamberty, G., Jenkins, R., McAdoo, H., Crnic, K., Wasik, B., & Vazquez Garcia, H. (1996). An integrative model for the study of developmental competencies in minority children. *Child Development, 67*, 1891–1914.

Graham, S. (1991). Communicating low ability in thee classroom: Bad things good teachers sometimes do. In S. Graham & V. Folkes (Eds.), *Attribution theory: Applications to achievement, mental health, and interpersonal conflict* (pp. 11–52). Hillsdale, NJ: Lawrence Erlbaum Associates.

Graham, S. (1994). Motivation in African Americans. *Review of Educational Research, 64*, 55–118.

Graham, S., Taylor, A., & Hudley, C. (1998). Exploring achievement values among ethnic minority early adolescents. *Journal of Educational Psychology, 90*, 606–620.

Gray-Litttle, B., & Hafdahl, A. (2000). Factors influencing racial comparisons of self-esteem: A quantitative review. *Psychological Bulletin, 126*, 26–54.

Hemmings, A. (1996). Conflicting images? Being Black and a model high school student. *Anthropology & Education Quarterly, 27*, 20–50.

Hudley, C., & Graham, S. (2000). *Stereotypes of achievement strivings among early adolescents.* Manuscript submitted for publication.

Juvonen, J., & Wentzel, K. (Eds). (1996). *Social motivation: Understanding children's school adjustment.* New York: Cambridge University Press.

MacIver, D., Stipek, D., & Daniels, D. (1991). Explaining within-semester changes in student effort in junior high school and senior high courses. *Journal of Educational Psychology, 83*, 201–211.

Major, B., Spencer, S., Schmader, T., Wolfe, C., & Crocker, J. (1997). Coping with negative stereotypes about intellectual performance: The role of psychological disengagement. *Personality and Social Psychology Bulletin, 24*, 34–50.

Matute-Bianchi, M. (1991). Situational ethnicity and patterns of school performance among immigrant and nonimmigrant Mexican-descent students. In M. Gibson & J. Ogbu (Eds.), *Minority status and schooling* (pp. 205–247). New York: Garland.

McClelland, D., Atkinson, J., Clark, R., & Lowell, E. (1953). *The achievement motive.* New York: Appleton-Century-Crofts.

Mickelson, R. (1990). The attitude–achievement paradox among black adolescents. *Sociology of Education, 63*, 44–61.

Niemann, Y., Jennings, L., Rozelle, R., Baxter, J., & Sullivan, E. (1994). Use of free responses and cluster analysis to determine stereotypes of eight groups. *Personality and Social Psychology Bulletin, 20*, 379–390.

Ogbu, J. (1997). Understanding the school performance of urban blacks: Some essential background knowledge. In H. Walberg, R. Reyes, & R. Weissberg (Eds.), *Children and youth: Interdisciplinary perspectives.* Thousand Oaks, CA: Sage.

Osborne, J. (1997). Race and academic disidentification. *Journal of Educational Psychology*, 89, 728–735.

Pintrich, P., & Schunk, D. (1996). *Motivation in education: Theory, research, and applications.* Englewood Cliffs, NJ: Prentice-Hall.

Phillips, M., Crouse, J., & Ralph, J. (1998). Does the Black–White test score gap widen after children enter school? In C. Jencks & M. Phillips (Eds.), *The Black–White test score gap* (pp. 229–272). Washington, DC: The Brookings Institution.

Rainwater, L. (1966). The crucible of identity: The Negro lower class family. *Daedalus*, 95, 172–216.

Rohan, M. (2000). A rose by any other name? The values construct. *Personality and Social Psychology Review*, 4, 255–277.

Rokeach, M. (1973). *The nature of human values.* New York: Free Press.

Rosen, B. (1959). Race, ethnicity, and the achievement syndrome. *American Sociological Review*, 24, 47–60.

Rosen, B., & d'Andrade, R. (1959). The psychosocial origins of achievement motivation. *Sociometry*, 22, 185–217.

Ruble. D., & Martin, C. (1998). Gender development. In N. Eisenberg (Ed.), *Handbook of child psychology* (5th ed., Vol. 3, pp. 933–1016). New York: Wiley.

Sidanius, J., & Pratto, F. (1999). *Social dominance.* New York: Cambridge University Press.

Simmons, R., Black, A., & Zhou, Y. (1991). African American versus White children and the transition into junior high school. *American Journal of Education*, 99, 481–520.

Steele, C. (1997). A threat in the air: How stereotypes shape intellectual identity and performance. *American Psychologist*, 52, 613–629.

Steinberg, L., Dornbusch, S., & Brown, B. (1992). Ethnic differences in adolescent achievement: An ecological perspective. *American Psychologist*, 47, 723–729.

Stipek, D. (1998). *Motivation to learn: From theory to practice* (3rd ed.). Boston: Allyn & Bacon.

Stipek, D., & MacIver, D. (1989). Developmental change in children's assessment of intellectual competence. *Child Development*, 60, 521–538.

Suarez-Orozco, C., & Suarez-Orozco, M. (1995). *Transformations: Migration, family life, and achievement motivation among Latino adolescents.* Stanford, Ca.: Stanford University Press.

Turner, J. (1972). Structural conditions of achievement among Whites and Blacks in the rural south. *Social Problems*, 19, 496–508.

van Laar, C. (2000). The paradox of low academic achievement but high self-esteem in African American students: An attributional account. *Educational Psychology Review*, 12, 33–62.

Weiner, B. (2000). *Social emotions and personality inferences: A scaffold for a new research direction in the study of achievement motivation.* Unpublished manuscript, University of California, Los Angeles.

Wigfield, A., & Eccles, J. (1992). The development of achievement task values: A theoretical analysis. *Developmental Review*, 12, 265–310.

Wigfield, A., & Eccles, J. (1994). Children's competence beliefs, achievement values, and general self-esteem: Change across elementary and middle school. *Journal of Early Adolescence*, 14, 104–138.

Wigfield, A., Eccles, J., Yoon, K., Harold, R., Arbreton, A., Freedman-Doan, C., & Blumenfeld, P. (1997). Changes in children's competence beliefs and subjective task values across the elementary school years: A 3-year study. *Journal of Educational Psychology*, 89, 451–469.

Zhou, M. (1997). Growing up American: The challenge confronting immigrant children and children of immigrants. *Annual Review of Sociology*, 23, 63–95.

CHAPTER

6

The Development
of Self-Determination in Middle
Childhood and Adolescence

WENDY S. GROLNICK, SUZANNE T. GURLAND, KAREN F. JACOB,
AND WENDY DECOURCEY
Clark University, Worcester, Massachusetts

The Montessori classroom is a wonderful setting in which to view self-determination at work. Observe Katie—within 1 hr, she has chosen three different activities and engaged in each with vigor and persistence. Clearly, these are activities in which she is interested. Her excitement and curiosity are evident in her frequent smiles and laughter and in the intensity of her concentration on the activities. Notable in Katie's approach is that her movement through the classroom has been without adult intervention. By contrast, observe Jennifer, who begins the session by wandering around the room. One of the teachers spots her and tries to interest her in a sorting game. She plays with this for a few minutes then appears to lose interest. She continues this way until another adult intervenes.

Now consider two middle school students. Both are B+ students. Jared does only what is expected and no more. He finds the material boring and focuses on learning what will be on the test. By contrast, Corey, while he may not find the material interesting and prefers to go to recess, does his work because he wants to learn new things and feels what he is learning is worthwhile. He often goes beyond what is expected, adding material to a project or exploring school subjects on the computer.

These different styles of the approaches to learning on the part of students represent different motivational orientations. Some of the differences

The Development of Achievement Motivation

represent the level of motivation—for example, Katie appears to be more motivated to pursue learning activities than Jennifer. Beyond simply the level of motivation, however, is the issue of why children engage in their work. Here the issue is the type or quality of the motivation. Although he may work as hard as Corey on a particular assignment, Jared's orientation to the work is quite different. Jared engages in his work because of prompts and prods and lacks a sense of himself as the initiator of his actions. In contrast, Corey pursues his studies because he personally values them. The motivation to pursue his work thus comes from himself, i.e., he sees himself as engaging in it by choice. Another child may engage in work because of anxiety about failure. This approach also lacks a sense of choice.

How do we make sense of these different orientations to schoolwork? One dimension along which we can understand the quality of motivation is in the degree to which children experience autonomy or a sense of self-determination around their schoolwork. When people are self-determined, they experience themselves as the initiators of their own actions, feel they have a choice about engaging in the activity, and feel they are "behind" their actions (Deci & Ryan, 1985). By contrast, an individual who feels controlled, either by external forces, such as powerful others, or by strong internal forces, feels like a pawn and lacks a sense of self-determination.

This chapter focuses on the issue of self-determination—how children come to experience a sense of self-determination in the activities they pursue, whether this makes a difference in children's performance and well-being, what can prevent them from feeling a sense of self-determination, and how we, as educators and psychologists, can facilitate self-determination. When we consider the development of self-determination, we can approach it in at least two ways. First, we can think about how people in general move toward a sense of self-determination. In other words, we can try to understand the developmental process. Second, we can ask about individual differences: How is it that some individuals are self-determined and others are not for the very same activity? Of course, these two issues are linked in that, if one understands the general process through which development occurs, one begins to understand the origins of individual differences. We consider both of these issues, and their intersection, in our chapter.

SELF-DETERMINATION DEFINED

We begin by defining self-determination and differentiating it from other related concepts. According to self-determination theory (Deci & Ryan, 1985), self-determination involves the degree to which individuals experience themselves as autonomous or as having choice in their actions and behaviors, as opposed to being controlled or pressured. This approach builds on the work of deCharms (1968), who suggested a distinction between behaviors that are experienced as emanating from the self and those that are not. In the former case, people experience themselves as "origins" and in the latter case as "pawns." When self-determined, individuals have an internal, as opposed to an external, locus of causality (Heider, 1958) for their behavior. Thus, when individuals are self-determined they experience themselves as volitional initiators of their own actions.

One frequent source of confusion is the distinction between self-determination, which implies an internal locus of causality, and Rotter's (1966) concept of "locus of control." Locus of control concerns individuals' experience of control over outcomes or reinforcements. Thus, when individuals have an internal locus of control, they view successes and failures (i.e., outcomes) as contingent on their own behavior. The person believes he or she can reliably obtain outcomes, even if this means abiding by the contingencies set by others. By contrast, when individuals have an external locus of control, they view successes and failures as a function of chance, luck, or the whims of others that cannot be understood or anticipated. Thus, the person does not feel he can reliably control outcomes. Unlike locus of control, self-determination is not concerned with control over outcomes, but rather with the initiation and regulation of behavior. Having an internal locus of control does not assure a sense of self-determination. For example, a child can feel quite capable of achieving good grades in school and know how to make successes happen, but may feel pressured or coerced into engaging in school activities. Thus, locus of control concerns the issue of competence to obtain outcomes, while self-determination concerns one's willingness or sense of autonomy in engaging in behavior. Importantly, an internal locus of control is necessary but not sufficient for self-determination. If individuals do not believe that outcomes are attainable through their own actions, they are likely to feel helpless—an experience that is antithetical to self-determination.

Self-determination is also sometimes confused with independence. While self-determination refers to the extent to which an individual feels a sense of volition for acting, independence refers to behaviors that are conducted in isolation, without connection to others (Ryan, Deci, & Grolnick, 1996). These are orthogonal constructs: it is quite possible to choose to be connected with others, and it is equally possible to feel pressured to connect with others. In fact, as will be explicated later, because relatedness and self-determination are both inherent needs, individuals experience both choice and connection when they are functioning optimally.

THE EXPRESSION OF SELF-DETERMINATION

Having defined self-determination, we turn to the question of how it is expressed. What are the hallmarks of self-determined behavior? How might we characterize children's behavior when it is not self-determined? Self-determination is manifested most vividly and purely in intrinsically motivated behavior. Intrinsic motivation refers to engagement in behavior for its own sake, not for the sake of rewards or goals separable from the behavior (Deci & Ryan, 1985). When intrinsically motivated, people choose to engage in activities that provide opportunities for mastery and enjoyment. We see intrinsic motivation in the curiosity and play of young children. Most children need no inducements to play, for example. They do it simply for the love of the activity itself; they follow their interest, becoming absorbed in the activity without any bribes or promises of rewards.

Intrinsic motivation is also evident, though perhaps not as often as we would like, in the school environment. When a child takes on a project out of interest and pursues it avidly, without external prompts or pushes, the child is displaying intrinsic motivation, the prototype of self-determination.

Surely, however, not all activities are inherently interesting or would be spontaneously pursued by all children. Learning multiplication tables, picking up toys, and going to bed on time are activities that few children enjoy. It is hard to imagine a child who cleans his or her room for the pure enjoyment he or she receives in the activity! Rather, such activities are pursued for the sake of goals external to the activity itself, and are thus referred to as extrinsically motivated.

However, not all extrinsically motivated behaviors are alike. Within the category of extrinsically motivated behaviors, there is variation in the extent to which behaviors are self-determined. Thus, while intrinsically motivated behaviors are, by definition, experienced as self-determined, extrinsically motivated behaviors vary along a continuum of less to greater self-determination.

At the least self-determined end of the continuum is *external regulation*. When externally regulated, people behave because of contingencies in their environments such as rewards and punishments. A child may engage in schoolwork, for example, because he will get in trouble if he fails to complete it, or because he wants to earn a sticker. In this case, the child does not experience the initiation of schoolwork as having originated by choice from within himself, but rather from factors external to himself (e.g., the sticker) that push him to do the work.

Somewhat further along the self-determination continuum is *introjected regulation*. In this form of regulation, contingencies are taken in by the individual and self-administered. The individual engages in behavior because of these self-imposed pressures or "shoulds," or to escape negative self-directed affects such as shame and guilt. A child might do her schoolwork, for example, because she would feel guilty otherwise. It is true that, in introjected regulation, initiation of the behavior comes from within the individual, but it is nevertheless not experienced as truly self-initiated. Rather, the individual feels pressured by self-administered affects or contingencies.

Still further along the continuum is regulation through identification. In *identified regulation*, individuals identify with the value or worth of the behavior and engage in it accordingly. They themselves feel that the behavior is in accord with their own values or beliefs, and they therefore want to engage in it, even though it may not be perceived as fun or enjoyable. For example, a child who exhibits identified regulation with regard to his schoolwork might do his homework assignment because he feels it is important to his understanding of the material. Identified regulation thus includes a sense of felt autonomy or self-determination.

Finally, behaviors that are extrinsically motivated have the potential to become integrated. *Integrated regulation* is the most autonomous form of extrinsic motivation. When regulating in an integrated way, individuals not only engage in the behavior out of a personal valuing or endorsement, but also integrate the behavior into a larger constellation of related behaviors and values.

Thus, in this theory, self-determination is evident in both intrinsically motivated behavior and in some forms of extrinsically motivated behavior, specifically that which is regulated through identification or integration. It should be noted that other theories have components that capture a dimension similar to self-determined motivation. Pintrich and De Groot (1990), in their theory of self-regulated learning, propose that there are three motivational components to self-regulated learning; an expectancy component, which includes beliefs about one's ability to perform a task, a value component, which includes students' beliefs about the value and interest of the task, and an affective component, which represents students' emotional reactions to the task. The value component, conceptualized as reasons for doing the task, is closest to our concept of self-determination. Eccles et al. (1983), in their theory of motivation, specified both competence beliefs and subjective task values as crucial to task choice and performance. Subjective task value includes individuals' interest in the task, its importance to them, and its utility for them. Subjective task value is thus highly related to self-determination.

Much of this chapter is concerned with the process of how children move toward a greater sense of self-determination. However, before tackling this issue, we ask whether children's levels of self-determination have important concomitants. Does it really matter how self-determined children are for the activities in which they engage? Does children's level of self-determination make a difference for their behavior and adjustment?

Does Self-Determination Make a Difference?

A variety of studies have shown that children who are more intrinsically motivated in school show higher levels of achievement, lower levels of anxiety, and higher perceptions of competence (Gottfried, 1982, 1985). Clearly there are ongoing cycles in which children's motivation fuels their persistence which, in turn, facilitates successful outcomes. These successes then further facilitate children's intrinsic motivation (Harter & Connell, 1984). How about children's placement along a continuum of self-determination for extrinsic motivation? In a series of studies in the academic domain, it has been found that children who are further along the continuum cope more actively and display more positive affect in school. Children who are high in external regulation, for example, use more defensive styles of coping with setbacks in school, such as projection, in which blame for failure is externalized, and denial, in which the significance of failure is minimized or avoided (Connell & Wellborn, 1991). Children high in external regulation also have a low sense of academic competence and self-worth. Because they do not see their behavior in school as self-initiated, it appears that they do not derive a sense of satisfaction or worth from their actions. Children who are high in introjected regulation, which is associated with negative self-related feelings such as guilt, experience high levels of anxiety in school and respond to failure with further self-disparagement and worry. Finally, children high in identification, who accept the value of school activities, report high levels of perceived competence and self-esteem and low levels of anxiety. Further, they tend to use more positive coping strategies such as asking the teacher for help (Connell & Wellborn, 1991).

One way of representing children's level of autonomy is to weight children's scores on each of the types of self-regulation and combine them to form a relative autonomy index. Children higher on the relative autonomy index are reported by their teachers to be more engaged in class and to show higher levels of school performance. At-risk students are significantly lower on the relative autonomy index than non-at-risk children (Connell & Wellborn, 1991). With regard to behavioral outcomes, children who believe a task is interesting and important engage in more metacognitive activity, more cognitive strategy use, and more effective effort management (e.g., Eccles, et al. 1983; Meece, Blumenfeld, & Hoyle, 1988) for that task. Pintrich and De Groot (1990) asked children about their interest in their coursework and whether they believed it was important, as well as about their preference for challenge and their mastery goals. Together, these components made up a score for intrinsic value for school activities. Higher levels of intrinsic value were correlated with greater use of self-regulation strategies including planning, skimming and comprehension monitoring, and persistence at difficult or boring tasks. Intrinsic value was also associated with higher student achievement.

The consequences of self-determination extend to domains other than the academic, as well. Ryan and Connell (1989) found that more autonomous regulation in the pro-social domain was associated with greater empathy, more mature moral reasoning, and more positive relatedness to others.

Thus, the results of a variety of converging studies conducted across domains indicate that children's degree of self-determination in the pursuit of their activities has important consequences for their experience and behavior within that domain. A second issue we explore before addressing the development of self-determination is whether there are gender differences in self-determination.

Sex Differences

Research on gender differences in self-determination has shown mixed findings. On the one hand, several studies have reported no gender differences in intrinsic motivation. Gottfried, using the Children's Academic Intrinsic Motivation Inventory, found no differences in intrinsic motivation in reading, math, social studies, and science in a sample of fourth through seventh graders (Gottfried, 1985). She also found no gender differences in intrinsic motivation for reading, math, and general academics in a sample of first through fourth graders (Gottfried, 1990). In three of our own samples of children ranging in grade from third through seventh, we found no consistent gender differences on the Relative Autonomy Index. Similarly, Pintrich and DeGroot (1990) found that girls and boys did not differ on their reported intrinsic value for school.

On the other hand, gender does make a difference in some specific domains and at specific ages. Wigfield et al. (1997), in a longitudinal study of first through sixth grade children, found that girls valued reading and instrumental music more than boys. Boys valued sports more than girls. There were no perceived differences in the value of math by gender. Harter and Jackson (1992) found a sharp decline in intrinsic motivation for science and math between fifth and sixth grade for girls but not boys. It is likely that this difference is due to the different socialization messages girls and boys receive about these subjects (e.g., different attributions for their successes and failures, gender role expectations) at this time (Yee & Eccles, 1988). This discrepancy in intrinsic motivation may go on to affect career choices; girls are more likely to pursue careers that they like (and they do not like math related careers as much as boys), while boys are more likely to pursue careers for money or power reasons (Eccles, 1989; Eccles, Barber & Jozefowicz, 1998).

Further, there is some evidence that girls may be particularly vulnerable to the undermining of their intrinsic motivation. For example, Boggiano, Main, and Katz (1991) had girls and boys complete a shape–matching game under one of two feedback conditions: a high controlling condition in which the children were told they "should" and "ought to" perform well, and a low controlling condition, in which children's feelings were reflected and supportive feedback was offered. In a subsequent free play session, children could pursue the challenging tasks or switch to something easier. Girls in the high controlling condition, particularly those who reported an extrinsic motivational style prior to the tasks, were most likely to pursue the easier tasks relative to those in the low controlling condition. There was no effect of the manipulation for boys. The authors suggest that girls' strong social orientation may make them more vulnerable to the particular style of the teacher or parent. Further, while overall boys' and girls' orientations to school do not differ, there is some evidence that girls use more self-regulated learning strategies (defined by the performance of the behaviors themselves, not children's expe-riences of the behaviors), including more goal setting and planning, keeping records and self-monitoring, and environmental structuring (Zimmerman & Martinez-Pons, 1990). Integrating our findings of no differences in overall self-determination for school with these results, we suggest that there may be a less direct link between feelings of self-determination and behavior for girls; girls may be more likely to engage in strategies advocated by the teacher even when they do not feel autonomous themselves. In other words, they may engage in good study behaviors not because they enjoy the topic or wish to learn more, but because they want to please others.

Overall, one is most struck in examining the literature on sex differences by their dearth. Self-determination seems more likely to be a function of indi-vidual differences, the development of which we describe in the next section. This situation is in contrast to that for perceived competence where stronger sex differences, particularly by domain, are observed. For example, boys have significantly higher math and sports ability perceptions than girls, while girls have higher English ability perceptions (Wigfield, Eccles, MacIver, Reuman, & Midgley, 1991). The dynamics of how girls' and boys' self-determination varies as a function of subject area, attributions made for successes and fail-ures, and feedback received is clearly an area needing further investigation.

In light of the convergent findings supporting the benefits of greater self-determination, and in light of the robustness of these findings across gender, it is important to discuss how self-determination develops. The following sec-tions are therefore devoted to considerations of how children move toward greater self-determination for both intrinsically motivated and extrinsically motivated tasks.

THE DEVELOPMENT OF SELF-DETERMINATION

Self-determination, or autonomy, has been considered a stage in some the-ories, with the issue of autonomy tied to a certain age range. For example, though he discussed all developmental issues as negotiated over the life span, Erikson (1950) identified autonomy vs. shame and doubt as a stage dur-ing the second year of life. Others have identified autonomy as an issue nego-tiated primarily during adolescence (Freud, 1958). Our conceptualization of self-determination, by contrast, views self-determination as a life-long issue and as an innate need shared by individuals throughout the life course. As such, self-determination is as applicable to the newborn baby as it is to the elderly adult. Consistent with this notion, our approach is not to focus on a particular age or stage in understanding the development of self-determina-tion, but to focus instead on the process by which individuals move toward a greater sense of self-determination in their activities and behaviors. Such movement is the result of a dialectic between an active organism and a dynamic environment, such that the environment not only acts on the individual, but is also shaped by the individual. We will explicate this process separately for intrinsic and extrinsic motivation.

Intrinsic Motivation

Self-determination theory posits that humans have innate needs for self-determination (or autonomy), competence, and relatedness. This is an assumption of the theory that, though not refutable itself, leads to a set of hypotheses that can be empirically evaluated. Behind behaviors oriented to fulfilling these needs is an energy source called intrinsic motivation. Intrinsic motivation is the energy source that fuels growth and development and participation in activities that satisfy innate needs. Thus, individuals are born with intrinsic motivation to exercise their abilities, develop skills, and master both their internal and external environments. Such a view is consistent with many organismic theories, which suggest that development is at least partially energized by the developing individual. For example, Piaget (1952) suggested that individuals naturally elaborate their structures. One difference between the theories, however, is that self-determination theory specifies the source of this elaboration and growth— in this case, intrinsic motivation.

If intrinsic motivation fuels organismic growth and development, then what facilitates intrinsic motivation? According to this theory, individuals are born with intrinsic motivation. We see examples of such inborn motivation in the curiosity and exploration of even newborn infants. While clearly children are born with intrinsic motivation, however, the actual levels of intrinsic motivation they express for particular activities can be differentially enhanced or undermined by a variety of factors. First, to express intrinsic motivation, individuals require opportunities to exercise their natural propensities, and the environment must afford such opportunities. In particular, there must be opportunities that provide optimal challenge so that children can stretch themselves in the zone of proximal development (Vygotsky, 1978). Second, the environment must allow children to master their environments autonomously, i.e., the environment must support children's autonomy. We discuss each of these issues in turn.

Optimal Challenge

There is much evidence that intrinsic motivation is facilitated when tasks to be pursued are optimally challenging, or just above the current level of ability. Danner and Lonky (1981) used the Piagetian model to determine the cognitive complexity of three tasks. Children were assessed to see which Piagetian level they were at and then given opportunities to engage with the three tasks. The amount of time children engaged in the tasks was recorded unobtrusively. These authors found that children engaged in and described as most interesting the task that was one step ahead of their pretested level. Harter (1978) similarly found that, given the choice, children worked on and found most enjoyable tasks that were just above their current ability level rather than too easy or too hard. Csikszentmihalyi's (1975) work suggests that people experience flow, involved periods of high attention, and smooth action when their skills match the challenges posed by the activities, that is, when the activities are optimally challenging.

Having said that the affordance of optimal challenges is crucial for children to exercise their self-determination, we would like to make the additional point that the content of those challenges will vary greatly across cultures. For example, opportunities to increase hunting skills may be available and socially valued in some cultures, cooking skills may be highly valued in others. Further, within the same culture, opportunities provided within families certainly differ. In some homes, sports are valued and available, while in others, musical activities might be most accessible. Thus, a critical ingredient for children's intrinsic motivation is the provision of optimal challenges in activities that are interesting to them, but the particular pool of activities from which children select and identify their interests will differ across cultures, families, neighborhoods, schools, etc.

Even within the same family or school, however, children's level of interest in different activities is a complex function of many factors. Certainly innate talents play a role. For example, though opportunities for singing may be available, not all children are given to musical abilities, and some may become frustrated by the inability to increase their skills. Thus, the particular activities in which children seek out optimal challenges will likely follow from their natural talents and interests. Innate talents and environmental opportunities to exercise capacities are, however, only one set of variables necessary for intrinsic motivation to develop. Such opportunities must be provided in a setting that allows autonomous mastery rather than controlling children's behavior.

The Role of Autonomy Support in Fostering Intrinsic Motivation

Initial studies of the degree to which environments facilitated or undermined intrinsic motivation focused on tangible rewards. In several early studies, it was found that when individuals were rewarded for engaging in an activity, their subsequent motivation to pursue the activity when on their own was attenuated (Deci, 1971). While several studies found this for adults, Lepper and Greene (1975) showed that children who were given a "good player" award for engaging in an art activity spent less time playing with the same art materials in a later free choice session than those given no reward. Many subsequent studies have come to the same conclusion—namely, that rewards change the locus of causality for behavior from internal to external, and thereby undermine intrinsic motivation.

While rewards, deadlines, and other contextual "events" may be quite important in affecting intrinsic motivation, the most salient aspect of the environment is the interpersonal one. Thus, a key factor in intrinsic motivation is likely to be the degree to which adults and others pressure children to behave in particular ways, and solve problems for them, instead of allowing children to solve problems for themselves and supporting their initiations. We will review research on two particular contexts—home and school—later in the chapter.

Differentiating the Level of Motivation

We have discussed how innate talents and contextual factors facilitate intrinsic motivation. However, we have not yet differentiated at what level this occurs. Consider the example of a mathematics problem. We can focus on the quality of motivation for doing this particular math problem at this particular time, or we can take a broader perspective, and consider the child's motivation for the whole domain of math, or even for academic work more generally. At an even broader perspective yet, we can consider the child's tendency to approach all activities in a more or less self-determined way.

Vallerand (1997) has developed a hierarchical model incorporating these three levels—namely, the situational or task, the contextual or domain, and the global or personality. Vallerand and his colleagues have shown that it is possible to measure the degree of self-determination at each level. For example, one can measure motivation for a particular task; one can measure motivation for a series of domains, including academic, leisure, work, and interpersonal relationships; and one can also measure people's general orientation toward approaching the world. People's motivation varies dramatically across domains. Further, motivation for an activity will be a function of social experiences at each level. For example, motivation for a school task will be influenced by the conditions immediately surrounding the task itself (e.g., whether it is presented in a controlling or autonomy-supportive manner), motivation for school, which is a function of one's experiences of autonomy support to control in school settings over time, and one's overall environment (e.g., parents, peers). The individual, then, in this model, is a collection of motivations at different levels.

Presumably, motivation at higher levels affects that at lower levels. For example, motivation in a particular domain will affect task motivation in that domain. Chantel, Guay, and Vallerand (1996), for example, in a sample of adolescents, found that only reported motivation for the educational domain, not the leisure domain, accounted for a significant amount of the variance in motivation for an educational task. In a compelling test of the model, Chantel et al. presented children with a word association task. Half the children were led to believe that the task was related to exercises they had done in their French class. The other half were led to believe that the task was a game similar to ones they engaged in at their leisure. Participants engaged in the task for 20 min. They also completed academic motivation and leisure motivation scales. The extent to which they were self-determined for each domain was calculated.

Results revealed that, in the condition where participants were presented the task as being relevant to education, motivation toward education was the only significant determinant of their motivation for the task. The more self-determined the domain-specific motivation, the more self-determined was the task-specific motivation, as well. Similarly, when the task was presented as a leisure activity, leisure motivation was the only determinant of task motivation.

Most theorists have accepted that self-determination is domain specific. First, average levels of self-determination vary by domain. Research by Graef, Csikszentmihalyi, and Gianninno (1983) showed high levels of extrinsic motivation for work and household chores, but high levels of intrinsic motivation for meals and socialization with friends. Further, individual differences in self-determination clearly depend on the context in that domain.

In summary, we have thus far discussed the development of intrinsic motivation. We have seen how intrinsic motivation, as the prototype of self-determination, fuels organismic growth and development, and is facilitated by opportunities for optimal challenge and by environmental support for autonomy. Additionally, we have explored hierarchically organized levels of motivation, noting that individuals have an overall tendency to be more or less self-determined, and that they express domain-specific motivation within that overall tendency and task-specific motivation within domains. It is now time to turn our attention to extrinsic motivation.

Facilitating Self-Determination for Extrinsically Motivated Activities

How do children move along the continuum of self-determination described earlier? Within the sphere of extrinsic motivation, movement from less to more self-determined regulation of behavior occurs through the process of internalization (Kelman, 1961; Schaefer, 1968). Internalization is the process through which behaviors that were originally externally regulated and non-self-determined are taken in by the individual and transformed into personally valued, self-determined behaviors. For example, while initially a child may clean his room because he is not allowed to go outside until it is clean, he may, over time, see the benefits of a clean room (being able to find his toys), and take on the value of a clean room himself. Then, room cleaning will be self-initiated and choicefully conducted.

How does this process occur? Movement toward greater self-determination is seen as a natural process, part of the organism's innate tendency to master the environment and integrate aspects of it with aspects of the self. As a natural process of growth, development, and mastery, the process of internalization is theorized to be energized by intrinsic motivation. Thus, children naturally internalize behaviors and values around them, and progressively integrate them.

While the process of internalization is a natural one, because it is energized by intrinsic motivation, it is subject to many of the same factors that undermine intrinsic motivation. Thus, the internalization process will be impeded by strong controls in the environment. Controlling environments undermine the active process of internalization and keep regulation tied to external contingencies. Autonomy supportive environments, on the other hand, facilitate the process of internalization and encourage movement toward more autonomous forms of self-regulation.

The process of internalization, however, requires more than autonomy support. First, the content to be internalized must be meaningful and understandable to the child. Thus, the rationales parents provide that they hope children will internalize must be age appropriate and clear. Rules and guidelines cannot be too complex and must match the cognitive level of the child. For example, children at age 5 cannot understand the value of a clean room for the houses they will manage as adults because they are unable to imagine themselves in the distant future. A more reasonable rationale for a young child might be that a clean room will allow them space to play on the floor. Further, because children have needs to be connected to others, internalization will be most likely when the interpersonal context is characterized by warm, involved caretakers. Such connections with others lead children to actively take on the values and behaviors modeled or advocated by those others.

Thus far, we have argued that children are intrinsically motivated to explore and master their environments and to internalize the regulation of extrinsically motivating activities. They require no prompting to engage in these natural processes of growth and development. According to self-determination theory, however, particular contexts can differentially facilitate or thwart these processes, depending on the extent to which they fulfill children's needs through the provision of autonomy support, structure, and involvement. Looking at two primary socializing contexts in children's lives—school and home—one may ask, "What is the evidence that the fulfillment of children's psychological needs facilitates positive self-determination?" We first review evidence relevant to the facilitative school context, and then the home environment.

Facilitating Self-Determination in School

Using the "Problems in School" questionnaire, Deci, Schwartz, Sheinman, and Ryan (1981) showed that school teachers vary along a dimension of a control vs. autonomy orientation in their teaching styles. Self-determination theory would predict that the classroom environment provided by autonomy-oriented teachers would be more facilitative of children's motivation and self-determination than that provided by control-oriented teachers. Consistent with the theory, late elementary school students who had more autonomy-oriented teachers showed greater perceived competence and greater intrinsic motivation than students of control-oriented teachers (Deci, Schwartz, Sheinman, & Ryan, 1981). Grolnick and Ryan (1989) examined changes in children's regulatory styles over a 5-month period, as a function of their teachers' attitudes toward autonomy support vs. control. Children in classrooms of autonomy-oriented teachers increased more in their identification with the value of achievement-related behaviors than did students in classrooms of more control-oriented teachers. Furthermore, within classrooms, children who were reported by their teachers to be less pressured and to be allowed to take more responsibility were more likely to report self-determined styles of regulation at the follow-up assessment. Thus, teachers whose classroom style is supportive of student autonomy have students who are more intrinsically interested in pursuing their schoolwork and who are more autonomously self-regulating with regard to achievement than students of more controlling teachers.

While teachers' styles on the dimension of autonomy to control can be reliably measured (Deci, Schwartz, Sheinman, & Ryan, 1981) and show associations with important student outcomes, these styles are not necessarily perceived by all children in the same way. Differences in children's perceptions are directly relevant to questions of facilitative school contexts, as it is not some invariant property of a teacher's style alone that is thought to affect student motivation and self-determination, but rather the functional significance of that style for the individuals exposed to it (Ryan & Grolnick, 1986). Ryan and Grolnick (1986) demonstrated this point in an investigation of children's perceptions of their classrooms as having an "origin climate" (i.e., autonomy supportive) or a "pawn climate" (i.e., controlling; deCharms, 1976). The 140 participants were from nine different classrooms, yet even children within a single classroom varied on their ratings of the origin vs. pawn climate of their classroom. Moreover, these individual differences in perception of the classroom climate were related to a variety of school-relevant outcomes. Specifically, children who perceived their classrooms as having a more origin climate also reported greater self-worth, perceived competence, and mastery motivation. These students also reported greater internal control over outcomes, and a better general understanding of who or what controls outcomes. While a significant amount of the variance in school-relevant outcomes was also explained by classroom effects, these results make the important point that children bring their past histories and interpretive lenses to bear on what they encounter in the classroom. Thus, the classroom can be said to represent both a shared and a unique context for each child. In both its shared and unique respects, however, the autonomy orientation of the teacher or the students' perceived origin climate are associated with more positive school-related outcomes for children than are teachers' control orientations or children's perceptions of a pawn climate.

Beyond the evidence that the overall orientation of the teacher or the overall perception of the student facilitates positive school outcomes, there is further evidence that the relative degree of autonomy support vs. control in the way a particular task is introduced can also facilitate or undermine school-relevant outcomes. For example, even the brief provision of autonomy support and structure by a researcher as part of an experimental manipulation was sufficient to result in greater internalization of a boring, monotonous task, as indexed by engagement in the task during a free choice period, as well as greater feelings of freedom and enjoyment during the task (Deci, Eghrari, Patrick, & Leone, 1994). Participants performed the boring task under one of eight conditions, formed by the factorial crossing of the presence vs. absence of three facilitating behaviors: providing a meaningful rationale for the task, acknowledging the participant's boredom, and emphasizing choice. Later, participants were measured on how much time they voluntarily spent engaging in the task when they had not been asked to, on their reports of feeling freedom and enjoyment in the task, and on how important they rated the task. Since the task was uninteresting, it was reasoned that those who engaged in it during the free choice period did so because they had internalized the value of the activity. In fact, the participants who originally performed the task in the presence of more of the facilitating behaviors subsequently spent more free time voluntarily performing the task, and reported more positive feelings than did the participants whose conditions included fewer of the facilitating behaviors. Thus, providing a rationale (structure) and supporting participants' autonomy by reflecting their feelings increased the likelihood that a regulation would be internalized. Grolnick and Ryan (1987) compared the learning of groups of children who had been introduced to a reading comprehension and recall task in either a controlling or a noncontrolling way. The children who learned under the controlling condition showed poorer conceptual learning as well as greater deterioration in rote recall at 1-week follow-up than their peers who learned in the noncontrolling condition. Thus, presenting a task in a noncontrolling way appears to increase internalization of regulation and integration of material, presumably by increasing self-determination.

Other research relevant to motivational outcomes, although conducted from within other theoretical frameworks, has produced findings consistent with self-determination theory's predictions. For example, children who are experimentally induced to focus on performance goals, given the choice, prefer to work on relatively easy problems that will safeguard their chances of performing well. By contrast, children who are experimentally induced to focus on learning goals tend to select progressively more challenging problems, thus striving to extend their own abilities, and ultimately performing better than their performance-focused peers (Dweck & Leggett, 1988).

Viewing these findings from within self-determination theory, we can understand a performance orientation as communicating to children that the important goals of school are getting good grades and high scores, and earning the teacher's praise by showing how smart one is. This orientation may foster in children an external style of regulation with regard to their schoolwork, since it encourages them to do their work for the sake of the reward (e.g., the praise) instead of for reasons that are more identified (e.g., schoolwork is important to me because it is in line with my aspiration of becoming an engineer) or intrinsic (e.g., I do my schoolwork because I love to learn new things). Children focused on performance would therefore be expected to choose easy problems that virtually guarantee them a strong performance and the external reward of praise. A learning orientation, by contrast, may communicate to children that the important goals of school are challenging oneself and striving to master new skills. This orientation would foster more autonomous styles of regulation in children, as it suggests that the very activity of learning, with no separable external reward or goal, is worth doing for its own sake. Thus, these children would be unafraid to try new and challenging problems, and would indeed seek them out for the intrinsic enjoyment of learning and mastering new skills.

Facilitating Self-Determination at Home

Despite the many differences between teacher–student relationships and parent–child relationships, the same stylistic dimensions are beneficial to children in both contexts. Just as teachers' autonomy support is associated with children's greater self-determination and positive school-related outcomes, parental autonomy support, too, is associated with greater self-determination and positive motivational and socialization-relevant outcomes. In a study of infant mastery motivation, for example, infants whose mothers supported their autonomy explored more and showed more persistence at a play task than did their peers whose mothers were controlling (Grolnick, Bridges, & Frodi, 1984). In another study, 5- and 6-year-old children played with their mothers at building/construction tasks. Children whose mothers were more autonomy supportive during the joint play session later showed greater intrinsic motivation to engage with the tasks when alone (Deci, Driver, Hotchkiss, Robbins, & Wilson, 1993).

Parental autonomy support, as assessed by both children's reports and observer ratings, was associated with children's more autonomous styles of self-regulation, greater competence in school, higher school achievement, fewer acting out problems in school, and decreased likelihood of learning difficulties (Grolnick & Ryan, 1989; Grolnick, Ryan, & Deci, 1991). In addition, parental autonomy support and involvement have been associated with children's greater control understanding with regard to school outcomes (Grolnick, Ryan, & Deci, 1991) and more nurturant object representations (Avery & Ryan, 1988).

Grolnick and Ryan (1989) conducted individual interviews with 114 mothers and fathers of third through sixth grade children regarding the ways in which these parents motivated their children to engage in school-related activities like homework. Data yielded from independent ratings of the interviews were then related to classroom data collected on the children. Parental autonomy support was associated with children's reports of autonomous self-regulation, with teacher ratings of the students' competence and adjustment, and with the children's grades and achievement scores. Furthermore, parents who were more autonomy oriented had children who were less likely, by teacher report, to act out in school, and less likely to have learning difficulties. Of course, in this and other studies, the direction of effects is unclear. While parents rated as controlling may undermine children's self-regulation, children who are lower in self-regulation may pull for more control from their parents. Undoubtedly, the relations uncovered are a result of bidirectional and cyclical pathways.

Grolnick, Ryan, and Deci (1991) tested whether children's motivation mediates the relationship between parenting environment and school-related outcomes. They found that children who rated their parents as more autonomy supportive and involved showed more autonomous regulation in school, higher perceived competence, and greater control understanding with regard to school outcomes. The children's motives and perceptions, in turn, predicted school achievement.

Avery and Ryan (1988) collected data on late-elementary age, urban, minority children with regard to their reports of parental autonomy support and involvement, their object representations of their parents as measured by projective tests, and their classroom adjustment. Higher ratings of parental autonomy support and involvement were associated with more nurturant object representations, and object representations were, in turn, associated with better classroom adjustment.

In a recently completed study (Grolnick, Gurland, DeCourcey, & Jacob (in press), mothers interacted with their third grade children on two homework-like tasks—a poem task and a map task. The children then worked on similar tasks alone, without having their mothers available. The study focused on both contextual factors and individual differences in understanding how autonomy supportive vs. controlling mothers would be in interacting with their children in the laboratory. Even more pertinent to our current discussion, however, is that the study also investigated the relation between mothers' autonomy support vs. control in interacting with their children and their children's subsequent (later in the same session) performance on the school-like tasks when they were alone. Specifically, we predicted that children whose mothers were more controlling during the parent–child interaction would be less likely to have internalized the information they worked on with their mothers and would therefore be less able on similar tasks when on their own. Indeed, consistent with our prediction, mothers who were more autonomy supportive during the task had children who wrote more accurate quatrain poems when they were alone. Further, we were interested in whether mothers' levels of controllingness would be related to the creativity of the poems children wrote when on their own. Creativity has been linked to intrinsic motivation in that it requires an openness, freedom of expression, and flexibility characteristic of an autonomous orientation (Amabile, 1983). Consistent with predictions, mothers who were more autonomy supportive during the task had children who later wrote more creative poems. This result held even when statistically controlling for children's competence in school (i.e., children's grades).

Such cooperation on homework-like tasks is one way in which parents can be involved in their children's schooling and create a facilitative context for the interplay between home and school. A variety of other forms of parent involvement have also been studied, and found to affect children's self-determination. Grolnick and Slowiaczek (1994) delineated three types of parental involvement in children's schooling: behavior (e.g., attending a school play or open house), cognitive/intellectual (e.g., visiting a museum), and personal (e.g., expressing positive feelings toward the child's school experience). Their findings supported a mediational model in which the relation between two types of involvement, behavioral and cognitive/intellectual, and children's school performance was mediated by the motivational resources of perceived competence and control understanding.

In summary, evidence from a multitude of studies supports the idea that at school and at home, the provision of autonomy support, structure, and involvement facilitates children's self-determination and helps them move toward more autonomous forms of regulation for extrinsically motivated tasks. Further, we have seen that greater self-determination is associated with more positive behavior and adjustment-related outcomes for children. To illustrate how the development of self-determination actually plays out in children's lives, we now take a closer look at self-determination during critical transitions in children's lives, and then address questions regarding the mutability of self-determination across contexts.

SELF-DETERMINATION AND TRANSITIONS

Researchers have defined transitions in diverse ways. Across theories, however, most agree that transitions involve a life change and that there is the potential for anxiety and distress. One way of minimizing distress is to acknowledge and accommodate to the change involved.

Self-determination is particularly important during times of change because self-determination facilitates problem solving and flexible strategies in new situations. Specifically, individuals who are more self-determined may be more likely to solve problems autonomously and thus adapt more easily.

For children, school transitions are perhaps the most salient transitions. The transition to junior high has, in particular, been described as a point of vulnerability. Occurring when children are simultaneously experiencing biological changes, the transition to junior high often involves movement from a small, intimate setting in which children know their teachers well, to a large bureaucratic institution where children have multiple teachers (Midgley, Feldlaufer, & Eccles, 1988). While there is controversy over whether all or most children experience disruptions in their self-esteem and school adjustment over the transition, it is clear that some children do experience such disruptions. Further, how children weather the transition to junior high has implications for later adjustment at the end of high school and possibly beyond (Eccles, Lord, Roeser, Barber, & Jozefowicz, 1999).

What personal resources facilitate adjustment to the transition? Several studies have found that children's competence, both perceived and actual (grades) can be facilitative. Lord, Eccles, & McCarthy (1996) showed that children with more positive perceptions of themselves in the sixth grade in the academic, peer, and athletic domains, and who saw themselves as physically attractive, showed gains in self-esteem over the transition while others declined. Can self-determination facilitate negotiation of the transition? In one study, we examined predictors of adjustment to the junior high transition in 60 children (Grolnick, Kurowski, Dunlap, & Hevey, 2000). We measured various motivational resources in the children in the spring of sixth grade, and again in the spring of seventh grade. We also collected information on various indicators of adjustment, including grades and behavior problems in the classroom, at the two time points. Among the motivational resources we examined were perceived competence, autonomy, and control understanding. Autonomy was computed by weighting children's levels of different types of self-regulation (which lie along a continuum from less to greater autonomy) and computing the relative autonomy index, which captured children's level of autonomy in school. We found that only children's autonomy in school predicted adjustment to the transition. Children who increased in autonomy from sixth to seventh grade were those who increased in reading and math performance and decreased in learning problems over the same period.

Further, in a more indirect look at autonomy at the transition, we examined family factors that might facilitate adjustment to the transition. In particular, we reasoned that children would make the transition most successfully when their parents provided resources of involvement and autonomy support. In this regard, we were interested both in the effects of levels of these resources parents provided during sixth grade and whether they maintained (or decreased) their levels over the transition. Our results showed strong effects of parental resources in sixth grade. First, higher involvement at sixth grade buffered children against declines in grades and perceived competence over the transition. Mothers who were more autonomy supportive when their children were in sixth grade showed lesser increases in behavior problems across the transition. Further, children of mothers who increased their autonomy support over the transition did not show the same negative declines in self-worth, control understanding and reading grades as did other children. These results are consistent with those of Lord, Eccles, and McCarthy (1994), who showed that adolescents of parents who were attuned to the adolescents' needs for decision making and used democratic decision making practices were less likely to decrease in self-esteem across the transition than those whose parents were less attuned and used fewer democratic practices. Thus, these studies show that when parents provide autonomy support to their children, children are most able to negotiate the transition successfully.

SELF-DETERMINATION IN MULTIPLE CONTEXTS

We have argued that self-determination is key to successful adaptation in multiple domains, including periods of transition in children's lives. But how difficult is it to change self-determination? What is the likelihood that changes in self-determination in one context will generalize to another context? How closely do those contexts have to match? Questions such as these are at the heart of key controversies in the field of motivation—is motivation an individual phenomenon or a property of the individual within context?

One side of this debate lies in the sociocultural approach. Within this approach, the contents of mind—skills, norms and discursive practices—arise in social interaction. The unit of analysis is not the individual but the activities in which the person is engaged, or the activity system. The person is always engaged in a practice and can be understood only in relation to it. For example, both Cole (1998) and Rogoff (1990) describe participation within a community of practice as the appropriate method of understanding internalization or regulation. As such, it would be inappropriate to think about the individual's self-determination outside the particular practice.

In an ongoing study (Grolnick, Sohmer, & Valsiner, 1999), we are combining the motivational and sociocultural approaches to ask some fundamental questions about self-determination. In this study, a group of middle school students are participating in an after-school science program held at Clark University known as the Investigators' Club. The children participating in the study are seventh grade students who, on a variety of indices, are at risk for school problems. These children come to Clark 3 days per week for 15 weeks and engage in active, hands-on activities in which they are the investigators. In the intervention, students are presented with a problem and then make predictions about what will happen. For example, students are asked what will happen to the weight of a soccer ball (increase, decrease, or remain the same) when air is pumped into it. Students then give their theories in a round-robin format. The experiment is then conducted and finally, students engage in a discussion about the outcome. The intervention is designed to provide students with the "tools" of science but in a manner that is motivationally facilitative (i.e., autonomy supportive).

At each session, students complete questionnaires designed to assess their levels of self-determination and perceptions of competence. Our analyses will focus on several key questions. Will students increase in self-determination in the Investigators' Club over time? Will participation in the Investigators' Club lead to changes in self-determination in science class? In school in general? Will these changes be associated with other positive changes including increased grades and engagement in the classroom?

SUMMARY AND CONCLUSIONS

In this chapter, we have explored the development of self-determination in middle childhood and adolescence, noting that while this period is characterized by unique challenges and transitions for children, the development of self-determination is actually equally relevant and important across the life span for individuals of all ages. We now summarize key points from our discussion and offer some parting thoughts.

As discussed, self-determination is the experience of oneself as a volitional initiator of one's own actions. When self-determined, individuals experience choice, feel unencumbered by external pressures, and feel that they are the origins of their behavior. We have seen that the behaviors in which individuals engage can be usefully categorized into those that are intrinsically motivated and those that are extrinsically motivated. Intrinsically motivated behaviors are done out of choice, for their own sake, and are the prototype of self-determination. Extrinsically motivated behaviors can be undertaken with varying levels of self-determination, depending on how those behaviors are regulated.

Intrinsic motivation fuels organismic growth and development, and is facilitated by opportunities for optimal challenge and by contextual autonomy support. Internalization, the process by which individuals move toward greater self-determination for extrinsically motivated activities, is itself intrinsically motivated. That is, people have an innate tendency to master their environments and integrate aspects of it into the self.

The degree to which children are self-determined has important consequences for their achievement, coping, preference for challenge, moral reasoning, and other important outcomes. Greater self-determination is associated with more positive behavior- and adjustment-related outcomes, including at difficult times of transition in children's lives, such as entry to junior high school. Thus, the facilitation of children's self-determination is an important goal of parents and educators.

There is strong evidence that self-determination is facilitated by the provision of autonomy support, structure, and involvement, and that these social-contextual "nutriments" also help children move toward more autonomous forms of regulation for extrinsically motivated tasks. Such findings are largely robust across gender, although much work remains to be done in further exploring whether girls and boys may differ, for example, in their vulnerability to having their self-determination undermined.

We opened this chapter with a description of some hypothetical students who differ in their quality of motivation and level of self-determination for school-related activities. Katie and Corey tend toward the more autonomously regulated (i.e., self-determined) end of the continuum. Katie guides her behavior on the basis of her interests and curiosity. Corey identifies with the value of his schoolwork. Jennifer and Jared, by contrast, tend toward the less self-determined end. Jennifer does not make many choices about her activities, but rather, waits for an adult to guide her. Jared does his work because of external factors, such as grades, instead of for the sake of the activity of learning itself.

The ideas presented in this chapter provide a framework for understanding the differences among these children. They also suggest possible antecedents of the children's different motivational styles, including contextual affordances, as well as individual differences. Furthermore, our discussion of the development of self-determination suggests contextual nutriments that can facilitate children's internalization, and might help Jared and Jennifer become more self-determined for their school behaviors.

Whether children like Jared and Jennifer can become more self-determined for particular activities or domains, however, remains an open question that is currently being addressed with new research projects, such as the Investigators' Club study cited above. Such studies will yield important information about the mutability and generalizability of children's and adolescents' self-determination. Recall, further, the study cited earlier in which children's level of motivation for a new task depended on the domain to which the task had been linked (i.e., whether the children were told the task resembled an exercise from French class vs. a game). Might it be that we can maximize children's self-determination for a new task or a new domain by combining two approaches: providing autonomy support, structure, and involvement to facilitate internalization, and linking the new task or domain to one in which the children are already expressing self-determination?

By pursuing these lines of thinking, and leveraging our knowledge about the development of self-determination, we hope that children's mental health, achievement, preference for challenge, and other outcomes will be positively affected. Further, new studies may teach us ways to intervene with at-risk children to restore their enjoyment of learning and their self-determination around school-related and other tasks. It is encouraging to imagine a classroom of children, fully engaged in their work, following their interests and natural curiosity, and extending themselves, out of a love of learning, beyond the minimum required of them. Such a classroom is the promise of future work on self-determination.

Acknowledgment

The preparation of this chapter was supported by a grant to WSG from the Spencer Foundation.

References

Amabile, T. M. (1983). *The social psychology of creativity*. New York: Springer-Verlag.

Avery, R. R., & Ryan, R. M. (1988). Object relations and ego development: Comparison and correlates in middle childhood. *Journal of Personality*, 547–569.

Boggiano, A. K., Main, D. S., & Katz, P. (1991). Mastery motivation in boys and girls: The role of intrinsic versus extrinsic motivation. *Sex Roles*, 25, 511–520.

Chantel, Y., Guay, F., & Vallerand, R. J. (1996). *A structural analysis of the motivational consequences*: A *test of the specificity hypothesis*. Manuscript in preparation.

Cole, M. (1998). *Cultural psychology: A once and future discipline*. Cambridge, MA: Harvard University Press.

Connell, J. P., & Wellborn, J. G. (1991). Competence, autonomy, and relatedness: A motivational analysis of self-system processes. In M. Gunnar & A. Sroufe (Eds.), *Self-processes in development: Minnesota Symposium on Child Psychology* (Vol. 23). Hillsdale, NJ: Lawrence Erlbaum.Associates.

Csikszentmihalyi, M. (1975). *Beyond boredom and anxiety*. San Francisco: Jossey-Bass.

Danner, F. W., & Lonky, E. (1981). A cognitive–developmental approach to the effects of rewards on intrinsic motivation. *Child Development*, 1043–1052.

deCharms, R. (1968). *Personal causation: The internal affective determinants of behavior*. New York: Academic Press.

deCharms, R. (1976). *Enhancing motivation: Change in the classroom*. New York: Irvington.

Deci, E. L. (1971). Effects of externally mediated rewards on intrinsic motivation. *Journal of Personality and Social Psychology*, 18, 105–115.

Deci, E. L., Driver, R. E., Hotchkiss, L., Robbins, R. J., & Wilson, I. M. (1993). The relation of mothers' controlling vocalizations to children's intrinsic motivation. *Journal of Experimental Child Psychology*, 55, 151–162.

Deci, E. L., Eghrari, H., Patrick, B.C. & Leone, D. R. (1994). Facilitating internalization: The self-determination theory perspective. *Journal of Personality*, 62, 119–142.

Deci, E. L., Nezlek , J., & Sheinman, L. (1981). Characteristics of rewarder and intrinsic motivation of rewardee. *Journal of Personality and Social Psychology*, 40, 1–10..

Deci, E. L., & Ryan, R. M. (1985). *Intrinsic motivation and self-determination in human behavior*. New York: Plenum Press.

Deci, E. L., Schwartz, A. J., Sheinman, L., & Ryan, R. M. (1981). An instrument to assess adults' orientations toward control versus autonomy with children: Reflections on intrinsic motivation and perceived competence. *Journal of Educational Psychology*, 73, 642–650.

Dweck, C. S., & Leggett, E. (1988). A social–cognitive approach to motivation and personality. *Psychological Review*, 95, 256–273.

Eccles, J. S. (1989). Gender roles and women's achievement related decisions. *Psychology of Women Quarterly*, 11, 135–172.

Eccles, J., Adler, T. F., Futterman, R., Goff, S. B., Kaczala, C. M., Meece, J., & Midgley, C. (1983). Expectancies, values and academic behaviors. In J. T. Spence (Ed.), *Achievement and achievement motives* (pp. 75–146). San Francisco: Freeman.

Eccles, J. S., Barber, B., & Jozefowicz, D. M.(1998). Linking gender to educational, occupational, and recreational choices. In W. B. Swann, J. H. Langlois, & L. A. Gilbert (Eds.), *Sexism and stereotypes in modern society: The gender science of Janet Taylor Spence* (pp.153–192). Washington, DC: APA Press.

Eccles, J. S., Lord, S. E., Roeser, R. W., Barber, B. L., & Jozefowicz, D. M. (1999). The association of school transitions in early adolescence with developmental trajectories through high school. In J. Schulenberg, H. Maggs, & K. Hurrelmann (Eds.), *Health risks and developmental transitions during adolescence.* New York: Cambridge University Press.

Erikson, E. H. (1950). *Childhood and society.* New York: Norton.

Freud, A. (1958). Adolescence. In R. S. Eissler, A. Freud, H. Hartmann, and M. Kris (Eds.), *Psychoanalytic study of the child* (Vol. 13, pp. 255–278). New York: International Universities Press.

Gottfried, A. E. (1982). Relationships between academic intrinsic motivation and anxiety in children and adolescents. *Journal of School Psychology, 20,* 205–215.

Gottfried, A. E. (1985). Academic intrinsic motivation in elementary and junior high school students. *Journal of Educational Psychology, 77,* 631–645.

Gottfried, A. E. (1990). Academic intrinsic motivation in young elementary school children. *Journal of Educational Psychology, 82,* 525–538.

Graef, R., Csikszentmihalyi, M., & Gianninno, S. M. (1983). Measuring intrinsic motivation in everyday life. *Leisure Studies, 2,* 155–168.

Grolnick, W. S., Bridges, L., & Frodi, A. (1984). Maternal control style and the mastery motivation of one-year-olds. *Infant Mental Health Journal, 5,* 72–82.

Grolnick, W. S., Gurland, S. DeCourcey, W. M., & Jacob, K. (in press). Antecedents and consequences of mothers' autonomy support: An experimental investigation. *Developmental Psychology.*

Grolnick, W.S., Kurowski, C.O, Dunlap, K. & Hevey, C. (2000). Parental resources and the transition to junior high. *Journal of Research on Adolescence, 10,* 465–488.

Grolnick, W. S., & Ryan, R. M. (1987). Autonomy in children's learning: An experimental and individual difference investigation. *Journal of Personality and Social Psychology, 52,* 890–898.

Grolnick, W. S., & Ryan, R. M. (1989). Parent styles associated with children's self-regulation and competence in school. *Journal of Educational Psychology, 81,* 143–154.

Grolnick, W. S., Ryan, R. M., & Deci, E. L. (1991). The inner resources for school achievement: Motivational mediators of children's perceptions of their parents. *Journal of Educational Psychology, 83,* 508–517.

Grolnick, W. S., & Slowiaczek, M. (1994). Parents' involvement in children's schooling: A multidimensional assessment and motivational model. *Child Development, 65,* 237–252.

Grolnick, W.S., Sohmer, R., & Valsiner, J. (1999). Socializing motivation and academic efficacy: The power of a practice. Grant funded by the Spencer Foundation.

Harter, S. (1978). Pleasure derived from optimal challenge and the effects of extrinsic rewards on children's difficulty level choices. *Child Development, 49,* 788–799.

Harter, S., & Connell, J. P. (1984). A comparison of alternative models of the relationships between academic achievement and children's perceptions of competence, control and motivational orientation. In J. Nicholls (Ed.), *The development of achievement-related cognitions and behaviors.* Greenwich, CT: JAI Press.

Harter, S., & Jackson, B. K. (1992). Trait vs. non-trait conceptualization of intrinsic/extrinsic motivational orientation. *Motivation and Emotion, 16,* 209–231.

Heider, F. (1958). *The psychology of interpersonal relations.* New York: Wiley.

Kelman, H. C. (1961). Processes of attitude change. *Public Opinion Quarterly, 25,* 57–78.

Lepper, M. R., & Greene, D. (1975). Turning play into work: Effects of adult surveillance and extrinsic rewards on children's intrinsic motivation. *Journal of Personality and Social Psychology, 31,* 479–486.

Lord, S., Eccles, J. S., & McCarthy, K. (1994). Risk and protective factors in the transition to junior high school. *Journal of Early Adolescence, 14,* 162–199.

Meece, J. L., Blumenfeld, P. C., & Hoyle, R. H. (1988). Students' goal orientations and cognitive engagement in classroom activities. *Journal of Educational Psychology, 80,* 514–523.

Midgley, C., Feldlaufer, H., & Eccles, J. S. (1988). The transition to junior high school: Beliefs of pre- and post-transition teachers. *Journal of Youth and Adolescence, 17,* 543–562.

Piaget, J. (1952). *The origins of intelligence in children.* New York: International Universities Press.

Pintrich, P. R., & DeGroot, E. V. (1990). Motivational and self-regulated learning components of classroom academic performance. *Journal of Educational Psychology, 82,* 33–40.

Rogoff, B. (1990). *Apprenticeship in thinking: Cognitive development in social context*. New York: Oxford University Press.

Rotter, J. B. (1966). Generalized expectancies for internal versus external control of reinforcement, (pp. 1–28). *Psychological Monographs*, 80 (1,Whole No. 609).

Ryan, R. M., & Connell , J. P. (1989). Perceived locus of causality and internalization: Examining reasons for acting in two domains. *Journal of Personality and Social Psychology*, 57, 739–761.

Ryan, R. M., & Grolnick, W. S. (1986). Origins and pawns in the classroom: Self-report and projective assessments of individual differences in children's perceptions. *Journal of Personality and Social Psychology*, 50, 550–558.

Ryan, R. M., Deci, E. L., & Grolnick, W. S. (1996). Autonomy, relatedness and the self: Their relation to development and psychopathology. In D. Cicchetti & D. J. Cohen (Eds.), *Developmental psychopathology: Vol. 1. Theory and methods* (pp. 618–655). New York: Wiley.

Schaefer, E. S. (1968). A circumplex model for maternal behavior. *Journal of Abnormal and Social Psychology*, 59, 226–235.

Vallerand, R. J. (1997). Toward a hierarchical model of intrinsic and extrinsic motivation. In M. P. Zanna (Ed.), *Advances in Experimental Social Psychology* (pp. 271–360). New York: Academic Press.

Vygotsky, L. S. (1978). *Mind in society: The development of higher mental processes*. Cambridge, MA: Harvard University Press.

Wigfield, A., Eccles, J. S., MacIver, D., Reuman, D. A., & Midgley, C. (1991). Transitions during early adolescence: Changes in children's domain specific self-perceptions and general self-esteem across the transition to junior high school. *Developmental Psychology*, 27, 552–565.

Wigfield, A., Eccles, J. S., Yoon, K. S., Harold, R. D., Arbreton, A. J. A., Freedman-Doan, C., & Blumenfeld, P. C. (1997). Change in children's competence beliefs and subjective task values across the elementary school years: A 3-year study. *Journal of Educational Psychology*, 89, 451–469.

Yee, D. K., & Eccles, J. S. (1988). Parent perceptions and attributions for children's math achievement. *Sex Roles*, 19, 317–333.

Zimmerman, B. J., & Martinez-Pons, M. (1990). Student differences in self-regulated learning: Relation of grade, sex, and giftedness to self-efficacy and strategy use. *Journal of Educational Psychology*, 82, 51–59.

CHAPTER

7

Student Interest and Achievement: Developmental Issues Raised by a Case Study

K. ANN RENNINGER

Swarthmore College, Swarthmore, Pennsylvania

SUZANNE HIDI

Ontario Institutes for Studies in Education of the University of Toronto, Toronto, Canada

In the minds of many, a person's interest is linked to his or her achievement with a particular subject content such as ballet, mathematics, etc. Such links are likely to be appropriate if the type of interest being discussed is a well-developed individual interest (Renninger, 2000; see also Krapp & Fink, 1992). The links are less likely to be accurate if "interest" refers to or is determined solely by measures of evaluation of positive or negative liking, preference, or attraction (Hidi, 2000).

Over the last 10 years, there have been an increasing number of studies which have included the study of interest as an independent variable. Findings from these investigations are sometimes contradictory, possibly because of the various ways in which interest has been conceptualized and measured (Hidi & Harackiewicz, 2000; Renninger, 1998b). Some researchers have equated interest with positive affect that stems from ongoing examination of subject matter, whereas others have equated the positive affect that stems from an initial contact with the same subject matter with interest. The present chapter suggests there are different types of interest and achievement relations, depending on the type of interest a student holds for a subject content. The chapter further suggests students can be supported to develop interest and work with subject content for which they initially have a less-developed interest.

Interest refers to a psychological state of having an affective reaction to and focused attention for particular content and/or the relatively enduring predisposition to re-engage particular classes of objects, events, or ideas (see discussions in Krapp et. al., 1992, 1998; Hidi, et. al., 1992). Various types of interest have been identified. These different types of interest can generally be categorized as assessing situational or individual interest (see discussions in Alexander 1997; Alexander, et. al., 1995; Krapp et. al., 1992, Krapp, 1999; Hidi, 1990; Schiefele, 1991; Renninger, 1990). Situational interest describes those interests that are triggered in the moment, such as by a sudden sound, the opportunity to work with friends on a project, a cartoon illustrating a text. Individual interest refers to a person's relatively enduring predisposition to re-engage and persevere in work with particular content over time.

Although individual interest and intrinsic motivation may appear to describe similar outcomes, including the enjoyment of focused and continued engagement with a task for the sake of the task itself, individual interest refers to a particular person and content relation, whereas intrinsic motivation more typically refers to a person's approach to a range of contents both in the moment and over time (see extended discussions in Hidi, 2000; Hidi & Harackiewicz, 2001, and Renninger, 2000). Both situational interest and individual interest refer to a psychological state of being interested, however they vary in the particular relation of stored knowledge and stored value they hold. A situational interest may involve little knowledge and is not necessarily associated with positive value. It may be triggered in a person who has little information about cloning seeing a video-clip on the subject, or a cartoon of Napoleon in a text about the French Revolution. An individual interest for history, on the other hand, would suggest that a student has both stored knowledge and positive value for history that leads to informed re-engagement and the ability and desire to work with difficulties that might arise (Corno, 1994; Paris & Winograd, 1990; Neumann, 1999; Prenzel, 1992; Renninger, 1989, 1990, 2000). Thus, a student for whom history is a well-developed interest maintains and deepens his or her interest in spite of frustrating or potentially difficult situations such as an ineffective history teacher, a research assignment that requires major revision, and the need to forego another activity in order to take advantage of an unassigned presentation related to topics currently being covered in the history class. Presumably, the student with a well-developed interest has a richer sense about possible questions, directions, etc., at least in part because working through difficulty leads to a stretching of what is known (see discussion in Renninger, 2000).

Although clearly influenced by genetics, the development of interest is supported through the student's interaction with his or her environment. The presence of others who think mathematically, a school in which students are encouraged to ask and pursue curiosity questions in addition to thinking about performance issues, teachers who work to understand what a student comprehends, all extend and constrain the sets of possibilities available to a student (Sansone & Smith, 2000). This role of culture, or what Valsiner (1984) has labeled the zone of potential action, is a significant influence on how and why students connect to particular contents rather than others. Depending on opportunities available and support to pursue particular content, a situational interest may evolve into individual interest (Hidi, 1990; Hidi & Anderson, 1992; Krapp, 1999), or individual interest will become well-developed (Renninger, 2000; Renninger et. al., 2001). It is also the case that some situational interests never become individual interests. Conditions that enable the development of interest include both what the student brings to and what he or she understands the environment to afford (see Renninger, 1989, 1990). If someone points out the humor in the cartoon of Napoleon, for example, there is more likelihood that the cartoon can provide a scaffold to a developing interest for any of a number of possible topics: Napoleon, pompous leaders, cartooning, and so forth. A student's response is a function of prior experience, personal preference, and the lens provided by his or her individual interest.

Almost all students have situational and individual interest for some contents (Travers, 1978). Furthermore, these types of interest may co-occur and evolve, frequently supporting the emergence of other interests. For example, at one time, Sam (a pseudonym) has well-developed interests for soccer, reading, and his friends. In addition, he has a triggered situational interest for the animal behavior project that he has been assigned in his seventh grade science class (Hidi & Baird, 1986; Hidi and Berndorff, 2002; Mitchell, 1993).

The case study of Sam is detailed below in order to: (1) illustrate the relation between student interest and achievement, (2) provide a basis for revisiting research on both interest and achievement motivation; and (3) consider the possibilities and conditions of interest development. These topics are addressed concurrently rather than sequentially. A concluding discussion follows.

In depth analysis of one student focuses attention on the range of interest and achievement relations that characterize student's lives. Sam's case is profiled because the school he attends allows for differences in student interest and the possibility of changed interest for school content.

SAM, A SEVENTH GRADER

Well-Developed Individual Interest and Achievement

Sam is a white, middle-class boy who spends most of his free time training for or playing soccer. Even though he is not supposed to play ball inside his home, he kicks and fools around with balls of all sizes as he moves around his house. Sam can also often be found reading before he goes to sleep, when he wakes up, and when he retrieves something from his room—despite the fact that he has his own reasons to get back downstairs. Sam also enjoys opportunities to hang-out with his friends, and he has many of them. He has friends on the different teams with which he plays; he has friends in the neighborhood, at camp, and at school. Even when he sees friends at school or at practice, Sam communicates with most of them via instant messenging (IM) every day.

Not surprisingly, Sam plays on a premier club soccer team and gets his highest marks in courses that have reading as their basis. More surprising, possibly, is the fact that he is likely to tell everyone that his interest is soccer but would only mention that he did any reading or had friends as an interest, if asked directly.

The fact that Sam identifies himself as having an interest for soccer is age, gender, and culture-appropriate (Bergin, 1999; Föllings-Albers & Hartinger, 1998; Todt & Schreiber, 1998). Sam is a young adolescent male who lives in a culture where recognition of athletes is visible and a regulator of status among young people (Eckert, 1996). That Sam is not aware of his well-developed interest for reading and for his friends is consistent with points made by Renninger (i.e., 1992, 1998, 2000) who suggests that students are not always aware of individual interest—especially if the interest in question is well-developed. Sam knows that he plays soccer better than most, that he likes to read whereas some of his friends have to be bribed to do their summer reading, and that he is more comfortable with people than are others in his age group. However, he does not appear to use information about his interest(s) as a basis for setting goals for himself (Harackiewicz & Elliot, 1993; Pintrich, 2000). Rather, he appears to engage soccer, reading, and his friends—his well-developed interests—without conscious evaluation of expectancy and value (Eccles-Parsons et. al., 1983; Wigfield, 1994; Wigfield and Eccles, 1992). Take, for example, Sam's interest for reading.

> Sam almost always does his reading assignments first. He is surprised that his friends have difficulty preparing for essay tests and sometimes do poorly in Language Arts (reading and writing) and social studies classes. For example, in the car pool one morning, Sam was asked about the meaning of the title of the novel he and the other students had been reading. The other students listened to him and wrote down what he said in their notebooks while Sam found a radio station that he wanted to listen to.
>
> Sam ended up doing very well on the test without either worrying about it or feeling like he needed to study for it. However, as part of the ongoing assignment, Sam had already read the novel very carefully and had written the assigned chapter summaries using far more detail than the other students. Neither his ability to read carefully, nor the quality of his chapter summaries were evaluated. Instead, the teacher checked periodically to see if the summaries had been written. Sam does not feel that he is exerting special effort to write thorough summaries. In fact, he does not seem to be aware that he is doing so.

Sam has characteristics of a mastery-oriented student (Ames, 1992; Dweck & Leggett, 1988). He puts a lot of work into his understanding of the novel and appears confident about his performance on the test. In contrast to students whose motivation might be identified as approach mastery because they have a strong belief in the role of effort (see summary, Linnenbrink & Pintrich, 2000), however, Sam is seemingly unaware that he is exerting effort on the reading assignment because for him reading is a well-developed interest.

> Even though Sam was confident about the test on the book, he is not self-efficacious about all other aspects of his performance. For example, he assumes that his method of approaching the chapter summaries is the same as the other students. His method includes rereading sections of the book as he writes and is not aware that others may not do so. From talking with other students he knows that they regularly finish the chapter summary assignment in about 20 minutes. It sometimes takes him as long as 2 hours to write a summary. He has an inaccurate sense that he is less able than the others as a result.

Thus, while Sam has feelings of self-efficacy and confidence in his test performance (Bandura, 1986; Zimmerman, 2000), he also has doubts about his abilities to process text efficiently. He does not consciously connect the detailed chapter summaries to his successful test performance. It is possible that without feedback on this point, his interest for reading may eventually be negatively affected. Sam may need support and feedback from others in order to stabilize his feelings of self-efficacy and to maintain his interest for reading, even though his interest for reading is well-developed (Renninger, 2000).

There is general agreement in the research literature on interest that heightened attention, concentration, and positive affect characterize the psychological state of relatively enduring interest (e.g., Krapp *et. al.*, 1992; Pekrun, 2000; Prenzel, 1992; Schiefele, 1998). It might also be expected that with heightened attention, concentration, and positive affect or interest, students would have more developed metacognitive strategies and achievement (Zimmerman & Martinez-Pons, 1990). Sam is disciplined in his work with the text but his metacognitive awareness is not what might be expected. He reads, but he is not metacognitively aware that he uses particular strategies to do so, nor does he think that others' strategies are different from his. Moreover, as the information available about his approach to and engagement with soccer suggests, Sam has a variety of challenges with which he is working that are in an ongoing process of being revised. At best, Sam might be said to have an idiosyncratic perception of the utility, importance, and personal relevance of contexts like reading or soccer for which he has a well-developed individual interest (Wigfield & Eccles, 1992). From Sam's perspective, he just plays soccer or reads.

One might wonder about students with less-developed interest for reading who do not prepare detailed chapter summaries, who have not reviewed what they have read, and who then need to cram for the test. For them, the Language Arts teacher's instructional method may be lacking. For them, developing skills in summarization is essential (Hidi & Anderson, 1992), as is reflecting on their approach to and strategies for reading (Beck & McKeown, 2001; Skinner & Belmont, 1993; Zimmerman & Martinez-Pons, 1990).

The divergence between Sam's behaviors and what might have been hypothesized may be related to Sam's having a well-developed, rather than a less-developed interest for reading. He does not need to be motivated to get to a task for which he has a well-developed interest because he is already engaged in and working on the types of challenges it represents.

Less-Developed Interest and Achievement

In all likelihood because Sam has effective-enough strategies and reading is a well-developed interest, there is little contradiction for him between what he wants to do when he is working on preparing chapter summaries and what he is supposed to do (Krapp, 1993). The lack of explicit direction and feed-back means that Sam experiences the writing of chapter summaries as something that he generates on his own. In this way, the assignment may be quite effective for Sam. However, Sam's work with the assigned novel and required chapter summaries can be distinguished from other learning that he is required to do in school, such as the science project for which he has only a triggered situational interest.

> In science class, Sam and two other boys chose to study the Indonesian Box Turtle because a teacher in the next room had one and it meant that they did not have to locate an animal to study.
>   The group's assignment was an open one, with the expectation that groups of three students would work together to care for an animal, write daily observations, and con-duct an experiment. The goals of their work and the expectation for the final write-up were laid out in rubric. Sam ended up volunteering to keep the turtle over the two weekends of the project, because one boy's parents are separated and he shuttles between homes, and the other boy was preparing for his Bar Mitzvah. The first week-end, Sam had to be reminded to do the feeding and observations keeping the turtle entailed, but once he did he seemed amused that his cat sat up on the table and watched the turtle too. He also noticed that as the turtle got comfortable in its new location, it started moving around, looked back at him or the cat and turned its head when spoken to. The second morning after observing that the turtle had trouble nego-tiating the stick in the aquarium and needed to be lifted into the Tupperware pool that he and his group had fashioned, Sam got some soil from the garden and built the tur-tle a ramp to get into the water. Much to Sam's delight, the turtle not only used the ramp but did so repeatedly. The turtle swam and spent a good deal of time in the water for the rest of the weekend.

Sam took the turtle home because the other boys could not, and he had to be reminded to do the assigned observations (i.e., what and how much the turtle ate, how much the turtle weighed). Given support to do the required observations, however, his situational interest was triggered by the cat's attentativeness, the turtle's responsiveness, and the turtle's need for a ramp. His decision to get soil and build a ramp for the turtle was rewarded by the turtle's use of the ramp.

Even though they held situational interest, each of Sam's connections to the science project were tenuous. Together these connections may have made the project more palatable but they did not appear to push Sam to engage seriously with the deeper purposes of the project. They had little to do with understanding the life cycle generally, or the Indonesian Box Turtle more specifically. At this point in the project, Sam was focused on getting aspects of the task done (e.g., feeding the turtle).

Support from the environment does appear to have initiated Sam's re-engagement with the project, however, and facilitated his finding a connection to it (Bergin, 1999; Gutherie & Cox, 2001). Without this support, it is unlikely that Sam would have noticed the cat's attentiveness or the turtle's need for a ramp.

Sam clearly can attend to, or connect with school content and does. The type of connection he makes to this kind of assigned project for which he has a less-developed interest, however, is related to his sense of its purpose. Sam needed both teacher and parental input about the project's goals and his immediate obligations (e.g. taking responsibility for the turtle observation over the weekend).

> The next weekend, Sam's parents suggested putting the turtle on the back porch so it did not smell up the house. However, the turtle never seemed to acclimatize. It remained hidden in a corner of the little house the boys had fashioned for it in the aquarium. Sam was very concerned that maybe the turtle was dying. He worried that the turtle's death would mean that he and his group would fail the project. He was also concerned that the turtle belonged to another teacher (the one he would have next year) and that that teacher would "kill him" for not taking care of the turtle. Sam checked on the turtle almost continuously, offering it more food and more water but his notes indicated that none of these efforts made any difference.
>
> When he went back to school Monday, he got his group together, explained the situation, and they all went to talk with the science teacher in whose room the turtle normally lived. The science teacher told them that the turtle looked like it was healthy. He suggested taking the turtle out of the aquarium for a bit and allowing it to crawl around on the grass outside. Outside on the grass, the turtle did start to move and moved very quickly.
>
> Sam was fascinated by how much faster the turtle moved on the grass outside. He and his group decided to clock the distance and the time of the turtle's movements and then devised a set of experiments to assess the turtle's ability to climb. Sam particularly enjoyed creating conditions to test the turtle's ability to climb. Based on information his dad located for him on the Internet, Sam later figured out that turtle probably did not move when it was put on the porch because the weather had been cool over the weekend. This type of turtle preferred to be warm.

It may have been predictable that the aspects of the project with the turtle that captured Sam's attention centered on conditions of movement and activity. He may have identified in some way with the turtle's speed and agility. He definitely found the increased activity of the turtle on the grass engrossing, and it was on this that he focused his subsequent observations and hypothesis testing. Sam also felt responsible for the turtle the weekend that it appeared to have stopped moving, however. The situational interest that the possible death of the turtle triggered probably caused him to spend more time focusing on the turtle and the conditions it needed for survival, in turn, priming him for being so attentive to the turtle's movement once he and the group had a lead on what the turtle needed.

Importantly, Sam's situational interest was triggered by a negative feeling, his anxiety (Iran-Nejad, 1987; Pekrun, 2000; Hidi & Harackiewicz, 2000). His anxiety led him to begin assuming responsibility for the turtle without being reminded to do so. He was worried that the turtle might die. With a purpose and autonomous action (Deci & Ryan, 1985, 1987; Krapp, 2000; Skinner et. al., 1990), however, Sam's feelings became more positive. The information his father found for him contributed to his understanding of the turtle's behavior but his interest for the turtle was now maintained and he no longer needed his parents' support in order to take responsibility for doing the assigned observations and turtle care. Once he began generating questions out of curiosity he was ready to extend his knowledge and this also resulted in the kind of valuing that also led him to return to the project on his own (see discussion in Renninger, 2000).

> Sam and the other two boys had each requested to work with the Box Turtle, although there was little in Sam's past experiences that might have predicted this choice. Since all groups of students worked with different animals, this meant that no group had exactly the same sets of observations or experiments to conduct. Thus, Sam and his group were responsible for figuring out how to work with the turtle themselves.

Faced with students like Sam who have little interest for their subject matter, a key issue for teachers is how to establish open-ended enough tasks that students both want to do and through which they will do substantial learning. Tasks that fit this description are typically complex, may focus on real problems, and lead students to use and develop skills through work with multiple resources, including peers (Blumenfeld et. al., 1991; Brown et. al., 1989; Resnick, 1987; Bransford et. al., 1999). The design of the science project Sam was assigned is an example of this type of project. Although it held little interest for him initially, it did involve working with friends, which for him was a well-developed interest. As the project evolved, others (parents, teachers, and peers) provided him with the kind of support or scaffolding that meant that Sam was able to pick up on the instances of situational interest the project afforded (Hidi, 1990; Mitchell, 1993), and that his situational interest was maintained.

> Sam's group received high marks on their turtle project. Sam had even chosen to miss a soccer practice so he could work on the written report that was required. The group worked over a weekend and after school for two nights in order to write their report. They talked about the effort they were expending and that they were doing a good job. One of the boys supervised the proofreading, redrafting and development of each section of the paper, and its alignment when printed out. Sam did his part to type, develop the content, and ensure that their copy was polished. He also cleaned up the aquarium for their final presentation, which now included a broccoli plant he had brought in from home in order to make the aquarium look more like the rice paddies of the turtle's homeland.

The type of interest a student holds for a given subject content appears to be related to both his or her activity and achievement. Even though Sam started out with little interest for the science project, he became attentive to the turtle, and ended up voluntarily spending long hours perfecting the report. He had the support of the other boys to continue working on the project and the intensity of the effort they put into it was buoyed by their sense that what they were doing was good. Sam had also identified turtle movement as a meaningful aspect of turtle behavior and had attempted to study it systematically, which also meant that he had something to write about in the report.

Later, however, Sam commented that even though their group got high marks on the project, he was not sure that all of the time it required was worth it. For him, the science project represented a qualitatively different type of engagement from those for which he has a well-developed interest.

Characteristics of Interest and Achievement

Sam's case suggests that the interest-achievement relation differs depending upon the type of interest a student holds. Even though Sam's interest for the science project was maintained, and he prioritized it over soccer for 1 week, he was also conscious of the time that he spent on the project.

Sam is most successful with subject contents for which he has a well-developed interest, in the sense that he has a sustained ability to work at and be challenged by these activities. Sam does not appear to need explicit target or academic goals (Linnenbrink & Pintrich, 2000) if he has a well-developed interest. Instead, he engages in a fluid process of generating and revising answers to the challenges he sets for himself as the process or flow of his activity (Csikszentmihalyi, 1990). This behavior is like that of expert problem solvers who can, when asked, explain their actions but who would never break down their actions in terms of particular goals to be pursued in the process of doing them because it would hamper their activity (Chi et. al., 1988). In fact, the effort that Sam does exert in the process of playing soccer, reading, or hanging out with friends feels effortless, even though he spends long hours honing his skills as a soccer player, reading, and talking and playing with friends. He enjoys the challenges that these contents represent and likes trouble shooting the complications they introduce. As a result, he does not count the hours that he puts into these activities.

The example of the science project demonstrates that Sam can develop a connection to content for which he has a less-developed interest and that he can experience success if (1) support for him is in place (Hidi et. al., 1998; Goldman et. al., 1998; Renninger, 2000; Sansone & Smith, 2000; Sansone et. al.,

1992) and (2) if he decides to commit some "effort" to developing this con-nection (Corno, 1994; Renninger, in press).

There were some aspects of the science project, like the conditions of the turtle's movement and its climbing ability, that Sam probably would not have realized without input from more expert-others, such as the science teachers and his dad. Furthermore, the final push to finish the paper and clean-up the aquarium might not have been undertaken without both the rubric for a fin-ished product supplied by his teacher and the support and expectations of others, including his peers. In fact, it seems likely that the presence of others working on the turtle project may have accounted for the kind of effort and hard work Sam invested in the project. The other students modeled possible work habits, strategies, and standards, and they, as friends, were also a well-developed interest for Sam.

The issue here is not simply that Sam needed support, but that he got the kind of support that enabled him to move a little closer to understanding life cycles and habitats, as well as what doing a good job on this kind of project involved (Grolnick & Ryan, 1989; Grolnick, Ryan, & Deci, 1991; Jacobs & Eccles, 2000; Skinner, 1995). The kind of support he received from more expert-oth-ers and peers built on his own strengths, needs, and interest. It was concrete and led to inquiry: the Box Turtle is not dying, try taking it outside. The anxi-ety Sam and the other boys felt was alleviated by the teacher's comment and although this pointed them to a next action, they had no idea what to expect.

Without support to further develop his understanding, Sam probably would have enjoyed hanging out with the two other boys in his group. It is unlikely, however, that he would have: (1) generated and answered his own question about the conditions in which the Box Turtle needed to live, (2) embarked on a set of systematic experiments, or (3) had a benchmark for knowing what a fully-developed report of the project entailed. The presence of others on the project provided camaraderie, and guidance from the teach-ers meant that the students worked together, providing each other with feed-back and models as they worked on the different parts of the project (Brown & Campione, 1994; Renninger, 1998a).

Even activities for which a person has a well-developed interest require feedback. For example:

> Sam was mostly fooling around at the school soccer game his dad was able to attend. When questioned about his behavior, Sam readily said that the team really wasn't any good, since they had no defenders. Sam needed his father's help to recognize the chal-lenge of covering both the goal and defense for his school soccer team by himself. His father's comments about what Sam might do helped Sam shift his focus for the remaining school games, even though he continued to need to talk about how hard the situation was when he felt particularly frustrated.

Sam is cognitively challenged by soccer, especially when the level of other team members' play is high. He can also be helped to figure out a way to chal-lenge himself as a soccer player, when the level of other team members' play is low. While these challenges typically involve figuring out how to work with shots that are at different angles, etc., the effects are not only cognitive. Sam appears to experience more extreme feelings about soccer and other subject content for which he has a well-developed interest than he does about other contents without such interest. For Sam, soccer is a mixture of elation, hard work, and frustration. His frustration invariably appears to yield hard thinking about what did not work and why, and to fuel the potential for improved performance (Neumann, 1999; Renninger, 2000).

In contrast, on the science project, Sam did not appear to experience frustration, nor did he seem to have any questions he wanted to answer until the health of the turtle was in question. He was willing to do some work on the project but even with the teacher's rubric for the project, he did not seem to have a clear idea about what the project required him to learn. Once he had questions about the health of the turtle, he began talking with his group about possible experiments, the write-up they were going to do, and its accuracy, etc. He needed content, not just an assignment in order to do work on the project. . He liked the project well enough. He just was not invested in it the same way that he would invest himself in activities for which he has well-developed interest (Renninger, 2000; Renninger, *et. al.*, 2002).

> Sam thinks and talks about plays in soccer games, or practices for his team after they have occurred. Even though Sam has soccer practices every day after school and two evenings a week with his team, he sometimes asks his dad or a friend to go out and practice with him some more, even in the evening under outdoor lights they set up for just this purpose.
>
> Many of the boys on Sam's school soccer team have positive feelings for soccer, including the boy who led Sam's group to redraft and develop the written version of the science report. However, their positive feelings for soccer are not the same as Sam's. Neither is the level of their play (or achievement), and they are not setting the types of challenges for themselves in soccer that Sam sets. And, even though their parents may be providing them with some feedback, this support may not lead them to challenge themselves in soccer and/or they may not have the physical coordination necessary to respond to the kinds of challenges that Sam identifies when he plays soccer.

Students with a less-developed interest for soccer play the game until it is over. Typically, they are not rethinking and analyzing past plays. Similarly, Sam's work with the science project begins as a project that needs to be finished. In the process of working with the other members of his group to explain the experiments they did, Sam appears to get caught up in the fervor of the group's recognition that they were doing a good job with the project (Sansone & Smith, 2000). His triggered situational interest had at this point been maintained.

Sam needed support to focus on what the project required and to find a question to answer. The health of the turtle triggered a situational interest, and once Sam's question about the turtle's health was addressed, he found a new set of questions in the movement of the turtle. This kind of connection to content gave the project more meaning. It also meant that the specification in the rubric to conduct a set of experiments could be met. Once the required set of experiments had meaning, Sam could then focus on achieving the goals laid out for him in the rubric for the project (Baron & Harackiewicz, 2000; Linnenbrink & Pintrich, 2000).

Conditions and Possibilities for Interest Development

> Like other students of his age, in the school he attends, Sam likes receiving good grades and is only beginning to understand that his strengths and interests translate into good grades. Recently, Sam proudly told his parents that his Language Arts teacher told his class that he and another boy had written the best "boy papers" in the seventh grade.

Sam's pride following recognition of his writing may have counterbalanced his concern about being slow when he writes chapter summaries. The extremes of emotion that Sam feels for writing about what he reads have their parallels in the highs and lows that he experiences with soccer. Both reading and soccer are contents of well-developed interest for him. Even when he is worried about the turtle's death or excited by the turtle's ability to move, Sam's does not appear to experience the same range of emotions in his work with the science project.

Recognition provides support for Sam to feel a sense of efficacy in his Language Arts class. It may also have encouraged Sam to continue writing detailed chapter summaries (Sansone & Smith, 2000). The technique of acknowledging strong "boy" papers as well as strong "girl" papers serves to recognize boys for work with a subject that often is considered to be a feminine strength and not necessarily one associated with male athletes. Since boys are often less-developed writers than are girls in middle school (Hidi & Berndorff, 1998, 2002), it may also be important to demonstrate to boys that they can also write well and get recognition for their particular strength as readers and writers (Gottfredson, 1981; Todt & Schreiber, 1998). Like the assignment to write chapter summaries that are then not evaluated, however, this technique may only be an effective approach for students who have a well-developed interests for reading and for writing about what they read. Students who have difficulty with writing and reading may not gain from this approach (Ainley, et. al., submitted).

Although the process of interest development is dependent on students' cognitive development as suggested by Eccles, et. al., (1998), it is also the product of the students' culture, a culture that supports, empowers, and constrains the development of some interests as opposed to others (Anderson & Maehr, 1994; Eccles & Midgley, 1990). By middle school, students begin to have a sense of themselves as strong in particular ways and not in others and their interest for particular topics rather than others begins to emerge (Krapp, 2000; Todt & Schrieber, 1998). Based on Sam's case, it appears that the role of school culture in shaping the emergence and maintenance of interest needs to be acknowledged.

The school Sam attends self-describes as emphasizing excellence in academics, athletics, and the arts. Sam has not really identified himself as having specific subject matter preferences and at this point in his life, he does well in most subjects. In fact, asked to describe the school subjects that he liked best, Sam wrote:

"I have several favorite subjects: reading, math, history, science, sports, woodshop, art, and music. What I like about reading is the fact that I can get a picture in my mind of a story without it being visual. I like math because I am pretty good at it and I like the challenge of tough math problems. I also like history because I like learning about what life was like in past years and we probably can learn some lessons from it. I like science because I like seeing how things work. I like sports because I like getting my energy out and I am pretty good at them. I like woodshop because I like building things. I like art because I like working with my hands and creating objects out of clay. I like music because I like playing all kinds of instruments and I like learning about the different kinds of music in the world."

Sam's listing of his favorite subjects suggests that he could achieve in his work with each of them were he supported to do so. The list is relatively undifferentiated, although he provides reasonable support for the inclusion of each subject on his list. His inclusion of science may seem unwarranted based on his work with the science project—however, it could be that following its completion the project left him with positive feelings and that having maintained a situational interest for science during the project, he now is in the early stages of developing an individual interest for science.

Sam's list of favorite subjects may be relatively undifferentiated because the organization of his school experience does not lead him to compare his work with that of other students. At the school he attends, students talk about the assignments they do and even help each other to do them, but they do so focused on the content, as in the example of Sam's telling his friends about what the title of the novel meant before the Language Arts test. There is little effort to best the next person. When the Language Arts teacher announces that Sam's writing is of high quality, Sam is rightfully proud, although he is not given any details to help him understand for what he was being recognized.

In fact, most of the students in the school Sam attends do well. These are normal students, who distribute in terms of IQ, background, etc. Some have need for support to pursue careful work in some subjects, while others need that support in other subjects. The expectation in this school is that students will do well and there are multiple opportunities to see themselves as doing well. For example, when Sam receives a report card, his teachers assign him five grades for each subject. He is graded on completion of homework assignments, projects, tests, class participation, and concern for community (in-class behavior). As a result, Sam's report card includes a total of 35 grades and written comments. This means he not only has many opportunities to do well, but that it is likely he will do well in some aspect of each subject, and because of this he is positioned to feel efficacious even if he has skills to master.

When students falter, teachers work with them individually during study halls, after and/or before school. It may be that the combination of this approach to providing students with opportunities to do well, the teachers' commitment to having their students learn the material being covered, and the project-oriented nature of the curriculum leads students to develop a broad array of interests and accounts for the number of favorite subjects that Sam lists.

Findings from Rudolph, *et. al.*, (2000) do suggest that students' perceptions of experience are likely to serve as filters through which they process the behaviors and responses of others. Thus, experiencing academic difficulty does not necessarily lead to decreased self-esteem, increased negative affect, or depression unless students are given negative feedback or their academic difficulties set up negative perceptions of academic demands or the way school is perceived. If students' positive feelings and willingness to work with different subjects is facilitated, they may be supported to develop a broader array of interest for school contexts.

As Wigfield (1994) points out, however, competence and task value beliefs are often relatively independent of each other, leading younger students to pursue contents to which they are attracted regardless of how well they are able to do them. Over time, Sam might be expected to begin to attach more value to activities that he is able to do well, in turn enabling himself to maintain a positive sense of self-efficacy and self-esteem (Eccles-Parsons, *et. al.*, 1983; Eccles Wigfield, & Schiefele, 1998; Harter, 1998). An important question that has not been answered is whether ability necessarily maps onto achievement, and/or interest. Most students have the ability necessary to work with grade-level materials. Many of them do not have or know how to seize the opportunity to make the necessary connections to the requirements of the tasks they are assigned (cf., Renninger, 1998a; Schoenfeld, 1992). Ideally, such connections would mean that they could use their own words to describe what a task or project requires and what the realization of it's goals includes. Sam's case suggests that such connections can be facilitated by one or more triggered situational interests.

Until very recently, it has been assumed that there is a decline in interest for school-based subject content among students of Sam's age. Many studies suggest that as children get older, their interest and attitude toward school in general and specific content areas in school begin to decline (Eccles & Wigfield, 1992; Eccles, *et. al.*, 1998; Epstein & McPartland, 1976; Haladyna & Thomas, 1979; Hidi & Harackiewicz, 2000; Gardner, 1998). Decline in interest for school subject content during adolescence has been attributed to a more general developmental process in which adolescents discover new and different pursuits leading to a lessened interest for school content (Eder & Parker, 1987).

Hoffmann (2001) proposes that declines in students' interest for school content may be a commentary on the constraints of curricula that do not include choice during middle school and high school years. She suggests that both elementary school-age students and college students may evidence less decline in their interest for school content then students in middle or high schools because they are given choice about the subjects they study. It may be that choice provides a basis for increasing a student's feelings of autonomy about their learning (Deci & Ryan, 1987; Deci, 1992), although some types of choice are constrained by curricula (Hoffmann & Häussler, 1998; Hoffmann, 2002), parents and their beliefs about students' needs (Jacobs & Eccles, 2000; Sigel, 1982; Sigel, et. al., 1992), as well as by students' perceptions about the utility of subject matter and its personal relevance for them (Wigfield, 1994; Eccles, et. al., 1998).

Although Sam has a fixed set of courses he needs to take, within each of these he was also given opportunities to make choices too (Cordova & Lepper, 1996; Schraw et. al., 1998; Schraw et. al., 2001). For example, he figured out the focus for each of his chapter summaries and also how detailed they would be. He chose the animal on which to focus in science, designed the experiment, and wrote up the report with his group in the way they thought best approximated the directions given in the rubric, and so forth. It may be because of these types of choices, that Sam felt some autonomy about his learning and for this reason he came to identify science as one of his favorite subjects. What he said he liked about science is understanding how things work. In fact, once Sam was able to focus on how the "turtle worked," so to speak, Sam began assuming responsibility for completing the assigned requirements more independently (Baron & Harackiewicz, 2000). Based on findings from Renninger and Shumar (2002), it is likely that it is the combination of autonomy, opportunities to build his knowledge, and interaction with his peers and expert-others that together provided support for his changed perception of science and may have paved the way for him to develop another individual interest (see related discussions in Deci, 1992; Deci & Ryan, 1987, 2002; Krapp, 1998, 1999, 2000).

INTEREST AND ACHIEVEMENT

Sam's case demonstrates that the types of interest a student holds for particular subject content is related to his or her activity and achievement. A student with a well-developed interest for subject matter might be expected to have high achievement whereas a student with a less well-developed interest is less likely to experience high achievement. The student with a triggered situational interest, for example, might only connect to a portion of an assignment. A student with a maintained situational interest or even an emerging individual interest may have positive feelings about the content generally but may not set challenges for him or herself that lead them to stretch their understanding or persevere through frustration to new understanding.

The level of a person's achievement, however, is not necessarily synonymous with the type of interest held. Students with well-developed interest for content will do well, as Sam's case suggests, when they are in schools that emphasize problem posing and problem solving in recognizing achievement. This type of achievement is different from the type of learning and standards for achievement in schools that emphasize more rote methods of instruction. It has been suggested that school cultures contribute to the types of goals students develop (Anderman & Maehr, 1994). It also appears that school culture may influence the development of student interest. In more traditional settings, it is likely there will be students with a well-developed interest for content who are not high achievers and do not connect to the content being taught, and students who are high achievers because they are good at applying algorithms, but who have less-developed interest for the content being covered (Renninger et. al., 2002).

Sam's case was selected as the focus of the present chapter because the school he attends emphasizes student learning. Sam is provided with many different ways to be acknowledged for the work he does and he and his peers share an expectation that school involves finding answers to questions. He is allowed to have and pursue contents of well-developed interest, he is involved with contents for which he has less-developed interest and given opportunities to connect to these.

That Sam cited reading first in describing his favorite subjects is consistent with the findings of Renninger and Wozniak (1985) who reported that young children were more likely to first shift attention, recognize, and recall contents of well-developed individual interest as opposed to contents of less-developed interest. Renninger (1990) interpreted these findings to suggest that well-developed individual interest gates students' attention by mediating to what and how a student attends.

As Sam's case illustrates, the attention and memory that characterizes a well-developed individual interest for subject matter also enables focused work and is characterized by flow-like engagement and strong feelings that are primarily positive. In fact, interest has been associated with the automatic (spontaneous) attention and this may account for why students working with content for which they have a well-developed interest efficiently process information (Hidi, 1990, 1995, 2001).

Sam's work on content for which he has a well-developed individual interest does not feel effortful and he does not necessarily have a target goal, an awareness of utility and importance, unwavering self-efficacy, or developed metacognitive awareness of the strategies he employs. Sam has curiosity questions and pursues challenges that can be quite frustrating in his work with this type of content. Furthermore, Sam's understanding of the conditions and possibilities for continued work with such content is reinforced by others, his school culture, and his own connections to the content(s) in question. Sam is acknowledged as having achieved, and the feedback he receives enables him to continue to stretch his abilities.

Just as important, even though Sam achieves in contents that are of well-developed interest, he does not appear to have a clear sense of what his strengths and strategies are. He does not know why he does not need to study for the test on the novel, or why he was singled out as a good writer. He seems to garner a sense that he is good or smart from his performance and others' recognition of him, and it may be that this is sufficient to lead him to begin to identify with reading (Language Arts) as a subject he likes because he does well in it. On the other hand, despite feelings of efficacy, he also harbors doubts about his abilities and thinks that maybe he is unusually slow.

Sam may doubt his abilities in reading, for example, because he does not have a basis for knowing what an effective performance on the different assignments would look like. On the other hand, it also appears that it is important that he has the opportunity to define for himself how to write a chapter summary and that he may be more thorough in completing it than he would have been were he told exactly what needed to be done.

Sam clearly has some ideas about his abilities to achieve when working with contents of well-developed interest and it appears likely that these provide a foundation for pursuing the challenges he sets for himself with these contents. That he is not always as realistic as he might be in setting these challenges may be influenced by what he wants to be able to do. His ambition and lack of realism may also account for the highs and lows of emotion he appears to experience. In working with content for which he has well-developed individual interest, Sam needs to continue to receive support and feedback that enables him to continue to refine, develop, and sustain his interest.

Sam's case suggests further, however, that interest for subject areas for which a student has less-developed interest can be facilitated (Hidi, 1990, 1995, 2001). In particular, it appears that support for students' attention to and achievement in working with less well-developed interest might usefully include multiple instances of triggered situational interest and the inclusion of individual interest (e.g., opportunities to work with friends).

Sam's work with the animal behavior project for which he had a less-developed interest required a lot of effort, even though the task was broken into discrete chunks and was not onerous. With support as Sam's case suggests, individuals with triggered situational interest can identify meaning for established goals, as well as some utility, importance, and personal relevance. With support they may be positioned to begin shifting their understanding of what a subject area includes and being able to make meaningful connections to the tasks they are assigned. This meaning is not global in the same sense that it appears to be for contents of well-developed interest. Instead, meaning is at least initially attached to singular goals linked to particular questions (i.e., How can I keep the turtle alive? How fast will the turtle move?) generated by the student. Importantly, these questions appear to be elicited by situational interest(s), not through an assignment to develop questions or hypotheses.

In order for Sam to do the project, he needed support to engage the goals (e.g., noting how much food was consumed, what the turtle was fed, weighing the turtle twice a day) and a purpose (keeping the turtle alive) of the project. While there were moments that might have been flow-like such as when the turtle began moving fast and the boys began generating experiments, the project did not evoke strong feelings from him one way or another. It was a school assignment and it needed to be done. He harbored few doubts about his work on the project and felt efficacious enough, probably because he felt confident that he had some peers as collaborators.

Interestingly, even though his interest for the project was less-developed, Sam's type of achievement goals map onto those of the hypothesized approach mastery student as summarized by Linnenbrink and Pintrich (2000). He had strong beliefs in effort—although he did not really link effort to achievement in the sense of success on the project, but rather on project completion. He had adaptive efficacy judgments in the sense that he assumed he could do the project; he just was not particularly concerned about how well he did until there was some question about the turtle's health. He became more self-regulated in his approach to the project, as he had purpose. He clearly persisted to complete the project and expended effort to do so.

Unlike the description of the student with approach mastery goals, however, Sam neither experiences high elation nor low anxiety; and he does not experience high interest and task value for the science project. While Sam has positive feelings for the project and he receives a high mark on it, the quality of his valuing and the nature of the work he is able to do in science is quite different than that undertaken with either soccer or reading. It is likely that Sam's positive feelings about his work on the project would offset any negative associations he might have developed prior to the project for science and/or animal behavior. A critical and unanswered question is whether Sam's positive feelings and the learning that he did undertake in working with the science project made a lasting impact on his learning.

DISCUSSION

It is important to point out that Sam's is one case. Examination of Sam's case was not intended to address all differences between students such as race, ethnicity, gender, or SES. Instead, Sam's case provides a basis for exploring the relation between different types of interest and achievement in a school environment that recognizes differences in interest as part of student learning, and as such allows for its study.

Sam's case underscores the importance of considering the role and type of a student's interest for different subject matter in assessing individual interest, task value, and emotional response. It suggests that interest can develop and that even well-developed interest needs to be supported. It also highlights the importance of recognizing that earlier stages of interest development may map more accurately onto research conducted on achievement motivation because triggered and maintained situational interest, and even emerging individual interest for content, addresses the processes involved in students making connections to content to be learned. Students with well-developed individual interest for subject content, in contrast, have established one or more connections to such content and are engaged in a qualitatively different process of further developing these connections. As such, they tend to be engaged in and get recognized for their achievement—provided that their environment does not constrain the development of their interest and such recognition.

Acknowledgments

We thank Sam his willingness to allow us to examine some of his in- and out-of-school experiences so that we could learn. We appreciate the help of Karina Kacala and Dagamar Berndorff in preparing this chapter for publication; and gratefully acknowledge research support from the Humboldt Foundation, the Joel Dean Foundation, the Social Sciences and Humanities Research Council of Canada, and the Swarthmore College Faculty Research Fund.

References

Ainley, M. D., Hidi, S., & Berndorff, D. (submitted). Interest, learning and the psychological processes that mediate their relationship.

Alexander, P. A. (1997). Mapping the multidimensional nature of domain learning: The interplay of cognitive, motivational, and strategic forces. In M.L. Maehr, & P. R. Pintrich (Eds.), *Advances in motivation and achievement*, Vol. 10 (pp. 213–250). Greenwich, CT: JAI Press.

Alexander, P. A., Jetton, T. L., & Kulikowich, J. M. (1995). Interrelationship of knowledge, interest, and recall: Assessing a model of domain learning. *Journal of Educational Psychology*, 87, 559–575.

Ames, C. (1992). Classrooms: Goals, structures, and student motivation. *Journal of Educational Psychology*, 84, 261–271.

Anderman, E. M., & Maehr, M. L. (1994). Motivation and schooling in the middle grades. *Review of Educational Research*, 64, 287–309.

Bandura, A. (1986). *Social foundations of thought and action: A social cognitive theory*. Englewood Cliffs, NJ: Prentice-Hall.

Barron, K. E., & J. M. Harackiewicz (2000). Achievement goals and optimal motivation: A multiple goals approach. In C. Sansone & J. M. Harackiewicz (Eds.), *Intrinsic and extrinsic motivation: The search for optimal motivation and performance* (pp. 231–256). New York: Academic Press.

Beck, I. L., & McKeown, M. G. (2001). Inviting students into the pursuit of meaning. In K. A. Renninger, & S. E. Wade (Guest Eds.), Student interest and engagement. *Educational Psychology Review*, 13 (3), pp. 225–242.

Bergin, D. A. (1999). Influences on classroom interest. *Educational Psychologist*, 34, 87–98.

Blumenfeld, P., Soloway, E., Marx, R., Krajcik, J., Guzdial, M., & Plinscar, A. (1991). Motivating project-based learning: Sustaining the doing, supporting the learning. *Educational Psychologist*, 26 (3& 4), 369–398.

Brown, A.L., & Campione, J. C. (1994). Guided discovery in a community of learners. In K. McGilly (Ed.), *Classroom lessons* (pp. 229–270). Cambridge, MA: MIT Press.

Brown, J. S., Collins, A., & Duguid, P. (1989). Situated cognition of learning. *Educational Researcher*, 18, 32–42.

Bransford, J. D., Brown, A. L., & Cocking, R. R. (1999). *How people learn: Brain, mind, experience, and school.* Washington, DC: National Academy Press.

Chi, M., Glaser, R., & Farr, M. (Eds.) (1988). *The nature of expertise.* Hillsdale, NJ: Lawrence Erlbaum Associates.

Cordova, D. I., & Lepper, M. R. (1996). Intrinsic motivation and the process of learning: Beneficial effects of contextualization, personalization, and choice. *Journal of Educational Psychology,* 88, 715–730.

Corno, L. (1994). Student volition and education: Outcomes, influences, and practices. In B. J. Zimmerman, & D. H. Schunk (Eds.). *Self-regulation of learning and performance* (pp. 229–254). Hillsdale, NJ: Lawrence Erlbaum Associates.

Csikszentmihalyi, M. (1990). *Flow: The psychology of optimal experience.* New York: Harper Collins.

Deci, E. L. (1992). The relation of interest to the motivation of behavior: A Self-Determination Theory perspective. In K. A. Renninger, S. Hidi, & A. Krapp (Eds.), *The role of interest in learning and development* (pp. 43–70). Hillsdale, NJ: Lawrence Erlbaum Associates.

Deci, E. L., & Ryan, R. M. (1985). *Intrinsic motivation and self-determination in human behavior.* New York: Plenum Press.

Deci, E. L., & Ryan, R. M. (1987). The support of autonomy and the control of behavior. *Journal of Personality and Social Psychology,* 53(6), 1024–1037.

Deci, E. L. & Ryan, R. M. (2000). The "what" and "why" of goal pursuits: Human needs and the self-determination of behavior. *Psychologica Inquiry,* 11 (4), 227–268.

Dweck, C. S., & Leggett, E. L. (1988). A social-cognitive approach to motivation and personality. *Psychological Review,* 95, 256–273.

Eccles, J. S. (1993). School and family effects on the ontogeny of adolescents' interests, self-perceptions, and activity choice. In J. Jacobs (Ed.), *Nebraska Symposium on Motivation: Vol. 40. Developmental perspectives on motivation* (pp. 145–208). Lincoln: University of Nebraska Press.

Eccles, J. S., & Midgley, C. (1990). Changes in academic motivation and self-perceptions during early adolescence. In R. Montemayor, G. R., Adams, & T. P. Gullotta (Eds.), *Advances in adolescent development: Vol. 2. From childhood to adolescence* (pp. 134–155). Newbury Park, CA: Sage Publications.

Eccles, J. S., Wigfield, A., & Schiefele, U. (1998). Motivation to succeed. In N. Eisenberg (Ed.), *Social, emotional, and personality development* (vol. 3). In W. Damon (Gen. Ed.), *Handbook of child psychology* (5ᵗʰ ed., pp. 1017–1095). New York: John Wiley & Sons.

Eccles- Parsons, J., Adler, T.F., Futterman, R. Goff, S.B., Kaczala, C.M., Meece, J.L., & Midgley, C. (1983). Expectancies, values, and academic behaviors. In J.T. Spence (Ed.), *Achievement and achievement motivation* (pp. 75–146). San Francisco: Freeman.

Eckert, P. (1989). *Jocks and burnouts: Social categories and identity in the high school.* New York, NY: Teachers College Press.

Eder, D., & Parker, S. (1987). The cultural production and reproduction of gender: The effect of extracurricular activities on peer-group culture. *Sociology of Education,* 60, 200–214.

Epstein, J.L., & McPartland, J.M. (1976). The concept and measurement of the quality of school life. *American Educational Research Journal.* 13, 15–30.

Föllings-Albers, M., & Hartinger, A. (1998). Interest of girls and boys in elementary school. In L. Hoffmann, A. Krapp, K.A. Renninger, & J. Baumert (Eds.), *Interest and learning: Proceedings of the Seeon conference on Interest and Gender* (pp. 175–183). Kiel, Germany: IPN.

Gardner, P. L. (1998). The development of males' and females' interests in science and technology. In L. Hoffmann, A. Krapp, K.A. Renninger, & J. Baumert (Eds.), *Interest and learning: Proceedings of the Seeon conference on Interest and Gender* (pp. 41–58). Kiel, Germany: IPN.

Grolnick, W. S., Deci, E. L., & Ryan, R. M. (1997). Internalization within the family: The self-determination theory perspective. In J. E. Grusec, & L. Kuczynski (Eds.), *Parenting and children's internalization of values: A handbook of contemporary theory* (pp. 135–161). New York: John Wiley & Sons.

Grolnick, W. S., & Ryan, R. M. (1989). Parent styles associated with children's self-regulation and competence in school. *Journal of Educational Psychology,* 81, 143–154.

Gutherie, J. T., & Cox, K. E. (2001). Classroom conditions for motivation and engagement in reading. In K. A. Renninger, & S. E. Wade (Guest Eds.), Student interest and engagement. *Educational Psychology Review,* 13 (3), pp. 283–302.

Haladyna, T., & Thomas, G. (1979). The attitudes of elementary school children toward school and subject matters. *Journal of Experimental Education*. 48, 18–23.

Harackiewicz, J. M., & Elliot, A. J. (1993). Achievement goals and intrinsic motivation. *Journal of Personality and Social Psychology*, 65, 1905–1915.

Harter, S. (1998). The development of self-representations. In N. Eisenberg (Ed.), *Social, emotional, and personality development* (vol. 3). In W. Damon (Gen. Ed.), *Handbook of child psychology* (pp. 553–618). New York: John Wiley & Sons.

Hidi, S. (1990). Interest and its contribution as a mental resource for learning. *Review of Educational Research*, 60, 549–571.

Hidi, S. (1995). A re-examination of the role of attention in learning from text. *Educational Psychology Review*, 7, 323–350.

Hidi, S. (2000). An interest researcher's perspective: The effects of extrinsic and intrinsic factors on motivation. In C. Sansone, & J. M. Harackiewicz (Eds.), *Intrinsic and extrinsic motivation: The search for optimal motivation and performance* (pp. 309–339). New York: Academic Press.

Hidi, S. (2001). Interest, reading, and learning: Theoretical and practical considerations. In K. A. Renninger, & S. E. Wade (Guest Eds.), Student interest and engagement. *Educational Psychology Review*, 13 (3), pp. 191–210.

Hidi, S., & Anderson, V. (1992). Situational interest and its impact on reading and expository writing. In K. A. Renninger, S. Hidi, & A. Krapp (Eds.), *The role of interest in learning and development* (pp. 215–238). Hillsdale, NJ: Lawrence Erlbaum Associates.

Hidi, S., & Baird, W. (1986). Interestingness—a neglected variable in discourse processing. *Cognitive Science*, 10, 179–194.

Hidi, S., & Berndorff, D. (1998). Situational interest and learning. In L. Hoffmann, A. Krapp, K. A. Renninger & J. Baumert (Eds.), *Interest and learning* (pp. 74–90). Kiel, Germany: IPN.

Hidi, S., & Berndorff, D. (2002). Improvements in children's argument writing, interest and self-efficacy: An intervention study. *Learning and Instruction*.

Hidi, S., & Harackiewicz, J. M. (2000). Motivating the academically unmotivated: A critical issue for the 21st century. *Review of Educational Research*. 70, 151–179.

Hidi, S., Renninger, K. A., & Krapp, A. (1992). The present state of interest research. In K. A. Renninger, S. Hidi, & A. Krapp (Eds.), *The role of interest in learning and development* (pp. 433–446). Hillsdale, NJ: Lawrence Erlbaum Associates.

Hidi, S., Weiss, J., Berndorff, D., & Nolan, J. (1998). The role of gender, instruction and a cooperative learning technique in schience education across formal and informal settings. In L. Hoffmann, A. Krapp, K. A. Renninger, & J. Baumert (Eds.), *Interest and learning* (pp. 215–227). Kiel, Germany: IPN.

Hoffmann, L.(2002). Promoting girls' learning and achievement in physics classes for beginners. *Learning and Instruction*.

Hoffmann, L., & Häussler, P. (1998). An intervention project promoting girls' and boys' interest in physics. In L. Hoffmann, A. Krapp, K. A. Renninger, & J. Baumert (Eds.), *Interest and learning* (pp. 301–316). Kiel, Germany: IPN.

Jacobs, J. E., & Eccles, J. S. (2000). Parents, task values, and real-life achievement-related choices. In C. Sansone, & J. M. Harackiewicz (Eds.), *Intrinsic and extrinsic motivation: The search for optimal motivation and performance* (pp. 405–439). New York: Academic Press.

Krapp, A. (1993). Die psychologie lernmotivation. *Zeitschrift für Pädagogik*, 39, 185–206.

Krapp, A. (1998). Entwicklung und Förderung von Interessen im Unterricht. *Psychologie in Erziehung*, 45, 186–203.

Krapp, A. (1999). Interest, motivation, and learning: An educational-psychological perspective. *Learning and Instruction*, 14 (1), 23–40.

Krapp, A. (2000). Interest and human development during adolescence: an educational–psychological approach. In J. Heckhausen (Ed.), *Motivational psychology of human development* (pp. 109–128). London: Elsevier.

Krapp, A., & Fink, B. (1992). The development and function of interests during the critical transition from home to preschool. In K. A. Renninger, S. Hidi, & A. Krapp (Eds.), *The role of interest in learning and development* (pp. 397–429). Hillsdale, NJ: Lawrence Erlbaum Associates.

Krapp, A., Hidi, S., & Renninger, K.A. (1992). Interest, learning, and development (pp. 3-25). In
    K.A. Renninger, S. Hidi, & A. Krapp (Eds.), *The role of interest in learning and development* (pp.
    361–395). Hillsdale, NJ: Lawrence Erlbaum Associates.

Krapp, A., Renninger, K. A., & Hoffmann, L. (1998). Some thoughts about the development of a
    unifying framework for the study of individual interest. In L. Hoffmann, A. Krapp, K. A. Ren-
    ninger, & J. Baumert (Eds.), *Interest and learning* (pp. 455–468). Kiel, Germany: IPN.

Linnenbrink, E.A., & Pintrich, P.R. (2000). Multiple pathways to learning and achievement: The
    role of goal orientation in fostering adaptive motivation, affect, and cognition. In C. Sansone,
    & J. M. Harackiewicz (Eds.), *Intrinsic and extrinsic motivation: The search for optimal motivation and per-
    formance* (pp. 196–230). New York: Academic Press.

Mitchell, M. (1993). Situational interest: Its multifaceted structure in the secondary school math-
    ematics classroom. *Journal of Educational Psychology*, 85(3), 424–436.

Murphy, P. K., & Alexander, P. A. (2000). A motivated exploration of motivation terminology. *Con-
    temporary Educational Psychology*, 25, 3–53.

Neumann, A. (1999, April). *Passionate talk about passionate thought: The view from professors at early mid-
    career.* Paper presented at the 80th-annual meeting of the American Educational Research
    Association. Montreal, Canada.

Paris, S. G., & Winograd, P. W. (1990). How metacognition can promote academic learning and
    instruction. In B. J. Jones & L. Idol. (Eds.), *Dimensions of thinking and cognitive instruction* (pp.
    15–51). Hillsdale, N. J.: Lawrence Erlbaum Associates.

Pekrun, R. (2000). A social-cognitive, control-value theory of achievement emotions. In J. Heck-
    hausen (Ed.), *Motivational psychology of human development.* Oxford, UK: Elsevier.

Pintrich, P.R. (2000). An achievement goal theory perspective on issues in motivation terminol-
    ogy, theory and research. *Contemporary Educational Psychology*, 25, 92–104.

Prenzel, M. (1992). The selective persistence of interest. In K. A. Renninger , S. Hidi, & A. Krapp
    (Eds.), *The role of interest in learning and development* (pp. 71–98). Hillsdale, NJ: Lawrence Erlbaum
    Associates.

Renninger, K. A. (1989). Individual differences in children's play interests. In L.T. Winegar (Ed.),
    Social interaction and the development of children's understanding (pp. 147–172). Norwood, NJ: Ablex.

Renninger, K. A. (1990). Children's play interests, representation, and activity. In R. Fivush & J.
    Hudson (Eds.), *Knowing and remembering in young children* (pp. 127–165), Emory Cognition Series,
    Vol. III. New York, NY: Cambridge University Press.

Renninger, K. A. (1992). Individual interest and development: Implications for theory and prac-
    tice. In K.A. Renninger, S. Hidi, & A. Krapp (Eds.), *The role of interest in learning and development*
    (pp. 361–395). Hillsdale, NJ: Lawrence Erlbaum Associates.

Renninger, K. A. (1998a). Developmental psychology and instruction: Issues from and for prac-
    tice. In I. E. Sigel, & K. A. Renninger (Vol. Eds.), *Child psychology and practice* (vol. 4). In W. Damon
    (Gen. Ed.), *Handbook of child psychology* (5th ed., pp. 211–274). New York: John Wiley & Sons.

Renninger, K. A. (1998b). The roles of individual interest(s) and gender in learning: An overview of
    research on preschool and elementary school-aged children/students. In L. Hoffmann, A. Krapp,
    K. A. Renninger, & J. Baumert (Eds.), *Interest and learning* (pp. 165–174). Kiel, Germany: IPN.

Renninger, K. A. (2000). Individual interest and its implications for understanding intrinsic moti-
    vation. In C. Sansone, & J. M. Harackiewicz (Eds.), *Intrinsic and extrinsic motivation: The search for
    optimal motivation and performance* (pp. 375–407). New York: Academic Press.

Renninger, K. A. (in press). Interest and effort. In J. W. Gutherie (Gen. Ed.), *The encyclopedia of edu-
    cation, Second edition.* New York: Macmillan.

Renninger, K. A., Ewen, L., & A.K. Lasher (2002). Individual interest as context in expository text
    and mathematical word problems. *Learning and Instruction.*

Renninger, K. A., & Shumar, W. (2002). Community building with and for teachers at *The Math
    Forum.* In K. A. Renninger, & W. Shumar (Eds.), *Building virtual communities: Learning and doing in
    cyberspace* (pp. 99–142). New York: Cambridge University Press.

Renninger, K. A., & Wozniak, R. H. (1985). Effect of interest on attentional shift, recognition, and
    recall in young children. *Developmental Psychology*, 21, 624–632.

Rudolph, K. D., Lambert, S.F., Clark, A.G., & Kurlakowsky, K.D. (2001). Negotiating the transition to middle school: The role of self-regulatory processes. *Child Development*, 72 (3), 929–946.

Sansone, C., & Smith, J. L. (2000). Interest and self-regulation: The relation between having to and wanting to. In C. Sansone, & J. M. Harackiewicz (Eds.), *Intrinsic and extrinsic motivation: The search for optimal motivation and performance* (pp. 341–372). New York: Academic Press.

Sansone, C., Weir, C., Harpster, L., & Morgan, C. (1992). Once a boring task always a boring task? Interest as a self-regulatory mechanism. *Journal of Personality and Social Psychology*, 63, 379–390.

Schiefele, U. (1991). Interest, learning, and motivation. *Educational Psychologist*, 26 (3&4), 299–323.

Schiefele, U. (1998). Individual interest and learning-What we know and what we don't know. In L. Hoffmann, A. Krapp, K. A. Renninger, & J. Baumert (Eds.), *Interest and learning* (pp. 91–104). Kiel, Germany: IPN.

Schraw, G., Flowerday, T., & Reisetter, M. (1998). The role of choice in reader engagement. *Journal of Educational Psychology*, 90, 705–714.

Schraw, G., Flowerday, T., & Lehman, S. (2001). Increasing situational interest in the classroom. In K. A. Renninger, & S. E. Wade (Guest Eds.), Student interest and engagement. *Educational Psychology Review*, 13 (3), pp. 211–224.

Sigel, I. E., (1982). The relationship between parental distancing strategies and the child's cognitive behavior. In L. M. Laosa, & I. E. Sigel (Eds.), *Families as learning environments for children* (pp. 47–86). New York: Plenum Press.

Sigel, I. E., McGillicuddy-DeLisi, A.V., & Goodnow, J. J. (1992). In I. E. Sigel (Ed.), *Parental belief systems: The psychological consequences for children*. Hillsdale, NJ: Erlbaum.

Skinner, E. A. (1995). *Perceived control, motivation, and coping*. Thousand Oaks, CA: Sage.

Skinner, E.A., & Belmont, M.J. (1993). Motivation in the classroom: Reciprocal effects of teacher behavior and student engagement across the school year. *Journal of Educational Psychology*, 85, 571–581.

Skinner, E. A., Wellborn, J. G., & Connell, J. P. (1990). What it takes to do well in school and whether I've got it: A process model of perceived control and children's engagement and achievement in school. *Journal of Educational Psychology*, 82, 22–32.

Todt, E., & Schreiber, S. (1998). Development of interests. In L. Hoffmann, A. Krapp, K. A. Renninger, & J. Baumert (Eds.), *Interest and learning: Proceedings of the Seeon Conference on Interest and Gender* (pp. 25–41). Kiel, Germany: IPN.

Travers, R. M. W. (1978). *Children's interests*. Kalamazoo, MI: Michigan State University, College of Education.

Valsiner, J. (1984). Construction of the zone of proximal development in adult-child joint action: The socialization of meals. In B. Rogoff, & J.V. Wertsch (Eds.), *Children's learning in the "Zone of Proximal Development"* (pp. 65–76). New Directions for Child Development. San Francisco: Jossey-Bass.

Wigfield, A. (1994). Expectancy-value theory of achievement motivation: A developmental perspective. *Educational Psychology Review*, 6, 49–78.

Wigfield, A., & Eccles, J. (1992). The development of achievement task values: A theoretical analysis. *Developmental Review*, 12, 265–310.

Zimmerman, B. J., & Martinez-Pons, M. (1990). Student differences in self-regulated learning: Relating grade, sex, and giftedness to self-efficacy and strategy use. *Journal of Educational Psychology*, 82, 51–59.

Zimmerman, B. J. (2000). Self-efficacy: An essential motive to learn. *Contemporary Educational Psychology*, 25, 82–91.

CHAPTER

8

The Development of Goal Orientation

ERIC M. ANDERMAN, CHAMMIE C. AUSTIN,
AND DAWN M. JOHNSON
The University of Kentucky, Lexington, Kentucky

Students often mention different reasons for doing academic work. Whereas some of their reasons surely vary by subject matter, the "rationale" for doing one's schoolwork certainly changes with age. The present chapter presents a review of research on developmental shifts in students' achievement goal orientations. Specifically, we argue that changes in goal orientations are quite predictable. Nevertheless, these changes primarily can be linked to the changing contexts in which children, adolescents, and adults encounter learning situations.

WHAT IS A "GOAL ORIENTATION"?

Goal orientations have to do with students' reasons for engaging in academic tasks. Whereas some goals are related specifically to what a student is trying to achieve (e.g., the goal of getting an A in a chemistry course), *goal orientations* deal with students' reasons for taking the chemistry course in the first place (Urdan, 1997). As noted in a special issue of *Contemporary Educational Psychology*, there is much confusion in the achievement motivation literature with regard to terminology (Murphy & Alexander, 2000). This confusion is particularly evident in the literature on achievement goal orientations (Pintrich, 2000).

Defining Goal Orientations

Researchers have identified several types of goal orientations. Although most definitions share a common underlying theme, there are subtle differences in these terms and in their interpretations. In addition, these different terms have evolved historically via different programs of research.

Goal Orientations Concerned with Learning, Effort, and Improvement

First, goal orientation researchers have identified an orientation in which the learner is focused on task mastery, improvement, and self-comparison. These goals have been operationalized and defined somewhat differently by various researchers. Dweck and her colleagues (e.g., Dweck & Leggett, 1988) discuss *learning goals*. They suggest that when students adopt learning goals, their goal when doing an academic task is "to increase their competence" (Dweck & Leggett, 1988, p. 256). Using this operationalization, Dweck and her colleagues have demonstrated that the adoption of learning goals is associated with the belief that one's intelligence is malleable (Dweck & Leggett, 1988).

Ames and her colleagues have referred to *mastery* goals in their program of research (e.g., Ames, 1992). Ames and her colleagues identified the parameters of classrooms that are associated with holding mastery goals. Specifically, Ames has argued that a classroom climate conducive to mastery goals is a classroom in which the teacher and students define success in terms of progress and improvement, place a high value on effort and learning, feel a sense of satisfaction from taking on challenges, and view mistakes as a part of the learning process (Ames & Archer, 1988). In addition, teachers in mastery-oriented classrooms are focused on how students are learning, rather than on how they are performing relative to others.

Maehr, Midgley, and their colleagues also have studied students' mastery goals. Their conception of goals relates to students' reasons for engaging in academic tasks (similar to the work of Ames and Dweck). Their research has focused on the development of reliable and valid measures of various types of achievement goals. Their operationalization of mastery goals focuses on the mastery-related reasons that students give for doing their school work (e.g., doing school work because one likes to learn new things, doing school work because one enjoys it, doing school work because one wants to get better at it, etc.) (see Midgley et al., 1998, 2000). In 2000 Midgley and her colleagues updated their measure of mastery goals to eliminate items that assessed intrinsic value and that made references to students' behavior (see Midgley et al., 2000).

Nicholls and his colleagues (e.g., Nicholls, Cobb, Wood, Yackel, & Patashnick, 1990) have operationalized their construct of *task orientation* somewhat differently from the previously mentioned researchers. Specifically, Nicholls and his colleagues have focused on the extent to which students report feeling successful or pleased when they engage in various tasks (e.g., how pleased they report feeling when they solve a problem by working hard, or when they feel the problems they are working on makes them "think hard") (Nicholls, Cobb, Wood, Yackel, & Patashnick, 1990, p. 115).

Goal Orientations Concerned with Performance, Extrinsic incentives, and Ability

Researchers have identified several types of goal orientations that are related to performance, ability, and extrinsic incentives. Dweck and her colleagues defined *performance goals* as goals "in which individuals are concerned with gaining favorable judgments of their competence" (Dweck & Leggett, 1988, p. 256). Their program of research has demonstrated that individuals who hold performance goals are likely to believe that their intelligence is a fixed entity that is resistant to change.

Ames defines performance goals somewhat differently. As they did with mastery goals, Ames and her colleagues have defined performance goals in terms of the characteristics of classrooms that are conducive to performance goals. Specifically, a classroom that is performance-oriented is a classroom in which success is defined by high grades, value is placed on high ability, satisfaction is derived from doing better than others, mistakes invoke anxiety in students, and the attention of students and teachers alike is focused on students' performance relative to others.

Nicholls and his colleagues (e.g., Nicholls, Cobb, Wood, Yackel, & Patashnick, 1990) have identified both an *ego orientation* and a *work-avoidance* construct. Students report being ego oriented when they feel pleased that they know more than others, or when they are the only ones who can answer a question. Work avoidance is characterized by being pleased when one does not have to work hard or when academic tasks are perceived as being "easy" (Nicholls, Cobb, Wood, Yackel, & Patashnick, 1990, p. 117).

Unconfounding Performance Goals

Through much of the 1980s and early 1990s, many of the foregoing constructs were confounded; specifically, a number of different ideas often were measured under the general rubric of a "performance goal" (Elliott, 1997). Recent research has distinguished among these various constructs. First, it should be noted that Elliot and Harackiewicz (1996) pointed out that most achievement goal orientation researchers focus exclusively on mastery and performance goals. Specifically, they argue that most motivation researchers focus on the "approach" components of mastery and performance goals. However, as noted by early motivation researchers (e.g., Atkinson, 1957; McClelland, 1951), learners are motivated both to attain success and to avoid failure. Thus, the "avoidance" component largely has been ignored in research on achievement goal orientations.

Elliot and Harackiewicz (1996) proposed and demonstrated that performance goals can be broken down into both *performance–approach* and *performance–avoid* goals. Approach-type performance goals involve the goal of demonstrating one's competence relative to others; individuals with these goals are interested in demonstrating their ability relative to others. In contrast, avoidance-type performance goals involve the goal of avoiding looking incompetent at a task. Other researchers (e.g., Middleton and Midgley, 1997) have demonstrated that the approach–avoidance distinction for performance goals applies to adolescents as well.

For example, Midgley and her colleagues describe performance–approach goals in this way:

> When oriented to performance–approach goals, students' purpose or goal in an achievement setting is to demonstrate their competence. Attention is focused on the self. A performance–approach orientation has been associated with both adaptive and maladaptive patterns of learning. (Midgley et al., 2000, p. 11).

In contrast, performance–avoid goals are described in the following manner:

> When oriented to performance–avoid goals, students' purpose or goal in an achievement setting is to avoid the demonstration of incompetence. Attention is focused on the self. A performance–avoid orientation has been associated with maladaptive patterns of learning. (Midgley et al., 2000, p. 12).

In addition, Pintrich (2000) suggests that mastery goals might be broken down into mastery–approach and mastery–avoid states. In a mastery–approach state, students would be focused on task mastery, learning, and understanding, whereas in a mastery–avoid state, students would be focused on avoiding misunderstanding or not learning the specific task (Pintrich, 2000).

Some goal orientation theorists also have identified an extrinsic goal orientation (Anderman, 1994; Anderman, Maehr, & Midgley, 1999; Maehr & Midgley, 1991, 1996; Pintrich, Smith, Garcia, & McKeachie, 1993; Wolters, Yu, & Pintrich, 1996). Students who are extrinsically goal oriented are particularly focused on earning rewards and good grades.

Reconciling Differences between the Various Definitions

Although there is much similarity between and among the constructs that have been developed by various researchers, there are some subtle yet important differences. For example, Nicholls' model of goal orientations includes aspects of timing—when students *feel* particularly successful at a given task, whereas other goal orientation models (e.g., Ames & Archer, 1988; Dweck &

Leggett, 1988; Maehr & Midgley, 1996) focus more on students' specific reasons for engaging in a task (Nicholls, et al., 1990; Maehr & Midgley, 1996; Midgley et al., 1998).

Thorkildsen and Nicholls (1998) have argued that some of these differences emanate from the theoretical frameworks of some of the researchers. For example, Thorkildsen and Nicholls have suggested that Ames' work emanates from a social psychology perspective, whereas Dweck's work emanates from a personality psychology perspective. Consequently, differences in definitions and formulations of goal orientation theory may be related to differences in the training and worldviews of the various psychologists who study these orientations.

In the present chapter, we adopt the terms "mastery goals" and "performance goals." We make the distinction between performance–approach and performance–avoid goals whenever that distinction is possible (whenever the researchers made that distinction in the research being reviewed). In addition, because some studies reviewed in this chapter focus on extrinsic goals, we use the term "extrinsic goals" when appropriate to describe goal orientations that focus on engaging in academic tasks to earn some type of reward or to avoid some type of punishment (e.g., Anderman, 1994; Maehr & Midgley, 1991, 1996; Pintrich, Smith, Garcia, & McKeachie, 1993; Wolters, Yu, & Pintrich, 1996).

The Importance of Goal Orientations

Why should we care about the development of goal orientations? Basically, we should be concerned about goal orientations because they predict important and valued educational outcomes. Indeed, students' reasons for engaging in various academic tasks are directly related to the types of cognitive strategies they use, as well as to how well newly learned material is stored in long-term memory.

Many studies have used a goal orientation framework over the past 20 years. For mastery goals, the results have been fairly consistent: The endorsement of mastery goals generally is related to positive educational outcomes, such as long-term learning, the use of deep cognitive strategies, and relating material to prior knowledge (e.g., Ames & Archer, 1988; Anderman & Young, 1994; Meece, Blumenfeld, & Hoyle, 1988; Nolen, 1988; Nolen & Haladyna, 1990; Pintrich, 2000; Pintrich & De Groot, 1990; Pintrich & Garcia, 1991; Pintrich & Schunk, 1996; Urdan, 1997). For performance goals, the results have been less consistent. This is primarily because prior to the mid-1990s, many researchers confounded the various types of performance goals (e.g., approach, avoid, extrinsic, etc.) (Elliott, 1997; Elliot & Harackiewicz, 1996; Middleton & Midgley, 1997). Harackiewicz, Elliot, and their colleagues have conducted a series of laboratory-based experiments, which demonstrate that the adoption of performance goals can lead to increased intrinsic motivation in college students. However, these effects depend on the effects of moderators. For example, in one study (Elliot & Harackiewicz, 1994), intrinsic motivation was related to performance goals for achievement-oriented participants, whereas intrinsic motivation was related to mastery goals for individuals low in achievement orientation.

In a study of college students, Harackiewicz, Barron, Carter, Lehto, and Elliot (1997) found that both mastery and performance goals may be beneficial to college students. Specifically, these researchers found that students who endorsed mastery goals in introductory psychology classes at the beginning of the semester were more likely to indicate high levels of interest in the course material at the end of the semester. The endorsement of performance goals predicted higher course grades. Mastery goals were unrelated to grades, and performance goals were unrelated to interest. Interactions between mastery and performance goals also were examined, but none were found. Other studies (e.g., Elliot & Harackiewicz, 1996) have found that performance–avoid goals may be related to decrements in intrinsic motivation in college-aged students, whereas performance–approach goals do not appear to have the same negative effects.

Pintrich (2000) examined mastery and performance–approach goals in a sample of eighth and ninth grade students. Results indicated that mastery goals were related to a host of positive outcomes. However, results also indicated that when students endorsed both performance–approach goals and mastery goals, the results proved to be equally adaptive for students.

In a recent review of the literature on performance–approach goals, Midgley, Kaplan, and Middleton (2001) conclude that the results of studies on the relations of performance–approach goals to a variety of outcomes are mixed. In some studies, these goals are related to adaptive outcomes, whereas in other studies, they are related negatively or inversely related to the same outcomes. Midgley and her colleagues conclude that additional research on performance–approach goals is needed. As an example, researchers need to more carefully examine of the effects of performance–approach goals on students when they face a setback (Midgley, Kaplan, & Middleton, 2001).

Other studies also have suggested that the patterns of goal endorsement in students are related to academic outcomes for children and adolescents. For example, Meece and Holt (1993) examined the mastery, ego, and work-avoidant goal orientations of fifth and sixth graders. Using cluster analysis, they found that students who were high in mastery goals (compared to the other two goal orientations) displayed the most positive achievement profiles (e.g., strategy usage, grades, achievement test scores), whereas students who were high on mastery and ego goals did not do as well in school. Students who reported being low on both mastery goals and ego goals displayed the most discouraging achievement profiles.

Goal Orientations and School Practices

Results of various studies of variables related to goal orientations have extremely important implications for the education of children and adolescents. Research clearly indicates that schools have a profound impact on students (e.g., Maehr, 1991; Roeser, Eccles, & Sameroff, 2000). In terms of goal orientation theory, goal orientations are related strongly to the practices of schools (Anderman & Maehr, 1994; Anderman, Maher, & Midgley, 1999; Maehr, 1991; Maehr & Anderman, 1993; Midgley, Anderman, & Hicks, 1995). When school personnel use practices that encourage social comparison and make ability differences salient, performance goals become significant; in contrast, when school personnel use practices that focus on improvement, effort, and self-comparisons, mastery goals become prominent (Maehr & Midgley, 1996). These issues will be addressed in greater detail later in this chapter.

THE DEVELOPMENT OF GOAL ORIENTATION

There are a number of important reasons for examining goal orientations from a developmental perspective. First and foremost, as evidenced by the chapters in this book, there is a tremendous amount of evidence indicating that academic motivation develops and changes over time. The intrinsic curiosity toward just about everything that is often noticed in very young children often gives way to interest in specific types of activities during later childhood and adolescence. In addition, a growing concern with grades and performance almost inevitably develops as students move through the educational system (Anderman & Maehr, 1994; Eccles, Lord, & Midgley, 1991; Eccles, Wigfield, Harold, & Blumenfeld, 1993; Harter, 1975).

Second, children, adolescents, and adults all move through different educational context at different times. These contexts have powerful effects on student motivation, and it is only in recent years that researchers have developed methods for carefully and appropriately measuring and understanding the effects of these contexts on educational outcomes (e.g., Lee, 2000; Turner & Meyer, 2000). Consequently, the inclusion of educational contexts into studies of goal orientation inherently must allow for developmental perspectives, since the nature of these contexts changes throughout development.

Third, developmental studies allow for the corroboration of various cross-sectional studies, as well as for an in-depth examination of the results of more sophisticated longitudinal studies.

GOAL ORIENTATIONS IN YOUNG CHILDREN

There has been very little research on achievement goal orientations with young children. Nevertheless, some related work suggests that motivational variables are important even among very young children. For example, Stipek and her colleagues (e.g., Stipek, Recchia, & McClintic, 1992) have demonstrated that preschool-aged children experience feelings of shame in the face of failure at some tasks; thus, even children who have not yet attended school may have some concerns about their performance and abilities.

However, work by Carol Dweck and her colleagues has examined young children's motivational patterns. Dweck has distinguished between two patterns of learning: a *mastery-oriented* pattern and a *helpless* pattern (e.g., Diener & Dweck, 1978; Dweck & Reppucci, 1973). The helpless pattern "is characterized by an avoidance of challenge and a deterioration of performance in the face of obstacles" (Dweck & Leggett, 1988, p. 256), whereas the mastery-oriented pattern "involves the seeking of challenging tasks and the generation of effective strategies in the face of obstacles" (Dweck & Leggett, 1988, p. 257). Dweck's research on achievement goal orientations differs from that of others in that Dweck focuses on goal orientations as a function of individual characteristics, whereas others (e.g., Ames, 1992; Maehr & Midgley, 1996) focus on goal orientations partially as a function of school contexts.

Although early studies suggested that young children probably do not experience the helpless pattern (e.g., Miller, 1985), there now is evidence that young children may experience the helpless motivational pattern. Cain and Dweck (1991) asked children in first, third, and fifth grades to complete various puzzles. The children also were classified as either helpless or mastery oriented. Results indicated that children in all three grade levels (including the first graders) could be classified as helpless. Helpless children in the first and third grades also reported lower expectations for the future. Most importantly, first graders who were classified as helpless were more likely than those classified as mastery oriented to be concerned with the performance *outcomes* of tasks (e.g., the observable results), rather than on controllable *processes*.

Dweck also has argued that individuals' beliefs about intelligence are related to motivational patterns. Perceiving one's intelligence as a fixed, unchangeable *entity* has been associated with performance goals, whereas perceiving one's intelligence as malleable and changeable (*incremental*) has been associated with mastery (learning) goals (Dweck & Leggett, 1988). Such beliefs about intelligence have been identified in children as young as kindergartners (Bempechat, London, & Dweck, 1991). In Dweck et al.'s (1991) study of motivational development in first, third, and fifth graders, they found that by the fifth grade, the helpless children were more likely than the mastery-oriented children to hold an entity view of intelligence; however, this relation did not emerge in the younger children. Dweck and her colleagues suggest that developmentally, an early focus on academic *outcomes* (e.g., grades or high marks) may be related to the subsequent development of an entity view of intelligence.

Dweck and her colleagues have demonstrated that young children respond differently to learning- and performance-oriented tasks. Specifically, they argue that students with learning goals will display a mastery pattern of motivation regardless of their confidence in their ability to perform a task (e.g., Smiley & Dweck, 1994). However, students with performance goals will demonstrate the helpless pattern when their confidence is low and an attenuated mastery-oriented pattern when their confidence is high. This model has been validated on children between the ages of 4 and 11 years (Buhrans & Dweck, 1995; E. Elliott & Dweck, 1988; Smiley & Dweck, 1994).

These findings are particularly important in that they indicate that the pursuit of learning goals may help young children to overcome fears about their abilities in certain domains. This finding has extremely important implications for educators who work with young children and develop curricula for elementary school aged children. As noted by Harter (1981), perceptions of academic self-competence in children should lead to intrinsic motivation. Specifically, a young child who lacks confidence in his or her ability in a particular domain (e.g., reading) might benefit greatly from learning to read in a classroom where learning goals are supported and encouraged. Indeed, for such students, a focus on learning goals might lead to long-term benefits, such as increased self-efficacy in reading and greater valuing of reading.

More recently, Mueller and Dweck (1998) studied the effects of praise on elementary students' achievement goals. Specifically, they found that fifth graders who were praised for their intelligence after engaging in problem-solving tasks were more likely to endorse performance goals on future tasks; in contrast, fifth graders who were praised for effort when engaging in these tasks were more likely to endorse mastery goals on future tasks. In addition, children who had been praised for their intelligence were interested in learning about the performance of other students, whereas students who were praised for effort were interested in finding out about strategies that could be used in problem solving.

Other important research on goal orientations in children has been conducted by Carole Ames and her colleagues. In one study, Ames (1984) asked children to solve puzzles in performance-oriented (competitive) conditions and in mastery-oriented (noncompetitive) conditions. The children who were in the performance-oriented condition were more likely to make attributions to ability, whereas the children in the mastery-oriented condition were more likely to make attributions to personal effort.

Nicholls and his colleagues (e.g., Nicholls, Cobb, Wood, Yackel, & Patashnick, 1990) examined task and ego orientation in mathematics in second graders. They presented the questionnaires to these young students by reminding them that their opinions would be assessed on the basis of their responses and that it was natural for opinions to vary. Results indicated that endorsement of a task (mastery) orientation was related to believing that success in math was related to effort, and to cooperation with peers. Endorsement of an ego (performance) orientation was related to believing that success was related to ability and to beating others. Interestingly, perceived ability was unrelated to either goal orientation.

Results of a recent study indicated that children's valuing of mathematics and reading declined when students' teachers reported emphasizing performance goals (Anderman et al., 2001). In this study, children completed measures developed by Eccles and her colleagues regarding their valuing of mathematics and reading. In addition, teachers reported their use of mastery and performance-oriented instructional strategies. Using hierarchical linear modeling techniques (which separated between and within classroom variance), the results indicated that the valuing of both reading and mathematics declined over the course of one academic year when students' teachers reported that they emphasized performance-oriented instructional strategies (e.g., emphasizing high test scores and emphasizing that students should try to do as well as the students who were doing best in the class). Interestingly, changes in the valuing of mathematics and reading were unrelated to the reported use of mastery-oriented instructional strategies (e.g., emphasizing personal improvement).

Nevertheless, other research indicates that performance goals may not always be related to negative outcomes in children. Using a large sample of fifth and sixth grade students, Meece and her colleagues (Meece , Blumenfeld, & Hoyle, 1988) found that both mastery goals and ego–social goals (demonstrating one's ability) were related positively to active cognitive engagement in science. Using structural equation modeling, they found that intrinsic motivation positively predicted task mastery goals and negatively predicted ego–social goals. In turn, task mastery goals positively and strongly predicted active cognitive engagement, whereas ego–social goals positively predicted cognitive engagement, but not nearly as strongly as did task mastery goals.

Self-Perceptions of Ability and Goal Orientations during Childhood

Because achievement goals deal primarily with the reasons why students engage in academic tasks, one must always consider students' self-evaluations of ability. Indeed, if a student chooses to engage in an academic task to pursue mastery goals, then it is probable that the student perceives that he or she has the ability to work on the given task.

Nicholls and his colleagues have demonstrated that children's conceptions of ability change throughout childhood. Young children tend to equate effort with ability, whereas at about the age of 11 or 12 children are able to differentiate among concepts such as effort, ability, and performance (Nicholls, 1978; Nicholls & Miller, 1984).

Self-perceptions of ability may be related to goal orientations in children in important ways. Dweck (1986) has argued that when performance goals are salient, children's perceptions of their own ability must be high before children will be willing to engage in a complex, challenging task. When children are young and equate effort with ability, they may be more likely to be mastery oriented, because ability and effort are essentially the same thing. In contrast, as children approach early adolescence and develop distinct understandings of concepts such as ability, effort, and performance, they may be more likely to consider the adoption of performance goals (since "performance" now has more actual meaning for these older children).

Summary

Research on goal orientations in children is growing. What is becoming increasingly clear is that young children are aware of and responsive to environments that emphasize either mastery or performance goals, and that children respond in predictable ways to these environments. Because it is particularly difficult to administer survey measures to young children, researchers often have had to utilize different types of methodologies with children. Nevertheless, the research on goal orientations during adolescence delineates more predictable patterns of change.

GOAL ORIENTATION IN ADOLESCENTS

In recent years, there has been much research on goal orientations during adolescence. Much of this research is based on Eccles and Midgley's discussion of stage–environment fit (Eccles & Midgley, 1989). Specifically, Eccles, Midgley, and their colleagues have argued and demonstrated that for many early adolescents, learning environments change dramatically as students make the transition from elementary to middle school. The typical middle school often provides the type of environment that is antithetical to the developmental needs of early adolescents; consequently, during early adolescence, there often is a decline in academic motivation (see also Anderman & Maehr, 1994).

Influences of Goal Orientations during Adolescence

Does endorsing a mastery or performance goal orientation lead to different outcomes for students? Do mastery and performance goals interact in the prediction of various outcomes? Research indicates that during the adolescent years, the endorsement of mastery and performance goals becomes particularly important because they lead to different types of outcomes for adolescents. These outcomes include the use of differing cognitive processing strategies, different effects on learning, and differing approaches to academic tasks.

Nolen (1988) examined the relations between adolescents' goal orientations and the use of deep- and surface-level cognitive processing strategies.

A task (mastery) orientation was related strongly and positively to the use of deep processing strategies, and less strongly to the use of surface processing strategies. In contrast, an ego (performance) orientation was related positively only to the use of surface-level strategies.

In a similar study with high school students, Nolen and Haladyna (1990) found that the belief in the usefulness of deep-processing strategies was related more strongly to a task (mastery) orientation than to an ego (performance) orientation. Similar results have been found in other studies (e.g., Anderman & Young, 1994).

Some research indicates that performance goals are related to some seemingly negative outcomes for early adolescents. For example, Urdan, Midgley, and Anderman (1998) examined a large sample of fifth graders and found that the use of self-handicapping strategies (e.g., fooling around, procrastinating, etc.) was related to perceptions of an emphasis on performance goals in the classroom, as well as to teachers' reported use of performance-oriented instructional strategies. Other studies (e.g., Midgley, Arunkumar, & Urdan, 1996) also indicate that performance goals may be related to the use of self-handicapping strategies in older adolescents.

Anderman, Griesinger, and Westerfield (1998) found that during adolescence, academic cheating may be related to performance goals and to extrinsic goals. Using a sample of sixth, seventh, and eighth graders, Anderman et al. found that self-reported cheating behaviors in science were predicted by perceiving the science classroom as extrinsically oriented and by perceiving the school as a whole as performance oriented. In addition, they found that the beliefs in the acceptability of cheating were related to personal extrinsic goals and to perceiving science classrooms as being extrinsically oriented.

Pajares and his colleagues (Pajares, Britner, & Valiante, 2000) examined mastery, performance–approach, and performance–avoid goal orientations in middle school students, in both writing and science. One of the more intriguing results of this study was that performance–approach goals were unrelated to the writing beliefs (e.g., self-efficacy, self-concept, self-regulation) of sixth grade students, but were related to writing self-efficacy and science self-concept in seventh grade students, and to self-regulatory beliefs in eighth grade students. These results suggest that performance–approach goals may serve a more adaptive purpose for older adolescents than for younger adolescents (see also Middleton & Midgley, 1997).

Classroom Influences on Goal Orientations during Adolescence

Much of the research on achievement goal orientations during adolescence has focused on students' perceptions of the goal stresses in the classroom.

As Eccles and Midgley (1989) noted, there is a shift in the focus of classrooms as students move from elementary schools into middle schools. Middle schools often are perceived as focusing more on ability and performance, whereas elementary schools are perceived as focusing more on mastery and intrinsic motivation.

Research indicates that students' endorsements of mastery and performance goals changes during the adolescent years. In general, research indicates that students tend to endorse performance goals more, and mastery goals less, as they progress through adolescence. This is particularly true of research on changes in students' goal orientations across the transition from elementary to middle school (e.g., Anderman & Anderman, 1999). In general, results of a number of studies indicate that these shifts in goal orientations are due to changes in school goal stresses.

Midgley and her colleagues have done much of the research on classroom goal stresses during adolescence. In a cross-sectional study, Midgley et al. (1995) compared elementary and middle school teachers and students. They found that elementary school teachers reported using instructional practices that emphasized mastery goals more than did middle school teachers. In addition, elementary school teachers endorsed mastery-oriented achievement goals for their students more than did middle school teachers.

In a longitudinal study, Anderman and Midgley (1997) examined students' perceptions of classroom goal structures (mastery and performance) before and after the transition to middle school. Students reported that their fifth grade elementary school classes were more focused on mastery than were their sixth grade middle school classes. In addition, they found that in sixth grade, students perceived their classrooms as more focused on performance and ability than during the fifth grade.

In a different longitudinal study, Anderman and Anderman (1999) found that changes in individual achievement goals across the middle school transition were related to perceptions of the classroom goal structures in middle school classrooms. An increase in a perceived classroom mastery–goal structure across the transition from elementary to middle school was associated with perceiving both a mastery and a performance goal structure in posttransition classrooms; in contrast, an increase in performance goals across the transition was related to perceptions of a performance goal structure in middle school classrooms.

Ames and Archer (1988) found that perceptions of an emphasis on mastery goals in the classroom were related to positive outcomes, such as the use of more effective strategies, and the belief that academic success is due to effort. In contrast, perceptions of an emphasis on performance goals in their classrooms were related to negative outcomes, such as attributing failure to a lack of ability.

Why Does the Goal Stress Change after the Middle School Transition?

The aforementioned studies converge on the finding that students tend to become more concerned with grades and relative ability, and somewhat less concerned with mastery, effort, and improvement, after the middle school transition. This leads to the obvious question of *why* these changes occur after this transition.

Various reviews of the literature on motivation during early adolescence (e.g., Anderman & Maehr, 1994; Eccles & Midgley, 1989; Eccles et al., 1993) indicate that the instructional practices of middle school teachers differ from those of elementary school teachers. Indeed, the methods used to instruct middle school students differ greatly from those used to teach elementary school students. Eccles, Midgley, and their colleagues (1993) have described the middle school environment as being characterized by rules and discipline, poor relationships between teachers and students, few opportunities for students to be involved in making decisions, and strict grading practices. In addition, the use of ability grouping increases after the middle school transition. This stands in sharp contrast to the environment of the elementary school, which is characterized by strong teacher–student relationships, opportunities to pursue creative projects, and less grouping of students by ability (Eccles & Midgley, 1989; Eccles et al., 1993). However, current research suggests that the quality of teacher–student relationships after the middle school transition may be improving. For example, a large-scale study by Midgley and her colleagues (Midgley et al., 1998) found that students did not report a decline in the quality of teacher–student relationships over the middle school transition.

For many students, this transition represents an abrupt change. Consequently, it is not terribly surprising that students often become more focused on performance and relative ability after the transition; indeed, they are entering an environment that stresses these factors as being extremely important. Thus, for many students, the purpose of learning changes from one of inquiry and learning for intrinsic reasons to learning in order to demonstrate ability and to prove that one is academically competent (Maehr & Midgley, 1996).

In addition, the differences in classroom goal stresses between elementary and middle schools may in part have historical explanations. Junior high schools were created early in the twentieth century to meet the unique developmental needs of early adolescents. Junior high schools eventually became "miniature high schools" (Clark & Clark, 1993, p. 450). The middle school movement of the 1960s through 1980s eventuated in many arguments regarding appropriate grade configurations for schools serving early adolescents, but in actuality there was little difference in the practices used by middle school and junior high school educators (Lounsbury, 1991). With the release of the Carnegie Council's report on the education of young adolescents in 1989 (Carnegie Council on Adolescent Development, 1989), the focus returned to the developmental needs of early adolescents—specifically, the need to critically examine the *practices* used by schools serving early adolescents.

Consequently, different schools probably emphasize different goals for their students, due in part to historical changes within school systems. Some schools clearly still operate in the "mini high school" mode and probably are highly focused on grades and performance, whereas other schools have adopted recommendations of developmental researchers (e.g., Eccles & Midgley, 1989; Maehr & Midgley, 1996) and have instituted reforms that permit a focus on the true developmental needs of early adolescents. Nevertheless, there is still a need for systematic research that carefully describes relations between school reform efforts, school policies, and goal stresses.

School Influences on Goal Orientations during Adolescence

Maehr (1991) has written extensively about the "psychological environment" of the school. Specifically, Maehr and his colleagues (e.g., Anderman & Maehr, 1994; Maehr & Buck, 1993; Maehr & Midgley, 1991, 1996) have demonstrated that school environments can be perceived as promoting both a mastery-oriented culture and a performance-oriented culture. A mastery-oriented school environment is one in which students perceive that all students can learn, that understanding what is learned is of primary importance, and that errors are acceptable as long as learning is occurring. In contrast, a performance-oriented school culture is one in which students perceive that the students who get the highest grades are treated better than other students, that teachers care more about the "smart" students than about other students and that the school has given up on some of its students.

Research has demonstrated that students' perceptions of the school culture are related to personal goal orientations during adolescence. Using a large sample of eighth graders, Roeser, Midgley, and Urdan (1996) demonstrated that students who perceived their school as stressing performance (ability) goals were likely to endorse personal performance (relative ability) goals; however, perceiving the environment as being mastery (task) focused was related to the endorsement of personal mastery (task) goals. Results of this study also indicated that the endorsement of personal performance goals was related to self-consciousness, whereas the endorsement of personal mastery goals was related to academic self-efficacy and to positive school affect.

Midgley et al. (1995) used samples of both elementary and middle school students to examine the relations between perceived school culture and personal achievement goal orientations. They found that perceptions of a school-wide performance goal stress positively predicted personal performance goals in elementary school students, and positively predicted personal performance goals *and* negatively predicted personal mastery goals in middle school students. Perceptions of a schoolwide mastery goal stress positively predicted personal mastery goals and self-efficacy in elementary students, whereas they positively predicted both performance and mastery goals (as well as self-efficacy) in middle school students.

Changing School Goal Stresses during Adolescence

Maehr, Midgley, and their colleagues have argued that the specific policies and practices of school can be changed in order to promote a mastery-focused school culture over a performance-focused school culture (Maehr & Midgley, 1996). Specifically, they demonstrated that when the policies and practices of schools are alligned with the tenets of goal orientation theory, students will adopt personal achievement goals in line with the theory. Maehr, Midgley, and their colleagues worked collaboratively with both elementary and middle schools in order to change policies and practices so that the schools would be perceived by students as emphasizing mastery goals, rather than performance goals.

Results of their work with one middle school are particularly relevant to the present chapter. In their research, they met weekly for 3 years with administrators, parents, and teachers from a middle school in a working-class community in the Midwest. The purpose of these meetings was to critically examine the practices of the school, and to examine strategies that school personnel could use to move the school culture more toward a mastery-oriented culture and away from being perceived as a performance-oriented culture. Some of the instructional practices that were changed over the course of the collaboration included the incorporation of team teaching into the sixth and seventh grades, some use of interdisciplinary units, increased opportunities for students to make important decisions, an emphasis on recognizing students for effort and improvement, the elimination of some ability grouping, and the creation of a "small house" or school within the school (Anderman, Maehr, & Midgley, 1999; Maehr & Midgley, 1991, 1996).

In order to evaluate the collaboration, students were followed longitudinally for 3 years. All students in the district were surveyed while in elementary school, in the fifth grade (prior to the middle school transition). Students then moved into one of two middle schools—the middle school collaborating with the university, and another middle school that had agreed to serve as a comparison school.

Students completed the *Patterns of Adaptive Learning Survey* (PALS) (Midgley et al., 1998; Midgley et al., 2000) at the end of the fifth grade (prior to the transition to middle school), and again at the end of the sixth and seventh grades (after the transition). Analyses indicated that students who attended the comparison school reported higher levels of personal performance goals and personal extrinsic goals after the transition from elementary to middle school than did the students in the collaborating school. In addition, students who moved into the comparison school exhibited an increase in their perceptions of an emphasis on performance goals between the fifth and sixth grades (Anderman, Maehr, & Midgley, 1999).

Goal Orientations in High School

Surprisingly little research has examined longitudinal changes in achievement goals across the transition from middle school to high school. During the high school years, many students consider dropping out of school altogether, whereas others consider future employment opportunities or college. Consequently, because some students are focused on getting into college, one might hypothesize that high schools would be perceived as being even more performance oriented and less mastery oriented than middle schools.

However, recent research suggests otherwise. Midgley and her colleagues followed a large sample of students from middle school to high school and examined changes in their perceptions of the goals stressed in their schools. High school students reported no change in their perceptions of an emphasis on mastery goals, and they reported a decrease in their perception of an emphasis on performance goals after the high school transition (Gheen, Hruda, Middleton, & Midgley, 2000). They also found that changes in perceptions of the goal stress across the transition were related in predictable ways to other variables. For example, when students perceived an increased emphasis on mastery after the transition, they also reported using self-regulatory strategies more (Gheen, et al., 2000).

DISCUSSION

Individuals' achievement goal orientations change in a variety of ways throughout childhood, adolescence, and adulthood. However, research is delivering more and more evidence that these changes are a function of changing learning environments, rather than enduring personality traits of individual learners.

As students move through most educational systems, the systems tend to demand more and more of students. Whereas early childhood programs and elementary schools often do not focus on children's ability and on ability differences, as students progress through elementary school and move into secondary schools, there is an increasing emphasis on ability, performance, and grades (Eccles & Midgley, 1989). Not all students move on to college, but those who do often face highly competitive environments there (Harackiewicz, Barron, Carter, Lehto, & Elliot, 1997). Because students tend to adopt the types of achievement goal orientations fostered by their learning environments (Maehr, 1991), students often tend to endorse performance goals more as they progress through the educational system. Nevertheless, recent research suggests that these changes may at least level off as students enter high school (Middleton, Midgley, Gheen, & Kumar, in press).

Unfortunately, we lose many students to this system. Dropout rates are exceedingly high (e.g., Supik & Johnson, 1999; U.S. Department of Education, 1990). Although research does indicate that performance goals can be adaptive and useful, particularly for college students (e.g., Elliot & Harackiewicz, 1996), one must question the utility of performance goals within a larger developmental perspective. Whereas performance goals may be adaptive for college students, one must remember that college students are in many ways the products of elementary, middle, and high schools; those students who make it to college have learned to adapt to the increasingly performance-oriented demands of schooling. Nevertheless, one cross-sectional study suggests that older adults may be more mastery oriented than are younger adults. Using a sample of college students of diverse ages (17 through 59), Burley, Turner, and Vitulli (1999) examined mastery (learning) and performance goal orientations. Results suggested that the older students were more mastery oriented than were the younger students. These researchers suggest that the grouping of older learners with younger learners may lead to increased mastery goals in the younger learners.

What about those students who do not enroll in college? What about those who do not graduate from high school? In our view, this is an important future direction for goal orientation theory research. From a developmental perspective, we know that goal orientations change as a function of changing school environments. However, we do not know much about students' abilities to cope with and adapt to these changes. We hope that future research will examine these important developmental issues.

New Areas of Inquiry

Research on the development of goal orientation is still nascent; indeed, there are many promising areas for exploration. Two areas that are particularly promising are (1) the study of gender and ethnic differences in goal orientations and (2) the study of domain differences in goal orientations.

Gender and Ethnic Differences in Goal Orientations

Few studies have addressed gender and ethnic differences in goal orientations. Although some research has been done on these topics, there are still areas that have not been explored in depth. Nevertheless, there is some research that indicates that achievement goal orientations may operate differently for different students.

There are mixed results regarding gender differences in goal orientations. Results of some studies suggest that males are more performance oriented than females; however, results of other studies indicate no gender differences. For example, Middleton and Midgley (1997) found no relation between gender and mastery, performance–approach, and performance–avoid goals, in a large sample of adolescents. However, Anderman and Anderman (1999) found that male adolescents were more performance–approach oriented than females. Using a different sample, Anderman and Midgley (1997) also found that males were more performance–approach oriented than females. Other studies (e.g., Roeser, Midgley, & Urdan, 1996; Ryan, Hicks, & Midgley, 1996) also support the notion that males are more performance oriented than are females.

Although the results of studies of gender and goal orientations appear to be mixed, there appears to be growing evidence that in many learning situations, males may be somewhat more performance oriented than females. Nevertheless, the null results of other studies involving gender differences (e.g., Middleton & Midgley, 1997) indicate clearly that additional research is necessary.

How might these discrepancies in gender differences be resolved? Perhaps the most promising solution would be for researchers to develop studies *specifically designed to examine gender differences*. Most of the studies of gender differences that have been reported in the literature were not designed specifically to examine gender differences; rather, they were designed to study goal orientations, and gender often was included as a control variable. Thus the gender differences that have been reported often have been intriguing, but they often have been sidebars in those research studies, rather than the actual purpose of the research. In addition, most gender differences that have been reported have been the result of survey-based studies. It would be very fruitful for researchers to incorporate more qualitative methods into gender-related studies of goal orientations, to better understand females' and males' reasons for adopting various goal orientations.

Even less research has been conducted to examine ethnic differences in achievement goal orientations. Middleton and Midgley (1997) examined differences between African-American and European-American adolescents. They found no differences for either performance–approach or performance–avoid goals. However, they found a small relation between ethnicity and mastery (task) goals, with African-American students reporting slightly higher mastery goals than did European-American students.

One important area for future inquiry will be studies that involve students of other ethnicities. Would similar or different patterns emerge for Latino-American, Asian-American, or Native American students? As an example, research from an attribution theory perspective has suggested that students of Asian descent often attribute academic achievement to effort rather than to ability (e.g., Holloway, 1988). Consequently, Asian-American students who exhibit this attributional style might react differently from European-American students to mastery- and performance-oriented environments. Indeed, it is possible that Asian-American students who attribute success to effort are immune to some of the possible negative effects of performance–avoid goal orientations. This will be a very important area for future studies.

Domain Differences

Another area that has only received minimal attention to date concerns the domain specificity of achievement goals. Some researchers measure goal orientation using general constructs that assess students' overall goal orientations across a variety of learning situations, whereas others assess goal orientations within specific academic subject domains. In recent years, studies have tended to include more domain specific than general measures of goal orientation, given the growing sensitivity to the importance of instructional contexts (Anderman & Anderman, 2000). Researchers have examined goal orientations in various subject domains, including mathematics, English, social studies, science, writing, current events, and psychology (e.g., Anderman & Midgley, 1997; Anderman & Johnston, 1998; Harackiewicz et al., 1997; Pajares, Britner, & Valiante, 2000; Wolters, Yu, & Pintrich, 1996).

Nevertheless, little research to date has examined developmental shifts in achievement goals across a variety of domains. However, there is evidence suggesting that this may be a particularly important area for future research. For example, Duda and Nicholls (1992) examined goal orientations in schoolwork and sports in a sample of high school students and found some important domain differences in the relations of goal orientations to other indices. In their study, regression analyses indicated that a task orientation was a significant and positive predictor of satisfaction and enjoyment with *schoolwork*, whereas perceived ability was a strong positive predictor of satisfaction and enjoyment of *sports*.

Wolters et al. (1996) examined goal orientations in middle school students for English, math, and social studies. They found no differences in the ways that goal orientations predicted outcomes across the three subject domains. However, other studies of adolescents using goal orientation theory do suggest that some domain differences may exist. For example, Anderman and Midgley (1997) found that adolescents reported being more performance oriented in math than in English. Anderman and Midgley (1997) also found an interaction of time by subject (math and English) by ability for perceiving classrooms as being mastery oriented. Specifically, they found that perceptions of classrooms as being mastery oriented declined between the fifth and sixth grades for both high and low ability students in math, but not in English. One of the differences between the findings from the Wolters et al. (1996) study and the Anderman and Midgley (1997) study was that the Wolters study examined students' personal goal orientations, whereas the Anderman and Midgley study examined personal goals and perceptions of the classroom goal stresses.

CONCLUSIONS

There are still many unanswered questions in the study of the development of achievement goal orientations. The purpose of this chapter was to outline some of the developmental knowledge base that is available, in order to examine developmental trends.

One important and optimistic note is that students clearly adopt the types of goals that are stressed in their schools and classrooms. This is a note of "optimism" because research also has demonstrated that classroom and school goal structures can be manipulated (Maehr & Midgley, 1996). Consequently, the continued study of the development of achievement goals must be interwoven with the study of classroom and school contexts (e.g., Turner & Meyer, 2000).

References

Ames, C. (1984). Achievement attribution and self-instructions under competitive and individualistic goal structures. *Journal of Educational Psychology, 76*, 478–487.

Ames, C. (1992). Classrooms: Goals, structures, and student motivation. *Journal of Educational Psychology, 84*, 261–271.

Ames, C., & Archer, J. (1988). Achievement goals in the classroom: Students' learning strategies and motivation processes. *Journal of Educational Psychology, 80*, 260–267.

Anderman, E. M. (1994). *Achievement goals and the transition to middle grades school.* Unpublished doctoral dissertation, University of Michigan, Ann Arbor.

Anderman, E. M., Eccles, J. S., Yoon, K.S., Roeser, R. W., Wigfield, A., & Blumenfeld, P. C. (2001). Learning to value math and reading: Individual differences and classroom effects. *Contemporary Educational Psychology, 26*, 76–95.

Anderman, E. M., Griesinger, T., & Westerfield, G. (1998). Motivation and cheating during early adolescence. *Journal of Educational Psychology, 90*, 84–93.

Anderman, E. M., & Johnston, J. (1998). TV news in the classroom: What are adolescents learning? *Journal of Adolescent Research, 13*, 73–100.

Anderman, E. M., & Maehr, M. L. (1994). Motivation and schooling in the middle grades. *Review of Educational Research, 64*, 287–309.

Anderman, E. M., Maehr, M. L., & Midgley, C. (1999). Declining motivation after the transition to middle school: Schools can make a difference. *Journal of Research and Development in Education. 32*, 131–147.

Anderman, E. M., & Midgley, C. (1997). Changes in achievement goal orientations, perceived academic competence, and grades across the transition to middle-level schools. *Contemporary Educational Psychology, 22*, 269–298.

Anderman, E. M., & Young, A. J. (1994). Motivation and strategy use in science: Individual differences and classroom effects. *Journal of Research in Science Teaching, 31*, 811–831.

Anderman, L. H., & Anderman, E. M. (1999). Social predictors of changes in students' achievement goal orientations. *Contemporary Educational Psychology, 25*, 21–37.

Anderman, L. H., & Anderman, E. M. (2000). Considering contexts in educational psychology: Introduction to the special issue. *Educational Psychologist, 35*, 67–68.

Atkinson, J. W. (1957). Motivational determinants of risk-taking behavior. *Psychological Review, 64*, 359–372.

Bempechat, J., London, P., & Dweck, C. S. (1991). Children's conceptions of ability in major domains: An interview and experimental study. *Child Study Journal, 21*, 11–35.

Buhrans, K. K., & Dweck, C. S. (1995). Helplessness in early childhood: The role of contingent worth. *Child Development*, 66, 1719–1738.

Burley, R. C., Turner, L. A., & Vitulli, W. F. (1999). The relationship between goal orientation and age among adolescents and adults. *Journal of Genetic Psychology*, 160, 84–88.

Cain, K. M., & Dweck, C. S. (1991). The relation between motivational patterns and achievement cognitions through the elementary school years. *Merrill-Palmer Quarterly*, 41, 25–52.

Carnegie Council on Adolescent Development. (1989). *Turning points: Preparing American youth for the 21st century* (Report of the Task Force on Education of Young Adolescents). New York: Author.

Clark, S. N., & Clark, D. C. (1993). Middle level school reform: The rhetoric and the reality. *Elementary School Journal*, 93, 447–460.

Diener, C. I., & Dweck, C. S. (1978). An analysis of learned helplessness: Continuous changes in performance, strategy, and achievement cognitions following failure. *Journal of Personality and Social Psychology*, 36, 451–462.

Duda, J. L., & Nicholls, J. G. (1992). Dimensions of achievement motivation in schoolwork and sport. *Journal of Educational Psychology*, 84, 290–299.

Dweck, C. S. (1986). Motivational processes affecting learning. *American Psychologist*, 41, 1040–1048.

Dweck, C. S., & Leggett, E. L. (1988). A social–cognitive approach to motivation and personality. *Psychological Review*, 95, 256–273.

Dweck, C. S., & Repucci, N. (1973). Learned helplessness and reinforcement responsibility in children. *Journal of Personality and Social Psychology*, 25, 109–116.

Eccles, J. S., Lord, S., & Midgley, C. (1991). What are we doing to early adolescents? The impact of educational contexts on early adolescents. *American Journal of Education*, 99, 521–542.

Eccles, J. S., & Midgley, C. (1989). Stage/environment fit: Developmentally appropriate classrooms for early adolescents. In R. E. Ames & C. Ames (Eds.), *Research on motivation in education* (Vol. 3, pp). New York: Academic Press.

Eccles, J. S., Midgley, C., Wigfield, A., Miller-Buchannan, C., Reuman, D., Flanagan, C., & MacIver, D. (1993). Development during adolescence: The impact of stage–environment fit on young adolescents' experiences in schools and families. *American Psychologist*, 48, 90–101.

Eccles, J. S., Wigfield, A., Harold, R., & Blumenfeld, P. (1993). Age and gender differences in children's self- and task perceptions during elementary school. *Child Development*, 64, 830–847.

Elliot, A. J. (1997). Integrating the "classic" and "contemporary" approaches to achievement motivation: A hierarchical model of approach and avoidance achievement motivation. In M. L. Maehr & P. R. Pintrich (Eds.), *Advances in motivation and achievement* (Vol. 10, pp. 143–179). Greenwich, CT: JAI Press.

Elliot, A. J., & Harackiewicz, J. M. (1994). Goal setting, achievement orientation, and intrinsic motivation: A mediational analysis. *Journal of Personality and Social Psychology*, 66, 968–980.

Elliot, A. J., & Harackiewicz, J. M. (1996). Approach and avoidance achievement goals and intrinsic motivation: A mediational analysis. *Journal of Personality and Social Psychology*, 70, 461–475.

Elliott, E., & Dweck, C. (1988). Goals: An approach to motivation and achievement. *Journal of Personality and Social Psychology*, 54, 5–12.

Gheen, M. H., Hruda, L. Z., Middleton, M. J., & Midgley, C. (2000). *Using goal orientation theory to examine the transition from middle to high school.* Paper presented at the annual meeting of the American Educational Research Association, New Orleans.

Harackiewicz, J. M, Barron, K. E., Carter, S. M., Lehto, A. T., & Elliot, A. (1997). Predictors and consequences of achievement goals in the college classroom: Maintaining interest and making the grade. *Journal of Personality and Social Psychology*, 73, 1284–1295.

Harter, S. (1975). Developmental differences in the manifestation of mastery motivation on problem-solving tasks. *Child Development*, 46, 370–378.

Harter, S. (1981). A new self-report scale of intrinsic versus extrinsic orientation in the classroom: Motivation and informational components. *Developmental Psychology*, 117, 300–312.

Holloway, S. D. (1988). Concepts of ability and effort in Japan and the United States. *Review of Educational Research*, 58, 327–345.

Lee, V. E. (2000). Using hierarchical linear modeling to study social contexts: The case of school effects. *Educational Psychologist*, 35, 125–141.

Lounsbury, J. H. (1991). *As I see it.* Columbus, OH: National Middle School Association.

Maehr, M. L. (1991). The "psychological environment" of the school: A focus for school leadership. In P. Thurstone & P. Zodhiates (Eds.), *Advances in educational administration* (Vol. 2, pp. 51–81). Greenwich, CT: JAI Press.

Maehr, M. L. & Anderman, E. M. (1993). Reinventing schools for early adolescents: Emphasizing task goals. *Elementary School Journal*, 93, 593–610.

Maehr, M. L., & Buck, R. (1993). Transforming school culture. In H. Walberg & M. Sashkin (Eds.), *Educational leadership and school culture: Current research and practice* (pp. 40–57). Berkeley, CA: McCutchan.

Maehr, M. L., & Midgley, C. (1991). Enhancing student motivation: A schoolwide approach. *Educational Psychologist*, 26, 399–427.

Maehr, M.L., & Midgley, C. (1996). *Transforming school cultures.* Boulder, CO: Westview Press.

McClelland, D. C. (1951). *Personality.* New York: The Dryden Press.

Meece, J. L., Blumenfeld, P. C., & Hoyle, R. H. (1988). Students' goal orientations and cognitive engagement in classroom activities. *Journal of Educational Psychology*, 80, 514–523.

Meece, J. L., & Holt, K. H. (1993). A pattern analysis of students' achievement goals. *Journal of Educational Psychology*, 85, 582–590.

Middleton, M., & Midgley, C. (1997). Avoiding the demonstration of lack of ability: An underexplored aspect of goal theory. *Journal of Educational Psychology*, 89, 710–718.

Middleton, M., Midgley, C., Gheen, M., & Kumar, R. (in press). Stage/environment fit revisited: A goal theory approach to examining school transitions. In C. Midgley (Ed.), *Goals, Goal Structures, and Patterns of Adaptive Learning.* Hillsborough, NJ: Lawrence Erlbaum Associates.

Midgley, C., Anderman, E., & Hicks, L. (1995). Differences between elementary and middle school teachers and students: A goal theory approach. *Journal of Early Adolescence*, 15, 90–113.

Midgley, C., Arunkumar, R., & Urdan, T. (1996). "If I don't do well tomorrow, there's a reason": Predictors of adolescents' use of academic self-handicapping strategies. *Journal of Educational Psychology*, 88, 423–434.

Midgley, C., Kaplan, A., & Middleton, M. (2001). Performance–approach goals: Good for what, for whom, under what circumstances, and at what cost? *Journal of Educational Psychology*, 93, 77–86.

Midgley, C., Kaplan, A., Middleton, M., Maehr, M. L., Urdan, T., Anderman, L. H., Anderman, E., & Roeser, R. (1998). The development and validation of scales assessing students' achievement goal orientations. *Contemporary Educational Psychology*, 23, 113–131.

Midgley, C., Maehr, M. L., Gheen, M., Hruda, L., Middleton, M., & Nelson, J. (1998). *The Michigan Middle School Study: Report to participating schools and districts.* Ann Arbor: University of Michigan.

Midgley, C., Maehr, M. L., Hruda, L., Anderman, E. M., Anderman, L., Freeman, K. E., Gheen, M., Kaplan, A., Kumar, R., Middleton, M. J., Nelson, J., Roeser, R., & Urdan, T. (2000). *Manual for the Patterns of Adaptive Learning Scales* (PALS). Ann Arbor: University of Michigan.

Miller, A.T. (1985). A developmental study of the cognitive basis of performance impairment after failure. *Journal of Personality and Social Psychology*, 49, 529–538.

Mueller, C. M., & Dweck, C.S. (1998). Praise for intelligence can undermine children's motivation and performance. *Journal of Personality and Social Psychology*, 75, 33–52.

Murphy, P. K., & Alexander, P. A. (2000). A motivated exploration of motivation terminology. *Contemporary Educational Psychology*, 25, 3–53.

Nicholls, J. (1978). The development of the concepts of effort and ability, perceptions of own attainment, and the understanding that difficult tasks require more ability. *Child Development*, 48, 800–814.

Nicholls, J. G., Cobb, P., Wood, T., Yackel, E., & Patashnick, M. (1990). Assessing students' theories of success in mathematics: Individual and classroom differences. *Journal for Research in Mathematics Education*, 21, 109–122.

Nicholls, J., & Miller, A. (1984). Development and its discontents: The differentiation of the concept of ability. In J. Nicholls (Ed.), *The development of achievement motivation* (pp. 185–218). Greenwich, CT: JAI Press.

Nolen, S. B. (1988). Reasons for studying: Motivational orientations and study strategies. *Cognition and Instruction*, 5, 269–287.

Nolen, S. B., & Haladyna, T. M. (1990). Motivation and studying in high school science. *Journal of Research in Science Teaching*, 27, 115–126.

Pajares, F., Britner, S. L., & Valiante, G. (2000). Relation between achievement goals and self-beliefs of middle school students in writing and science. *Contemporary Educational Psychology*, 25, 406–422.

Pintrich, P.R. (2000). An achievement goal theory perspective on issues in motivation terminology, theory, and research. *Contemporary Educational Psychology*, 25, 92–104.

Pintrich, P. R., & De Groot, E. V. (1990). Motivational and self-regulated learning components of classroom academic performance. *Journal of Educational Psychology*, 82, 33–40.

Pintrich, P. R., & Garcia, T. (1991). Student goal orientation and self-regulation in the college classroom. In M. L. Maehr & P. R. Pintrich (Eds.), *Advances in motivation and achievement: Goals and self-regulatory processes* (Vol. 7, pp. 371–402). Greenwich, CT: JAI Press.

Pintrich, P. R., & Schunk, D. H. (1996). *Motivation in education: Theory, research, and applications*. Englewood Cliffs, NJ: Prentice Hall.

Pintrich, P. R., Smith, D.A.F., Garcia, T., & McKeachie, W. J. (1993). Reliability and predictive validity of the Motivated Strategies Learning Questionnaire (MSLQ). *Educational and Psychological Measurement*, 53, 801–813.

Roeser, R. W., Eccles, J. S., & Sameroff, A. J. (2000). School as a context of early adolescents' academic and social–emotional development: A summary of research findings. *Elementary School Journal*, 100, 443–471.

Roeser, R. W., Midgley, C., & Urdan, T. C. (1996). Perceptions of the school psychological environment and early adolescents' behavioral functioning in school: The mediating role of goals and belonging. *Journal of Educational Psychology*, 88, 408–422.

Ryan, A. M., Hicks, L., & Midgley, C. (1997). Social goals, academic goals, and avoiding seeking help in the classroom. *Journal of Early Adolescence*, 17, 152–171.

Smiley, P. A., & Dweck, C. S. (1994). Individual differences in achievement goals among young children. *Child Development*, 65, 1723–1743.

Stipek, D. J., Recchia, S., & McClintic, S. (1992). Self-evaluation in young children. *Monographs of the Society for Research in Child Development*, 57 (1, Serial No. 226).

Supik, J. D., & Johnson, J. R. (1999). *Missing: Texas Youth. Dropout and Attrition Rates in Texas Public High Schools. A Policy Brief.* Intercultural Development Research Association, San Antonio, TX.

Turner, J. C., & Meyer, D. K. (2000). Studying and understanding the instructional contexts of classrooms: Using our past to forge our future. *Educational Psychologist*, 35, 69–85.

U.S. Department of Education (1990). *National goals for education* (Publication No. 455-B-2). Washington, DC: U.S. Government Printing Office.

Urdan, T. (1997). Achievement goal theory: Past results, future directions. In M. L. Maehr & P. R. Pintrich (Eds.), *Advances in motivation and achievement*, (Vol. 10 pp. 99–141). Greenwich, CT: JAI Press.

Urdan, T., Midgley, C., & Anderman, E. M. (1998). Classroom influences on self-handicapping strategies. *American Educational Research Journal*. 35, 101–122.

Wolters, C. A., Yu, S. L., & Pintrich, P. R. (1996). The relation between goal orientation and students' motivational beliefs and self-regulated learning. *Learning and Individual Differences*, 8, 211–238.

The Contribution of Social Goal Setting to Children's School Adjustment

KATHRYN R. WENTZEL

University of Maryland, College Park, Maryland

The social worlds of children are challenging and complex. Each day at home, children are expected to learn and follow family rules, interact with their parents and siblings in an appropriate manner, and generally contribute to family processes that support emotional health and safety. Similarly, children must negotiate their way through the school day, adhering to classroom rules, maintaining and making new friendships, and seeking out situations that allow them to thrive as members of the school community. Given these challenges, interesting questions arise concerning how and why children strive to achieve these social outcomes:

- What kinds of social goal setting do children engage in?
- Which goals must children pursue in order to be competent students?
- How do contexts provided by parents and teachers support or undermine the achievement of children's social needs?

My goal for this chapter is to provide some insight into these social motivational issues. Toward this end, I will describe several traditions for studying social goals and discuss social and relationship factors likely to have an impact on children's choice and pursuit of social goals. In addition, the implications of this work for understanding children's school adjustment will be considered.

PERSPECTIVES ON SOCIAL GOALS

What are social goals? Although definitions vary slightly as a function of theoretical perspective, goals are generally referred to as cognitive representations of future events that are powerful motivators of behavior (Austin & Vancouver, 1996; Bandura, 1986; Ford, 1992; Pervin, 1983). An underlying assumption of this definition is that people do set goals for themselves and in the case of social goals, to achieve specific social outcomes (e.g., making a friend) or to interact with others in certain ways (e.g., helping someone with a problem). Despite this common definition, researchers have studied social goals from three fairly distinct perspectives. First, researchers have investigated children's knowledge about and choice of social goals as a social–cognitive skill. Based on models of social information processing (e.g., Crick & Dodge, 1994; Dodge, 1986; Ford, 1984), this perspective highlights children's interpretations of social situations and their knowledge of which goals are appropriate or inappropriate to pursue under which conditions. In addition, the pursuit of social goals has been studied as a motivational process related to situation-specific competence. In this case, the extent to which children try to achieve certain prescribed goals is examined as a predictor of social competence and person–environment fit (Ford, 1982; 1992; Wentzel, 1991a, 1991b, 1993). Finally, social goals have been construed as motivational orientations that guide children's behavioral responses to social opportunities and challenges. For the most part, these more global social goals or needs are believed to function independently of context.

In this section, I will describe each of these perspectives and discuss how each might inform our understanding of children's motivation to achieve socially and academically at school.

Social Goal Setting as a Social–Cognitive Skill

Given that social situations are inherently ambiguous and ill defined, a major social–cognitive challenge for children is to discern which goals they should pursue in order to be socially accepted and to avoid conflict with others (see Parkhurst & Asher, 1985). Therefore, models of social information processing (Crick & Dodge, 1994; Dodge, 1986; Ford, 1984) have recognized the setting of social goals as a fundamental psychological process that contributes to behavioral competence. According to Crick and Dodge (1994), goals serve a critical psychological function in social decision making. Although not defined explicitly, these authors refer to goals as affectively charged beliefs concerning what an individual should do in response to specific social cues; goals are derived from past experiences with specific individuals or situations. Therefore, as part of an individual's history of social interactions, goals have a motivational function in that they predispose individuals to interpret information and act on it in certain ways. Goal setting is described further by Dodge as a component process of social decision making that acts in tandem with other social–cognitive processes, including encoding and interpretation of social cues, and generation and evaluation of possible responses, to eventually determine behavior.

Research on Social Goal Setting as a Social–Cognitive Process

Research on social goal setting as a social–cognitive process has focused on two related issues. First, researchers have sought to document the quality of goals that socially competent and incompetent children set in specific social situations. In addition, these goal-setting skills have been related to other information processing skills such as choice of problem-solving strategies and affect regulation. To study these issues, researchers have focused primarily on elementary school-aged children's reactions to hypothetical situations in which conflict between peers is described. Typically, children are asked to generate goals they would pursue in these situations or asked to choose goals that represent specific dimensions of behavior, such as hostile or benign (e.g., Slaby & Guerra, 1988).

Some of the earliest work on social–cognitive aspects of goal setting was conducted by Renshaw and Asher (1983), who demonstrated that children respond to a variety of hypothetical social situations (initiating peer interaction, peer group entry, making friends, resolving conflict) in predictable ways. In this research, children typically articulated goals to be friendly and outgoing, to accommodate the interests of others, to be compliant with social rules, to avoid negative consequences, and to be hostile. Moreover, these authors found that children's goal setting was related to their social status among peers, with more popular children generating a wider variety of nonhostile goals in the conflict resolution situation than less popular children. Similarly, Slaby & Guerra (1988) found that aggressive adolescents were more likely to endorse hostile goals than nonaggressive adolescents. More recently, researchers have extended these findings by linking goal setting to other self-regulatory skills. In general, these researchers have shown that endorsement of positive or benign goals is related positively to adaptive approaches to problem solving, general levels of social–behavioral competence, and anger management (Chung & Asher, 1996; Erdley & Asher, 1996; Murphy & Eisenberg, 1996).

Few studies have investigated this aspect of social goal setting in school contexts. One exception is an ethnographic study by Allen (1986) in which ninth grade students were interviewed about their school-related goals. Allen found that two major goals were mentioned by almost all students: to socialize with peers and to pass the course. Students believed these goals could be accomplished by trying to figure out the teacher, having fun, giving the teacher what he or she wants, minimizing work, reducing boredom, and staying out of trouble. When given a list of possible social and academic goals to pursue at school, high school students have reported trying to achieve social goals to have fun and to be dependable and responsible, in addition to task-related goals to learn new things and to get good grades (Wentzel, 1989).

Implications for Understanding School Adjustment

Although the majority of these studies have focused on issues related to social problem solving, this perspective has interesting implications for understanding the basic underpinnings of students' motivation. For instance, we often assume that students understand how they are supposed to behave and what it is they are supposed to accomplish while at school. However, for some students these expectations are not always immediately obvious. In particular, young children who are just beginning school and students being raised in cultures with goals and values dissimilar to those espoused by American educational institutions might need explicit guidance with respect to the school-related goals they are expected to achieve at school (Ogbu, 1985). In addition, teachers do not always clearly communicate their own goals for their students. In two studies of middle school students, almost half the participants reported that teachers did not have clear rules for them to follow and did not explain clearly what would happen if rules were broken (Wentzel, 2000; Wentzel, Battle, & Cusick, 2000). Therefore, the more explicit and clearly defined we can make the social expectations of school contexts, the more likely it is that students will at least understand the goals they are expected to achieve.

Based on social information processing models, interventions designed by Oden and Asher (1977) have demonstrated that helping children to replace inappropriate goals with ones that will facilitate social competence can lead to improved behavioral skills when interacting with peers. Similarly, it is reasonable to expect that school-based interventions that provide children with a clear set of socially acceptable goals to strive for might help alleviate school adjustment problems. In this regard, providing children with a more balanced set of goals might be especially beneficial. Rabiner and Gordon (1992) asked boys to generate goals for hypothetical situations that required coordination of competitive and cooperative goals to resolve a conflict. In this case, aggressive boys who also were rejected by their peers tended to generate goals that were focused on personal needs and interests, whereas nonaggressive and socially accepted boys were more likely to generate responses that reflected a balance between personal goals, goals that focused on the needs of others, or goals to maintain interpersonal relationships. Together, these studies support the notion that students trained to identify and subsequently coordinate multiple social goals might also develop more positive interactions with peers as well as teachers.

What is missing from this research is an examination of which goals children pursue in real-life situations and the consequences of not pursuing school-related goals that are valued by adults and peers. Theoretical and empirical issues related to this perspective are discussed in the next section.

Social Goal Pursuit as an Aspect of Competence

A second perspective on social goals is based on the assumption that pursuit of specific social goals is a critical aspect of situational competence. In contrast to the social–cognitive approach, this perspective does not focus on children's understanding of which goals are appropriate in a given social situation but rather on the extent to which pursuit of certain socially valued goals contributes to situation-specific competence. Indeed, Bronfenbrenner (1989) argues that competence can be understood only in terms of context-specific effectiveness, that is, mastery of culturally and socially defined tasks. Therefore, competence is not only the achievement of personal goals, but of ways in which an individual contributes to the smooth functioning of the social group. With respect to goal pursuit, this implies that effective functioning in social settings requires the achievement of goals that result in approval and acceptance by the social group, as well as those resulting in the achievement of personal competence and feelings of self-determination (see Bronfenbrenner, 1989; Ford, 1992). With respect to classroom competence, research is typically focused on the latter set of self-focused goals. However, if one takes into account the social ecology of the classroom, the pursuit of socially integrative goals such as to be cooperative and compliant should be equally important for understanding school success.

Using this competence-based perspective, I have explored the degree to which school-related success can be predicted by the degree to which children pursue specific social goals to behave in pro-social and socially responsible ways. I define personal goals with respect to their content, that is, as a cognitive representation of *what* it is that an individual is trying to achieve in a given situation (see also Ford, 1992). Context goals would be defined as what it is that individuals should be trying to achieve if they are to be competent and successful within that situation.

Goals to be prosocial and responsible are of particular interest given the increasing recognition among scholars that children's overall adjustment and success at school requires a willingness as well as ability to meet social as well as academic challenges (Hinshaw, 1992; Ladd, 1989; Wentzel, 1991b). Being a successful student is dependent on conforming to rules for social conduct such as to pay attention, to cooperate with others, and to restrain from aggressive or disruptive behavior. Students also must conform to rules and conventions for completing learning activities; teachers provide students with procedures for accomplishing academic tasks and dictate specific criteria and standards for performance. Moreover, teachers prefer to have students in their class who behave in socially responsible ways (Wentzel, 1991a, 1994).

Research on Prosocial and Socially Responsible
Goal Pursuit

In my research, I have typically asked students to report how often they try to pursue specific goals while at school. For instance, in a study of high school students, 62% of students reported always trying to be dependable and responsible and 42% reported always trying to be helpful to others. Girls reported trying to be helpful significantly more often than did boys (Wentzel, 1989). In a series of follow-up studies, social goal pursuit was operationalized more specifically as students' self-reported efforts to help, share, and cooperate with teachers and peers (prosocial goals) and to follow rules and keep interpersonal promises and commitments (social responsibility goals). In this case, girls tended to report more frequent pursuit of these goals than did boys (Wentzel 1991a, 1994), and the frequency with which these goals were pursued decreased from sixth to eighth grade (Wentzel, 1997). Interestingly, adolescents in middle school reported trying to achieve social goals to behave appropriately more frequently than goals to learn or to socialize with peers (Wentzel, 1991b, 1992).

Does pursuit of socially valued goals predict school-related competence? Work on prosocial and social responsibility goals has related motivation to achieve these outcomes with various aspects of social as well as academic success. With respect to social competence, middle school students who frequently pursue these goals are better liked by their peers and teachers than are students who report infrequent pursuit of these goals (Wentzel, 1994). In addition, as predicted by an ecological perspective, there is ample evidence that students who pursue certain social goals at school also succeed academically. For example, pursuit of goals to be prosocial and responsible is related positively to classroom grades (Wentzel, 1989, 1991a, 1993, 1996, 1997, 1998) as well as to IQ (Wentzel, 1991a). For the most part, these relations are mediated by students' displays of prosocial and socially responsible behavior at school (Wentzel, 1991a, 1994).

These goals also have been examined as part of a coordinated effort to achieve multiple social and academic goals. I have found that high and low achieving high school students can be distinguished on the basis of the sets of goals they pursue or do not pursue at school (Wentzel, 1989). In particular, 84% of the highest achieving students reported always trying to be a successful student, to be dependable and responsible, and to get things done on time; only 13% of the lowest achieving students reported always trying to achieve these three goals. Moreover, although the highest achieving students reported frequent pursuit of academic goals (i.e., to learn new things, to understand things), less frequent pursuit of these goals did not distinguish the lowest achieving from average achieving students. Rather, an unwillingness to try to conform to the social and normative standards of the classroom uniquely characterized the lowest achieving students. These low achieving students also reported frequent pursuit of other types of social goals such as to have fun and to make and keep friendships. In a follow-up study of middle school students (Wentzel, 1993), two academic goals reflecting efforts to master new and challenging tasks and to earn positive evaluations and two social goals reflecting efforts to be prosocial and to be socially responsible were investigated. Pursuits of these social and academic goals were significant, independent predictors of classroom effort over time, even when other motivational variables such as self-efficacy and values were taken into account (Wentzel, 1996).

Implications for Understanding School Adjustment

This perspective on social goal setting can provide researchers with a rich description of the multiple goals that students try to achieve at school, as well as a basis for understanding person–environment fit as it relates to classrooms and schools (Eccles, 1993). In other words, an examination of which goals a student is trying to achieve and the degree to which these goals are compatible with the requirements of the classroom can explain, in part, students' overall success and adjustment at school.

Several important issues, however, remain for further study. First, greater focus on development and testing of theoretical models that explain links between social competence and academic achievement is needed. For instance, it is likely that pursuit of prosocial and social responsibility goals is related to academic outcomes for several reasons. Positive relations might reflect the possibility that students are rewarded for their social efforts with good grades. In addition, when students are behaving appropriately, it is likely that their attention will be focused on instructional activities and therefore, will likely learn more than if they are misbehaving. It also is reasonable to expect that pursuit of social goals can result more directly in intellectual gains. Goals to be socially competent should lead to displays of cooperative and helpful behavior with peers (Wentzel, 1992, 1994). In turn, constructivist theories of development (Piaget, 1965; Youniss & Smollar, 1989) propose that positive social interactions (e.g., cooperative and collaborative problem solving) can create cognitive conflict that hastens the development of higher order thinking skills and cognitive structures (e.g., DeBaryshe, Patterson, & Capabaldi, 1993; Slavin, 1987; Wentzel, 1991a).

This perspective also raises questions concerning how students coordinate their own social and academic goals with those promoted within individual classrooms. For instance, some students who try to pursue multiple goals might be unable to coordinate the pursuit of their goals into an organized system of behavior, and as a consequence become distracted or overwhelmed when facing particularly demanding aspects of tasks that require focused concentration and attention. An example of this problem occurs when students want to achieve social goals *and* academically related goals. Students who are unable to coordinate these goals might opt to pursue social relationship goals with peers (e.g., to have fun) in lieu of task-related goals such as to complete class assignments. Students with more effective goal coordination skills would likely find a way to achieve both goals, for instance, by doing homework with friends. An identification of specific self-regulatory strategies that enable students to accomplish more than one task at a time seems essential for helping students coordinate demands to achieve multiple and often conflicting goals at school.

It also is worth noting that only a limited number of social goals have been studied in relation to academic outcomes. However, a broad array of goals that reflect social concerns and influences are highly relevant for understanding students' academic motivation and general adjustment to school. Ford (1992) has identified three general categories of goals that require input from or interaction with the social environment: integrative social relationship goals, self-assertive social relationship goals, and task goals. The social relationship goals identified by Ford are perhaps most relevant to the social motivational issues raised thus far, with goals to benefit the welfare of others and the social group (integrative social relationship goals) having been studied most frequently (e.g., Ford, 1996; Wentzel, 1991a, 1993, 1994). However, a focus on self-assertive social relationship goals (e.g., obtaining help or resources from others) reminds us of the potential benefits of relationships to the individual. An inclusion of these goals in studies of academic motivation (e.g., A. M. Ryan & Pintrich, 1997) would provide added insight into issues of how individuals derive personal benefits from working and learning with others.

Social Goals as Generalized Motivational Orientations

Social goals also have been defined as relatively enduring aspects of personality that orient an individual toward achieving specific outcomes in social situations. McClelland's identification of need for affiliation as a powerful explanatory construct represents some of the earliest work on social orientations and needs (see McClelland, 1987). According to McClelland, people with a high need for affiliation tend to display a "concern over establishing, maintaining, or restoring a positive, affective relationship with another person or persons" (p. 347). Work based on this definition demonstrated that individuals with a high need for affiliation are more sensitive to affiliative cues, are more interested in and learn more about social relationships more quickly, and interact with others more frequently than those with a low need for affiliation.

Subsequent work in this area identified the need for social approval as an important social motivator of children's classroom learning (e.g., Maehr, 1983; Veroff, 1969). More recently, Dweck proposed that children have social goal orientations that guide problem solving in social situations (Dweck & Leggett, 1988). These goal orientations are hypothesized to result in individuals interpreting situations as either providing opportunities for positive evaluation and gaining social approval or avoiding social disapproval (social performance goals) or providing opportunities to learn and form new relationships (social learning goals).

Social needs also have gained prominence in the work of Connell and his colleagues (Connell & Wellborn, 1991; Deci & Ryan, 1991). In this work, motivation is defined in terms of three basic needs, competence, autonomy, and relatedness. Of relevance for the present discussion is the need for relatedness, defined as "the need to feel securely connected to the social surround and the need to experience oneself as worthy and capable of love and respect" (Connell & Wellborn, 1991, p. 51). According to these authors, individuals experience a positive sense of self, emotional well-being, and beliefs that the social environment is a benevolent and supportive place when this need for relatedness is met. Moreover, they suggest that a sense of social relatedness contributes to the adoption of goals promoted by social groups or institutions, whereas a lack of relatedness or disaffection can lead to a rejection of such goals. In other words, the pursuit of social goals that promote group cohesion and positive interpersonal interactions (such as to be prosocial and responsible), depends in large part on feeling like one is an integral and valued part of the social group.

Research on Social Orientations and Needs

There is not a cohesive body of research on social orientations and needs, although some consistent findings have been reported. For instance, studies of need for affiliation established consistent links between this social need and a variety of social and academically related outcomes (see McClelland, 1987). Of particular interest is that students with high need for affiliation appear to benefit from certain types of classroom environments. Specifically, McKeachie, et al. (1966) found that college students with high need for affiliation worked harder and got better grades when their instructor was socially supportive and friendly than when the instructor was not affiliative.

Researchers of children's needs for approval also have found fairly consistent results in that orientations to gain social approval tend to be antagonistic to learning. For instance, Kozeki and Entwistle (1984; Entwistle & Kozeki, 1985; Kozeki, 1985) found that elementary school-aged students concerned with moral outcomes such as compliance and responsibility reported learning styles that were less conducive to conceptual learning than did students with more intrinsic and task-related orientations. Similarly, Crandall (1966) found that elementary school-aged children who expressed a high need for social approval did less well academically than children with a low need for approval. However, she also found that older students who had strong needs for social approval performed better than their peers who were less concerned with social evaluation. One explanation for these contradictory findings is that the ability of older children to coordinate social and learning goals enhances school performance, whereas younger children's relative inability to focus on multiple goals simultaneously results in performance decrements.

Dweck and her colleagues (Erdley, Cain, Loomis, Dumas-Hines, & Dweck, 1997) examined children's social goal orientations within the context of making friends. Using an experimental format in which children experienced failure when trying to obtain a pen pal, these authors demonstrated that children endorse goals to learn about and develop new relationships (social learning goal orientations) and to obtain social approval or to avoid social disapproval (social performance goal orientations) in response to hypothetical social situations. They further demonstrated that these social goal orientations were related to their behavioral responses to failure. Children with social performance goal orientations tended to react with helpless types of responses in reaction to social rejection (e.g., decreased effort to obtain a pen pal), whereas those with social learning goal orientations reacted to rejection with increased effort and persistence. Goal orientations in the social domain have not been linked to those operating in academic or task-related domains of functioning.

Systematic research that has assessed social relatedness has not been forthcoming, although Connell and Wellborn (1991) report significant relations between a sense of relatedness and student engagement. However, aspects of social and emotional well-being that are reflected in Connell and Wellborn's definition of relatedness have been related consistently to academic outcomes. For instance, studies have linked psychological distress and depression to interest in school (Wentzel, Weinberger, Ford, & Feldman, 1990) as well as to academic performance (Harter, 1990; Wentzel, Weinberger, Ford, & Feldman, 1990). Negative emotional states have been related to negative attitudes, poor adjustment to school (see Dubow & Tisak, 1989), and ineffective cognitive functioning (e.g., Jacobsen, Edelstein, & Hoffmann, 1994). In addition, interventions designed to create classrooms that address the social and emotional needs of elementary school-aged children also have increased levels of academic as well as social competence in students (Watson, Solomon, Battistich, Schaps, & Solomon, 1989).

Implications for Understanding School Adjustment

Personality approaches to social motivation offer a unique perspective on what compels individuals to behave as they do. Specifically, the study of goal orientations and needs is focused on factors that reflect and validate one's sense of self and meet basic social needs. Moreover, it is expected that these personality-level goals will be pursued in systematic fashion across multiple contexts. Therefore, rather than posing the question of "What does this person want to do?" a researcher might ask "What does this person want to be like?" Or, rather than asking the question, "How does an individual's social goal pursuit contribute to situation-specific competence?" a researcher might ask, "How does the context contribute to the achievement of an individual's social needs?"

These are interesting and important questions, especially for understanding children who tend to display problematic behavior in many and diverse social situations, or for those who consistently choose to pursue situation-specific goals that are inappropriate or antithetical to those valued by others. Adopting this approach, however, is problematic for several reasons. First, researchers have adopted multiple definitions of social needs, including basic orientations toward social problem solving (Dweck & Leggett, 1988), one's ability to regulate affect and other physiological states (Eisenberg & Fabes, 1992), motivational qualities of the emotional attachment, or affective bond, that has developed between two individuals (Connell & Wellborn, 1991) and the need to validate one's sense of worth (Covington, 1992). However, clear distinctions between these various definitions need to be maintained as they represent quite different outcomes. In addition, given that these definitions reflect complex psychological processes, it is not clear that equating them with a generalized goal orientation or need is useful for understanding their contribution to behavior.

More general criticisms of personality approaches to motivation have typically centered around the fact that an individual's behavior is rarely consistent across situations. For instance, a child who is aggressive with peers might be compliant among adults; a student who is attentive and engaged in math class might be inattentive and disruptive in social studies class. It has been argued, therefore, that these variations in behavior cannot be explained by traitlike orientations but rather by idiosyncratic influences such as social expectations, social cues, and opportunities that uniquely determine goal setting in each situation. One could counter, however, that individuals have multiple orientations and needs that regulate behavior. Indeed, adopting Connell's perspective, one might expect children to become engaged in a context to the extent that it provided opportunities to meet needs of relatedness, competence, or autonomy. In other words, it is possible that children engage academically in one classroom because relatedness needs are being met, they might cooperate with peers in another because this allows them to demonstrate competence, and they might act out in another to achieve some level of personal autonomy.

In summary, as with a competence-based perspective described earlier, understanding the motivational significance of social needs requires an examination of contexts and the degree to which they afford the satisfaction of these needs. Without a clear understanding of how children perceive a situation and its various provisions for goal attainment, it is difficult to predict which goals they will pursue, much less why. This is a critical issue for understanding the contribution of social goals to school success that will be discussed further in the next section.

Coordinating Multiple Perspectives on Social
Goal Setting

Thus far, I have described three somewhat unique perspectives on social goals, each with different implications for understanding school adjustment. However, a more coherent understanding of social goals might be possible if these perspectives are considered to be part of an interrelated system of motivational processes. Indeed, it is likely that these perspectives are not mutually exclusive but rather reflect various levels of generality at which goals and their contribution to motivation might be studied. This section describes ways to integrate these various perspectives into a more cohesive picture of social goal setting at school.

In what ways might these three approaches be compatible with each other? At the most basic level, social goal setting can be viewed as a response to how we perceive and understand our social worlds. Most often these perceptions reflect the demands of the social situations we are experiencing at a given moment, and our understanding of what can and cannot be accomplished given situational constraints and affordances. At this level of psychological functioning, goals are likely to reflect a wide range of possible outcomes that potentially can be achieved rather than outcomes that are actively pursued. It is likely that we then use this knowledge to choose goals that will allow us to accomplish some level of situation-specific competence or at least some level of compatibility with the demands of the situation. As Ford (1992) suggests, these choices might be based on our beliefs and expectations about our own abilities to achieve a goal in this particular context, as well as our knowledge of what is appropriate and inappropriate conduct. It also is likely that our choice of these situation-specific goals will reflect desires to achieve more basic social needs.

If viewed in this manner, each aspect of goal setting makes a unique contribution to decisions concerning which goals will be pursued in a given situation. Although described in hierarchical fashion, these levels of decision making reflect an iterative process; for instance, social orientations are likely to determine, in part, how we perceive a situation and the degree to which we strive to be socially competent. This integrated approach is particularly useful for understanding children's classroom motivation. For instance, students are likely to view the classroom as affording the achievement of multiple goals, many of which are social. Students are also likely to understand that the achievement of some of these goals is more desirable than others if they want to be successful at school. How students ultimately define success (e.g., gaining adult or peer approval, developing new relationships, helping classmates) and the degree to which and how they think their classroom affords them the opportunity to achieve that success (e.g., opportunities to compete for grades, opportunities to collaborate with peers) will ultimately determine which goals they will decide to pursue.

Beyond explanations of why students behave as they do, these complex goal systems can also inform our understanding of students' efforts to achieve academically. A student's pursuit of goals that results in person–environment fit might reflect a desire to conform to the demands of the situation, that is, to achieve positive intellectual and performance outcomes. In addition, however, a student might perceive the goal of getting a good grade as a classroom requirement and therefore, a responsible thing to do. In this case, a student might excel academically because this type of achievement fulfills a more global social need for adult approval. The important point is that if we are to understand the relevance of social goal setting for academic outcomes, each perspective must be acknowledged: What kinds of goals and needs does the individual child bring to the classroom? Which goals do teachers expect students to achieve, and to what extent does the child understand these expectations? And does the student have effective strategies for coordinating multiple goals?

From a methodological perspective, however, addressing each of these questions is not a simple task. For instance, researchers of social–cognition often assess goal setting qualitatively by first asking "What would you do?" (responses are considered as strategies) and then "Why would you do this?" (responses are considered as goals). To study this type of goal setting, researchers present subjects with hypothetical situations that require goal coordination and conflict resolution skills. What is needed in this regard is a clearer distinction between strategies and goals, and a better understanding of how children perceive and respond to problems in real classroom settings. In my own work (see Wentzel, 1993), I ask students to report how often they try to accomplish something in their classes at school (e.g., "In this class, how often do you try to share what you've learned with your classmates?"). What is needed here is an identification of which goals students are expected to achieve in a classroom. For instance, do teachers really expect students to help each other with their work and do they provide meaningful opportunities to do so? Finally, social orientations and needs are assessed using a variety of self-report instruments designed to tap general beliefs about the self (e.g., "Do you always help people who need help?" [Crandall & Katkovsky, 1965]). In this case, scales that tap specific social orientations (e.g., cooperation, compliance, affiliation) need to be developed. Although these methodological problems require careful and systematic work to resolve, such work will be necessary to understand the entire range of processes involved in social goal setting.

THE DEVELOPMENT OF SOCIAL GOALS

How do children's social goals change over time? Interestingly, few researchers have addressed this question longitudinally. However, another way to think about development is to consider why children's goals change over time. In this case, the challenge is to identify the socialization processes that lead children to pursue certain goals and not others, and to adopt specific social orientations that direct behavior across multiple contexts and over time. Indeed, this is the central concern of educators and parents alike. One common explanation for how social influence occurs focuses on the motivational significance of children's social relationships. In general, it is hypothesized that children are more likely to adopt and internalize goals that are valued by adults when their relationships are nurturant and supportive as opposed to harsh and critical (see Grusec & Goodnow, 1994). The role of interpersonal relationships with parents and teachers in explanations of why students pursue social goals will be the focus of this section. Specifically, I will discuss ways in which models of socialization offer some insight into how parents and teachers motivate children to engage in each type of social goal setting described in the previous sections.

Social Orientations and Needs

Although children pursue goals for many reasons, the question of what leads students to pursue goals for their own sake without the need for external prompts or rewards lies at the heart of research on motivation (e.g., Maehr, 1984; R. M. Ryan & Stiller, 1991). One way to understand this phenomenon is to consider social orientations and needs as types of internalized goals. In other words, goals that have been internalized are those which a student will pursue consistently across many learning situations. These goals could represent outcomes in which a student is intrinsically interested or those for which he or she has acquired personal value (e.g., R. M. Ryan, 1993).

If specific socialization experiences promote the development of these social orientations, how does this influence occur? For the most part, mechanisms that link parenting styles to children's internalization of specific goals have not been the target of empirical investigations. However, Lewin was able to document that children granted developmentally appropriate levels of autonomy and personal control by adults displayed greater persistence at assigned tasks in the absence of adults than did children who interacted with over- or undercontrolling adults (e.g., Lewin, Lippitt, & White, 1939). These findings were especially important for their implication that certain socialization experiences might result in behavior motivated by internalized goals and values rather than by mere compliance.

Diana Baumrind extended this work to the study of parent–child interactions and socialization within the family. Based on extensive observations of parents and children, Baumrind concluded that specific dimensions of parent–child interactions could reliably predict children's social, emotional, and cognitive competence (Baumrind, 1971, 1991). In general, these dimensions reflect consistent enforcement of rules, expectations for self-reliance and self-control, solicitation of children's opinions and feelings, and expressions of warmth and approval. Of interest for the present discussion is that they also have been useful in establishing links between parenting behavior and children's academic motivation, including intrinsic interest (Ginsberg & Bronstein, 1996; Rathunde, 1996) and goal orientations toward learning (Hokoda & Fincham, 1995). Although these studies provide little evidence that specific parenting practices promote the consistent pursuit of specific social goals much less degrees of internalization, they do indicate that motivational processes may be a critical link between socialization experiences and academic outcomes. Moreover, this literature supports a conclusion that parent socialization processes can have an impact on children's motivation to achieve in contexts outside the home.

A more specific model of influence proposed by R. M. Ryan (1993; see also Grolnick, Gurland, Jacob, & Decourcey, Chapter 6, this volume) recognizes the importance of parenting styles similar to those identified by Baumrind and speaks directly to the issue of why children adopt and internalize socially valued goals (for similar arguments, see Deci & Ryan, 1991; Connell & Wellborn, 1991; Ford, 1992; Grolnick, Kurowski, & Gurland, 1999; Lepper, 1983). Ryan argues that within the context of a secure parent–child relationship in which caregivers provide contingent feedback, nurturance, and developmentally appropriate structure and guidance, young children develop a generalized positive sense of social relatedness, personal competence, and autonomy when presented with new experiences and challenges. These positive aspects of self-development then support the internalization of socially prescribed goals and values, that is, "the transformation of external controls and regulations into internal ones" (R. M. Ryan, 1993, p. 29). In contrast, children who do not experience secure relationships tend to enter situations with detachment or high levels of emotional distress.

Ryan's perspective on parent socialization implies that students' orientations toward achieving socially valued outcomes in the classroom, including academic success, might be part of an overarching or more global motivational system derived from early socialization experiences. Although limited, research supports this notion. For instance, young children's initial orientations toward achievement at academic tasks appears to be grounded in a child's fundamental view of themselves as morally and socially acceptable human beings (Dweck, 1991; Heyman, Dweck, & Cain, 1992; see also, Benenson & Dweck, 1986; Burhans & Dweck, 1995). Further, Heyman and Dweck (1998; Heyman, Dweck, & Cain, 1992) report that these beliefs are related to children's reports of how they think their parents will react to their successes and failures, with children expressing performance orientations also reporting high levels of parental criticism, and those expressing mastery orientations reporting positive and supportive parental responses.

At a more general level, researchers have related aspects of parenting to young children's sense of relatedness, personal competence, and autonomy (Grolnick & Slowiaczek, 1994; Grolnick & Ryan, 1989). Research on adolescents also has established that perceived social and emotional support from parents is related positively to perceived academic competence, a sense of relatedness to peers, and academic effort and interest in school (Cauce, Felner, & Primavera, 1982; Connell, Spencer, & Aber, 1994; Felner, Aber, Primavera, & Cauce, 1985; Harter, 1987; Wentzel, 1998; Wenz-Gross, Siperstein, Untch, & Wideman, 1997).

An important gap in this literature is that few studies have established links between teachers' communication of rules and norms, and students' acceptance and internalization of these expectations in the form of valued goals. R. M. Ryan's (1993) model of internalization poses the intriguing hypothesis that the foundations for internalization can only be laid within the context of early socialization experiences and that later social interactions outside the family are likely to have little influence in this regard. However, it is clear that teachers can influence which classroom-specific goals children choose to pursue, primarily by defining appropriate types of classroom behavior and standards for social as well as academic competence. The literature that supports this conclusion will be discussed in the next section.

Context-Specific Competence and Goal Pursuit

Much research on socialization practices at school has focused on issues pertaining to classroom management (e.g., Doyle, 1986) and classroom reward structures (e.g., Ames, 1992). More specifically, an extensive literature documents that teachers actively teach social norms and expectations for classroom behavior. For instance, teachers tend to have a core set of expectations for their students. Trenholm and Rose (1981) identified six categories of student behavior deemed necessary for success by elementary school teachers: appropriate responses to academic requests and tasks, impulse control, mature problem solving, cooperative and courteous interaction with peers, involvement in class activities, and recognition of appropriate contexts for different types of behavior.

LeCompte (1978a, 1978b) reports similar findings from observations of elementary school classrooms. In these studies, teachers held expectations that children should conform to authority, follow schedules and not waste time, equate academic achievement with personal worth, keep busy, and maintain order. Moreover, teachers actively communicate these expectations to their students, regardless of the teachers' instructional goals, teaching styles, and ethnicity, and most students understand that these are important rules to obey (see also, Blumenfeld, Hamilton, Bossert, Wessels, & Meece, 1983; Hargreaves, Hester, & Mellor, 1975). Teachers also communicate expectations for students' interactions with each other. High school teachers promote adherence to interpersonal rules concerning aggression, manners, stealing, and loyalty (Hargreaves, Hester, & Mellor, 1975), and elementary school teachers tend to focus on peer norms for sharing resources, being nice to each other, working well with others, and harmonious problem solving (Sieber, 1979).

In addition teachers provide students with contexts that support the adoption of these goals. In studies of elementary school-aged students, teacher provisions of structure, guidance, and autonomy have been related to a range of positive, motivational outcomes (e.g., Skinner & Belmont, 1993). When teachers are taught to provide students with warmth and support, clear expectations for behavior, and developmentally appropriate autonomy, their students develop a stronger sense of community, increase displays of socially competent behavior, and show academic gains (Schaps, Battistich, & Solomon, 1997; Watson, Battistich, Schaps, & Solomon, 1989).

Teachers also structure learning environments in ways that make certain goals more salient to students than others. For example, cooperative learning structures can be designed to promote the pursuit of social goals to be responsible to the group and to achieve common objectives (Ames & Ames, 1984; Cohen, 1986; Solomon, Schaps, Watson, & Battistich, 1992). Finally, teachers also provide students with evaluation criteria and design tasks in ways that can focus attention on goals to learn and develop skills (task-related and intellectual goals) or to demonstrate ability to others (performance goals) (see Ames, 1992; Blumenfeld, 1992).

Social Cognition and Goal Setting

Few researchers have examined socialization processes that might influence social–cognitive aspects of social goal setting, especially the degree to which students believe that classrooms afford opportunities to achieve social goals. However, these beliefs are likely to reflect to some degree cultural or social orientations towards goal pursuit and situational affordances learned at home (see, e.g., Fordham & Ogbu, 1986; Okagaki & Sternberg, 1993; Phelan, Davidson, & Cao, 1991). If students' beliefs about appropriate school-related goals do not match those of the classroom, they are likely to feel alienated and to disengage. To illustrate, students who come to school with strong motives to behave prosocially rather than competitively (e.g., Knight & Kagan, 1977) might develop a generalized belief that classrooms are antagonistic to their social needs. This would be especially true if they have a history of interacting with teachers who have rewarded demonstrations of superiority rather than equality. These students are likely to perceive the classroom as an unsupportive if not hostile environment.

Research on perceived social support also underscores the important role that a students' perceptions and interpretations of their teacher's behavior plays in their active pursuit of appropriate classroom goals. For instance, teachers vary in the degree to which they are perceived as socially supportive and caring by their students (Wentzel, 1994, 1997). In turn, these perceptions are related to students' pursuit of social goals to be cooperative and responsible as well as to learn (Wentzel, 1991a, 1994). In addition, Eccles and her colleagues (Feldlaufer, Midgley, & Eccles, 1988; Midgley, Feldlaufer, & Eccles, 1989) have found that young adolescents report declines in the nurturant qualities of teacher–student relationships after the transition to middle school; these declines correspond to declines in academic motivation and achievement. These findings are especially interesting in that they document the interrelated role of students' perceptions and social needs (i.e., social support and belongingness) in predicting classroom-specific motivation.

The literature on social relatedness suggests that a fruitful avenue of research would be to extend our understanding of the underlying belief systems that are reflected in students' perceptions of social support at school (see Wentzel, 1997, in press). Interestingly, by middle school, adolescents have fairly clear notions of what a supportive and caring teacher is like. When asked to characterize teachers who care, middle school students describe teachers who demonstrate democratic and egalitarian communication styles designed to elicit student participation and input, develop expectations for student behavior and performance in light of individual differences and abilities, model a "caring" attitude and interest in their instruction and interpersonal dealings with students, and provide constructive rather than harsh and critical feedback. Moreover, students who perceive their teachers to display high levels of these characteristics also tend to pursue appropriate social and academic classroom goals more frequently than students who do not (Wentzel, 2000).

Future research might also focus on identifying additional student characteristics that predispose students to perceive relationships with adults and peers in either positive or negative ways. The literature on peer relationships suggests that children who are socially rejected tend to believe that others are out to harm them when in fact they are not, and they choose to pursue inappropriate and often antisocial goals in social situations (see Dodge & Feldman, 1990; Erdley, 1996). Over time, these children develop relationships with their peers marked by mistrust and hostility. Similar research has not been conducted on student–teacher relationships. However, it is possible that students who believe that teachers do not like them might also be perceiving and interpreting these adult relationships in ways that are biased and unfounded. Therefore, efforts to promote perceptions that peers and teachers are caring and supportive are likely to be most successful if students themselves are targets of intervention.

Implications for Understanding School Adjustment

There is growing evidence that models of socialization might be well suited for understanding which goals children pursue at school and the degree to which these goals have been internalized and represent personal values. Socialization models are especially important to consider with respect to the content of students' goals, given that successful students must achieve social and academic objectives that are imposed externally by adults. In this regard, it is important to note that some students reject these goals outright. It is likely that other students merely comply with these expectations and present the impression that they are interested in achieving what is required when in fact, they are not (see Juvonen, 1996; Sivan, 1986). Some students, however, are likely to have internalized adult-valued goals and are committed to achieving them regardless of competing expectations. Therefore, identifying the precise socialization experiences that lead to these fundamentally different orientations toward learning remains a significant challenge to the field.

Several other issues remain unresolved with respect to teacher influences on student goal setting. First, teachers tend to focus on different issues depending on the age of their students. For instance, teachers of early elementary and junior high school students tend to spend more of their time on issues related to social conduct than do teachers at other grade levels (Brophy & Evertson, 1978). In addition, the contribution of various socialization agents to the development and internalization of goals and values might also change with age. Whereas parents and teachers might facilitate the learning and adoption of goals in young children, peers might play an increasingly important role as children reach adolescence. It is likely that developmental influences and changes that orient children to either adults or peers for guidance are central to explanations of context-specific goal pursuit, and to the question of how the content of students' goals changes with age. One obvious direction for future research would be an examination of changes in the degree to which adult and peer norms are complementary or compatible with each other as well as with personal goals (e.g., Phelan, Davidson, & Cao, 1991).

The reward structures teachers establish in their classrooms also might have differential impact depending on how old the students' are and the family environment. Ames (1984, 1992) has identified several classroom reward structures that communicate the value of goals to compete with others, to improve one's own personal performance, and to cooperate with group efforts. However, middle and high school students might be more attuned to evaluation practices that are competitive and normative than elementary school-aged children (see Harter, 1996; Ruble, 1983). Students from families who stress mastery over performance might also be less susceptible to teacher practices that focus on performance and ability (Ames & Archer, 1987). In addition, teachers are likely to differ in their promotion of specific classroom goals as well as beliefs concerning what it means to be a successful student. For example, a student who pursues social needs for relatedness and therefore chooses to adopt classroom goals valued by her teacher might learn that being better than others (pursuing competitive goals) defines success, whereas the same student might learn from another teacher that progressively mastering a subject (achieving individualistic goals) or perhaps even behaving cooperatively (achieving prosocial goals) defines success (see Ames, 1984, 1992). Therefore, it is difficult to predict which students will be most successful without knowing the content of goals and belief systems being communicated by individual teachers.

Issues of goal coordination also are relevant for discussions of socialization influences, especially when we consider the potentially negative motivational effects of competing, incongruent goals across family, peer, and classroom contexts often experienced by minority students (Phelan, Davidson, & Cao, 1991). Children from minority cultures often are expected to adapt to normative expectations for behavior that are inconsistent with those espoused by their families and communities. Ogbu (1985; Fordham & Ogbu, 1986) describes how failing to achieve academically can be interpreted by some minority children as an accomplishment rather than a failure. In such cases, noncompliance with the majority culture's institutional norms and standards for achievement can lead to acceptance within the minority community but social rejection and academic failure at school. Indeed, goal pursuit can explain, in part, significant gender and ethnic differences in classroom behavior and achievement (Wentzel, 1991a).

Little is known about cultural influences on goal setting. However, when Knight and Kagan (1977) attempted to deduce goals from how children distribute rewards between themselves and peers in experimental, game-playing formats, they found that Mexican-American children became increasingly prosocial and cooperative in their distribution of rewards with age (5–6 years vs. 7–9 years), whereas Anglo-American children became more competitive. These findings were robust for children of high as well as low socioeconomic status and regardless of the school they attended. Although not directly relevant to school performance, these findings suggest that a student's cultural background might also influence his or her choice of goals in classroom settings, especially with respect to competing with peers for social or academic rewards.

CONCLUSION

Social goal setting is a multifaceted and complex process. As described in this chapter, goal setting involves interpreting social situations and deciding which goals are appropriate or inappropriate to pursue under which conditions; it involves choices that can lead to socially competent or incompetent behavior, and it requires coordination of global social needs and the demands of specific situations. In the classroom, this process is translated into one of gaining knowledge about the social expectations, rules, and norms in individual classrooms, choosing to adhere to those that will bring success as a student, and achieving social needs in the form of classroom goals that have taken on personal value.

How and why these social goal setting processes develop is not well understood. Indeed, even the most basic descriptive research has not been done. However, we are beginning to gain some insight into socialization factors that can promote social competence in the classroom. In particular, caregiving styles on the part of teachers marked by democratic and respectful interactions, expectations for performance based on individual differences, and constructive, nurturing feedback seem to promote children's pursuit as well as internalization of adult-valued goals. Children's ability to coordinate the multiple demands of teachers, parents, and peers with their own personal needs appears to be one of the most critical skills to develop in dealing with these often competing social influences.

The impact of other social context factors such as gender, race, and culture also needs to be incorporated into research designs. As noted throughout this chapter, little work has been conducted on ways in which these factors might influence social goal pursuit. It is reasonable to believe that group differences exist. For instance, girls are more likely to try to behave prosocially than are boys (Wentzel, 1989, 1991a, 1994), and students of Hispanic descent often pursue cooperative goals more often than Caucasian students (Knight & Kagan, 1977). The more interesting question, however, is whether these differences have implications for overall adjustment to school. In this case, the answer probably lies in the complex interactions between the goals of an individual student, the expectations of his or her teachers and peers, and the degree to which he or she can clearly identify and effectively coordinate these multiple demands when pursuing classroom goals. Similarly, the degree to which relations between social goal pursuit and academic accomplishments are influenced by a student's gender or race remains an unanswered question. On the one hand, if indices of academic performance are based in part on rewards for social behavior, then these individual differences might well have an impact on relations between social motivation, social behavior, and academic outcomes. On the other hand, existing models of cognitive development based on social interactions and skills (see, e.g., Hinde, Perret-Clermont, & Stevenson-Hinde, 1985) would not posit moderating influences of race and gender on relations between social and cognitive outcomes, but would rather suggest more universal processes of development. Theoretical and empirical advances that will challenge and test these hypotheses remain an exciting challenge for the field.

References

Allen, J. D. (1986). Classroom management: Students' perspectives, goals, and strategies. *American Educational Research Journal, 23,* 437–459.

Ames, C. (1984). Competitive, cooperative, and individualistic goal structures: A cognitive–motivational analysis. In R. Ames & C. Ames (Eds.), *Research in motivation in education* (Vol. 1, pp. 177–208). New York: Academic Press.

Ames, C. (1992). Classrooms: Goals, structures, and student motivation. *Journal of Educational Psychology*, 84, 261–271.

Ames, C., & Ames, R. (1984). Systems of student and teacher motivation: Toward a qualitative definition. *Journal of Educational Psychology*, 76, 535–556.

Ames, C., & Archer, J. (1987). Mothers' beliefs about the role of ability and effort in school learning. *Journal of Educationsl Psychology*, 79, 409–414.

Austin, J. T., & Vancouver, J. B. (1996). Goal constructs in psychology: Structure, process, and content. *Psychological Bulletin*, 120, 338–375.

Bandura, A. (1986). *Social foundations of thought and action: A social–cognitive theory*. Englewood Cliffs, NJ: Prentice-Hall.

Baumrind, D. (1971). Current patterns of parental authority. *Developmental Psychology Monograph*, 4, (1, Pt. 2).

Baumrind, D. (1991). Effective parenting during the early adolescent transition. In P. A Cowan & M. Hetherington (Eds.), *Family transitions* (pp. 111–164). Hillsdale, NJ: Lawrence Erlbaum Associates.

Benenson, J. F., & Dweck, C. S. (1986). The development of trait explanations and self-evaluations in the academic and social domains. *Child Development*, 57, 1179–1187.

Blumenfeld, P. C. (1992). Classroom learning and motivation: Clarifying and expanding goal theory. *Journal of Educational Psychology*, 84, 272–281.

Blumenfeld, P. C., Hamilton, V. L., Bossert, S. T., Wessels, K., & Meece, J. (1983). Teacher talk and student thought: Socialization into the student role. In J. M. Levine & M. C. Wang (Eds.), *Teacher and student perceptions: Implications for learning*, (pp. 143–192). Hillsdale, NJ: Lawrence Erlbaum Associates.

Bronfenbrenner, U. (1989). Ecological systems theory. In R. Vasta (Ed.), *Annals of child development* (Vol. 6, pp.187–250). Greenwich, CT: JAI Press.

Brophy, J. E., & Evertson, C. M. (1978). Context variables in teaching. *Educational Psychologist*, 12, 310–316.

Burhans, K. K., & Dweck, C. S. (1995). Helplessness in early childhood: The role of contingent worth. *Child Development*, 66, 1719–1738.

Cauce, A. M., Felner, R. D., & Primavera, J. (1982). Social support in high-risk adolescents: Structural components and adaptive impact. *American Journal of Community Psychology*, 10, 417–428.

Chung, T., & Asher, S. R. (1996). Children's goals and strategies in peer conflict situations. *Merrill-Palmer Quarterly*, 42, 125–147.

Cohen, E. G. (1986). *Designing group work: Strategies for the heterogeneous classroom*. New York: Teachers College Press.

Connell, J. P., Spencer, M. B., & Aber, J. L. (1994). Educational risk and resilience in African-American youth: Context, self, action, and outcomes in school. *Child Development*, 65, 493–506.

Connell, J. P., & Wellborn, J. G. (1991). Competence, autonomy, and relatedness: A motivational analysis of self-system processes. In M. R. Gunnar & L. A. Sroufe (Eds.), *Self processes and development: The Minnesota Symposia on Child Development* (Vol. 23, pp. 43–78). Hillsdale, NJ: Lawrence Erlbaum Associates.

Covington, M. V. (1992). *Making the grade: A self-worth perspective on motivation and school reform*. New York: Cambridge University Press.

Crandall, V. C. (1966). Personality characteristics and social and achievement behaviors associated with children's social desirability response tendencies. *Journal of Personality and Social Psychology*, 4, 477–486.

Crandall, V. C., Crandall, V. J., & Katkovsky, W. (1965). A children's social desirability questionnaire. *Journal of Consulting Psychology*, 29, 27–36.

Crick, N., & Dodge, K. A. (1994). A review and reformulation of social information-processing mechanisms in children's social adjustment. *Psychological Bulletin*, 115, 74–101.

DeBaryshe, B. D., Patterson, G. R., & Capabaldi, D. M. (1993). A performance model for academic achievement in early adolescent boys. *Developmental Psychology*, 29, 795–804.

Deci, E. L., & Ryan, R. M. (1991). A motivational approach to self: Integration in personality. In R. Dienstbier (Ed.), *Nebraska Symposium on Motivation 1990* (pp. 237–288). Lincoln: University of Nebraska Press.

Dodge, K. A. (1984) A social information processing model of social competence in children. In M. Perlmutter (Ed.), *Minnesota symposium on child psychology* (Vol. 18, pp. 77–126). Hillsdale, N. J., Lawrence Erlbaum Associates.

Dodge, K. A., & Feldman, E. (1990). Issues in social cognition and sociometric status. In S. R. Asher & J. D. Coie (Eds.), *Peer rejection in childhood* (pp. 119–155). New York: Cambridge University Press.

Doyle, W. (1986). Classroom organization and management. In M. C. Witrock (Ed.), *Handbook of research on teaching* (pp. 392–431). New York: Macmillan.

Dubow, E. F., & Tisak, J. (1989). The relation between stressful life events and adjustment in elementary school children: The role of social support and social problem-solving skills. *Child Development*, 60, 1412–1423.

Dweck, C. S. (1991). Self-theories and goals: Their role in motivation, personality, and development. In R. Dienstbier (Ed.), *Nebraska Symposium on Motivation* (Vol. 38, pp. 199–236). Lincoln: University of Nebraska Press.

Dweck, C. S., & Leggett, E. L. (1988). A social–cognitive approach to motivation and personality. *Psychological Review*, 95, 256–272.

Eccles, J. (1993). School and family effects on the ontogeny of children's interests, self-perceptions, and activity choices. In J. Jacobs (Ed.), *Developmental perspectives on motivation* (Vol. 40, pp. 145–208). Lincoln: University of Nebraska Press.

Eccles, J., Wigfield, A., & Schiefele, U. (1998). Motivation to succeed. In W. Damon (Series Ed.) and N. Eisenberg (Vol. Ed.), *Handbook of child psychology* (5th ed., Vol. 3, pp. 1017–1095). New York: Wiley.

Eisenberg, N., & Fabes, R. A. (1992). Emotion, regulation, and the development of social competence. In M. S. Clark (Ed.), *Review of personality and social psychology: Vol. 14. Emotional and social behavior* (pp. 119–150). Newbury Park, CA: Sage.

Entwistle, N. J., & Kozeki, B. (1985). Relationships between school motivation, approaches to studying, and attainment, among British and Hungarian adolescents. *British Journal of Educational Psychology*, 55, 124–137.

Erdley, C. A. (1996). Motivational approaches to aggression within the context of peer relationships. In J. Juvonen & K. Wentzel (Eds.), *Social motivation: Understanding children's school adjustment* (pp. 98–125). New York: Cambridge University Press.

Erdley, C. A., & Asher, S. R. (1996). Children's social goals and self-efficacy perceptions as influences on their responses to ambiguous provocation. *Child Development*, 67, 1329–1344.

Erdley, C. A., Cain, K. M., Loomis, C. C., Dumas-Hines, F., & Dweck, C. S. (1997). Relations among children's social goals, implicit personality theories, and responses to social failure. *Developmental Psychology*, 33, 263–272.

Feldlaufer, H., Midgley, C., & Eccles, J. S. (1988). Student, teacher, and observer perceptions of the classroom before and after the transition to junior high school. *Journal of Early Adolescence*, 8, 133–156.

Felner, R. D., Aber, M. S., Primavera, J., & Cauce, A. M. (1985). Adaptation and vulnerability in high-risk adolescents: An examination of environmental mediators. *American Journal of Community Psychology*, 13, 365–379.

Ford, M. E. (1982). Social cognition and social competence in adolescence. *Developmental Psychology*, 18, 323–340.

Ford, M. E., (1984). Linking social–cognitive processes with effective social behavior: A living systems approach. In P. C. Kendall (Ed.), *Advances in cognitive–behavioral research and therapy* (Vol. 3, pp. 167–211). New York: Academic Press.

Ford, M. E. (1992). *Motivating humans: Goals, emotions, and personal agency beliefs*. Newbury Park, CA: Sage.

Ford, M. E. (1996). Motivational opportunities and obstacles associated with social responsibility and caring behavior in school contexts. In J. Juvonen & K. Wentzel (Eds.), *Social motivation: Understanding children's school adjustment* (pp. 126–153). New York: Cambridge University Press.

Fordham, S., & Ogbu, J. U. (1986). Black students' school success; Coping with "the burden of 'acting white.'" *The Urban Review*, 18, 176–206.

Ginsberg, G. S., & Bronstein, P. (1993). Family factors related to children's intrinsic/extrinsic motivational orientations and academic performance. *Child Development*, 64, 1461–1474.

Grolnick, W. S., Kurowski, C. O., & Gurland, S. T. (1999). Family processes and the development of children's self-regulation. *Educational Psychologist*, 34, 3–14.

Grolnick, W. S., & Ryan, R. M. (1989). Parent styles associated with children's self-regulation and competence in school. *Journal of Educational Psychology*, 81, 143–154.

Grolnick, W. S., & Slowiaczek, M. L. (1994). Parents' involvement in children's schooling: A multidimensional conceptualization and motivational model. *Child Development*, 65, 237–252.

Grusec, J. E., & Goodnow, J. J. (1994). Impact of parental discipline methods on the child's internalization of values: A reconceptualization of current points of view. *Developmental Psychology*, 30, 4–19.

Hargreaves, D. H., Hester, S. K., & Mellor, F. J. (1975). *Deviance in classrooms*. London: Routledge & Kegan Paul.

Harter, S. (1987). The determinants and mediational role of global self-worth in children. In N. Eisenberg (Ed.), *Contemporary issues in developmental psychology*. New York: Wiley.

Harter, S. (1990). Self and identity development. In S. S. Feldman & G. R. Elliott (Eds.), *At the threshold: The developing adolescent* (pp. 352–387). Cambridge, MA: Harvard University Press.

Harter, S. (1996). Teacher and classmate influences on scholastic motivation, self-esteem, and level of voice in adolescents. In J. Juvonen & K. Wentzel (Eds.), *Social motivation: Understanding children's school adjustment* (pp. 11–42). New York: Cambridge University Press.

Heyman, G. D., & Dweck, C. S. (1998). Children's thinking about traits: Implications for judgements of the self and others. *Child Development*, 69, 391–403.

Heyman, G. D., Dweck, C. S., & Cain, K. M. (1992). Young children's vulnerability to self-blame and helplessness: Relationship to beliefs about goodness. *Child Development*, 63, 401–415.

Hinde, R. A., Perret-Clermont, A., & Stevenson-Hinde, J. (1985). *Social relationships and cognitive development*. Oxford, U.K.: Clarendon Press.

Hinshaw, S. P. (1992). Externalizing behavior problems and academic underachievement in childhood and adolescence: Causal relationships and underlying mechanisms. *Psychological Bulletin*, 111, 127–155.

Hokoda, A., & Fincham, F. D. (1995). Origins of children's helpless and mastery achievement patterns in the family. *Journal of Educational Psychology*, 87, 375–385.

Jacobsen, T., Edelstein, W., & Hofmann, V. (1994). A longitudinal study of the relation between representations of attachment in childhood and cognitive functioning in childhood and adolescence. *Developmental Psychology*, 30, 112–124.

Juvonen, J. (1996). Self-presentation tactics promoting teacher and peer approval: The function of excuses and other clever explanations. In J. Juvonen & K. R. Wentzel (Eds.), *Social motivation: Understanding children's school adjustment* (pp. 43–65). New York: Cambridge University Press.

Knight, G. P., & Kagan, S. (1977). Development of prosocial and competitive behaviors in Anglo-American and Mexican-American children. *Child Development*, 48, 1385–1394.

Kozeki, B. (1985). Motives and motivational style in education. In N. Entwistle (Ed.), *New directions in educational psychology: Vol. 1. Learning and teaching* (pp. 189–199). Philadelphia: Falmer Press.

Kozeki, B., & Entwistle, N. J. (1984). Identifying dimensions of school motivation in Britain and Hungary. *British Journal of Educational Psychology*, 54, 306–319.

Ladd, G. W. (1989). Children's social competence and social supports: Precursors of early school adjustment? In B. H. Schneider, G. Atilli, J. Nadel, & R. P. Weissberg (Eds.), *Social competence in developmental perspective* (pp. 277–291). Dordrecht, The Netherlands: Kluwer.

LeCompte, M. (1978a). Establishing a workplace: Teacher control in the classroom. *Education and Urban Society*, 11, 87–106.

LeCompte, M. (1978b). Learning to work: the hidden curriculum of the classroom. *Anthropology and Education Quarterly*, 9, 22–37.

Lepper, M. (1983). Social control processes, attributions of motivation, and the internalization of social values. In E. T. Higgins, D. Ruble, & W. Hartup (Eds.), *Social cognition and social development: A sociocultural perspective* (pp. 294–330). Cambridge, U.K.: Cambridge University Press.

Lewin, K., Lippitt, R., & White, R. K. (1939). Patterns of aggressive behavior in experimentally created "social climates." *Journal of Social Psychology*, 10, 271–299.

Maehr, M. L. (1983). On doing well in science: Why Johnny no longer excels; why Sarah never did. In S. G. Paris, G. M. Olson, & H. W. Stevenson (Eds.), *Learning and motivation in the classroom* (pp. 179–210). Hillsdale, NJ: Lawrence Erlbaum Associates.

Maehr, M. L. (1984). Meaning and motivation: Toward a theory of personal investment. In R. E. Ames & C. Ames (Eds.), *Research on motivation in education* (pp. 115–144). New York: Academic Press.

McClelland, D. C. (1987). *Human motivation.* New York: Cambridge University Press.

McKeachie, W. J., Lin, Y., Milholland, J., & Isaacson, R. (1966). Student affiliation motives, teacher warmth, and academic achievement. *Journal of Personality and Social Psychology, 4,* 457–461.

Midgley, C., Feldlaufer, H., & Eccles, J. (1989). Student/teacher relations and attitudes toward mathematics before and after the transition to junior high school. *Child Development, 60,* 981–992.

Murphy, B. C., & Eisenberg, N. (1996). Provoked by a peer: Children's anger-related responses and their relations to social functioning. *Merrill-Palmer Quarterly, 42,* 103–124.

Oden, S., & Asher, S. R. (1977). Coaching children in social skills for friendship making. *Child Development, 48,* 495–506.

Ogbu, J. U. (1985). Origins of human competence: A cultural–ecological perspective. *Child Development, 52,* 413–429.

Okagaki, L., & Sternberg, R. J. (1993). Parental beliefs and children's school performance. *Child Development, 64,* 36–56.

Parkhurst J. T., & Asher, S. R. (1985). Goals and concerns: Implications for the study of children's social competence. In B. B. Lahey & A. E. Kazdin (Eds.), *Advances in clinical child psychology* (pp. 199–228). New York: Plenum Press.

Pervin, L. A. (1983). The stasis and flow of behavior: Toward a theory of goals. In M. M. Page (Ed.), *Personality–Current theory and research* (pp. 1–53). Lincoln: University of Nebraska Press.

Phelan, P., Davidson, A. L., & Cao, H. T. (1991). Students' multiple worlds: Negotiating the boundaries of family, peer, and school cultures. *Anthropology and Education Quarterly, 22,* 224–250.

Piaget, J. (1965). *The moral judgment of the child.* New York: Free Press.

Rabiner, D. L., & Gordon, L. V. (1992). The coordination of conflicting social goals: Differences between rejected and nonrejected boys. *Child Development, 63,* 1344–1350.

Rathunde, K. (1996). Family context and talented adolescents' optimal experience in school-related activities. *Journal of Research on Adolescence, 6,* 605–628.

Renshaw, P. D., & Asher, S. R. (1983). Children's goals and strategies for social interaction. *Merrill-Palmer Quarterly, 29,* 553–574.

Ruble, D. N. (1983). The development of social comparison processes and their role in achievement-related self-socialization. In E. T. Higgins, D. Ruble, & W. Hartup (Eds.), *Social cognition and social development: A sociocultural perspective* (pp. 134–157). Cambridge, U.K.: Cambridge.University Press.

Ryan, A. M., & Pintrich, P. R. (1997). Should I ask for help? The role of motivation and attitudes in adolescents' help seeking in math class. *Journal of Educational Psychology, 89,* 329–341.

Ryan, R. M. (1993). Agency and organization: Intrinsic motivation, autonomy, and the self in psychological development. In J. Jacobs (Ed.), *Nebraska Symposium on Motivation,* Vol. 40, pp. 1–56. Lincoln: University of Nebraska Press.

Ryan, R. M., & Stiller, J. (1991). The social contexts of internalization: Parent and teacher influences on autonomy, motivation, and learning. In M. Maehr & P. Pintrich (Eds.), *Advances in motivation and achievement,* Vol. 7, pp. 86–114. Greenwich, CT: JAI Press.

Schaps, E., Battistich, V., & Solomon, D. (1997). School as a caring community: A key to character education. In A. Molnar (Ed.), *Ninety-sixth yearbook of the National Society for the Study of Education* (pp. 127–139). Chicago: University of Chicago Press.

Schunk, D. H. (1987). Peer models and children's behavioral change. *Review of Educational Research, 57,* 149–174.

Sieber, R. T. (1979). Classmates as workmates: Informal peer activity in the elementary school. *Anthropology and Education Quarterly*, 10, 207–235.

Sivan, E. (1986). Motivation in social constructivist theory. *Educational Psychologist*, 21, 209–233.

Skinner, E. A., & Belmont, M. J. (1993). Motivation in the classroom: Reciprocal effects of teacher behavior and student engagement across the school year. *Journal of Educational Psychology*, 85, 571–581.

Slaby, R. G., & Guerra, N. G. (1988). Cognitive mediators of aggression in adolescent offenders: 1. Assessment. *Developmental Psychology*, 24, 580–588.

Slavin, R. E. (1987). Developmental and motivational perspectives on cooperative learning: A reconciliation. *Child Development*, 58, 1161–1167.

Solomon, D., Schaps, E., Watson, M., & Battistich, V. (1992). Creating caring school and classroom communities for all students. In R. Villa, J. Thousand, W. Stainback, & S. Stainback (Eds.), *Restructuring for caring and effective education: An administrative guide to creating heterogeneous schools* (pp. 41–60). Baltimore: Brookes.

Trenholm, S., & Rose, T. (1981). The compliant communicator: Teacher perceptions of appropriate classroom behavior. *Western Journal of Speech Communication*, 45, 13–26.

Veroff, J. (1969). Social comparison and the development of achievement motivation. In P. C. Smith (Ed.), *Achievement-related motives in children*. New York: Russell Sage.

Watson, M., Solomon, D., Battistich, V., Schaps, E., & Solomon, J. (1989). The child development project: Combining traditional and developmental approaches to values education. In L. Nucci (Ed.), *Moral development and character education: A dialogue* (pp. 51–92). Berkeley: McCutchan.

Wentzel, K. R. (1989). Adolescent classroom goals, standards for performance, and academic achievement: An interactionist perspective. *Journal of Educational Psychology*, 81, 131–142.

Wentzel, K. R. (1991a). Relations between social competence and academic achievement in early adolescence. *Child Development*, 62, 1066–1078.

Wentzel, K. R. (1991b). Social and academic goals at school: Achievement motivation in context. In M. Maehr and P. Pintrich (Eds.), *Advances in motivation and achievement* (Vol. 7, pp. 185–212). Greenwich, CT: JAI Press.

Wentzel, K. R. (1992). Motivation and achievement in adolescence: A multiple goals perspective. In D. Schunk & J. Meece (Eds.), *Student perceptions in the classroom: Causes and consequences* (pp. 287–306). Hillsdale, NJ: Lawrence Erlbaum Associates.

Wentzel, K. R. (1993). Social and academic goals at school: Motivation and achievement in early adolescence. *Journal of Early Adolescence*, 13, 4–20.

Wentzel, K. R. (1994). Relations of social goal pursuit to social acceptance, classroom behavior, and perceived social support. *Journal of Educational Psychology*, 86, 173–182.

Wentzel, K. R. (1996). Motivation in context: Social relationships and achievement in middle school. In J. Juvonen & K. R. Wentzel (Eds.), *Social motivation: Understanding children's school adjustment*. New York: Cambridge University Press.

Wentzel, K. R. (1997). Student motivation in middle school: The role of perceived pedagogical caring. *Journal of Educational Psychology*, 89, 411–419.

Wentzel, K. R. (1998). Social support and adjustment in middle school: The role of parents, teachers, and peers. *Journal of Educational Psychology*, 90, 202–209.

Wentzel, K. R. (in press). *Are effective teachers like good parents? Interpersonal predictors of school adjustment in early adolescence*. Child Development.

Wentzel, K. R., Battle, A., & Cusick, L. (2000). *Teacher and peer contributions to classroom climate in middle school: Relations to school adjustment*. Unpublished manuscript, University of Maryland, College Park.

Wentzel, K. R., Weinberger, D. A., Ford, M. E., & Feldman, S. S. (1990). Academic achievement in preadolescence: The role of motivational, affective, and self-regulatory processes. *Journal of Applied Developmental Psychology*, 11, 179–193.

Wenz-Gross, M., Siperstein, G. N., Untch, A. S., & Widaman, K. F. (1997). Stress, social support, and adjustment of adolescents in middle school. *Journal of Early Adolescence*, 17, 129–151.

Youniss, J., & Smollar, J. (1989). Adolescents' interpersonal relationships in social context. In T. J. Berndt & G. Ladd (Eds.), *Peer relationships in child development* (pp. 300–316). New York: Wiley.

What Do I Need to Do to Succeed?

CHAPTER

10

The Development of Academic Self-Regulation: The Role of Cognitive and Motivational Factors

PAUL R. PINTRICH AND AKANE ZUSHO

The University of Michigan, Ann Arbor, Michigan

The development of the capability to self-regulate cognition, motivation, affect, and behavior is an important developmental task. It is clear from research on cognitive and emotional development that the capabilities to regulate cognition and affect are key for adaptive growth and development (Saarni, Mumme, & Campos, 1998; Schneider & Bjorklund, 1998; Thompson, 1998). Research on academic learning also has shown that students who are able to regulate their own learning in the face of the many distractions and difficulties in classrooms perform and learn better than students who lack self-regulatory capabilities (Pintrich, 2000c). Given the importance of self-regulation in general, and more specifically within classroom settings, it is surprising that there has been so little empirical research explicitly focused on the development of academic self-regulation. Accordingly, there are a number of important developmental questions that should be addressed in future research. Our goal in this chapter is to examine some of these questions and suggest future directions for research on the development of self-regulation in academic contexts.

At a global level, there are two key developmental questions: (1) What develops? and (2) What are the factors that facilitate or constrain development? In this chapter, we will focus on self-regulated learning that takes place in classroom settings. Accordingly, we will focus on the development of self-regulatory capabilities in school-age children. There is research on the development of self-regulation in younger infants and children (Saarni , Mumme, & Campos, 1998; Thompson, 1998), but we will focus on describing the developmental trajectories related to academic self-regulation in classroom contexts. We will discuss some of the personal cognitive characteristics (e.g., prior knowledge, theories) and motivational characteristics (efficacy, goals) that might facilitate or impede the development of self-regulation. We are fully aware that the role of these cognitive and motivational characteristics can be moderated by contextual factors, and moreover, that contextual factors can have a direct influence on self-regulatory development, but given space and page limitations, we will not discuss these contextual factors in this chapter.

The developmental questions will be addressed at two levels. First, there is the traditional age-graded maturational developmental perspective. This concerns the classic developmental question of how self-regulation changes with age and maturation. It is represented by general descriptions that suggest that younger children are generally less knowledgeable and capable than older children in many domains, including self-regulated learning (Paris & Byrnes, 1989). The key issue is that the age-related maturational changes are seen as general enabling conditions that allow for the development of knowledge, representations, strategies, metacognition, and beliefs. In this case, changes in development would be expected to show some common age-related shifts over time; in other words, age is relevant. The second perspective reflects an expertise or task–domain-specific approach that describes how self-regulation expertise might evolve over the course of different phases of doing a task or activity (Alexander, Jetton, & Kulikowich, 1995; Zimmerman, 2000; Zimmerman & Kitsantas, 1997). Under this perspective, which is focused more on learning than on development, age is not a relevant consideration, but expertise with the task or activity is crucial. We will consider both these perspectives in our discussion of the development of self-regulated learning.

WHAT DEVELOPS IN SELF-REGULATED LEARNING?

In our definition, self-regulated learning is an active, constructive process whereby learners set goals for their learning and then attempt to monitor, regulate, and control their cognition, motivation, and behavior in the service of those goals, guided and constrained by both personal characteristics and the contextual features in the environment (Pintrich, 2000c). This definition is similar to other models of academic self-regulated learning (e.g., Butler & Winne, 1995; Zimmerman, 1986; 1989, 1998a, 1998b, 2000), although there is great diversity in general models of self-regulation (see Boekaerts, Pintrich & Zeidner, 2000). Our definition is relatively simple, but the remainder of this section outlines the various processes and areas of regulation and their application to learning and achievement in the academic domain, which serves to define what develops in self-regulated learning.

Table 1 displays a framework for classifying the different phases and areas for regulation. The four phases that make up the rows of the table are processes that many models of regulation and self-regulation share (e.g., Zimmerman, 1998a, 1998b, 2000) and reflect goal setting, monitoring, and control and regulation processes. Of course, not all academic learning follows these phases, as there are many occasions for students to learn academic material in more tacit or implicit or unintentional ways without self-regulating their learning in such an explicit and goal-directed manner as suggested in the model. The phases are suggested as a heuristic to organize our thinking and research on self-regulated learning. Phase 1 involves planning and goal setting as well as activation of perceptions and knowledge of the task and context and the self in relation to the task. Phase 2 concerns various monitoring processes that represent metacognitive awareness of different aspects of the self and task or context. Phase 3 involves efforts to control and regulate different aspects of the self or task and context. The awareness and control/regulation processes involved in phases 2 and 3 are key developmental outcomes over the course of schooling. Finally, phase 4 represents various kinds of reactions and reflections on the self and the task or context.

The four phases do represent a general time-ordered sequence that individuals would go through as they perform a task, but there is no strong assumption that the phases are hierarchically or linearly structured such that earlier phases must always occur before later phases. In most models of self-regulated learning, monitoring, control, and reaction can be ongoing simultaneously and dynamically as the individual progresses through the task, with goals and plans being changed or updated based on the feedback from the monitoring, control, and reaction processes. In fact, much of the research suggests that the monitoring and control phases are very difficult to separate empirically, albeit clear conceptual distinctions can be made between these phases (Pintrich, Wolters, & Baxter, 2000; Pressley & Afflerbach, 1995).

The four columns in Table 1 represent different areas for regulation that an individual learner can attempt to monitor, control, and regulate. The first three columns of cognition, motivation/affect, and behavior reflect the traditional tripartite division of different areas of psychological functioning (Snow, Corno, & Jackson, 1996) and represent aspects of the individual's own cognition, motivation/affect, and behavior that he or she can attempt to "self-regulate" or control. Of course, other individuals in the environment such as teachers, peers, or parents can try to "other"-regulate an individual's cognition, motivation, or behavior by directing or scaffolding the individual in terms of what, how, and when to do a task. More generally, other task and contextual features (e.g., task characteristics, feedback systems, evaluation structures) can facilitate or constrain an individual's attempts to self-regulate learning. In this way, different aspects of the context can influence

TABLE I
Phases and Areas for Self-Regulated Learning

Phases	Areas for Regulation			
	Cognition	Motivation/Affect	Behavior	Context
Forethought, planning, and activation	Target goal setting Prior content knowledge activation Metacognitive knowledge activation	Goal orientation adoption Efficacy judgments Ease of learning judgments (EOLs), perceptions of task difficulty Task value activation Interest activation	Time and effort planning Planning for self-observations of behavior	Perceptions of task Perceptions of context
Monitoring	Metacognitive awareness and monitoring of cognition, judgments of learning (JOLs)	Awareness and monitoring of motivation and affect	Awareness and monitoring of effort, time use, need for help Self-observation of behavior	Monitoring changing task and context conditions
Control	Selection and adaptation of cognitive strategies for learning, thinking	Selection and adaptation of strategies for managing motivation and affect	Increase/decrease effort Persist, give up Help-seeking behavior	Change or renegotiate task Change or leave context
Reaction and reflection	Cognitive judgments Attributions	Affective reactions Attributions	Choice behavior	Evaluation of task Evaluation of context

self-regulation directly. At the same time, the individual can attempt to control and regulate the context (fourth column in Table 1) by taking different actions on the context that help the person reach his or her goals. The cells in the context column in Table 1 represent the latter case and list some possible ways the individual can try to control and regulate the context adaptively.

The cognition column in Table 1 concerns the different cognitive strategies individuals may use to learn and perform a task as well as the metacognitive strategies individuals may use to control and regulate their cognition. These strategies can be used at different phases to help control and regulate learning. For example, comprehension monitoring helps students become aware of their lack of understanding and can lead to attempts to repair their comprehension if regulatory strategies like rereading are then used. There are a great number of different cognitive and metacognitive strategies that can be used to regulate learning, and they are discussed in more detail elsewhere (e.g., Pintrich, 2000c; Pressley & Afflerbach, 1995; Weinstein & Mayer, 1986).

However, in terms of developmental trajectories, there is clear evidence that students do become more strategic or more capable of using various cognitive and metacognitive strategies with age (Schneider & Bjorklund, 1998; Schneider & Pressley, 1997). For example, some basic rehearsal or organizational strategies (e.g., repeating words; sorting into categories) for rather simple memory tasks seem to be in place by early elementary school, but more complex strategies for understanding text (e.g., identifying main ideas, summarizing or elaborating on ideas in text) may not emerge until middle or high school (Brown, Bransford, Ferrara, & Campione, 1983; Paris & Lindauer, 1982; Pressley, Forrest-Pressley, Elliot-Faust, & Miller, 1985; Schneider & Bjorklund, 1998). More important, as Schneider and Bjorklund (1998) point out, the developmental trajectory of strategy development for both simple memory strategies and more complex strategies is one of initial difficulties in use, including both production deficiencies (strategy is not used spontaneously) and utilization deficiencies (strategy is used, but benefits are not realized), and finally after much use and practice, more adaptive and successful use of the strategy.

These two general developmental patterns reflect the two developmental perspectives. First, there is a general age-graded developmental trajectory, with older students being more capable to regulate their cognition than younger students. Of course, it is important to note that it is general competence or capability to use these strategies that develops. It is still the case that many older students in high school or college may not know about various cognitive or metacognitive strategies or, more importantly may not use them, even if they have knowledge of them. This distinction between *competence* to use the strategies versus the actual *performance* or use of the strategies is an important consideration in any developmental discussion of self-regulation. Second, in line with the task-expertise developmental perspective, novice users of a strategy (regardless of age) may show less benefit from using the strategy than more experienced or knowledgeable students. This utilization deficiency (Miller, 1990, 1994; Miller & Seier, 1994) may appear for students of any age who are learning to use a strategy for the first time. It is likely that utilization deficiencies or problems will be common for many initial attempts at the use of self-regulatory strategies, beyond just use of cognitive and metacognitive strategies.

The motivation/affect column concerns the various motivational beliefs that individuals may have about themselves or the task, such as self-efficacy beliefs and values for the task. Interest in or liking of the task would be included in this column, as well as positive and negative affective reactions to the self or task. In terms of self-regulation, the key issue is the strategies that individuals may use to control and regulate their motivational beliefs and affect. It is not the motivational beliefs themselves, it is the individuals attempts to control and regulate their personal motivation that are the focus of self-regulated learning models. In contrast, self-determination models of motivation (see Grolnick, Gurland, Jacobs, & Decourcey, Chapter 6, this volume) discuss self-regulation in terms of a continuum of control or autonomy that goes from external control of an individual's motivation and behavior to self-determined control. Although much less investigated than the cognitive or metacognitive strategies, strategies to control motivation and affect are often called volitional control strategies (see Boekaerts, 1993, 1995; Boekaerts & Niemivirta, 2000; Corno, 1989, 1993; Kuhl, 1984, 1985; Pintrich, 1999b). For example, Wolters (1998) has shown that college students do attempt to control their interest in a task by invoking strategies to make the activity seem more gamelike. Students also may attempt to control their self-efficacy through positive self-talk (Bandura, 1997; Wolters, 1998). However, there has been little explicit developmental research on these motivational control strategies, at least in contrast to all the developmental research on cognitive and metacognitive strategies.

The behavior column of Table 1 reflects the general effort the individual may exert on the task as well as persistence, help-seeking, and choice behaviors. Some of the behavioral control strategies such as invoking positive self-talk (e.g., "You can do it, just stick to it, keep trying") to bolster effort and persistence also have been investigated under the rubric of volitional control strategies (Corno, 1989, 1993; Kuhl, 1984, 1985; Pintrich, 1999b). The fourth column in Table 1, context, refers to various aspects of the task environment or general classroom or cultural context where the learning is taking place that potentially could be controlled by the individual. Individuals do try to monitor and control their environment to some extent, and in fact, in some models of intelligence (e.g., Sternberg, 1985), attempts to selectively control and change the context are seen as very adaptable. As part of any attempt to control the context, an important process is the individual's perceptions of the context, hence the first cell in Table 1 under the context column reflects the individual's perceptions of the task or context, not the actual context itself. However, there has been little research on the developmental trajectories of these behavioral and contextual control strategies. Nevertheless, it would be expected that the use of these motivational, behavioral, and contextual control strategies would follow the same two developmental progressions noted for cognitive strategies with a general age-graded improvement over time as well as improvement that comes from experience and developing expertise with the task or domain.

In summary, the processes outlined in Table 1 provide a general description of what can develop in terms of self-regulated learning in academic settings. The adaptive use of these different kinds of cognitive, motivational, behavioral, and contextual regulatory strategies can be viewed as an important developmental task. As students become better able to use these strategies, they will become more successful and learn and perform better. Given their importance, it is useful to consider what factors can facilitate or constrain the development of these different strategies. We now turn to a discussion of the personal cognitive and motivational characteristics that seem to influence the development of self-regulated learning.

There are a number of different personal factors that might facilitate or impede the development of self-regulated learning. We will focus on several cognitive and motivational factors. Others, such as personality characteristics (i.e., temperament, Caspi, 1998; Rothbart & Bates, 1998; Snow, Corno, & Jackson, 1996; identity, Ferrari & Mahalingham, 1998; Paris, Byrnes & Paris, 2000) are clearly relevant but are not discussed due to space limitations.

THE ROLE OF COGNITIVE FACTORS IN THE DEVELOPMENT OF SELF-REGULATION

There are a number of personal cognitive factors that play a role in the development of self-regulation. These include traditional cognitive–developmental factors that are often associated with general maturational or age-related changes as well as other cognitive factors that change with expertise or experience. Of course, these factors are sensitive to contextual variations and can be shaped by contextual differences, but they may mediate any direct relations between contextual features and the development of self-regulation. Cognitive factors may play a role in the development of self-regulation through two main routes: (1) changing the goals or criteria that are used to guide self-regulatory processes, and (2) improving the speed and efficiency of the self-regulatory processes themselves.

The Role of Developmental Differences In Working Memory

As outlined in Table 1, self-regulated learning is a constellation of complex cognitive and metacognitive processes in which students set goals for themselves, monitor their progress toward their goals, and then attempt to control or regulate themselves in order to make better progress toward their goals. In this definition, self-regulated learning clearly implicates the basic cognitive system. One key aspect of any cognitive model, regardless of theoretical orientation, is that there are some limitations in cognitive resources, particularly in the amount of information that can be processed or attended to at any one point in time and the speed at which the cognitive system can operate on this information (Miyake & Shah, 1999; Schneider & Bjorklund, 1998; Siegler, 1998).

Current cognitive models propose that working memory (defined in various ways) represents the central theoretical construct that underlies and supports the maintenance of task-relevant information during the performance of a cognitive task (Shah & Miyake, 1999). In these models the operation of working memory is mainly responsible for the limitations in the use of cognitive resources such as capacity, attentional focus, and speed of processing. Given that self-regulated learning is a complex cognitive process that clearly involves the maintenance of task-relevant information during the performance of a cognitive task, then working memory functioning should be related to self-regulated learning. For example, most models of working memory include an individual's goals as an important aspect of what is in working memory during task performance. In addition, monitoring task performance is an important function of working memory (Miyake & Shah, 1999). Goal-setting and monitoring also are important components of self-regulated learning, so there should be some important linkages between working memory and self-regulated learning such that constraints on working memory also might impede self-regulated learning.

Developmentally, it might be expected that younger children would have smaller working memories (smaller capacities) than older children. Although this is certainly a reasonable developmental hypothesis, current research and models suggest that this is not the case, especially for children of school age on up to adults. Basically, the research suggests that developmental differences in working memory are a function of differences in prior knowledge, strategy use, and the affordances in speed and efficiency of processing that are generated by more knowledge and strategy use in older students (Schneider & Bjorklund, 1998; Schneider & Pressley, 1997; Siegler, 1998). Accordingly, it is not the case that younger elementary school-aged children have a structurally smaller working memory capacity than middle school or high school or even college students; rather, developmentally they are less able to use their cognitive resources as effectively or efficiently as older students. In this case then, the improvement of working memory processes such as attention and executive control processes with age and experience would afford better self-regulatory processes.

Given that a simple structural argument of limited capacity due to smaller working memory size is not supported, other explanations have focused on functional mechanisms that limit cognitive processing. This emphasis on functional aspects of working memory coincides with the rejection of the modal model of short-term memory as a separate information store or structure. For example, Miyake and Shah (1999) note that their volume on current models of working memory in cognitive psychology "marks the demise of the 'box' or 'place' metaphor of working memory" (p. 445). Along with the demise of the box metaphor, they also note that current research emphasizes that the operation of working memory is an active process in the service of complex cognition, not just memory for lists of words. Moreover, in line with the emphasis on complex cognition, they point out that working memory is "not really about 'memory' per se; it is about 'control' and 'regulation' of our cognitive action" (p. 446), which fits nicely with a self-regulatory perspective on learning focused on control and regulation. Finally, Miyake and Shah (1999) suggest that there is consensus across different models of working memory that capacity limitations are due to multiple factors (e.g., lack of knowledge, strategies, or skills; limits in speed or efficiency of processing; poor executive monitoring and control) and that the assumption of a single factor to explain memory limitations is no longer viable. The role of some of these factors is the focus of the next section.

The Role of Prior Content Knowledge in Working Memory Functioning and Self-Regulation

It is a well-accepted generalization that prior knowledge of a domain or a topic area has a positive effect on memory, learning, thinking, and problem solving. For example, developmental studies of novices and experts have shown that young children who are experts in a domain perform better on memory and learning tasks than adult novices, with the effect being shown on topics such as chess, dinosaurs, soccer, baseball, and Star Wars (Schneider & Bjorklund, 1998; Schneider & Pressley, 1997). In addition, there is a great deal of research on expertise in more academic domains such as physics, mathematics, history, and writing that clearly shows that experts in these domains are able to think, learn, and problem solve more effectively and flexibly than novices in these domains (Bransford, Brown, & Cocking, 1999).

In all this work on expertise, it is assumed that a deep and well-organized knowledge base affords experts several advantages over novices (Bransford, Brown, & Cocking, 1999; Schneider & Bjorklund, 1998; Schneider & Pressley, 1997). First, experts do not have to expend cognitive resources in searching for and retrieving the appropriate information. Their knowledge base is organized in a way that allows them to activate the appropriate knowledge automatically or with little attentional or mental effort (they do not need to use deliberate strategies to recall information), thereby freeing up working memory resources for other cognitive tasks such as thinking and reasoning. In addition, as the knowledge base becomes more elaborated with the growth of expertise, the speed of activation and use of knowledge is increased, providing more efficient use of cognitive resources, an example of the second route to development of self-regulation.

Given these affordances of prior knowledge, it would be expected that experts in a domain would be capable of more self-regulation and the research supports this view. Although not necessarily labeled self-regulation, the literature on expertise does note that experts are more likely to be metacognitive and think about their own thinking and regulate their thinking in the service of higher order goals like solving a problem effectively, rather than the simpler task of trying to retrieve relevant information (Bransford, Brown, & Cocking, 1999). Developmentally, it would be expected that older students, in comparison to younger students who lack prior knowledge, would benefit from the same affordances of prior knowledge on self-regulation. In this case, older students can think about their own thinking and regulate it, not because they are more mature or in a higher developmental stage, but because their cognitive resources are freed up for regulatory tasks in comparison to knowledge search or retrieval processes.

There is an interesting developmental paradox that arises from this interaction of prior knowledge, working memory, and self-regulation. Younger students or novices with less prior knowledge would be expected to have more difficulties in self-regulation due to working memory constraints. At the same time, within the self-regulated learning literature, use of the various planning, monitoring, and control processes often is endorsed as a way of increasing knowledge or expertise. It is often suggested that for younger children or novices to become more knowledgeable or skilled, they need to become more metacognitive and regulate their own learning. However, these students are the ones who may have the most difficulty in enacting the various regulatory strategies as use of these strategies will involve working memory at the same time their lack of knowledge also consumes working memory resources. Given this problem, it is not surprising that novices often have to be "other-regulated" initially through coaching, instructional supports, and teacher scaffolding before they can be self-regulating. Once they become more knowledgeable or skilled, then some of these supports can be faded or withdrawn, and they can use the various processes outlined in Table 1 in a more self-regulating manner.

The Role of Metacognitive Knowledge in the Development of Self-Regulation

Besides prior content knowledge in the domain or topic area, students also acquire knowledge about cognition over the course of development. This type of knowledge has been labeled metacognitive knowledge and includes declarative knowledge about person, task, and strategy variables that affect cognitive performance. Metacognitive knowledge is distinct from metacognitive processes such as awareness, monitoring, and control of cognition (Brown, Bransford, Ferrara, & Campione, 1983; Pintrich, Wolters, & Baxter, 2000). Knowledge about person variables includes knowledge about individual differences in cognitive performance (some people are better at memory tasks than others), as well as self-knowledge about one's own cognitive abilities (which overlaps with motivational variables such as self-concept and self-efficacy). Knowledge about task variables includes knowledge that certain tasks are harder than others (e.g., free recall tasks are harder than recognition tasks). Knowledge of strategy variables includes knowledge about the various cognitive strategies that can be used to facilitate cognitive performance. An important aspect of strategy knowledge includes conditional knowledge about when and why to use different cognitive strategies (Paris, Lipson, & Wixson, 1983).

Developmentally, there is research that shows that even preschool children have some metacognitive knowledge about person, task, and strategy variables, but of course older children have much more metacognitive knowledge than younger children (Schneider & Bjorklund, 1998; Schneider & Pressley, 1997). Although many elementary school children may have developed metacognitive knowledge about relatively simple memory tasks, the development of metacognitive knowledge about more sophisticated tasks (i.e., text comprehension) continues well beyond elementary school. More importantly, the development of metacognitive knowledge about how person, task, and strategy variables interact to influence cognitive performance continues to develop through adolescence (Schneider & Pressley, 1997). The development of metacognitive knowledge also would allow students to think more about their own learning and influence their strategy use and self-regulatory processes.

The Role of Theories in the Development of Self-Regulation

Another type of prior knowledge that may play a developmental role consists of various "theories" that might facilitate or constrain self-regulation. Research from the "theory theory" perspective suggests that individuals have framework theories in different domains (biology, physics, psychology) that provide them with distinctive ways of describing, explaining, predicting, and interpreting phenomena within that domain (Paris, Byrnes, & Paris, 2000; Wellman & Gelman, 1998). In terms of self-regulation, the research on children's theory of mind is the most relevant. Of course, at one level, the work on metacognitive knowledge discussed in the previous section represents specific knowledge that would be part of an individual's theory of mind (Paris, Byrnes, & Paris, 2000). On the other hand, the research on the theory of mind of young children (ages 3–5) suggests that preschool children have rather abstract and general framework knowledge about mental entities such as minds, beliefs, desires, and emotions as well as the potential causal relations among these entities (Wellman, 1990; Wellman & Gelman, 1998).

Moreover, it seems that by about the time children enter school (by age 5), they have in place a general theory of mind that reflects a representational or constructivist perspective where the general operating principle is that individuals operate on the world through their perceptions and constructions, their representation of reality, not reality itself (Wellman & Gelman, 1998). In addition, young children hold a general belief–desire–action causal framework or folk psychology that leads them to explain people's actions in terms of their desires, wants, or goals. As Wellman and Gelman (1998) state about this causal system, "Because an actor has certain beliefs and desires, he or she engages in certain intentional acts, the success or failure of which leads to emotions, revised beliefs, renewed desires, and so on" (p. 539). For most children, this system of beliefs or theory of mind seems to be in place by age 5. This type of development seems to be function of age–maturational changes more than the development of expertise.

In terms of self-regulation, this general theory of mind seems to have all the components necessary for self-regulation, including some notions about desires or goals, the importance of representations of reality, and some notion of an intentional actor who takes action in order to reach a goal or satisfy a desire. It appears that this rudimentary theory of mind would allow young elementary school children to be potentially self-regulating, at least in contrast to those who may not develop certain aspects of a theory of mind (e.g., autistic children, see Wellman & Gelman, 1998). For example, young elementary school children could understand that people who want to learn (desire) and try hard (action) usually do better in school than those who do not. If these general ideas were not in place, it seems logical that it may be difficult for students to regulate their behavior. In contrast to the development of working memory, which is tied to improved processing, the development of the theory of mind might be linked to changes in goal structures for self-regulation. Once a theory of mind is in place, children can begin to see how setting goals and then intentionally trying to attain them can help them actually obtain their goals. However, there is a need for empirical research to test these hypothesized relations between young children's theories of mind and their self-regulation attempts.

At the same time, it is likely that these very general beliefs that are privileged by an abstract theory of mind, while necessary, may not be sufficient for academic self-regulation. In particular, young children have to acquire more specific knowledge about school tasks and strategies in order to become self-regulating. In addition, more self-knowledge is probably necessary as well in order to become an academically self-regulating learner (Paris, Byrnes, & Paris, 2001). In this sense, development may proceed from the abstract to the more specific and concrete, from a general abstract theory of mind to specific theories about learning in academic contexts, a reversal of the usual concrete to abstract developmental story line. Finally, while the general and abstract ideas in young children's theory of mind can be applied to other people and their own simple thoughts and behaviors, it is not clear that young children are able to actively use these ideas to reflect on their own behavior and cognition in any dynamic, regulatory manner. This active control of cognition may be a rather late-developing phenomenon, coinciding with a developmental shift in adolescence that enables students to have their own thoughts not just as objects of their thinking, but also to control their own thinking (Harter, 1998; Paris, Byrnes, & Paris, 2001).

The epistemological theories of children and adolescents comprise another type of theory that may play a developmental role in self-regulation (Hofer & Pintrich, 1997, 2002). Hofer and Pintrich (1997) have suggested that individuals' theories about the nature of knowledge and knowing do play a role in learning and achievement. Epistemological theories include beliefs about the certainty and simplicity of knowledge, the role of authority in creating knowledge, and justifications for knowing such as the criteria for making knowledge claims, use of evidence, and reasoning (Hofer & Pintrich, 1997; Pintrich, 2002). There is some evidence to suggest that student beliefs about epistemology are related to their cognitive strategy use, reading comprehension, and academic performance (e.g., Schommer, 1990, 2002), although this work has used a broader definition of epistemological theories that includes theories of intelligence and beliefs about learning. Nevertheless, it is possible that theories about knowledge and knowing give rise to certain types of goals for learning (e.g., mastery, performance, completion) which then foster more or less self-regulatory strategy use (Hofer & Pintrich, 1997; Pintrich, 2002). Here again, it seems more likely that epistemological theories are working through changing the goals for self-regulation, like the theory of mind research, not the improvement of self-regulatory processing as afforded by developments in working memory and prior knowledge.

There is a great deal of research that shows a consistent developmental trend in the nature of epistemological theories and thinking over the course of adolescence into the college years. The general developmental trajectory is that epistemological theories become more sophisticated over time, with individuals starting from a more objectivist stance or perspective toward knowledge (e.g., "There is one right answer and authorities like teachers should tell it to me"), then moving to a relativistic phase (e.g., "All answers are equally good, and so my answer is just as good as the teacher's or anyone else's"). Finally, there is a more balanced end point of development on the objectivist–relativist continuum that recognizes diversity in viewpoints, but also the importance of evidence and reasoning in support of one's perspectives. Given this developmental trend, it might be expected that younger students who would be more likely to have an objectivist perspective toward knowledge would be less motivated to engage in the use of different cognitive strategies.

For example, if students believe there is basically one "right" answer to strive for, then this goal might lead them to curtail deeper cognitive processing or reflective thinking and reasoning in favor of more memorization or rote learning. In contrast, more sophisticated epistemological beliefs should encourage students to think deeply about the material to be learned, question it, reflect on it, and use various cognitive and metacognitive strategies for understanding (Hofer & Pintrich, 1997; Pintrich, 2002). Of course, there is still a need for empirical evidence for these developmental linkages, but they are logical hypotheses that can guide future research.

In addition, there is a need to examine the domain specificity of these epistemological beliefs and their linkages to self-regulated learning. Most of the empirical work on epistemological thinking has been guided by a general age–stage perspective, which has focused on the development of global stages or phases in epistemological thinking (Hofer & Pintrich, 1997; Pintrich, 2002). However, it seems plausible that students might think differently about the nature of knowledge and knowing in different disciplines. Hofer (2000), using a within-subjects design, has shown that there are some differences between natural science and social science disciplines in terms of how the same individuals think about them epistemologically. As would be expected, natural science is seen as being closer to the objectivist perspective, and social sciences are perceived as being more relativistic. These domain differences in epistemological thinking could then lead to differences in self-regulated learning. Accordingly, it may be that there are both general age-related and domain-specific trends in epistemological thinking that need to be considered as potential moderators of the development of self-regulated learning.

In summary, there are several different kinds of theories that might facilitate or inhibit the development of self-regulation. At the most general and abstract level, there are young children's theories of mind. It appears that by the age of 5, most children have in place a theory of mind that would allow for the possibility of self-regulation. However, it seems clear that given young elementary school-age children's lack of domain knowledge and metacognitive knowledge, which can burden working memory, they will still be less likely to be self-regulating. Accordingly, a sophisticated theory of mind may be necessary, but it is hardly sufficient to foster adaptive self-regulated learning. There is a need for research that examines how young children's theories of mind are linked developmentally with the growth in expertise and metacognitive knowledge about academic learning, and in turn with the development of self-regulation.

The research on epistemological theories has focused on much older students, generally adolescents and college-age students, in contrast to the theory of mind research. The epistemological research suggests that as individuals get older, they are more likely to become relativistic or constructivist in their thinking, which might facilitate attempts at self-regulation. However, it is an interesting paradox that the theory of mind research suggests that children aged 5 and older could be described as naive constructivists or relativists, given their reliance on a representational perspective which recognizes that individuals work off their perceptions of reality, not reality itself. However, the epistemological beliefs research has suggested that most pre-college-age students are objectivists. As Chandler, Hallet, and Sokol (2002) have pointed out, this state of affairs seems impossible on the face of the data and theories. They suggest that young children are constructivists in a narrow "retail" sense in terms of specific tasks or domains, while with the development of the ability of abstraction, adolescents become constructivists at the "wholesale" level, where their relativism pervades all their thinking and reasoning. In any event, it seems likely that an adoption of a more "constructivist" perspective would facilitate efforts at self-regulation, which relies on the construction of personal goals, judgments of one's own progress, and strategies to learn better. Clearly, however, there is a need for research on the developmental trajectories and intertwining of theories of mind and theories of knowledge and their linkages to self-regulation.

Self-Regulation as a Depletable Resource

The cognitive factors discussed to this point focus attention on the role of limited cognitive resources in terms of capacity of working memory and the costs or benefits associated with using cognitive resources to self-regulate. Prior knowledge, strategies, and different types of theories may facilitate self-regulation because they lessen the demands on working memory, allowing cognitive resources to be used for self-regulatory purposes, or change the goal structures that guide self-regulatory processes. More recently, there has been another model proposed that suggests that self-regulatory activity is a limited resource itself and can be depleted much in the way that a muscle can be depleted by exercise. Muraven and Baumeister (2000) have made this argument, given their analysis of empirical studies of self-control. For the most part, self-control is defined in their work in terms of avoiding unpleasant stimuli such as stress and negative affect or avoiding temptations. For example, self-control is used when a dieter avoids overeating and regulates her eating. In this case, the individual has decided to control her eating habits and uses self-control processes to help her maintain her diet. Muraven and Baumeister (2000) summarize studies of coping with stress, regulating mood, and delaying gratification to suggest that the self-control process may function much like a muscle.

They suggest that the muscle metaphor has several key assumptions and hypotheses (see Muraven and Baumeister, 2000). First, they assume that acts of volition and self-control require self-control strength just as lifting a barbell in the gym requires a certain amount of strength. Second, just as our muscles are limited in strength, self-control is limited and we can only use so much before it becomes depleted. Third, their model assumes that self-control strength is general, not domain specific, so that using self-control to obtain one goal diminishes overall self-control strength, leaving less self-control resources for other goals. This would fit with general folk theories about how coping with stress in one domain (e.g., stress due to divorce, illness, etc. in the personal domain) can make it harder to accomplish goals in other domains (school, work). Moreover, this domain-general assumption is not in line with the domain-specific perspective on the role of prior knowledge and expertise that assumes that much of cognition is domain specific. Fourth, Muraven and Baumeister assume that success or failure at self-control tasks depends on self-control strength with those who have more strength more likely to succeed. In addition, some tasks are harder and require more self-control resources, just as heavier barbells are harder to lift than lighter barbells. Fifth, these authors suggest that self-control resources are expended in self-control tasks, and after use there is a refractory period where resources must be replenished. This is not unlike muscle use in lifting barbells where an individual can usually lift them for a period of time, but then the muscle becomes fatigued and some time is needed for the muscle to recover before full strength is restored.

Muraven and Baumeister (2000) note that this strength capacity idea is different from working memory capacity as working memory capacity is fully restored as soon as the task is over, there is no refractory period necessary for the resource to be fully functioning. In contrast, the muscle metaphor suggests that there may be a period of rest necessary, or at least an unrelated task might be needed in order to give time for self-control resources to be restored. These authors also note that there may be individual differences with some individuals having more self-control strength than others, just as some people (e.g., bodybuilders) have stronger muscles than others. Finally, they note that another implication of the muscle metaphor is that individuals may be able to develop better self-control resources through the use of self-control processes over time, just as a weight lifting and training program can increase muscle strength. Although Muraven and Baumeister do not discuss developmental differences, their experiential hypothesis suggests that older children and adolescents will have had many more opportunities to exercise self-control than younger children, possibly affording the development of bigger reservoirs of self-control, or "bigger" muscles to follow the metaphor.

Although this model is relatively new and so far has only been applied to avoidance behaviors in nonacademic settings, there may be implications for self-regulation in academic settings. A key self-control process in much of this work is inhibition of undesired behavioral responses (eating to break diet) or cognitions (negative thoughts) or emotions (negative emotions, anxiety, or bad moods). Table 1 shows different regulatory strategies that are designed to inhibit undesirable academic behaviors such as not studying, unwanted negative thoughts such as low efficacy beliefs, and certainly unwanted emotions such anxiety. In addition, the work on academic delay of gratification (e.g., Bembenutty & Karabenick, 1998) suggests the importance of inhibition processes to control academic behavior in the service of academic goals rather than other social goals. Finally, Dempster and Corkill (1999) have shown how basic inhibition processes are related to a host of traditional academic and educational areas such as memory and attention, intelligence, problem solving, reasoning, and self-regulated learning.

It seems clear that an important aspect of self-regulated learning is inhibition or avoidance of unwanted behavior, cognitions, and emotions. If this is the case, and self-control processes do function as a muscle as suggested by Muraven and Baumeister (2000), then it could be predicted that use of self-regulated learning processes also would deplete the system and follow some of the hypotheses noted earlier for self-control. There does not seem to be very much empirical evidence on the depletion of resources notion in the self-regulated learning literature. Researchers have suggested that strategy use is a difficult and effortful task, and there is some implication that formal strategy training efforts and continued use of strategies over time may increase children's ability to regulate, akin to weight training to improve muscle strength (e.g., Schneider & Pressley, 1997), but there has been no explicit test of the resource depletion hypothesis. Most of the research has been based more on a working memory resource perspective than on a resource depletion model.

There are some interesting differential predictions that follow from these general models that should be explored in future research. For example, the working memory view would suggest that there would be difficulties in using self-regulatory strategies developmentally due to problems of low prior knowledge and lack of automaticity of strategy use, but that once some of these issues were resolved, self-regulatory strategies could be run almost continuously without resource depletion. Accordingly, young children or novices at a task would have some difficulties given their lack of expertise, but older children and adults with more expertise should be able to regulate for long periods of time on academic tasks. In contrast, a resource depletion model would suggest that there would be degradation of performance over time as the continual use of self-regulatory strategies would deplete the reservoir of self-control strength, regardless of expertise level. From a developmental task perspective then, the two models predict different patterns of self-regulatory use and other outcomes or side effects over the time spent working on an academic task or series of academic tasks. For example in classroom terms, the working memory capacity model would suggest that there would be no difficulty in having a series of tasks that tax the self-regulatory system as the children move from reading to math to other subject areas. In contrast, the resource depletion model would suggest the need to alternate or space out the demanding self-regulatory tasks in order for resources not to be depleted too quickly.

In addition, from an age-graded developmental perspective, the resource depletion model would predict that younger children would have less self-control strength than older children and adults, just as they have less muscle strength in general. Dempster (1992) has shown that inhibitory processes do follow a developmental sequence tied to age-related changes. The developmental work by Mischel and his colleagues on delay of gratification certainly suggest that younger children have a much harder time resisting temptation than older children and adults and that delay of gratification seems to emerge sometime after 4 years of age (Mischel, 1974; Mischel & Metzner, 1962; Mischel & Patterson, 1976, 1978). . Metcalfe and Mischel (1999) in their integration of the delay of gratification research, and their use of the construct of willpower more generally, suggest both an expertise and age–developmental progression of willpower to control cognition, emotions, and behavior. Nigg (2000) also has suggested that various inhibitory processes do show strong developmental trends. Given this work, it appears that self-control and inhibition processes do follow an age-graded developmental pattern.

In summary, the resource depletion self-control model offers some interesting hypotheses about the development of self-regulated learning that need to be tested empirically. Some of these hypotheses diverge from expectations that would be generated under working memory and expertise models that have been used more often in self-regulated learning research. At the same time, it is possible that there may be multiple systems operating, including multiple working memory systems (reflecting the domain-specificity principle) as well as a general self-control resource depletion system, and that self-regulated learning implicates both systems. In addition, the self-control research may apply more to problems of inhibition or avoiding unwanted goals, rather than of approaching desired goals. As self-regulated learning involves working towards desired goals of learning and understanding, not just avoiding negative goals, the resource depletion model may only apply to certain aspects of self-regulated learning. In addition, at this point, the theoretical base for the construct of self-control strength is rather fuzzy, and the history of research on cognition or learning as a general muscle (e.g., learning Latin will improve intelligence) casts doubt on some aspects of the construct. Nevertheless, some interesting hypotheses are generated, and future research is needed to determine if and how it can be applied to academic self-regulation. Moreover, it seems most useful for future research to focus on how the multiple factors of knowledge, expertise, and resource depletion may operate together or for different aspects of self-regulated learning across different tasks or developmental periods, rather than searching for a single cognitive factor that explains all the developmental differences in self-regulated learning.

THE ROLE OF MOTIVATIONAL FACTORS IN THE
DEVELOPMENT OF SELF-REGULATED LEARNING

There are a number of different motivational factors that could facilitate or constrain self-regulated learning. Given space considerations, we will focus on three general constructs: efficacy–competence judgments, interest and value beliefs, and goal orientations. In addition, we will focus on students' own personal beliefs and perceptions of motivation, although it is clear that all three of these general motivational constructs are heavily influenced by contextual factors in classrooms and schools. As with the cognitive factors, the motivational factors might influence the development of self-regulation through two basic avenues of changing goal structures and improving self-regulatory processing.

The Role of Efficacy and Competence Judgments

An important component of most models of self-regulation is the monitoring of performance (phase 2 in Table 1) in terms of progress towards a goal that provides information about the discrepancy between the goal and the current state (Pintrich, 2000c). In cognitive models this type of monitoring has been labeled judgments of learning or JOLs (Nelson & Narens, 1990; Pintrich, Wolters, & Baxter, 2000). It is assumed that as students judge their progress, their understanding, or their performance, they will then be able to use this information to help them control or change their behaviors or cognitions in order to reduce the discrepancy between the goals and the current state. In this sense, the control and regulation activities are assumed to be dependent on the metacognitive judgments of learning.

These judgments of learning are similar in many ways to judgments of competence or self-efficacy to do a task. Of course, JOLs are usually conceived of and studied as ongoing in the process of doing a task, although some studies ask individuals to study a set of materials and then make a judgment about their readiness for a test (Pintrich, 2000c). In contrast, self-efficacy judgments are often seen as being predictive and taken before one attempts a task. For example, students are shown a set of math problems, but not allowed to work on them, and asked for their judgments of their capabilities to solve them (Schunk, 1989, 1991, 1994). Finally, competence judgments are often more global measures of individuals' perceptions of their general ability to do something ("I'm good at math") and less tied to a specific task or direct progress on a task (Pintrich & Schunk, 1996). Although these differences are important, from a functional point of view, the key issue for self-regulation theory and research is that students are making some self-evaluation or judgment of their progress or competence. These judgments are functionally similar to monitoring processes (phase 2 in Table 1) in many ways and would be related to the second route of the improved functioning of self-regulatory processes.

The research on the links between self-efficacy and use of self-regulatory strategies has generated a fairly stable generalization. Both experimental and correlational studies have shown that self-efficacy judgments are positively correlated with self-regulation and actual performance (Pintrich, 1999a; Pintrich &

De Groot, 1990; Pintrich & Schrauben, 1992; Pintrich & Schunk, 1996; Schunk, 1989, 1991, 1994). Students who believe they have the capabilities to perform or learn the task are much more likely to report using self-regulatory strategies as well as do better on the task itself. The same general positive relation also has been found in research on children's competence perceptions and their links to academic performance (Harter, 1998). This generalization also seems to apply across a number of different tasks and domains.

However, there may be important developmental differences in the nature of this relation. Research on the development of children's self-competence perceptions has shown that there is a general developmental decline in the mean level of these ratings with age. Young elementary school children tend to have fairly high perceptions of their competence and believe they can master most tasks or think they are all near the top of their class on academic tasks (Eccles, Wigfield, & Schiefele, 1998; Harter, 1998). However, with age, students become more realistic or negative about their capabilities and perceptions of their competence drops, especially as they enter middle schools. This decline is related to developing cognitive competencies in understanding and interpreting feedback information as well as the use of social comparison information. In addition, the classroom context is changing and becoming more evaluative, competitive, and norm referenced, thereby providing more evaluative and social comparative information (Blumenfeld, Pintrich, Meece, & Wessels, 1982; Eccles, Wigfield, & Schiefele, 1998; Pintrich & Schunk, 1996).

Given these findings, younger children may be more unrealistic about their competencies, or less calibrated in terms of their judgments of competence relative to other measures of their actual performance (e.g., Wigfield, et al., 1997). In the case of younger students who would tend to be overestimators of their competence, they would then be less likely to see the need to regulate or change their behavior. In other words, younger students generally think they can read or write or do mathematics, and so would be less likely to see the need for change in self-regulatory behavior to improve their performance. After all, if a student thinks he is one of the better readers in the class, why would he need to do anything different in terms of regulating his reading strategies or behaviors? This lack of awareness would make younger students less likely to be self-regulating, providing another constraint on the development of self-regulation for younger students. As they get older and learn that they are not necessarily the best students in the class, that there may be some academic domains or tasks in which they are not as skilled as they need to be in order to be successful, then this dawning awareness might motivate them to try to change their self-regulatory strategies and behaviors. This awareness is most likely not sufficient for self-regulation to occur, given our discussion of the important cognitive factors, but the awareness may be necessary to motivate the use of self-regulatory strategies.

Of course, there are individual differences in calibration, besides the general developmental optimism of younger students. Some students are consistent overestimators and some are chronic underestimators. The research shows that students who underestimate their actual competence, who suffer from an "illusion of incompetence" (Phillips & Zimmerman, 1990), are more likely to be anxious, to have lower expectations for success, and are more likely to avoid challenging tasks because they believe they are not able to do the task. In contrast, overestimators also may avoid challenging tasks because they do not want to fail and do want to protect their sense of competence (Harter, 1998). In terms of underestimators, they may be less likely to self-regulate because they lack self-efficacy about their capabilities to change or learn how to do the task. Overestimators may not self-regulate because they may not see the need to change what they are doing. In any event, here is a situation where the trajectory of use of self-regulatory strategies is similar, but the motivational rationale for the pattern is quite different. There is a clear need for more research on the role of calibration in self-regulation, including both over- and underestimating one's competence.

Besides the role of actual judgments of self-competence, the definitions and theories that students have of ability and effort may play a role in the development of self-regulation. For example, Dweck and her colleagues (e.g., Dweck, 1999; Dweck & Leggett, 1988) have shown that individuals often adopt one of two theories of intelligence, an entity theory where ability is limited and fixed, and an incremental theory where ability is more malleable and can be changed through effort and learning. Moreover, these different theories can give rise to very different patterns of goals, effort, self-regulatory strategy use, affect, and achievement. The general finding from this research is that an entity theory gives rise to a concern with ability and demonstrating ability to others, leading to an adoption of a performance goal. Performance goals, in turn, can give rise to less effort, less adaptive strategy use, more negative affect, and lower levels of achievement (Dweck, 1999), although they do not have to lead to maladaptive outcomes in all cases (see Harackiewicz, Barron, & Elliot, 1998; Pintrich, 2000a, 2000b, 2000c). In contrast, an incremental theory leads the student to adopt a mastery or learning goal, where the focus is on self-improvement and learning. Mastery goals have been shown to lead to more effort, more adaptive strategy use, positive affect, and better achievement (Dweck, 1999; Pintrich, 2000a, 2000b, 2000c).

This theories $\longrightarrow$ goals $\longrightarrow$ outcomes pattern is one way for theories of intelligence to be related to self-regulated learning, reflecting the changing goal structure route. However, it may be that the mediational role of goals is not necessarily the only pathway from theories to self-regulation. It may be that there is a direct route, with theories of intelligence influencing the nature of self-regulation. If students believe that their general ability or intelligence is fixed and stable, they may be less motivated to engage in the effortful and time-consuming aspects of self-regulation regardless of their goals. In terms of the costs and benefits, students with an entity theory may assume that the costs of using various self-regulatory strategies to improve their learning and performance are too high, with little payoff, since their ability is not very malleable. In contrast, those with an incremental theory of intelligence should readily see the advantages of using various self-regulatory strategies in order to improve their skills, even if there are costs in terms of time and effort. Dweck (1999) summarizes research that supports this general hypothesis as well as the direct link between theories of intelligence and actual achievement as indexed by grades and course performance. The relative costs/benefits of engaging in self-regulation also reflect the goal structure route to self-regulation.

In terms of development, there is some evidence to suggest that younger children may be more likely to endorse incremental theories, while older children and adults may be more likely to hold entity theories (Dweck & Elliot, 1983; Pintrich & Schunk, 1996). Nicholls and his colleagues (Nicholls, 1978, 1990; Nicholls & Miller, 1983, 1984a, 1984b) have shown that children about 5 years old or younger do not differentiate the concepts of luck, skill, ability, and effort in the same manner as older children and adults. These younger children tend to see effort and ability as covarying positively, such that those who try hard are smart, and those who are smart also try hard. It is not until about 12 or 13 years of age that children start to develop the normative conception of ability and effort that involves the idea that ability and effort covary inversely, such that those who are smart do not have to try hard, and those who try hard probably lack ability. The developmental trajectory of this pattern is probably due to both changing cognitive developmental resources and contextual transitions in classrooms (Pintrich & Schunk, 1996).

Taken together, the research by Dweck and her colleagues and Nicholls and his colleagues suggests that there are important developmental differences in how children think about ability and effort. If older children and adults come to believe that effort and ability covary inversely, then this belief could lead them to think that individuals who have to use the various effortful self-regulatory strategies such as those defined in Table 1 are less able. This kind of belief or theory could make older children and adults less likely to choose to use self-regulatory strategies, especially if they want to preserve their perceptions of their own ability (Covington, 1992). Again, there seems to be a paradoxical developmental pattern, with older children more likely to have the cognitive resources that enable them to use self-regulatory strategies, but at the same time their developing theories of intelligence, ability, and effort may lead them to avoid using these strategies. There is a clear need for research on how these different developmental competencies interact to influence self-regulation. It may be that having the cognitive resources may be sufficient and it does not matter what the accompanying theories of intelligence are for an individual. On the other hand, given the problems of students who do seem to have the cognitive resources but still fail to use them, then there should be some role for theories of intelligence, ability, and effort that can set in motion certain types of goals that can guide, facilitate, or constrain self-regulation.

The Role of Interest and Value Beliefs

As noted above, self-regulation is an effortful and time-consuming activity. It takes much more mental effort and commitment to use some of the self-regulatory strategies listed in Table 1. Given this fact, it is not surprising that students who are more personally interested in a task or activity as well as those who see it as more important or useful to them (value) are more likely to use self-regulatory strategies (Pintrich, 1999a; Pintrich & De Groot, 1990; Pintrich & Schrauben, 1992). This generalization also seems to be fairly stable across different tasks and activities. In terms of self-regulation, it could be suggested that high interest and value beliefs lead students to construct goals for their learning that downplay some of the costs and highlight the benefits of self-regulation.

From a developmental perspective, there is evidence that children's reports of their interest in and value for academic domains decline across the school years. It appears that elementary students report liking and valuing school work more than middle school and high school students in general (Eccles, Wigfield, & Schiefele, 1998). This overall decline in interest and value for schoolwork would suggest that students would be less likely to be motivated to use self-regulatory strategies as they develop and move into the upper grades in school. This is an interesting paradox, since motivation that would facilitate self-regulation seems to be declining just at the time when cognitively the adolescent students are more capable of becoming self-regulating. From this general age–developmental perspective, this would help explain why it is difficult to motivate adolescents in general to become more self-regulating.

At the same time, from a developmental–task and individual differences perspective, there are clearly tasks and activities that individual students become very interested in as they grow older and begin to have some choices about how they spend their time. For example, a student who becomes very interested in athletics, or math, or science may chose to spend more time on these activities . As she spends more time on these activities, initially fostered by her personal interest, her expertise in the domain grows, as well as her skill at regulating her behavior in the domain. The interactions between interest, knowledge, and self-regulation can become mutually reinforcing and facilitate the further development of the individual (Alexander, Jetton, & Kulikowich, 1995). From this task–developmental perspective, it is clear that there can be large domain or individual differences in the role of interest and value in facilitating self-regulation.

The Role of Goal Orientation

There has been a great deal of research on the role of goal orientation in self-regulated learning (see Pintrich, 2000c, for a review). In general, this research has examined how approach mastery goals and approach–avoid performance goals are related to the use of a wide variety of self-regulatory strategies. There is good deal of converging evidence regarding the positive influence of mastery goals on the different components of self-regulated learning. That is, if individuals set their general criterion or standard for academic tasks to be learning and improving, then as they monitor their performance and attempt to control and regulate it, this standard should guide them towards the use of more self-regulatory processes. In fact, the vast majority of the empirical evidence from both experimental laboratory studies and correlational class-room studies suggest just such a stable generalization. Students who adopt or endorse an approach mastery goal orientation do engage in more self-regulated learning than those who do not adopt or endorse to a lesser extent a mastery goal (Ames, 1992; Pintrich, 1999a; 2000a, 2000b, 2000c; Pintrich & De Groot, 1990; Pintrich & Schrauben, 1992; Pintrich & Schunk, 1996).

The research on performance goals and self-regulated learning is not as easily summarized as the results for approach mastery goals. The original goal theory research generally found negative relations between performance goals and various cognitive, motivational, and behavioral outcomes (Ames, 1992; Dweck & Leggett, 1988; Pintrich & Schunk, 1996), although it did not discriminate empirically between approach and avoidance performance goals. The more recent research, which has made the distinction between approach and avoidance performance goals, does show some differential relations between approaching a task focusing on besting others and approaching a task focused on trying not to look stupid or incompetent. In particular, the general distinction between an approach and an avoidance orientation suggests that there could be some positive aspects of an approach performance orientation. If students are approaching a task trying to promote certain goals and strategies, this might lead them to be more involved in the task than students who are trying to avoid certain goals which could lead to more withdrawal and less engagement in the task (Harackiewicz, Barron, & Elliot, 1998; Higgins, 1997; Pintrich, 2000a, 2000b, 2000c).

Most of the research on performance goals that did *not* distinguish between approach and avoidance versions finds that performance goals are negatively related to students' use of deeper cognitive strategies (e.g., Meece, Blumenfeld, & Hoyle, 1988; Nolen, 1988; cf., however, Bouffard, Boisvert, Vezeau, & Larouche, 1995). This would be expected, given that performance goal scales that include items about besting others as well as avoiding looking incompetent would guide students away from the use of deeper strategies. Students focused on besting others may be less likely to exert the time and effort needed to use deeper processing strategies because the effort needed to use these strategies could show to others that they lack the ability, given that the inverse relation between effort and ability is usually operative under performance goals, and trying hard in terms of strategy use may signify low ability. For students who want to avoid looking incompetent, the same self-worth protection mechanism (Covington, 1992) may be operating, whereby students do not exert effort in terms of strategy use in order to have an excuse for doing poorly that can be attributed to lack of effort or poor strategy use.

However, more recent research with measures that reflect only an approach or avoidance performance goal suggests that there may be differential relations between these two versions of performance goals. For example, Wolters, Yu, and Pintrich (1996) in a correlational study of junior high students found that independent of the positive main effect of mastery goals, an approach performance goal focused on besting others was positively related to the use of deeper cognitive strategies and more regulatory strategy use. Pintrich (2000b) also found a similar pattern. However, Kaplan and Midgley (1997) in a correlational study of junior high students found no relation between an approach performance goal and adaptive learning strategies, but approach performance goals were positively related to more surface processing or maladaptive learning strategies. These two studies did not include separate measures of avoid performance goals. In contrast, Middleton and Midgley (1997) in a correlational study of junior high students found no relation between either approach or avoidance performance goals and cognitive self-regulation.

Nevertheless, it may be that approach performance goals could lead to deeper strategy use and cognitive self-regulation, as suggested by Wolters et al. (1996), when students are confronted with overlearned classroom tasks that do not challenge or interest them or offer opportunities for much self-improvement. In this case, the focus on an external criterion of "besting others" or being the best in the class could lead them to be more involved in these boring tasks and to try to use more self-regulatory cognitive strategies to accomplish this goal. On the other hand, it may be that approach performance goals are not that strongly related to cognitive self-regulation in either a positive or negative way as suggested by the results of Kaplan and Midgley (1997) and Middleton and Midgley (1997). Taken together, the conflicting results suggest that approach performance goals do not have to be negatively related to cognitive self-regulatory activities in comparison to avoidance performance goals. This conclusion, although not accepted by all researchers (see Midgley, Kaplan, & Middleton, 2001), suggests that there may be multiple pathways between approach and avoidance performance goals, cognitive strategy use and self-regulation, and eventual achievement. Future research should attempt to map out these multiple pathways and to determine how approach and avoidance performance goals may differentially relate to self-regulation activities.

Developmentally, there is little research on the age-related longitudinal changes in children's goal orientations (Eccles, Wigfield, & Schiefele, 1998). This is partially due to the assumption that goal orientations are very contextually sensitive, not personal traits of the individual. In this case, it is more important to understand the nature of the context and how the contextual features shape the adoption of different goal orientations than to understand how children's goal orientations change with age. Nevertheless, there may be both cognitive and contextual reasons to expect that mastery goals will become less dominant with age as performance goals become more salient to children. Dweck (1999; Dweck & Leggett, 1988) would predict that performance goals would become more important to children as they age, given the increasing switch to entity theories of intelligence with age. In addition, there is evidence to suggest that classrooms become more competitive and performance goal-focused as students make the transition from elementary to middle school (Eccles, Wigfield, & Schiefele, 1998). Both these personal and contextual factors would contribute to the adoption of or emphasis on performance goals with age.

If students are more likely to adopt performance goals as they develop, then normative goal theory would predict that this would constrain the development of self-regulation (Ames, 1992; Midgley, Kaplan, & Middleton, 2001; Pintrich, 2000a, 2000b, 2000c). However, more recent research from a revised goal theory perspective (Harackiewicz, Barron, & Elliot, 1998; Pintrich, 2000a, 2000b, 2000c) would suggest two alternative hypotheses. First, it can be predicted that if students adopt an avoid performance goal, then the probability of a maladaptive pattern of self-regulation developing is increased. Second, the adoption of an approach performance goal may not necessarily lead to maladaptive patterns; there may be some adaptive patterns of regulation that are fostered by approach performance goals. Future research needs to examine the possibility of multiple goals and multiple developmental pathways towards regulation that are fostered by different patterns of goals (Pintrich, 2000 a, 2000b, 2000c).

The Moderating Role of Gender and Ethnicity

Thus far, we have demonstrated how certain cognitive and motivational factors can facilitate or constrain the development of self-regulated learning. In this section, we extend this discussion by considering the role of gender and ethnicity as moderators of the relations between the cognitive and motivational factors and the development of self-regulatory processes. Given the preceding discussion, it would seem most reasonable to expect personal characteristics such as gender and ethnicity to have their greatest influence on self-regulated learning through their relation to motivational factors such as self-efficacy. In terms of the various cognitive factors, there is little evidence to suggest that systematic gender and ethnic differences exist in students' working memory or strategy use. There may be some differences in prior knowledge and theories, but the most consistent gender and ethnic differences seem to appear in the motivational constructs.

Briefly, motivational theorists have found female students to display somewhat less adaptive patterns of motivation in comparison to male students, although the results do vary by domain or task (Eccles, Wigfield, & Schiefele, 1998). Dweck (1986) for example, portrayed girls as suffering from low expectancies and decreased achievement strivings, particularly in the face of failure. Researchers have noted lower perceptions of academic competence among girls even in their early elementary years and especially in subjects such as mathematics and science, despite achievement levels comparable to (or even exceeding) those of their male counterparts (Entwisle & Baker, 1983; Eccles, Wigfield, & Schiefele, 1998). On the other hand, in some domains (reading/English) females rate their competence higher than males (Wigfield et al., 1997). Researchers also have noted some variation in student motivational processes according to ethnicity. Asian-American students, for example, have been found to exhibit lower levels of self-efficacy (e.g., Eaton & Dembo, 1997), while African-American students have been found to display great confidence in their academic competence (e.g., Graham, 1994).

Based on our earlier contention that higher levels of efficacy are typically associated with greater use of both cognitive and self-regulatory strategies, one could then hypothesize that males and African-American students should regulate their learning more than females and Asian-American students. However, a more complex picture of the role of ethnicity and gender in self-regulated learning emerges from the empirical work. Before we examine the various empirical findings in greater depth, several notes of caution are necessary. First, the scope of the literature is rather limited both in terms of the number of studies that have examined gender and ethnic differences in self-regulated learning and in terms of the samples of participants these studies have employed (almost all focus on late elementary to middle school students). In general, researchers have yet to systematically investigate gender and ethnic differences in self-regulatory processes. Much of the work to date on this topic has been done in a somewhat haphazard fashion, often taking the form of a secondary research question. Accordingly, the majority of findings concerning gender and ethnic differences have been somewhat mixed. As such, we feel that it would be somewhat peremptory to draw definitive conclusions about the role of gender and ethnicity in self-regulatory learning processes at this time. Nevertheless, the findings are certainly provocative.

First in terms of gender differences, several researchers have found female students to report greater use of self-regulatory strategies despite lower levels of self-efficacy (Ablard & Lipshultz, 1998; Zimmerman & Martinez-Pons, 1990). Such findings run counter to our general assertion that higher levels of self-efficacy should be related to greater self-regulatory strategy use. For example, Zimmerman & Martinez-Pons (1990) discovered comparatively more girls than boys to employ strategies that optimize immediate learning environments (e.g., record keeping and monitoring, environmental structuring) and personal regulation (e.g., goal setting). Ablard and Lipschultz (1998), who used a similar procedure to that of Zimmerman and Martinez-Pons, also found greater use of such strategies among girls in their sample, even after adjusting for covariates such as mastery goal orientation. At the same time, however, they found that use of these strategies by girls varied depending on the learning context. However, if we assume that the relatively lower perceptions of efficacy for females reflect the possibility that females are better calibrated than males (i.e., it is not so much that females are underestimators, but that males are overestimators), then it follows that females would be more likely to be self-regulating, given their better accuracy at monitoring their strengths and weaknesses.

In contrast to the above findings, a select number of researchers have reported little to no gender differences in student use of various learning and self-regulatory strategies (Anderman & Young, 1994; Meece & Jones, 1996; Wolters & Pintrich, 1998). Anderman and Young (1994), who investigated sixth and seventh grade student motivation and self-regulated learning in science, reported no gender difference in self-regulated learning. Wolters and Pintrich (1998) also found no gender differences in self-regulatory strategy use, although the female middle school students in their study did report greater use of cognitive strategies (e.g., rehearsal, organization). Finally, Meece and Jones (1996) found no differences in female and male self-regulated learning, except among female students of average ability, who reported greater use of active engagement strategies than did average ability boys.

In terms of ethnic differences in self-regulated learning, very few studies have examined how the process of self-regulated learning might be moderated by ethnicity. In fact, we do not know of any study that has methodically investigated differences in ethnic minority student self-regulatory processes. However, cross-cultural studies comparing Japanese and Australian student self-regulated learning have suggested some differences in the use of specific self-regulated learning strategies (Purdie & Hattie 1996; Purdie, Hattie, & Douglas, 1996). The most common finding is that Japanese students tend to rely more on memorization and rehearsal strategies than Australian students, strategies Western researchers generally associate with shallow learning. Unfortunately, one cannot assess the relationship of the use of these strategies by Japanese students to their efficacy levels, as these cross-cultural studies did not assess their competence judgments. However, if one considers the general finding that Asian students often have lower competence perceptions than American students (e.g., Stevenson & Stigler, 1992), then it may be an issue of calibration again, with the overestimating American students less likely to be self-regulating because they believe they are basically capable. The same argument might be relevant to African Americans if they have generally high perceptions of competence, even in the face of generally low levels of achievement (Graham, 1994). This suggests some problems in accuracy of calibration, which would make them less likely to self-regulate (Pintrich, 2000c).

In short, much work remains to be done on the role of gender and ethnic differences in self-regulated learning. In terms of ethnic differences, given the paucity of research on this topic to date, it is difficult to assess the actual role ethnicity has on self-regulatory processes at this time. On the other hand, the empirical work on gender and self-regulated learning seems to suggest that gender differences might exist in strategy use, with female students reporting greater use of certain cognitive and self-regulated learning strategies despite their lower ratings of their academic competence. However, this trend of greater strategy use among females seems to vary somewhat depending upon the type of strategy, the learning context, and the ability level. One should also note that all the findings reported in this section were based on student self-reports of their self-regulated learning. Consequently, it is difficult to ascertain whether these gender differences truly reflect differences in actual use of these strategies or merely differences in the level of awareness or self-reporting biases. At the very least, however, these findings underscore the need for self-regulated learning researchers to consider potential variation according to gender and ethnicity in their models of the development of self-regulated learning.

CONCLUSIONS AND FUTURE DIRECTIONS

The development of self-regulated learning capabilities is an important developmental task for all students. Students who can regulate their own cognition, motivation–affect, behavior, and their environment, are more likely to be successful in academic settings. The various processes and strategies outlined in this chapter and listed in Table 1 represent what develops in self-regulated learning. There are two important developmental trends in the acquisition and use of these self-regulatory strategies. First, there is a general increase in self-regulation capabilities with age. Young elementary school children will not be able to self-regulate as well as older middle school, high school, and college students. More importantly, however, there also are task-related developmental trajectories that show individual differences in development. Self-regulatory capabilities also increase as a student gains experience and expertise in doing a task. Accordingly, there are both general age–developmental as well as individual–task-related trajectories in the development of self-regulation.

In terms of the factors that drive these two developmental trends, both cognitive and motivational factors can facilitate and constrain the development of self-regulation in school contexts. In terms of the age-related changes in cognitive development, there is a general positive trend in the development of content knowledge, metacognitive knowledge, epistemological theories, self-knowledge, and expertise in strategy use that can "push" or propel the individual towards self-regulation. At the very least, it seems that with development, the cognitive resources of knowledge and expertise in strategy use increase, providing sufficient resources to self-regulate. Moreover, with the growth in constructivist and epistemological thinking in adolescence, these theories may privilege certain types of self-regulation or foster the goals that in turn increase self-regulatory processes. Finally, with age, there seems to be the development of better accuracy of competence judgments, better calibration or self-knowledge, which should lead to more adaptive attempts at self-regulation and control.

At the same time, however, there may be both cognitive and motivational factors that exert a countervailing "pull" or hold the individual back from self-regulation. There is evidence to suggest that as students get older, their theories of intelligence are more likely to become entity-like, a theory that might foster or privilege fewer or less adaptive self-regulation attempts. In addition, the possibility that with age, students become less interested in school and value it less would likely foster less adaptive self-regulation. Finally, the fact that schools become more competitive and could foster a greater emphasis on performance goals, than mastery goals, suggests that students may be less willing to engage in effortful self-regulatory activities.

Taken together, these two general developmental trends suggest the paradoxical conclusion that just as students are becoming cognitively able to self-regulate, their motivational beliefs and some aspects of the school context conspire to deflect them away from self-regulation activities. This is one reason that it is important to include both cognitive and motivational components in strategy training programs for students at all ages, but it may be particularly important in programs in middle schools, high schools, and colleges (Hofer, Yu, & Pintrich, 1998). Of course, there are individuals who negotiate these general developmental trajectories along different pathways, and there is a need for more research on the multiple pathways, that individuals can take to successful self-regulation.

In addition, from a task–developmental perspective, there is a need for more research on how these various cognitive and motivational factors interact to facilitate self-regulation over the course of developing expertise in a domain or on a specific class of tasks. There may be clear general age–developmental constraints on content knowledge and expertise in strategy use, but there also are significant task or domain effects that needed to be considered in our models. Finally, we have not really considered the implications of a strength model of self-regulation that could play an important role in the waxing and waning of self-regulation activities as one engages in a task over time.

These new perspectives on the developmental factors that might facilitate or constrain self-regulation should open up new avenues for research. In addition, there is a clear need to link these developments with changes in the nature of school and classroom contexts. Self-regulation is not just afforded or constrained by personal cognition and motivation, but also privileged, encouraged, or discouraged by the contextual factors. Besides integrating the cognitive and motivational factors in our models of self-regulation, we need to tie these developments to the social contextual factors in schools and classrooms.

Acknowledgment

We thank our colleagues at Michigan, Scott Paris and Alison Paris, for their helpful comments on an earlier draft of this chapter. In addition, Allan Wigfield provided very useful feedback that improved our chapter greatly. Of course, we take full responsibility for the ideas presented here.

References

Ablard, K. E., & Lipschultz, R. E. (1998). Self-regulated learning in high achieving students: Relations to advanced reasoning, achievement goals, and gender. *Journal of Educational Psychology*, 90, 94–101.

Alexander, P., Jetton, T., & Kulikowich, J. (1995). Interrelationship of knowledge, interest, and recall: Assessing a model of domain learning. *Journal of Educational Psychology*, 87, 559–575.

Ames, C. (1992). Classrooms: Goals, structures, and student motivation. *Journal of Educational Psychology*, 84, 261–271.

Anderman, E., & Young, A. (1994). Motivation and strategy use in science: Individual differences and classroom effects. *Journal of Research in Science Teaching*, 31, 811–831.

Bandura, A. (1997). *Self-efficacy: The exercise of control.* New York: Freeman.

Bembenutty, H., & Karabenick, S. A. (1998). Academic delay of gratification. *Learning and Individual Differences*, 10, 329–346.

Blumenfeld, P.C., Pintrich, P.R., Meece, J., & Wessels, K. (1982). The formation and role of self perceptions of ability in elementary classrooms. *Elementary School Journal*, 82, 401–420.

Boekaerts, M. (1993). Being concerned with well-being and with learning. *Educational Psychologist*, 28, 148–167.

Boekaerts, M. (1995). Self-regulated learning: Bridging the gap between metacognitive and metamotivation theories. *Educational Psychologist*, 30, 195–200.

Boekaerts, M., & Niemivirta, M. (2000). Self-regulated learning: Finding a balance between learning goals and ego-protective goals. In M. Boekaerts, P. R. Pintrich, & M. Zeidner (Eds.), *Handbook of self-regulation: Theory, research, and applications*, (pp. 417–450). San Diego: Academic Press.

Boekaerts, M., Pintrich, P. R., & Zeidner, M. (Eds.). (2000). *Handbook of self-regulation.* San Diego: Academic Press.

Bouffard, T., Boisvert, J., Vezeau, C., & Larouche, C. (1995). The impact of goal orientation on self-regulation and performance among college students. *British Journal of Educational Psychology*, 65, 317–329.

Bransford, J. D., Brown, A. L., & Cocking, R. R. (1999). *How people learn: Brain, mind, experience, and school.* Washington, DC: Academy Press.

Brown, A. L., Bransford, J. D., Ferrara, R. A., & Campione, J. C. (1983). Learning, remembering, and understanding. In J. H. Flavell & E. M. Markman (Eds.), *Handbook of child psychology: Vol. 3. Cognitive development*, 4th ed. (pp. 77–166). New York: Wiley.

Butler, D. L., & Winne, P. H. (1995). Feedback and self-regulated learning: A theoretical synthesis. *Review of Educational Research*, 65, 245–281.

Caspi, A. (1998). Personality development across the life course. . In W. Damon (Series Ed.) & N. Eisenberg (Vol. Ed.), *Handbook of child psychology: Vol. 3. Social, emotional, and personality development* (5th ed., pp. 311–388). New York: Wiley.

Chandler, M., Hallet, D., & Sokol, B. (2002). Competing claims about competing knowledge claims. In B. Hofer & P. R. Pintrich (Eds.), *Personal epistemology: The psychology of beliefs about knowledge and knowing* (pp. 145–168). Mahwah, NJ: Lawrence Erlbaum Associates.

Corno, L. (1989). Self-regulated learning: A volitional analysis. In B. J. Zimmerman & D. H. Schunk, (Eds.), *Self-regulated learning and academic achievement: Theory, research and practice* (pp. 111–141). New York: Springer-Verlag.

Corno, L. (1993). The best-laid plans: Modern conceptions of volition and educational research. *Educational Researcher, 22,* 14–22.

Covington, M. V. (1992). *Making the grade: A self-worth perspective on motivation and school reform.* Cambridge, U.K.: Cambridge University Press.

Dempster, F. (1992). The rise and fall of the inhibitory mechanism: Toward a unified theory of cognitive development and aging. *Developmental Review, 12,* 45–75.

Dempster, F., & Corkill, A. (1999). Interference and inhibition in cognition and behavior: Unifying themes for educational psychology. *Educational Psychology Review, 11,* 1–88.

Dweck, C. (1986). Motivational processes affecting learning. *American Psychologist, 41,* 1040–1048.

Dweck, C. (1999). *Self-theories: Their role in motivation, personality, and development.* Philadelphia: Psychology Press.

Dweck, C., & Elliot, E. S. (1983). Achievement motivation. In P. H. Mussen (Series Ed.) & E. M. Heatherington (Vol. Ed.), *Handbook of child psychology: Vol. 4. Socialization, personality, and social development,* (4th ed., pp. 643–691). New York: Wiley.

Dweck, C., & Leggett, E. L. (1988). A social–cognitive approach to motivation and personality. *Psychological Review, 95,* 256–273.

Eaton, M. J., & Dembo, M. H. (1997). Differences in the motivational beliefs of Asian American and non-Asian students. *Journal of Educational Psychology, 89,* 433–440.

Eccles, J. S., Wigfield, A., & Schiefele, U. (1998). Motivation to succeed. In W. Damon (Series Ed.) & N. Eisenberg (Vol. Ed.), *Handbook of child psychology: Vol. 3. Social, emotional, and personality development* (5th ed., pp. 1017–1095). New York: Wiley.

Entwisle, D. R., & Baker, D. P. (1983). Gender and young children's expectations for performance in arithmetic. *Developmental Psychology, 19,* 200–209.

Ferrari, M., & Mahalingam, R. (1998). Personal cognitive development and its implications for teaching and learning. *Educational Psychologist, 33,* 35–44.

Graham, S. (1994). Motivation in African Americans. *Review of Educational Research, 64,* 55–117.

Harackiewicz, J. M., Barron, K. E., & Elliot, A. J. (1998). Rethinking achievement goals: When are they adaptive for college students and why? *Educational Psychologist, 33,* 1–21.

Harter, S. (1998). The development of self-representations. In W. Damon (Series Ed.) & N. Eisenberg (Vol. Ed.), *Handbook of Child Psychology. Vol. 3. Social, emotional, and personality development* (5th ed., pp. 553–617). New York: Wiley.

Higgins, E. T. (1997). Beyond pleasure and pain. *American Psychologist, 52,* 1280–1300.

Hofer, B. K. (2000). Dimensionality and disciplinary differences in personal epistemology. *Contemporary Educational Psychology, 25,* 378–405.

Hofer, B. K., & Pintrich, P. R. (1997). The development of epistemological theories: Beliefs about knowledge and knowing and their relation to learning. *Review of Educational Research, 67,* 88–140.

Hofer, B. K. & Pintrich, P. R. (2002). *Personal epistemology: The psychology of beliefs about knowledge and knowing.* Mahwah, NJ: Lawrence Erlbaum Associates.

Hofer, B. K., Yu, S., & Pintrich, P. R. (1998). Teaching college students to be self-regulated learners. In D. H. Schunk & B. J. Zimmerman (Eds.), *Self-regulated learning: From teaching to self-reflective practice* (pp. 57–85). New York: Guilford Press.

Kaplan, A., & Midgley, C. (1997). The effect of achievement goals: Does level of perceived academic competence make a difference? *Contemporary Educational Psychology, 22,* 415–435.

Kuhl, J. (1984). Volitional aspects of achievement motivation and learned helplessness: Toward a comprehensive theory of action control. In B. Maher & W. Maher (Eds.), *Progress in experimental personality research*. (Vol. 13, pp. 99–171). New York: Academic Press.

Kuhl, J. (1985). Volitional mediators of cognition–behavior consistency: Self-regulatory processes and action versus state orientation. In J. Kuhl & J. Beckman (Eds.), *Action control: From cognition to behavior* (pp. 101–128). Berlin: Springer-Verlag.

Meece, J., Blumenfeld, P., & Hoyle, R. (1988). Students' goal orientation and cognitive engagement in classroom activities. *Journal of Educational Psychology*, 80, 514–523.

Meece, J. L., & Jones, M. G. (1996). Gender differences in motivation and strategy use in science: Are girls rote learners? *Journal of Research in Science Teaching*, 33, 393–406.

Metcalfe, J., & Mischel, W. (1999). A hot/cool system analysis of delay of gratification: Dynamics of willpower. *Psychological Review*, 106, 3–19.

Middleton, M., & Midgley, C. (1997). Avoiding the demonstration of lack of ability: An underexplored aspect of goal theory. *Journal of Educational Psychology*, 89, 710–718.

Midgley, C., Kaplan, A., & Middleton, M. (2001). Performance–approach goals: Good for what, for whom, under what circumstances, and at what cost? *Journal of Educational Psychology*, 93, 77–86.

Miller, P. H. (1990). The development of strategies of selective attention. In D. F. Bjorklund (Ed.), *Children's strategies: Contemporary views of cognitive development* (pp. 157–184). Hillsdale, NJ: Lawrence Erlbaum Associates.

Miller, P. H. (1994). Individual differences in children's strategic behavior: Utilization deficiencies. *Learning and Individual Differences*, 6, 285–307.

Miller, P. H., & Seier, W. L. (1994). Strategy utilization deficiencies in children: When, where, and why. In H. W. Reese (Ed.), *Advances in child development and behavior* (pp. 107–156). San Diego: Academic Press, Inc.

Mischel, W. (1974). Processes in delay of gratification. In L. Berkowitz (Ed.), *Advances in experimental social psychology* (Vol. 7, pp. 249–292). New York: Academic Press.

Mischel, W., & Metzer (1962). Preferences for delayed rewards as a function of age, intelligence, and length of delay interval. *Journal of Abnormal and Social Psychology*, 64, 425–431.

Mischel, W., & Patterson, C. (1976). Substantive and structural elements of effective plans for self-control. *Journal of Personality and Social Psychology*, 34, 942–950.

Mischel, W., & Patterson, C. (1978). Effective plans for self-control in children. In W. Collins (Ed.), *Minnesota Symposium on Child Psychology* (Vol. 11, pp. 199–230). Hillsdale, NJ: Lawrence Erlbaum Associates.

Miyake, A., & Shah, P. (1999). Towards unified theories of working memory: Emerging general consensus, unresolved theoretical issues, and future research directions. In A. Miyake & P. Shah (Eds.), *Models of working memory: Mechanisms of active maintenance and executive control* (pp. 442–481). New York: Cambridge University Press.

Muraven, M., & Baumeister, R. (2000). Self-regulation and depletion of limited resources: Does self-control resemble a muscle? *Psychological Bulletin*, 126, 247–259.

Nelson, T., & Narens, L. (1990). Metamemory: A theoretical framework and new findings. In G. Bower (Ed.), *The psychology of learning and motivation* (Vol. 26, pp. 125–141). New York: Academic Press.

Nicholls, J. (1978). The development of the concepts of effort and ability, perception of academic attainment, and the understanding that difficult tasks require more ability. *Child Development*, 49, 800–814.

Nicholls, J. (1990). What is ability and why are we mindful of it? A developmental perspective. In R. Sternberg & J. Kolligian (Eds.), *Competence considered* (pp. 11–40). New Haven, CT: Yale University Press.

Nicholls, J., & Miller, A. (1983). The differentiation of the concepts of difficulty and ability. *Child Development*, 54, 951–959.

Nicholls, J., & Miller, A. (1984a). Development and its discontents: The differentiation of the concept of ability. In J. Nicholls (Ed.), *Advances in motivation and achievement: The development of achievement motivation* (Vol. 3, pp. 185–218). Greenwich, CT: JAI Press.

Nicholls, J., & Miller, A. (1984b). Reasoning about the ability of self and others: A developmental study. *Child Development*, 55, 1990–1999.

Nigg, J. (2000). On inhibition/disinhibition in developmental psychopathology: Views from cognitive and personality psychology and a working inhibition taxonomy. *Psychological Bulletin*, 126, 220–246.

Nolen, S. (1988). Reasons for studying: Motivational orientations and study strategies. *Cognition and Instruction*, 5, 269–287.

Paris, S. G., & Byrnes, J. (1989). The constructivist approach to self-regulation and learning in the classroom. In B. J. Zimmerman and D. H. Schunk (Eds.), *Self-regulated learning and academic achievement: Theory, research, and practice* (pp. 169–200). New York: Springer-Verlag.

Paris, S. G., Byrnes, J., & Paris, A. H. (2001). Constructing theories, identities, and actions of self-regulated learners. In B. J. Zimmerman and D. H. Schunk (Eds.), *Self-regulated learning and academic achievement* (2nd ed., pp. 253–287). Mahwah, NJ: Lawrence Erlbaum Associates.

Paris, S. G., & Lindauer, B. (1982). The development of cognitive skills during childhood. In B. Wolman (Ed.), *Handbook of developmental psychology* (pp. 333–349). Englewood Cliffs, NJ: Prentice-Hall.

Paris, S. G., Lipson, M. Y., & Wixson, K. K. (1983). Becoming a strategic reader. *Contemporary Educational Psychology*, 8, 293–316.

Phillips, D. A., & Zimmerman, M. (1990). The developmental course of perceived competence and incompetence among competent children. In R. J. Sternberg & J. Kolligian (Eds.), *Competence considered* (pp. 41–66). New Haven, CT: Yale University Press.

Pintrich, P. R. (1999a). The role of motivation in promoting and sustaining self-regulated learning. *International Journal of Educational Research*, 31, 459–470.

Pintrich, P. R. (1999b). Taking control of research on volitional control: Challenges for future theory and research. *Learning and Individual Differences*, 11, 335–354.

Pintrich, P. R. (2000a). An achievement goal theory perspective on issues in motivation terminology, theory, and research. *Contemporary Educational Psychology*, 25, 92–104.

Pintrich, P. R. (2000b). Multiple goals, multiple pathways: The role of goal orientation in learning and achievement. *Journal of Educational Psychology*, 92, 544–555.

Pintrich, P. R. (2000c). The role of goal orientation in self-regulated learning. In M. Boekaerts, P. R. Pintrich, & M. Zeidner (Eds.), *Handbook of self-regulation* (pp. 451–502). San Diego: Academic Press.

Pintrich, P.R. (2002). Future challenges and directions for theory and research on personal epistemology. In B. Hofer and P. R. Pintrich (Eds.), *Personal epistemology: The psychology of beliefs about knowledge and knowing* (pp. 389–414). Mahwah, NJ: Lawrence Erlbaum Associates.

Pintrich, P. R., & De Groot, E. V. (1990). Motivational and self-regulated learning components of classroom academic performance. *Journal of Educational Psychology*, 82, 33–40.

Pintrich, P. R., & Schrauben, B. (1992). Students' motivational beliefs and their cognitive engagement in classroom tasks. In D. Schunk & J. Meece (Eds.), *Student perceptions in the classroom: Causes and consequences* (pp. 149–183). Hillsdale, NJ: Lawrence Erlbaum Associates.

Pintrich, P. R., & Schunk, D. H. (1996). *Motivation in education: Theory, research and applications*. Englewood Cliffs, NJ: Prentice Hall Merrill.

Pintrich, P. R., Wolters, C., & Baxter, G. (2000). Assessing metacognition and self-regulated learning. In G. Schraw & J. Impara (Eds.), *Issues in the measurement of metacognition* (pp. 43–97). Lincoln, NE: Buros Institute of Mental Measurements.

Pressley, M., & Afflerbach, P. (1995). *Verbal protocols of reading: The nature of constructively responsive reading*. Hillsdale, NJ: Lawrence Erlbaum Associates.

Pressley, M., Forrest-Pressley, D., Elliot-Faust, D., & Miller, G. (1985). Children's use of cognitive strategies, how to teach strategies, and what to do if they can't be taught. In M. Pressley & C. Brainerd (Eds.), *Cognitive learning and memory in children* (pp. 1–47). New York: Springer-Verlag.

Purdie, N., & Hattie, J. (1996). Cultural differences in the use of strategies for self-regulated learning. *American Educational Research Journal*, 33, 845–871.

Purdie, N., Hattie, J., & Douglas, G. (1996). Student conceptions of learning and their use of self-regulated learning strategies: A cross-cultural comparison. *Journal of Educational Psychology*, 88, 87–100.

Rothbart, M., & Bates, J. (1998). Temperament. In W. Damon (Series Ed.) & N. Eisenberg (Vol. Ed.), *Handbook of child psychology: Vol. 3. Social, emotional, and personality development* (5th ed., pp. 105–176). New York: Wiley.

Saarni, C., Mumme, D., & Campos, J. (1998). Emotional development: Action, communication, and understanding. In W. Damon (Series Ed.) & N. Eisenberg (Vol. Ed.), *Handbook of child psychology: Vol. 3. Social, emotional, and personality development* (5th ed., pp. 237–309). New York: Wiley.

Schneider, W., & Bjorklund, D. (1998). Memory. In W. Damon (Series Ed.) & D. Kuhn and R. S. Siegler (Vol. Eds.), *Handbook of child psychology: Vol. 2. Cognition, perception, and language* (5th ed., pp. 467–521). New York: Wiley.

Schneider, W., & Pressley, M. (1997). *Memory development between 2 and 20.* Mahweh, NJ: Lawrence Erlbaum Associates.

Schommer, M. (1990). Effects of beliefs about the nature of knowledge on comprehension. *Journal of Educational Psychology, 82,* 498–504.

Schommer, M. (2002). An evolving theoretical framework for an epistemological belief system. In B. Hofer and P. R. Pintrich (Eds.), *Personal epistemology: The psychology of beliefs about knowledge and knowing* (pp. 103–118). Mahwah, NJ: Lawrence Erlbaum Associates.

Schunk, D. H. (1989). Social cognitive theory and self-regulated learning. In B. J. Zimmerman & D. H. Schunk (Eds.), *Self-regulated learning and academic achievement: Theory, research, and practice* (pp. 83–110). New York: Springer-Verlag.

Schunk, D. H. (1991). Self-efficacy and academic motivation. *Educational Psychologist, 26,* 207–231.

Schunk, D. H. (1994). Self-regulation of self-efficacy and attributions in academic settings. In D. H. Schunk & B. J. Zimmerman (Eds.), *Self-regulation of learning and performance: Issues and educational applications* (pp. 75–99). Hillsdale, NJ: Lawrence Erlbaum Associates.

Shah, P., & Miyake, A. (1999). Models of working memory: An introduction. In A. Miyake & P. Shah (Eds.), *Models of working memory: Mechanisms of active maintenance and executive control* (pp. 1–27) New York: Cambridge University Press.

Siegler, R. S. (1998). *Children's thinking.* Upper Saddle River, NJ: Prentice Hall.

Snow, R., Corno, L., & Jackson, D. (1996). Individual differences in affective and conative functions. In D. Berliner & R. Calfee (Eds.), *Handbook of educational psychology* (pp. 243–310). New York: Macmillan.

Sternberg, R. (1985). *Beyond IQ: A triarchic theory of intelligence.* New York: Cambridge University Press.

Stevenson, H. W., & Stigler, J. W. (1992). *The learning gap.* New York: Summit Books.

Thompson, R. (1998). Early sociopersonality development. In W. Damon (Series Ed.) & N. Eisenberg (Vol. Ed.), *Handbook of child psychology: Vol. 3. Social, emotional, and personality development* (5th ed., pp. 25–104). New York: Wiley.

Weinstein, C. E., & Mayer, R. (1986). The teaching of learning strategies. In M. Wittrock (Ed.), *Handbook of research on teaching and learning* (pp. 315–327). New York: Macmillan.

Wellman, H. (1990). *The child's theory of mind.* New York: Cambridge University Press.

Wellman, H., & Gelman, S. (1998). Knowledge acquisition in foundational domains. In W. Damon (Series Ed.) & D. Kuhn and R. S. Siegler (Vol. Eds.), *Handbook of child psychology: Vol. 2. Cognition, perception, and language* (5th ed., pp. 523–573). New York: Wiley.

Wigfield, A., Eccles, J., Yoon, K., Harold, R., Arbreton, A., Freedman-Doan, K., & Blumenfeld, P. (1997). Changes in children's competence beliefs and subjective task values across the elementary school years: A three-year study. *Journal of Educational Psychology, 89,* 451–469.

Wolters, C. (1998). Self-regulated learning and college students' regulation of motivation. *Journal of Educational Psychology, 90,* 224–235.

Wolters, C. A., & Pintrich, P. R. (1998). Contextual differences in student motivation and self-regulated learning in mathematics, English, and social studies classrooms. *Instructional Science, 26,* 27–47.

Wolters, C., Yu, S., & Pintrich, P. R. (1996). The relation between goal orientation and students' motivational beliefs and self-regulated learning. *Learning and Individual Differences, 8,* 211–238.

Zimmerman, B. J. (1986). Development of self-regulated learning: Which are the key subprocesses? *Contemporary Educational Psychology, 16,* 307–313.

Zimmerman, B. J. (1989). A social cognitive view of self-regulated learning and academic learning. *Journal of Educational Psychology*, 81(3), 329–339.

Zimmerman, B. J. (1990). Self-regulated learning and academic achievement: An overview. *Educational Psychologist*, 25, 3–17.

Zimmerman, B. J. (1994). Dimensions of academic self-regulation: A conceptual framework for education. In D. H. Schunk & B. J. Zimmerman (Eds.), *Self-regulation of learning and performance: Issues and educational applications* (pp. 3–21). Hillsdale, NJ: Lawrence Erlbaum Associates.

Zimmerman, B.J. (1998a). Academic studying and the development of personal skill: A self-regulatory perspective. *Educational Psychologist*, 33, 73–86.

Zimmerman, B. J. (1998b). Developing self-fulfilling cycles of academic regulation: An analysis of exemplary instructional models. In D. H. Schunk & B. J. Zimmerman (Eds.), *Self-regulated learning: From teaching to self-reflective practice* (pp. 1–19). New York: Guilford Press.

Zimmerman, B. J. (2000). Attaining self-regulation: A social cognitive perspective. In M. Boekaerts, P. R. Pintrich, & M. Zeidner (Eds.), *Handbook of self-regulation: Theory, research, and applications* (pp. 13–39). San Diego: Academic Press.

Zimmerman, B. J., & Kitsantas, A. (1997). Developmental phases in self-regulation: Shifting from process to outcome goals. *Journal of Educational Psychology*, 89, 29–36.

Zimmerman, B. J., & Martinez-Pons, M. (1990). Student differences in self-regulated learning: Relating grade, sex, and giftedness to self-efficacy and strategy use. *Journal of Educational Psychology*, 82, 51–59.

CHAPTER

11

What Do I Need to Do to Succeed...When I Don't Understand What I'm Doing!?: Developmental Influences on Students' Adaptive Help Seeking

RICHARD S. NEWMAN

University of California, Riverside, California

INTRODUCTION

When facing difficult academic tasks, many elementary- and middle-school students exert little effort. They often give up prematurely, sit passively, or persist unsuccessfully on their own. Yet, other students exhibit curiosity, challenge, resilience, and eventual academic success. And, for other students, engagement depends on the specific academic domain or task; they might be actively engaged in certain situations but passive in others. When one considers that young children typically are described as innately curious, inquisitive, and eager to learn, two questions emerge: What happens that transforms many children into passive learners who do not take the initiative required to overcome adversity? and What happens that maintains in other children a determination to succeed in the face of potential failure?.

This chapter focuses on how students respond to academic difficulty, in particular, how they go about seeking necessary help from teachers and classmates. I examine individual differences—and the development of these differences—in the academic help seeking of elementary and middle school students. More specifically, I address the question, How do teachers and peers contribute to the socialization of students' attitudes and behavioral patterns of help seeking?

It is important to clarify at the outset that the focus of the chapter is *adaptive help seeking* (Newman, 1994; see also Nelson-Le Gall, 1981). When children monitor their academic performance, show awareness of difficulty they cannot overcome on their own, and exhibit the wherewithal and self-determination to remedy that difficulty by requesting assistance from a more knowledgeable individual, they are exhibiting mature, strategic behavior. Help seeking can maintain task involvement, avert possible failure, and optimize the chance for mastery and long-term autonomy. Indeed, help seeking can be viewed as a strategy of *self-regulated learning*. Current conceptualizations emphasize that self-regulated learners possess a repertoire of cognitive and social strategies for dealing with academic challenge and are motivated to use these strategies at the appropriate time (see Boekaerts, Pintrich, & Zeidner, 2000). This view of self-regulated learning converges with findings from earlier (i.e., from the 1970s and 1980s) cognitive–developmental research on children's memory strategies. "Strategies" are defined as an integration, or fusing, of "skill" and "will" (Paris, 1988). Underlying the present discussion is the notion that self-regulated learners possess certain competencies and motivational resources that energize and direct the use of these competencies. Adaptive help seeking involves:

1. *Cognitive competencies* (i.e., knowing when assistance is necessary; knowing how to frame a request that will yield precisely the action or information that is needed)

2. *Social competencies* (i.e., knowing that others can help; knowing who is the best person to approach for help; knowing how to carry out a request in a socially appropriate way)

3. *Motivational resources* (i.e., goals, attitudes, self-beliefs, and feelings that are associated with the child's sense of agency and control, desire for challenge, tolerance for task difficulty, willingness to admit personal difficulty, and desire for social interaction with teachers and more knowledgeable peers)

The important developmental question is, What socializing experiences help children develop these particular competencies and motivational resources? There has been little research directly addressing this question. Elsewhere (Newman, 2000), I have argued that *sociocultural theory* (Vygotsky, 1978) and *self-determination theory* (R. M. Ryan & Deci, 2000; see also Connell & Wellborn, 1991; Grolnick, Gurland, Jacob, & Decourcey, Chapter 6, this volume) are useful in thinking about socialization of adaptive help seeking. The two theories emphasize particular developmental processes that can be interpreted as mediating between socializers' actions and children's help seeking. In the case of sociocultural theory, social interaction can be viewed as a mediating factor; in the case of self-determination theory, satisfying certain psychological needs of the child can be seen as a mediator. In the chapter, I first discuss briefly aspects of the two theories that pertain to children's help seeking. Then, based on this theoretical perspective, I discuss developmental contributions of two major socializing agents for children—teachers and classmates. The chapter concludes with suggestions for future research on help seeking.

DEVELOPMENTAL THEORIES RELATED TO STUDENTS' HELP SEEKING

According to Vygotsky's sociocultural theory, children develop as a result of active participation in social interaction with other individuals. The child is not simply a passive recipient of knowledge from more skilled individuals. Assistance, coaching, and questioning are provided in the form of "scaffolding," whereby the adult or more knowledgeable peer carefully monitors how the child is doing and determines what support the child needs so that just the right amount and type of help can be given. As a result of scaffolded experiences, the child has an opportunity to master difficult tasks as well as to internalize others' patterns of behavior, goals, and values. So, for example, parent and child jointly participate in reading a book or solving a puzzle, with the parent taking the lead and gradually shifting more and more responsibility (for the talk and problem solving) to the child. The child internalizes patterns of discourse and problem-solving strategies so that, in time, he or she is able to use inner speech (i.e., "self-talk") and self-directed strategies to read and solve problems on his or her own. Children gradually come to regulate their own learning and development.

In portraying development in this fashion (i.e., as progression from "other-regulation" to "self-regulation"), one can potentially overlook a critical way in which children participate in regulating their own development, that is, *by learning how to obtain assistance from others*. Returning to other-regulation is a natural part of learning, and self-regulation is sometimes required to obtain other-regulation. When engaged in difficult tasks on their own, children occasionally must take the initiative to enlist the help of teachers and more knowledgeable peers. In fact, with development and its associated expectations of independence, the responsibility for obtaining assistance falls increasingly on the child's shoulders.

The chapter also draws on notions of development from self-determination theory. In particular, children have three innate, psychological needs that underlie self-regulated learning: *relatedness*, *autonomy*, and *competence*. First, children have a need to feel that others care about their well-being and success (cf. attachment, Bowlby, 1969). Second, children need to feel a sense of agency or volition (i.e., that they are in charge of their own actions; cf. construct of intrinsic motivation, Deci & Ryan, 1985). Third, children have a need to feel competent and to believe that their actions have a causal relation to successful outcomes (cf. perceived competence, Harter, 1982, and perceived control, Skinner, 1995). The extent to which children experience these needs being met is related to the development of inner, motivational resources that influence actions. These resources (i.e., self-perceptions of relatedness, autonomy, and competence) influence the degree to which children's actions in learning contexts reflect engagement and self-regulation, or alternatively, disaffection.

It follows that socializing agents, in order to facilitate the development of self-regulatory mechanisms, have three important tasks: to provide children with (1) *involvement* (e.g., dedication of resources such as shared activities, nurturance, and affective closeness), (2) *support for autonomy* (e.g., encouragement of the child's initiatives and efforts at independence; absence of extrinsic and coercive pressures), and (3) *support for competence* (e.g., rules, expectations, and lessons that instill a sense of competence and an understanding of contingency between actions and consequences). There presumably are experiences in which teachers and classmates accomplish these tasks so that children develop the competencies and motivational resources associated with adaptive help seeking.[1]

THE ROLE OF TEACHERS

Children entering school already exhibit individual differences in academic skills and attitudes about learning (see Paris & Cunningham, 1996). Given these individual differences, what role do teachers play in the further development of individual differences in skills and attitudes required for adaptive help seeking? In this section, I discuss how teachers' involvement, support for autonomy, and support for competence may influence students' help seeking.

Teacher Involvement

In classrooms in which teachers readily share with children their time, energy, and nurturance, students tend to be engaged in learning, as evidenced by their effort, attention, goal pursuit, self-expression, and interest (Skinner &

---

[1]It is noted that self-determination theory focuses on the development of motivational resources, including *self perceptions of competence*. To understand the development of adaptive help seeking, it is necessary to discuss the development of motivational resources as well as *actual competencies*. Hence, in this chapter, although employing the organizational scheme of self-determination theory, I discuss, where appropriate, how socializers help in the development of skills and knowledge children need for adaptive help seeking.

Belmont, 1993). With specific regard to adaptive help seeking, teacher involvement may be influential because of student–teacher intersubjectivity and students' beliefs about schooling.

When teachers are personally involved with their class, children tend to respect their teacher and experience a sense of belongingness in the classroom (Skinner & Belmont, 1993). Teachers who are perceived as caring typically provide a learning context characterized by "intersubjectivity" (i.e., attunement of teacher and child's purpose, focus, and affect; Noddings, 1992). Intersubjectivity presumably mitigates the power differential common to student–teacher relations. When teachers and students share a sense of purpose, teachers are especially able to take the child's perspective and understand his or her thinking (e.g., regarding a particular academic task) and, based on this understanding, appropriately guide the child's learning. Teachers who are perceived as friendly and caring have been described as having lines of communication open to students and as demonstrating "democratic interaction" styles (Wentzel, 1997; see also Wentzel, Chapter 9, this volume). Caring teachers tend to listen, ask questions, inquire if students need help, make sure students understand difficult material, and provide help in nonthreatening ways. It is likely that students who experience this type of communication learn that teachers are effective and trustworthy helpers (see later section on teacher support for competence).

A second, but related, way in which teacher involvement may influence help seeking involves students' beliefs about schooling. A child's sense of belongingness and respect vis-à-vis the teacher may become translated into a set of attitudes, beliefs, and feelings about teachers' helpfulness and *benefits* of help seeking, on the one hand, and about potential hassles and *costs* of help seeking, on the other hand. In the remainder of this section, I discuss how students in elementary and middle school feel about seeking help from their teachers and how these feelings may affect their help-seeking behavior.

Young children typically have a positive attitude about getting help from adults. When they approach their teacher for assistance, preschoolers, kindergartners, and first graders show an awareness and appreciation that teachers possess global, affective traits and competencies (e.g., niceness and kindness) that can help meet their needs (Barnett, Darcie, Holland, & Kobasigawa, 1982; Nelson-Le Gall & Gumerman, 1984). Young children reason that people are good helpers if they have been helpful in the past (Barnett, Darcie, Holland, & Kobasigawa, 1982). As they become better at understanding others' motives, abilities, and behaviors, children become aware of diverse ways in which teachers can meet their needs. By the middle and upper elementary grades, children judge a teacher as helpful according to his or her dependability (e.g., willingness to help), attunement (e.g., awareness of others' problems, abilities, and needs), and quality and dedication of resources (e.g., advice, time, and energy; Furman & Buhrmester, 1985). In spite of a generally positive view of adults' helpfulness, young children also have negative views. As early as grade 2, students fear negative reactions from their teacher (e.g., "I think she might think I'm dumb") if they ask for help with schoolwork (Newman & Goldin, 1990). Perceived costs of going to the teacher tend to be heightened when students experience teachers as unwilling to help. For example, during review lessons, teacher comments such as "If you had paid attention, you wouldn't need to ask that question" obviously discourage students (van der Meij, 1988). Because of their need for peer approval and to protect their self-worth, fear of "looking dumb" in front of teachers is especially salient among older students (Good, Slavings, Harel, & Emerson, 1987).

Children presumably integrate or weigh their beliefs about benefits and costs of help seeking. Over the school years, these beliefs influence in increasingly complex ways children's decisions about whether or not to take the initiative and ask for assistance when they encounter difficulty. In Newman's (1990) sample of third, fifth, and seventh graders, students at all grades were aware of benefits (e.g., "Asking questions can help you learn") and also were concerned about costs (e.g., "It's embarrassing") of going to the teacher. And, consistently across these grades, there was a positive relation between students' beliefs about benefits and the students' stated intentions of requesting help. It was not until grade 7 that there was a negative relation between students' beliefs about costs and the students' intentions. Thus, at middle school, beliefs about costs and benefits have competing influence. In spite of elementary school students being aware of potential costs, deciding whether to actually seek help apparently depends only on the degree to which students feel they will benefit from the teacher's help. With age and transition to middle school, thoughts and fears about costs take on a more prominent role in decision making. Students increasingly struggle in deciding what to do when they need assistance with their schoolwork.

Can positive beliefs about teachers' helpfulness and caring override the costs that children typically perceive with regard to help seeking? Although this question has not been directly addressed, the potential influence on help seeking of teacher involvement has been powerfully illustrated with students who are already disengaged at school. Children with poor self-perceptions of ability and low self-esteem, who often are low achievers, typically are reluctant to seek help in class (Newman, 1990; Newman & Goldin, 1990). Yet, it has been shown that avoidance of help seeking among sixth graders with poor self-perceptions is reduced in classrooms in which teachers believe their responsibility is to attend to students' social and emotional as well as academic needs (Ryan, Gheen, & Midgley, 1998). Further evidence of the importance of teacher involvement is provided by Newman and Schwager (1993). When elementary and middle school students were asked if—and why—they go to their teacher for help when they do not understand an assignment, perceptions of mutual liking and friendship with the teacher were predictive of help seeking at all grade levels. In addition, teachers' explicit encouragement and support of student questions also predicted help seeking at the upper elementary grades and at middle school. Hence, it appears that students at all grades appreciate the affective benefits of teacher involvement. As they get older, students increasingly acknowledge and appreciate specific, task-oriented ways in which teachers can help them.

Support for Autonomy

According to self-determination theory, self-regulated learners have a sense of autonomy. They take control and responsibility for their own learning. This does not mean they are self-sufficient and isolated from others. To the contrary, they feel comfortable asking for help when necessary. By creating a classroom environment that stresses autonomy and accommodates individual needs and goals, teachers potentially support students' efforts at adaptive help seeking.

Teachers establish in their classroom certain *contextual goals* (Ames, 1992). Goals are reflected in grading practices, competitive (vs. cooperative) activities, types of feedback, and other cues and structural features in the classroom. In a context that emphasizes *learning* (i.e., task-involved or mastery) *goals*, teachers stress the importance of long-term understanding and autonomy; they provide students with feedback tailored to, and supportive of, each individual child's intellectual and social development (Anderman, Austin, & Johnson, Chapter 8, this volume; Dweck, 1986). Students working under these conditions tend to be energized by challenge. When facing difficulty, they persevere and strategically attempt to overcome obstacles to learning. Elementary and middle school students working on difficult tasks in this sort of context tend to request task-related information that helps them debug errors, resolve difficulties, and proceed toward mastery (Newman & Schwager, 1995). If they choose not to seek help from the teacher, students in learning–goal contexts often explain that they would rather continue to persevere on their own (Butler & Neuman, 1995). In a context that emphasizes *performance* (i.e., ego-involved or ability) *goals*, teachers stress the importance of getting good grades and being judged competently; they provide students with feedback that stresses social comparison with classmates. Here, students tend to avoid challenge and difficulty in order to maintain their self-perceptions of ability relative to others. If they seek help at all, students often engage in expedient, noninquisitive patterns of questioning (e.g., immediately asking for the correct answer on difficult problems without first attempting the task on their own; Newman & Schwager, 1995). Or, they simply avoid asking for assistance altogether in an attempt to mask low ability (Butler & Neuman, 1995).

To fully understand how teachers may facilitate adaptive help seeking, it is necessary to consider not just contextual goals but also students' *personal goals*. These are trait-like orientations that students bring with them to the classroom

(Dweck & Leggett, 1988). Past research focusing on personal goals and help seeking has distinguished between personal learning goals (or intrinsic goal orientation) and personal performance goals (or extrinsic goal orientation). When faced with difficult math problems they cannot do on their own, fourth and fifth grade students with personal learning goals tend to request feedback about whether their work is right or not. Students with personal performance goals tend *not* to be interested in this sort of information (Newman, 1998). According to Harter (1981), and consistent with the notion of multiple goals (Wentzel, 1992), there are several different components of intrinsic goal orientation (e.g., striving for independent mastery, preference for academic challenge) and extrinsic goal orientation (overdependence on the teacher, preference for easy assignments). In a study of third and fifth grade African-American students working on a difficult vocabulary task, intrinsically oriented children (in particular, those who strive for independent mastery) were more likely to request assistance in ways that provided them an opportunity to figure out problems for themselves (e.g., requesting hints) than they were to simply request a direct answer. In contrast, extrinsically oriented children (in particular, those who are overly dependent on the teacher) showed no preference for one type of help over the other (Nelson-Le Gall & Jones, 1990).

Relations between different components of goal orientation and help seeking may differ with grade level. Newman (1990) found that the third and fifth graders who were most likely to seek assistance when they did not understand math assignments had a "combination" of intrinsic orientation (i.e., preference for challenge) and extrinsic orientation (i.e., dependence on the teacher). Among seventh graders, on the other hand, those most likely to seek help were intrinsically oriented, both in terms of preference for challenge and striving for independent mastery. Thus, across the elementary and middle school grades, preference for challenge seems to motivate children's help seeking. In addition, younger students may go to the teacher because of dependency needs, whereas older students may do so because they are truly interested in learning and, in the long term, being able to work independently. Perhaps, at middle school, students who have dependency needs turn to classmates rather than the teacher.

Given that both contextual and personal goals are related to help seeking, it is important to consider situations where goals coincide and where they differ. In general, the "fit" between person and environment variables influences students' attitudes toward learning, task performance, and actual school success (Eccles & Midgley, 1989). How does the way in which teachers accommodate students' personal goals influence help seeking? One possible answer is found in a recent study by Newman (1998), who addressed interactions between contextual and personal goals among fourth and fifth graders. Findings showed that a learning–goal context—in comparison to a performance–goal context—did not uniformly lead to more adaptive help seeking (i.e., task-relevant questions about how to solve difficult math problems). For students with personal goals that stressed performance, help-seeking efforts were facilitated in a context that stressed learning. However, there was no facilitation in this context for students who did not care about performance. When *both* personal and contextual goals emphasized grades and "looking smart," students were especially reluctant to seek help. When students who did care about performance were placed in a learning–goal context, they appeared to overcome, and perhaps compensate for, their personal tendencies (to avoid help seeking). Hence, by emphasizing learning goals in the classroom, teachers can potentially assist disengaged students who otherwise might avoid help and give up. Findings point to the importance of teachers being attuned to the personal goals and attitudes of individual children.

Finally, although research on personal goals and help seeking has largely relied on orthogonal measures (e.g., extrinsic and intrinsic orientations), self-determination theory posits a continuum of extrinsic-to-intrinsic motivation (R. M. Ryan & Deci, 2000; Grolnick, Gurland, Jacob, & Decourcey, Chapter 6, this volume). Along this continuum, regulatory processes (cf. goals) that underlie one's behavior vary from *external* (i.e., operant control) to *introjected* (i.e., need to demonstrate ability to, or mask failure from, others) to *identified* (i.e., conscious valuing and acceptance of a goal) to *integrated* (i.e., a goal that is fully assimilated to the self) to *internal* (i.e., inherent satisfaction and interest in a task). This perspective provides an important reminder that "self-regulated learning" is a relativistic construct, and the degree to which one is self-regulated varies in relation to the particular regulatory process (i.e., on the continuum of extrinsic-to-intrinsic motivation) under which an individual is operating. The important classroom implication for facilitating adaptive help seeking is that the teacher's task is to position the child as far along the continuum—toward integrated and internal control—as possible. Helping children enjoy and become inherently interested in academic activities should result in students who are aware of when they need help and are able to ask "intelligent" questions that elicit answers that precisely meet their needs.

Support for Competence

According to self-determination theory, self-regulated learning is contingent on the child feeling academically competent. How can teachers foster in children cognitive and social competencies required for adaptive help seeking, and additionally, how can they help children appreciate the importance of help seeking as a means to achieve academic success?

First, teachers establish an overall context for the child's learning. I have already discussed the importance of classroom, or contextual, goals. In addition, teachers employ different activity structures in the classroom (e.g., individual, whole class, and small group), each of which can influence student–teacher interaction (Ames, 1992). During individual activity, which often involves practice and review exercises, teachers tend to expect students not to need assistance (van der Meij, 1988). During whole-class activity, questioning tends to flow in the direction of teacher-to-student rather than student-to-teacher (Cazden, 1986). In front of all their classmates, students tend to be concerned about social comparison and potential embarrassment (i.e., factors that inhibit help seeking; Rosen, 1983; Shapiro, 1983). Small-group activity, on the other hand, is explicitly designed to promote children collaborating with one another, for example, by requesting and giving help (see Webb & Palincsar, 1996). Students working in small groups, in contrast to those working individually or in a whole-class activity, are more likely to seek assistance from other students as well as from the teacher (Nelson-Le Gall & Glor-Scheib, 1985). When working collaboratively, children experience a relative lack of social comparison and presumably less inhibition against help seeking. In particular, when group composition emphasizes diversity and diffusion of status characteristics (e.g., ability level, gender, ethnicity), students tend to have their task-related questions successfully answered by peers (Webb, 1984). Collaboration gives students a sense of self-determination and opportunity to pursue their personal goals, and hence, potentially increases their personal incentive (i.e., identified, integrated, or internal goals) to be actively engaged in learning.

Second, teachers help establish in the classroom certain patterns of discourse that potentially facilitate the development of help-seeking skills. According to Vygotskian theory, children gradually internalize adults' patterns of discourse—for example, their use of questioning for the purpose of regulation. In "learning communities" that foster conversation, discussion, and inquiry, children participate by formulating and evaluating questions, hypotheses, evidence, and conclusions (Brown & Campione, 1994). Children presumably learn the value, usefulness, and skills of self-questioning and questioning of others. An important part of discourse, namely, teacher feedback, lets children know when they need help. Giving no more assistance than is necessary would seem to be important for teaching children to make distinctions between necessary (i.e., adaptive) and excessive (i.e., dependency-oriented) help seeking. Providing personally encouraging comments that focus on specific strengths and weaknesses in performance rather than global assessments or normative grades tends to maximize intrinsic motivation and, as a result, supports students' continued effort following failure (Butler, 1987). Questions and probes used to diagnose misconceptions may help students ask intelligent questions, both of themselves and of others. Explicitly encouraging students to strategically use the help that is given to them (e.g., going back to an incorrect problem and trying to resolve it) may help students continue to monitor their understanding and determine if they need additional assistance (see Webb & Palincsar, 1996).

Third, to the extent that teachers help the student learn, they may indirectly influence help-seeking competencies. As children become more knowledgeable in different academic subjects, there are associated improvements in cognitive and metacognitive capabilities that function as component skills of adaptive help seeking. With increased expertise, students are more aware of task difficulty, more accurate in monitoring their knowledge states, more attuned to when requests for help are necessary, and better at formulating questions that home in on precisely the information they need when they encounter difficulties (e.g., Nelson-Le Gall, Kratzer, Jones, & DeCooke, 1990). Although high achievers may need less help with their schoolwork than low achievers, it has been demonstrated across a number of different academic domains that when they *do* encounter difficulties, high achievers are especially likely to rely on others who are more knowledgeable (Zimmerman & Martinez-Pons, 1986).

Finally, the teacher influences not only the development of competencies but also awareness and appreciation that seeking help from more knowledgeable others can be an effective means—*under one's own control*—of achieving academic success (cf. perceived control; Skinner, 1995). Teachers help socialize students' expectancies for success. The frequency at which teachers call on students, the amount of time they wait for responses, and the amount and type of praise they give vary from student to student. It is likely that certain children (e.g., low achievers) learn not to volunteer questions in order to avoid negative feedback and embarrassment (Eccles & Wigfield, 1985; Weinstein, 1985). Classrooms in which teachers are the "experts" (e.g., those who present to the class an explanation, without discussion, and then expect students simply to practice, using workbooks that exclude any additional instruction) arguably support students' nonadaptive, dependency-oriented help seeking (see Stodolsky, 1988). On the other hand, teachers who respond to requests for help with hints and contingently scaffolded instruction, rather than direct and controlling answers, potentially help students learn that self-questioning and questioning of others are effective means for solving problems (Wood, 1989). To the extent that teachers demonstrate that problems, dilemmas, and uncertainty can be tolerated—and perhaps shared and even transformed into intellectual challenge—students may come to recognize that it is normal not to be able to solve all problems independently. They may come to appreciate the value of "co-regulation" through help seeking and help giving (McCaslin & Good, 1996). And, demonstrating to children that they deserve—and expect—answers to their questions arguably helps socialize children with a personal sense of empowerment and "voice" (see Gilligan, 1982; Harter, 1996); these are lessons that may be especially important for minority children (Nelson-Le Gall & Resnick, 1998).

How teachers socialize children's expectations for success and failure may help explain gender differences in help seeking. Newman and Goldin (1990) have observed consistently across the elementary grades that girls are more concerned than boys that their teacher will think they are "dumb" if they have to ask questions in math class; there was no gender difference in reading or English class. Math is a subject that traditionally has been sex-typed as male.

Teachers, along with parents and children themselves, often expect less success for girls than boys in math (Eccles, 1983; see also Sadker & Sadker, 1994). Perhaps because of low expectations for success, fear of embarrassment, and suppression of their own thoughts and ideas, one might expect that girls would be more likely than boys to refrain from seeking help in math class. And, if they do not get necessary assistance, girls may put themselves at a disadvantage in terms of math achievement at high school. Studies show, however, that elementary school-aged girls actually are more likely than boys to seek help in math class (Eccles & Blumenfeld, 1985; Ryan, Gheen, & Midgley, 1998). This is consistent with women being more likely than men to seek help in a variety of job- and health-related domains (Nadler, 1983). Perhaps, girls' relatively low expectation for success in math is accompanied by less threat to their self-esteem, hence less inhibition about revealing that they need assistance. That is, if girls are not expected—by others or by themselves—to do well in math class, it matters less what others think. It remains to be examined how individual children, regardless of gender, integrate or reconcile different feelings as they contemplate raising their hand to ask a question in class. How teachers contribute to gender differences in children's feelings about help seeking also needs to be further studied (cf. Eccles, 1983).

In sum, teachers play an obviously important role in fostering adaptive help seeking. Personal involvement with children can have a powerful, facilitating influence. Caring and responsive teachers may buffer children from inhibitions against help seeking. Inhibitions are especially salient at middle school, when students fear being perceived as "dumb" if they ask questions in class. Young elementary school children sometimes seek help because they feel dependent on the teacher. To the extent that classroom goals emphasize the importance of autonomy and intrinsic interest in learning rather than grades, "looking smart," and not "looking dumb," chances are that students will seek assistance when it is needed. Classrooms that stress learning may serve a compensatory function for students whose personal goals are introjected and who would otherwise avoid help seeking. As they become more knowledgeable, students are better attuned to when they need assistance and more skillful at framing questions that address their specific needs. How teachers manage the day-to-day operation of the classroom (e.g., with particular types of feedback and use of questioning) can have a bearing on cognitive and social competencies as well as motivational resources needed for adaptive help seeking.

THE ROLE OF PEERS

Children are important socializing agents for one another at school. Do children contribute to the development of one another's competencies and motivational resources required for adaptive help seeking? Although self-determination theory has not been applied to classmates as socializers, there are connections (i.e., involvement, support for autonomy, support for competence) that may prove useful in thinking about the role of peers. Of course, peer influence typically is constrained by classroom rules regarding students helping one another.

Peer Involvement

Schoolchildren spend many hours each day with their classmates, and over the course of frequent interactions, students influence one another—both positively and negatively—in multiple ways. A growing body of research on how peers influence students' school adjustment provides a basis for thinking about how peer involvement may be related to help seeking.

First, friendships influence help seeking. With friendships that satisfy their needs, children tend to be engaged in classroom learning, enjoy school, and do well academically (see Birch & Ladd, 1996). By definition, friends assist and support one another (Berndt, 1999). Among elementary and middle school students, "quality" friendships are characterized by help and support as well as by certain features that would seem to mediate students' efforts at help seeking (e.g., reliability, affection, intimacy, and lack of conflict and rivalry; Furman & Buhrmester, 1985). In close relationships, children tend to be relatively unconcerned about self-disclosure, threat to self-esteem, and indebtedness to those who help them (see Nadler, 1998). In a friendly context, children presumably find it easier to manage and negotiate social demands of interactions and perhaps then are better able to focus their mutual efforts on academic issues of learning and problem solving. With greater familiarity and friendship among students, help seeking is more likely to be successful (i.e., to result in requested information), and thereby reinforced as an effective learning strategy. While quality friendships provide a context in which children feel comfortable expressing their need for assistance and support, children in conflictual relationships typically are reluctant to disclose difficulties to one another. Most likely these children would not expect help to be forthcoming even if they requested it.

A second way in which peer involvement may influence help seeking has to do with students' social goals (cf. earlier discussion of academic goals; Wentzel, 1996, and Chapter 9, this volume). I discuss two particular goals, namely, *social affiliation* (i.e., desire for friendship and intimacy) and *social status* (i.e., desire for peer approval and popularity). Children who are successful at making and maintaining friendships and are well adjusted at school typically place importance on social affiliation (see Birch & Ladd, 1996). According to Ryan, Hicks, and Midgley (1997), the more strongly fifth grade children feel that social affiliation with classmates is important, the less they avoid asking questions (of teachers and/or peers) when they encounter academic difficulties. Children who care about maintaining friendships tend to view help seeking as a valued classroom activity. It is important to note, however, that social affiliation goals do not guarantee that help seeking is "adaptive." Factors such as social maturity and value of learning may moderate a relation between social affiliation goals and help seeking. One can envision situations where children appear to work together and request help from one another but are really just having fun or "goofing off." Requests can be socially inappropriate (e.g., shouting questions across the room or making domineering demands) as well as cognitively inappropriate (e.g., asking for unnecessary help). Also, social affiliation goals are not necessarily related to academic success. In a study of sixth graders working in collaborative math groups, Newman and Gauvain (1996) found that the more students were engaged within their groups and the more they liked to work and talk with their classmates, the more they reported seeking help from *group members*. The more important it was for students to do well academically, the more they reported seeking help from the *teacher*. Findings suggest that different goals (i.e., social affiliation vs. personal learning goals) may predict a student's choice of helper.

In addition to social affiliation, students often are motivated by a desire for social status. The more strongly children feel that social approval from classmates is important, the more they fear embarrassment in front of their peers and the more they avoid carrying out requests for help (Ryan, Hicks, & Midgley, 1997). One can speculate that influence of social status goals on help seeking is moderated by several factors, namely, self-esteem and a sense of what it takes to win social approval. If the child's self-esteem is easily threatened and if the child and his or her peer group do not value behaviors that typically lead to school success, striving for social approval from classmates is likely to inhibit help seeking. On the other hand, an inhibitory effect of social status goals may be buffered if the child has a strong sense of self and has a peer group that values learning and task mastery. At the transition to middle school, when students are especially concerned about maintaining a positive image in front of classmates, it is likely that social status goals play an especially important role in help seeking. Children who truly want to learn but feel peer pressure not to "look dumb" have to balance different goals as they decide what to do when facing academic difficulty. Goal coordination may be even more daunting for children who want to learn but whose peer group exerts pressure not to "look smart" (see Ogbu, 1987; Wentzel, 1996).

Support for Autonomy

Can students support, or undermine, one another's sense of autonomy needed for adaptive help seeking? In this section, I discuss social comparison among students. There are several ways social comparison may influence—both positively and negatively—children's initiatives at help seeking. A good deal of this discussion pertains to peer support for competence as well as autonomy.

Social comparison produces information (i.e., social referencing) that is useful for children as a benchmark for defining performance norms, and ultimately, for improving task performance and competence. During preschool years, children are sensitive to task failure. In spite of noticing when they are outperformed by peers, they generally have expectations for success that are unrealistically high (Stipek & Mac Iver, 1989). In time, one's internal system of self-monitoring becomes better calibrated and children develop a more accurate understanding of task difficulty. Social comparison information may help children begin to think about effort and persistence and make judgments about whether they have "tried enough" before asking for help. With age and expertise, children are increasingly able to sense when help is necessary on difficult tasks and increasingly able to adjust their help seeking according to task difficulty (Nelson-Le Gall, Kratzer, Jones, & DeCooke, 1990). Partially because of their overly optimistic view of competence—of both themselves and others—young children often make nondiscriminating and incorrect judgments about the quality of help from classmates. Over time, social comparison provides important information about others' strengths and weaknesses and thus permits children to more accurately evaluate peers' capacity to be effective helpers (Ruble & Frey, 1991). Social comparison can sometimes normalize help seeking. When upper elementary and middle school students compare their academic performance with that of classmates and realize that others also need assistance (i.e., it is "normal" to need help), embarrassment from asking the teacher questions tends to be minimized. At lower elementary grades, it matters much less to students whether they are alone or not in needing help (Newman & Schwager, 1993).

In addition to these positive aspects, social comparison conveys information that often inhibits help seeking. For preschoolers and kindergartners, it is natural to turn to peers for help. However, starting at ages 6 to 7, children begin to feel bad when receiving help from peers as well as teachers (Ruble & Frey, 1991). At second grade and beyond, students are more concerned that peers—in comparison to the teacher—might interpret a request for help as a sign of being "dumb" (Newman & Goldin, 1990). In their sample of second, fourth, and sixth graders, Newman and Goldin found that this difference in perceptions about peers and teachers (i.e., greater concern with negative reactions from peers) was especially significant among fourth grade girls and then, in the sixth grade, among both boys and girls. Thus, fear of embarrassment from looking silly or incompetent in the eyes of classmates may be salient for girls several years earlier than for boys. At the transition to middle school—around the same time that it becomes so important for students to be socially accepted by classmates—there is an increase in the degree of competitiveness in many classrooms (Eccles & Midgley, 1989). At this same time, there typically are changes in how children conceptualize ability, such that older students realize that a "smart" child who does not have to try very hard and a "dumb" child who has to work extra hard can get a similar grade on an assignment (Nicholls & Miller, 1984). Older students generally believe that children who need help are not very "smart." Expending too much effort, especially in a public way that is easily observed by peers, therefore puts adolescents' self-worth at considerable risk (see Covington, 1992).

Support for Competence

How might students support one another's sense of competence needed for adaptive help seeking? Assuming that classroom organization and norms allow it, for example, when activity includes small-group collaboration, children can turn to classmates rather than to the teacher when they need help. Within certain developmental constraints, collaboration can foster in children cognitive and social skills involved in questioning.

Young children generally lack sociolinguistic competencies required for truly collaborative learning. At preschool, children have opportunities to work and play together. Yet, they tend to operate "in parallel," dividing up tasks and working on the parts separately. As they become more mature and gain experience in working together, children become better at asking each other questions that address their academic needs. Requests for help are more skillfully executed. For example, second graders are more likely than kindergartners to check to see if the potential helper is paying attention to them before actually making a request for information (Cooper, Marquis, & Ayers-Lopez, 1982). Older and more skilled students tend to make requests to peers that are direct, sincere, and polite and make it relatively clear what is being requested (Wilkinson & Calculator, 1982). For more experienced students, requests for help are often revised and clarified if they are initially unsuccessful in obtaining a response. When students make vague requests but persist by reformulating and clarifying the requests, academic performance tends to improve. Asking for (and receiving) help is most likely to facilitate learning when the help is "elaborated" (e.g., explanations rather than direct answers) and when children then use the help in a constructive way (see Webb & Palincsar, 1996).

At upper elementary and middle school grades, collaborative activity provides students a chance to "think in public" and to exchange with one another their thoughts (Brown & Campione, 1994). Importance is placed on students questioning one another. Built into many collaborative activities are opportunities for children to ask—and be asked—questions for purposes of monitoring their own and others' understanding and for requesting clarification, justification, and elaboration of other students' ideas. Questions during collaboration potentially allow an exchange of perspectives among individuals who are working on relatively equal footing with one another. Children observe the effectiveness of peers' questions in resolving difficulties. Recognizing that different individuals can contribute unique skills and knowledge may help a child learn how, in the future, to choose effective helpers according to the peer competencies. An implicit goal of collaborative activity is for children to realize that help seeking is a normal and adaptive part of the learning process (McCaslin & Good, 1996).

In sum, classmates provide one another opportunities to experience and benefit from social aspects of learning. Friendships, in particular, support help seeking. Friends tend to feel comfortable sharing their difficulties with each other. Especially in the context of collaborative activity, children have opportunities to develop questioning skills needed for help seeking. Social comparison, an inevitable aspect of peer interaction, helps children know when assistance is needed, gives children an opportunity to identify individuals who might be able to help them in the future, and makes help seeking seem more a natural part of the learning process. To the extent they perceive social comparison information in these particular ways, one can argue that children support one another's developing sense of autonomy and competence needed for adaptive help seeking. However, social comparison can have a powerful, inhibiting effect on children's willingness to publicly admit they need assistance. This may be especially true for older students and for those children who strongly need social approval from their peers and whose personal achievement goals are introjected (e.g., emphasizing "looking smart").

CONCLUDING THOUGHTS AND IDEAS FOR FUTURE RESEARCH

In this chapter, I have presented a developmental perspective on how teachers and peers contribute—through their involvement and support for autonomy and competence—to children's competencies and motivational resources needed for adaptive help seeking. Because of the paucity of developmental research on help seeking, a good deal of the discussion has been speculative. Further work is clearly needed in order to advance our understanding of the development of adaptive help seeking. In the remainder of the chapter, I suggest three particular topics that should be addressed: (1) the role of parents, (2) the role of culture, and (3) research methodology.

How do parents contribute to children's competencies and resources needed for adaptive help seeking at school? Although there are no studies that relate home factors to academic help seeking, self-determination theory and its emphasis on involvement, support for autonomy, and support for competence suggest potential connections (see Grolnick, Kurowski, & Gurland, 1999; Newman, 2000; Ryan & Stiller, 1991). I imagine that children who experience supportive and caring parents are relatively likely to develop an internal representation, and accompanying expectation, of others as respectful, approachable, and helpful. Sensitivity to children's needs arguably lays the groundwork for, and sustains, students' ability to confidently approach others for assistance. It is reasonable to expect that responsiveness to requests for help during joint activities helps the child develop a sense of autonomy (e.g., "I am in charge of my own actions and able to enlist the help of others—for both solving difficult problems and regulating my feelings in the face of failure"). There may be specific types of parent involvement (e.g., participating in parent-teacher conferences) and shared intellectual activity (e.g., helping with homework) that are related to student help seeking. Discourse that resembles scaffolding (e.g., with prompts and questions rather than direct answers) and that models social appropriateness (e.g., parents listening, inquiring if the child needs help, using "please" and "thank you") may be related to intelligent questioning on the part of students. Research questions about the role of parents should be addressed both concurrently and longitudinally.

How is culture involved in the development of students' adaptive help seeking? Different cultures may have different standards and rules for schoolchildren and thereby different views about the role of help seeking in the learning process. In different cultures, teachers and parents may have different expectations for boys and girls. In certain classrooms, students are expected to work independently; getting help—however necessary—is considered to be a sign of weakness or perhaps even cheating; if anyone is allowed to help a student, it is the teacher, not classmates; students are rewarded for "looking smart" (and not "looking dumb") rather than for trying hard; and making mistakes is an embarrassment—not a normal part of the learning process and certainly not a valued opportunity from which the entire class can benefit (see Nelson-Le Gall & Jones, 1991; Nelson-Le Gall & Resnick, 1998; Stevenson & Stigler, 1992). Academic help seeking differs from most other strategies of self-regulated learning for it is a *social transaction* between a child and his or her teacher or classmates, within a particular sociocultural context of learning. Research on help seeking needs to take into account more seriously factors of culture, ethnicity, and gender.

Are there issues of methodology that need to be addressed in order to improve developmental research on help seeking? First and foremost is the question of construct validity of "adaptive" (cf. nonadaptive or overly dependent) help seeking. Nelson-Le Gall (1981), Newman (1994), and others have operationalized adaptiveness according to certain features (e.g., requests for information that are necessary, well phrased, and addressed to individuals who can potentially help). Instances of such requests for help are difficult to observe in naturalistic classroom settings. Most researchers use self-report measures (e.g., estimated likelihood of asking questions when one does not understand an assignment) or experimental procedures simulating one-to-one tutoring (e.g., giving the child a difficult task and an opportunity to request help from an adult experimenter). A major challenge is devising valid measures of adaptive help seeking—ones that capture different degrees of "adaptiveness," are observable in the classroom, and are appropriate at different grade levels.

A second methodological issue is the need for longitudinal research. I suggest focusing on points of transition in children's lives (e.g., entry to school, transition from elementary to middle or junior high school, transition to high school). These are times when students are often at risk in terms of school adjustment and achievement (see Eccles, Wigfield, & Schiefele, 1998). The following are examples of important questions regarding stability of individual differences in adaptive help seeking:

Do children who adaptively seek help at elementary school tend to do so at middle school? At high school?

Does the relative influence on children's help seeking from teachers' involvement, support for autonomy, and support for competence vary over time?

Also, there are questions regarding interindividual differences in development, for example:

At the point of transition from elementary to middle school, do girls more than boys decrease their frequency of help seeking in math class?

At transition points, do teachers provide girls with less involvement, support for autonomy, and support for competence than they provide for boys?

Are there particular parent–child or teacher–child experiences (e.g., regarding homework) and parent or teacher attitudes (e.g., regarding the value of studying and collaborating) that buffer different groups of students (e.g., low achievers) from negative help-seeking trajectories (e.g., marked by passivity and avoidance)?

Answers to research questions such as these may ultimately inform school and home interventions aimed at helping students deal more adaptively with academic difficulty.

References

Ames, C. (1992). Classrooms: Goals, structures, and student motivation. *Journal of Educational Psychology*, 84, 261–271.

Barnett, K., Darcie, G., Holland, C. J., & Kobasigawa, A. (1982). Children's cognitions about effective helping. *Developmental Psychology*, 18, 267–277.

Berndt, T. J. (1999). Friends' influence on students' adjustment to school. *Educational Psychologist*, 34, 15–28.

Birch, S. H., & Ladd, G. W. (1996). Interpersonal relationships in the school environment and children's early school adjustment: The role of teachers and peers. In J. Juvonen & K. R. Wentzel (Eds.), *Social motivation: Understanding children's school adjustment* (pp. 199–225). Cambridge, U.K.: Cambridge University Press.

Boekaerts, M., Pintrich, P. R., & Zeidner, M., (Eds.) (2000), *Handbook of self-regulation*. San Diego: Academic Press.

Bowlby, J. (1969). *Attachment and loss: Vol. 1*. New York: Basic Books.

Brown, A. L., & Campione, J. C. (1994). Guided discovery in a community of learners. In K. McGilly (Ed.), *Classroom lessons: Integrating cognitive theory and classroom practice*. Cambridge, MA: MIT Press.

Butler, R. (1987). Task-involving and ego-involving properties of evaluation: Effects of different feedback conditions on motivational perceptions, interest, and performance. *Journal of Educational Psychology*, 79, 474–482.

Butler, R., & Neuman, O. (1995). Effects of task and ego achievement goals on help-seeking behaviors and attitudes. *Journal of Educational Psychology*, 87, 261–271.

Cazden, C. B. (1986). Classroom discourse. In M. C. Wittrock (Ed.), *Handbook of research on teaching* (3rd ed.). New York: Macmillan.

Connell, J. P., & Wellborn, J. G. (1991). Competence, autonomy, and relatedness: A motivational analysis of self-system processes. In M. R. Gunnar & L. A. Sroufe (Eds.), *Self-processes in development: Minnesota Symposium on Child Psychology: Vol. 23*. Hillsdale, NJ: Lawrence Erlbaum Associates.

Cooper, C. R., Marquis, A., & Ayers-Lopez, S. (1982). Peer learning in the classroom: Tracing developmental patterns and consequences of children's spontaneous interactions. In L. C. Wilkinson (Ed.), *Communicating in the classroom*. New York: Academic Press.

Covington, M. (1992). *Making the grade: A self-worth perspective on motivation and school reform*. New York: Cambridge University Press.

Deci, E. L., & Ryan, R. M. (1985). *Intrinsic motivation and self-determination in human behavior*. New York: Plenum Press.

Dweck, C. (1986). Motivational processes affecting learning. *American Psychologist*, 41, 1040–1048.

Dweck, C. & Leggett, E. L. (1988). A social–cognitive approach to motivation and personality. *Psychological Review*, 95, 256–273.

Eccles, J. S. (1983). Expectancies, values, and academic behaviors. In J. T. Spence (Ed.), *Achievement and achievement motives: Psychological and sociological approaches*. San Francisco: Freeman.

Eccles, J. S., & Blumenfeld, P. (1985). Classroom experiences and student gender: Are there differences and do they matter? In L. C. Wilkinson & C. B. Marrett (Eds.), *Gender differences in classroom interaction* (pp. 79–114). New York: Academic Press.

Eccles, J. S., & Midgley, C. (1989). Stage–environment fit: Developmentally appropriate classrooms for young adolescents. In C. Ames & R. Ames (Eds.), *Research on motivation in education: Vol. 3*. New York: Academic Press.

Eccles, J. S., & Wigfield, A. (1985). Teacher expectations and student motivation. In J. B. Dusek (Ed.), *Teacher expectations* (pp. 185–226). Hillsdale, NJ: Lawrence Erlbaum Associates.

Eccles, J. S., Wigfield, A., & Schiefele, U. (1998). Motivation to succeed. In W. Damon (Ed.), *Handbook of child psychology: Vol. 3. Social, emotional, and personality development* (pp. 1017–1095). New York: Wiley.

Furman, W., & Buhrmester, D. (1985). Children's perceptions of the personal relationships in their social networks. *Developmental Psychology*, 21, 1016–1024.

Gilligan, C. (1982). *In a different voice*. Cambridge, MA: Harvard University Press.

Good, T., Slavings, R., Harel, K., & Emerson, H. (1987). Student passivity: A study of question asking in K–12 classrooms. *Sociology of Education*, 60, 181–199.

Grolnick, W. S., Kurowski, C. O., & Gurland, S. T. (1999). Family processes and the development of children's self-regulation. *Educational Psychologist*, 34, 3–14.

Harter, S. (1981). A new self-report scale of intrinsic versus extrinsic orientation in the classroom: Motivational and informational components. *Developmental Psychology*, 17, 300–312.

Harter, S. (1982). The perceived competence scale for children. *Child Development*, 53, 89–97.

Harter, S. (1996). Teacher and classmate influences on scholastic motivation, self-esteem, and level of voice in adolescents. In J. Juvonen & K. R. Wentzel (Eds.), *Social motivation: Understanding children's school adjustment*. (pp. 11–42). Cambridge, U.K.: Cambridge University Press.

McCaslin, M., & Good, T. L. (1996). The informal curriculum. In D. C. Berliner & R. C. Calfee (Eds.), *Handbook of educational psychology*. New York: Simon & Schuster Macmillan.

Nadler, A. (1983). Personal characteristics and help-seeking. In B. M. DePaulo, A. Nadler, & J. D. Fisher (Eds.), *New directions in helping: Vol. 2. Help seeking* (pp. 303–340). New York: Academic Press.

Nadler, A. (1998). Relationship, esteem, and achievement perspectives on autonomous and dependent help seeking. In S. A. Karabenick (Ed.), *Strategic help seeking: Implications for learning and teaching*. Hillsdale, NJ: Lawrence Erlbaum Associates.

Nelson-Le Gall, S. (1981). Help-seeking: An understudied problem-solving skill in children. *Developmental Review*, 1, 224–246.

Nelson-Le Gall, S., & Glor-Scheib, S. (1985). Help seeking in elementary classrooms: An observational study. *Contemporary Educational Psychology*, 10, 58–71.

Nelson-Le Gall, S., & Gumerman, R. (1984). Children's perceptions of helpers and helper motivation. *Journal of Applied Developmental Psychology*, 5, 1–12.

Nelson-Le Gall, S. & Jones, E. (1990). Cognitive–motivational influences on the task-related help-seeking behavior of Black children. *Child Development*, 61, 581–589.

Nelson-Le Gall, S. & Jones, E. (1991). Classroom help-seeking behavior of African American children. *Education and Urban Society*, 24, 27–40.

Nelson-Le Gall, S., Kratzer, L., Jones, E., & DeCooke, P. (1990). Children's self-assessment of performance and task-related help seeking. *Journal of Experimental Child Psychology*, 49, 245–263.

Nelson-Le Gall, S., & Resnick, L. (1998). Help seeking, achievement motivation, and the social practice of intelligence in school. In S. A. Karabenick (Ed.), *Strategic help seeking: Implications for learning and teaching* (pp. 39–60). Hillsdale, NJ: Lawrence Erlbaum Associates.

Newman, R. S. (1990). Children's help-seeking in the classroom: The role of motivational factors and attitudes. *Journal of Educational Psychology*, 82, 71–80.

Newman, R. S. (1994). Adaptive help seeking: A strategy of self-regulated learning. In D. H. Schunk & B. J. Zimmerman (Eds.), *Self-regulation of learning and performance: Issues and educational applications* (pp. 283–301). Hillsdale, NJ: Lawrence Erlbaum Associates.

Newman, R. S. (1998). Students' help seeking during problem solving: Influences of personal and contextual achievement goals. *Journal of Educational Psychology*, 90, 644–658.

Newman, R. S. (2000). Social influences on the development of children's adaptive help seeking: The role of parents, teachers, and peers. *Developmental Review*, 20, 350–404.

Newman, R. S., & Gauvain, M. (1996). *Mathematical communication and thinking: The role of peer collaboration in the classroom*. Paper presented at the annual meeting of the American Educational Research Association, New York.

Newman, R. S., & Goldin, L. (1990). Children's reluctance to seek help with schoolwork. *Journal of Educational Psychology*, 82, 92–100.

Newman, R. S., & Schwager, M. T. (1993). Student perceptions of the teacher and classmates in relation to reported help seeking in math class. *Elementary School Journal*, 94, 3–17.

Newman, R. S., & Schwager, M. T. (1995). Students' help seeking during problem solving: Effects of grade, goal, and prior achievement. *American Educational Research Journal*, 32, 352–376.

Nicholls, J. G., & Miller, A. (1984). Reasoning about the ability of self and others: A developmental study. *Child Development*, 55, 1990–1999.

Noddings, N. (1992). *The challenge to care in schools*. New York: Teachers College Press.

Ogbu, J. (1987). Variability in minority school performance: A problem in search of an explanation. *Anthropology and Education Quarterly*, 18, 312–334.

Paris, S. G. (1988). Motivated remembering. In F. E. Weinert & M. Perlmutter (Eds.), *Memory development: Universal changes and individual differences*. Hillsdale, NJ: Lawrence Erlbaum Associates.

Paris, S. G., & Cunningham, A. E. (1996). Children becoming students. In D. C. Berliner & R. C. Calfee (Eds.), *Handbook of educational psychology* (pp. 117–147). New York: Simon & Schuster Macmillan.

Rosen, S. (1983). Perceived inadequacy and help-seeking. In B. M. DePaulo, A. Nadler, & J. D. Fisher (Eds.), *New directions in helping: Vol. 2. Help seeking* (pp. 73–107). New York: Academic Press.

Ruble, D. N., & Frey, K. S. (1991). Changing patterns of comparative behavior as skills are acquired: A functional model of self-evaluation. In J. Suls & T. A. Wills (Eds.), *Social comparison: Contemporary theory and research*. Hillsdale, NJ: Lawrence Erlbaum Associates.

Ryan, A. M., Gheen, M. H., & Midgley, C. (1998). Why do some students avoid asking for help? An examination of the interplay among students' academic efficacy, teachers' social–emotional role, and the classroom goal structure. *Journal of Educational Psychology*, 90, 528–535.

Ryan, A. M., Hicks, L., & Midgley, C. (1997). Social goals, academic goals, and avoiding seeking help in the classroom. *Journal of Early Adolescence*, 17, 152–171.

Ryan, R. M., & Deci, E. L. (2000). Self-determination theory and the facilitation of intrinsic motivation, social development, and well-being. *American Psychologist*, 55, 68–78.

Ryan, R. M., & Stiller, J. (1991). The social contexts of internalization: Parent and teacher influences on autonomy, motivation, and learning. In P. R. Pintrich & M. L. Maehr (Eds.), *Advances in motivation and achievement: Vol. 7* (pp. 115–149). Greenwich, CT: JAI.

Sadker, M., & Sadker, D. (1994). *Failing at fairness: How America's schools cheat girls.* New York: Charles Scribner's Sons.

Shapiro, E. G. (1983). Embarrassment and help-seeking. In B. M. DePaulo, A. Nadler, & J. D. Fisher (Eds.), *New directions in helping: Vol. 2. Help seeking* (pp. 143–163). New York: Academic Press.

Skinner, E. A. (1995). *Perceived control, motivation, and coping.* Thousand Oaks, CA: Sage.

Skinner, E. A., & Belmont, M. J. (1993). Motivation in the classroom: Reciprocal effects of teacher behavior and student engagement across the school year. *Journal of Educational Psychology, 85,* 571–581.

Stevenson, H. W., & Stigler, J. (1992). *The learning gap: Why our schools are failing and what we can learn from Japanese and Chinese education.* New York: Summit Books.

Stipek, D., & MacIver, D. (1989). Developmental change in children's assessment of intellectual competence. *Child Development, 60,* 521–538.

Stodolsky, S. S. (1988). *The subject matters.* Chicago: University of Chicago Press.

van der Meij, H. (1988). Constraints on question asking in classrooms. *Journal of Educational Psychology, 80,* 401–405.

Vygotsky, L. S. (1978). *Mind in society: The development of higher psychological processes* (M. Cole, V. John-Steiner, S. Scribner, & E. Souberman, Eds.). Cambridge, MA: Harvard University Press.

Webb, N. M. (1984). Sex differences in interaction and achievement in cooperative small groups. *Journal of Educational Psychology, 76,* 33–34.

Webb, N. M., & Palincsar, A. S. (1996). Group processes in the classroom. In D. C. Berliner & R. C. Calfee (Eds.), *Handbook of educational psychology.* New York: Simon & Schuster Macmillan.

Weinstein, R. (1985). Student mediation of classroom expectancy effects. In J. Dusek (Ed.), *Teacher expectancies.* Hillsdale, NJ: Lawrence Erlbaum Associates.

Wentzel, K. R. (1992). Motivation and achievement in adolescence: A multiple goals perspective. In J. Meece & D. Schunk (Eds.), *Student perceptions in the classroom: Causes and consequences* (pp. 287–306). Hillsdale, NJ: Lawrence Erlbaum Associates.

Wentzel, K. R. (1996). Social goals and social relationships as motivators of school adjustment. In J. Juvonen & K. R. Wentzel (Eds.), *Social motivation: Understanding children's school adjustment* (pp. 226–247). Cambridge, U.K.: Cambridge University Press.

Wentzel, K. R. (1997). Student motivation in middle school: The role of perceived pedagogical caring. *Journal of Educational Psychology, 89,* 411–419.

Wilkinson, L. C., & Calculator, S. (1982). Effective speakers: Students' use of language to request and obtain information and action in the classroom. In L. C. Wilkinson (Ed.), *Communicating in the classroom.* New York: Academic Press.

Wood, D. (1989). Social interaction as tutoring. In M. H. Bornstein & J. S. Bruner (Eds.), *Interaction in human development* (pp. 59–80). Hillsdale, NJ: Lawrence Erlbaum Associates.

Zimmerman, B. J., & Martinez-Pons, M. (1986). Development of a structured interview for assessing student use of self-regulated learning strategies. *American Educational Research Journal, 23,* 614–628.

Motivation and Instruction

Good Instruction Is Motivating

DEBORAH STIPEK

Stanford University, Stanford, California

Researchers often lament the inattentiveness of practitioners to research findings, and some have sought ways to make their research more useful as well as more accessible to people who interact directly with children. In this chapter I argue that the typical research approach of studying isolated qualities of children and contexts can make findings difficult to apply in complex real-life settings inhabited by whole children.

Most studies assess very specific cognitive or social–motivational outcomes. Studies of factors in the environment that affect child outcomes are also usually very focused. Thus, research reports tend to provide information suggesting the effects of a narrowly defined aspect of children's experience on a narrowly defined child outcome. Furthermore, as the fields of psychology and education become increasingly complex and vast, researchers become more restricted in their expertise as well as their research focus.

Teachers, on the other hand, are required by the nature of their work to be generalists. They must be concerned with the effects of a variety of environmental inputs on children's development on many dimensions. It cannot be easy to make sense of research that divides environments and children into pieces in a context in which the needs of whole children are to be met.

This chapter attempts to integrate just two sets of child outcomes that are central to teaching and learning—academic skills and achievement motivation. As interrelated as these two dimensions are, most researchers study the effects of classroom or other factors on one or the other. Here we will examine both, with particular attention given to how well findings that suggest the value of particular classroom practices in one dimension support or contradict findings on the value of those same practices in the other dimension. I discuss first what we know about the effects of different instructional approaches on children's academic learning, and then move to the field of achievement motivation, focusing primarily on early childhood and elementary levels.

There is not now and probably will not ever be complete agreement on the most effective ways to teach children. But research on teaching has revealed fairly consistent evidence on instructional practices that promote subject matter learning. And considerable progress has been made in the last decade in developing consensus among researchers and expert practitioners about effective instructional practices in mathematics and literacy.

For example, the National Council of Teachers of Mathematics (NCTM, 1991, 1995, 2000) has issued guidelines for the teaching of mathematics, complemented by other reports at state and local levels (e.g., California State Department of Education, 1992). Recently, the National Academy of Science issued a set of guidelines for the teaching of reading (Committee on the Prevention of Reading Difficulties in Young Children, 1998). Guidelines for reading instruction are also included in a report of the National Council of Teachers of English and International Reading Association (1996), and the National Association for the Education of Young Children (NAEYC) has issued guidelines for teaching children from preschool through the third grade (Bredekamp, 1997; Bredekamp & Rosegrant, 1995). A substantial body of research on teaching and learning supports the recommendations for instruction made by these and other groups. The practices endorsed have been shown to support learning directly by providing children with coherent, meaningful input and opportunities to engage in intellectual activities that promote skills and understanding.

An examination of the achievement motivation literature suggests that the "best practices" described in various consensus documents also enhance students' learning indirectly, by enhancing their motivation—their self-confidence, enthusiasm, and desire to understand and develop skills. This increased motivation, in turn, leads to the kind of active engagement with academic tasks that maximizes learning. My conjecture is based both on theoretical analysis and empirical findings.

I will begin first with the analysis. Although the research literatures for teaching and learning and for achievement motivation are quite distinct, careful examination of the practices suggested by subject matter specialists to enhance learning reveals a striking resemblance to practices promoted by achievement motivation researchers. Consider first recommendations made by people who study teaching and learning in academic subjects.

TEACHING AND LEARNING LITERATURE

The NCTM standards advocate open-ended problem solving and deep conceptual analysis rather than memorizing procedures and getting correct answers. They also suggest giving students opportunities to engage in mathematical conversations that reveal their conceptual understandings, which teachers can then build upon. In addition, mathematics education experts promote students' autonomous, active engagement with mathematical ideas and the personal construction of mathematical concepts (see also Ball, 1993; Cobb, Wood, Yackel & McNeal, 1993; Fennema, Carpenter, Franke, & Carey, 1993; Lampert, 1991). In general, responsibility for student learning is shifted from the exclusive authority of the teacher to include the student in active inquiry (see also Carpenter & Fennema, 1991; Cobb, Wood & Yackel, 1993; Lampert, 1991; Prawat, Remillard, Putnam, & Heaton, 1992).

Similarly, although reading experts emphasize phonics and mechanics, they recommend embedding this learning into meaningful reading and writing activities when possible, and giving equal attention to comprehension and analysis. Teachers are encouraged to provide students with ample opportunity to read for meaning, and to teach analytic skills—for example, by asking students to make predictions, inferences, and connections to their own lives. A third component of effective reading instruction often mentioned in the literature is an emphasis on oral as well as written language—engaging children in "instructional conversations" about the substance of the reading material (See, e g , Committee on the Prevention of Reading Difficulties in Young Children, 1998; Gillet & Temple, 2000; National Council of Teachers of English and International Reading Association, 1996.)

Looking across subjects, Newmann and his colleagues (1992) recommend similar instructional approaches, based on their studies of schools that produce the best learning. They endorse, for example, "authentic" instruction that is connected to the real world (children's lives outside of school), as well as instruction that involves content-based discourse, in which the teacher elicits students' points of view and understandings and promotes substantive conversation among students. Their endorsement of instruction that involves challenging, "higher order thinking" requiring analysis and extrapolation is similar to mathematics reformers' support for an emphasis on deep conceptual knowledge and problem solving.

Turning to early childhood education, the general consensus, summarized in the NAEYC guidelines (Bredekamp, 1997; Bredekamp & Rosegrant, 1995), is that young children learn best when they have open-ended opportunities to explore concrete materials and to interact with each other. Teachers serve primarily as resources to children's self-initiated learning. To the degree that basic skills are taught, they are embedded in everyday, meaningful activities (e.g., cooking, reading stories) rather than using didactic, teacher-directed methods, such as flash cards or paper-and-pencil tasks.

ACHIEVEMENT MOTIVATION LITERATURE

The importance of motivation is explicitly recognized in some of the subject matter literature. For example, the NCTM standards (2000) refer to students' confidence in their ability to tackle difficult problems and take control over their own learning. Teachers engaged in reform-minded mathematics instruction are counseled in other documents as well to promote students' self-confidence as mathematics learners (Resnick, Bill, Lesgold, & Leer, 1991; see Schunk and Pajares, Chapter 1, this volume), willingness to take risks and approach challenging tasks (Fennema, Carpenter, Franke & Carey, 1993; Resnick, Bill, Lesgold, & Leer, 1991), enjoyment in engaging in mathematics activities (Fennema, Carpenter, Franke, & Carey, 1993; McLeod, 1992; Middleton, 1995; see Grolnick, Gurland, Jacob, & Decourcey, Chapter 6, this volume), and related positive feelings (e.g., pride in mastery) about mathematics (McLeod, 1992). And, in the early childhood education literature, many of the instructional approaches are endorsed specifically because they are believed to support children's intrinsic interest in learning.

The motivation goals referred to in the subject matter literature are usually recommended without explicit instructions on how they can be achieved or how motivation promotes learning. Implicit, however, is the notion that motivation is a key component of learning. When we turn to research in the achievement motivation literature we see evidence for the motivational value of the same instructional approaches that subject matter specialists endorse to enhance learning.

Focus on Challenging, Conceptual Thinking

There are several reoccurring themes in the recommended instructional approaches. The first theme concerns engaging children in challenging, conceptual thinking. This theme is central to the NCTM standards; it is also seen in the emphasis on meaning, analysis, and interpretation in reading instruction, and on open-ended activities in the NAEYC guidelines for early childhood education.

According to many motivation theorists, the challenging, conceptual, and analytic thinking promoted by subject matter specialists should foster greater feelings of competence than would isolated skill practice, in part because challenging work is more likely to result in discernible improvements in understanding. Mastering challenging concepts should also engender positive emotions, such as pride and satisfaction. Intrinsic motivation theorists claim that these feelings of competence and pride should, in turn, engender intrinsic interest and enjoyment (Deci, 1975; Deci & Ryan, 1985; White, 1959). Questionnaire studies support the assumption that children enjoy work that is challenging, conceptual, and framed around "big ideas" rather than isolated skills (Newmann, 1992; Zahorik, 1996).

Research by Csikszentmihalyi (1988) also supports the motivational value of challenging work, but demonstrates the importance of students feeling "up to the challenge." Using the experience sampling form (on which students report events and their feelings over the course of the day), students were asked to rate the level of challenge and their skills, independently. Analyses revealed that students rated situations in which both challenge and skills were relatively high as the most motivating. Turner, Meyer, Cox, Logan, DiCintio, and Thomas (1998) likewise found higher motivation for elementary school students who were challenged, but not beyond reach, than for students who were not challenged.

Focus on Learning and Understanding

A second theme, especially prominent in the mathematics instruction literature, concerns the focus on learning and developing understanding rather than on getting correct answers or performing better than others. This focus, according to goal theorists, should foster a mastery orientation rather than a performance orientation (Ames, 1992; Dweck, 1986; Meece, Blumenfeld, & Puro, 1989; see Anderman, Austin, & Johnson, Chapter 8, this volume). Previous research indicates that when teachers focus on gaining skills and understanding, students attend to the same. When learning is the student's goal, initial failures or performing poorly relative to classmates should not engender negative emotions such as embarrassment, shame, or hopelessness, nor should they breed helpless behavior. In contrast, when students who are focused on performing (looking smart) encounter difficulty, negative emotions and helpless behavior are common.

A focus on learning should also contribute to students' perceptions of their competencies. All students can be competent if competence is defined in terms of developing mastery and understanding. In contrast, when competence is defined competitively (e.g., based on how well students perform relative to classmates), failure (and the attendant low perceptions of competence and negative emotions) is guaranteed for some students.

Active Participation and Control

A third recommendation in the mathematics, reading, and early childhood literatures concerns the emphasis on active participation in learning. This notion is central to the consctuctivist learning theories that underlie many subject-matter expert recommendations. Again, there is overlap with the motivation literature. Motivation researchers have found that students enjoy activities that allow active participation more than they enjoy passive listening or reading (Mitchell, 1993).

Related to active participation is control. Many of the subject matter reports mentioned encourage teachers to give up some control, or at least to share control over the learning process with their students. They stress the importance of allowing students to take initiative and to experiment with their own problem-solving strategies. Autonomy is one of the three central ingredients in intrinsic motivation theory (Deci, 1975; Deci & Ryan, 1985), and it has been shown in many studies to promote intrinsic interest and enjoyment (e.g., Deci, Schwartz, Sheinman, & Ryan, 1981; see Stipek, 1998). Autonomy is also considered to be a basic need in self-systems theory, and previous studies suggest that when this need is met, students are more likely to be actively engaged in academic tasks (Connell & Wellborn, 1991; Skinner & Belmont, 1993; Skinner, Wellborn, & Connell, 1990).

Authenticity and Meaningfulness

A fourth theme in the recommendations concerns the authenticity of instruction. Teachers are encouraged to make connections between classroom instruction and children's lives outside of school and to take advantage of children's personal interests, so that instruction is personally meaningful. Motivation research on interest provides good evidence that text relevant to an individual's interests promotes attention and effort (Krapp, 1999; Renninger, Hidi, & Krapp, 1992; Schiefele & Krapp, 1996).

All these motivational benefits should be manifested in more active and more enthusiastic engagement in school tasks. For example, children who enjoy learning and are self-confident about their ability to succeed in academic tasks can be expected to exert more effort and persist longer in the face of difficulty than students who do not enjoy learning tasks and expect to fail. A learning orientation has been shown to foster productive learning behaviors, such as a willingness to take risks and ask for assistance when it is needed, as well as persistence in the face of difficulty (see Stipek, 1998). This greater engagement should, in turn, contribute to students' learning.

My point—that the kind of instruction that has been found to promote learning does so in part by enhancing motivation—may seem obvious. But research on teaching and learning and research on achievement motivation tend to be conducted by two rather distinct groups of researchers. Attempts to examine the overlap in recommendations made to teachers—who need to implement instructional practices that promote both motivation and learning—are rare.

I turn now to empirical evidence related to my point. If the kind of instruction that is recommended by subject matter specialists promotes learning in part by enhancing motivation, then the more teachers implement such instruction, the more motivated and engaged their students should be. Below I describe analyses from three studies that examined direct associations between practices advocated by subject matter specialists and children's motivation.

MATHEMATICS INSTRUCTION STUDY

The first set of data is from a study of mathematics instruction in the upper elementary grades, which I conducted with Maryl Gearhart and Geoffrey Saxe. We developed an intervention to help teachers implement the NCTM mathematics standards, using the California replacement units for fractions and measurement. The data reported below includes teachers who were committed to and learning to implement reform-minded mathematics teaching, and teachers from a control group, who implemented traditional, textbook-based instruction. The 21 teachers in this study, therefore, varied considerably in the degree to which they implemented the kind of mathematics instruction that is promoted by mathematics education experts.

The study was conducted in public schools in the greater Los Angeles area, all serving predominantly low-income children. All the teachers (one male, nineteen females) taught fourth, fifth, or sixth grade. Their levels of experience varied from 1 to more than 20 years. The 437 children in their classrooms were ethnically diverse: 64% Latino, 14% Caucasian, 8% African American, and 7% Asian.

Classroom Instruction

Two researchers visited classrooms during a lesson on part–whole relationships in fractions. One researcher videotaped the lesson and the other took detailed field notes. Evaluations of mathematics instruction were based on the videotapes and supplemented with information from field notes. Codes for two critical dimensions of classroom instruction, focusing on whole-class episodes, were used in the analyses described below.

The code, *integrated assessment*, captured students' opportunities to participate in classroom discussions involving questioning and problem solving that revealed their mathematical thinking. High scores were given if teachers asked students to explain their reasoning and compare their solution with other students' solutions, and if they extended conversations to explore students' understanding. The code for *conceptual issues* assessed the degree to which students had opportunities to engage in conceptual thinking and problem solving. (See Gearhart et al., 1999, for details of the coding system.[1])

---

[1] The coding system was developed by Maryl Gearhart and colleagues and is available by writing to Dr. Maryl Gearhart, Graduate School of Education, Tolman Hall 4413, University of California, Berkeley, CA 94720-1670.

Both scales had four points, with detailed descriptions accompanying each point on the scale. For example, to receive the highest score on conceptual issues, the following description had to apply to a lesson observed:

> A fundamental goal of the discussion appears to be to engage students in formalizing procedures the students have devised or engaging students in conceptual analysis of conventional procedures. The discussion may focus on the ways procedures address and can reveal part–whole relationships or operations on fractional quantities. Discussions generally entail consideration of conceptual relations among possible representations (graphic, numeric, linguistic) for fractional quantities or operations on fractional quantities.

Student Motivation

All students completed a questionnaire with questions related to motivation after they had completed both the fractions and measurement units. The questionnaire assessed

1. Students' *perceptions of their mathematics ability* (e.g., "How good are you at math?")
2. The degree to which they were *mastery orientated* (e.g., "How much do you care about really understanding math?")
3. *Positive emotions* they experienced while working on mathematics tasks (e.g., interested, proud)
4. *Negative emotions* (e.g., embarrassed, frustrated, upset)
5. *Enjoyment* (how much they liked working on math tasks and how boring they found math to be)

Findings

We ran regression analyses using the two codes reflecting the degree to which teachers implemented reform-minded mathematics instruction to predict motivation-related beliefs and emotions. Teachers' emphasis on conceptual issues predicted student motivation better than the integrating assessment dimension. The more students had opportunities to engage with conceptual issues underlying problem solving, the more motivated they tended to be to achieve mastery ($\beta = 0.08$, $p < 0.051$), the more they claimed to experience positive emotions while working on math ($\beta = 0.12$, $p < 0.01$), and the more they claimed to enjoy doing math ($\beta = 0.10$, $p < 0.05$). The integrated assessment scale of instructional practices predicted only children's negative emotions. The more teachers were observed integrating assessment into their instruction, the *less* children claimed to experience negative emotions while they worked on math tasks ($\beta = -0.09$, $p < 0.05$).

The findings are consistent with the hypothesis that instruction recommended by subject matter specialists to improve student learning also promotes beliefs and emotions associated with positive motivation. Furthermore, this study found that student motivation predicted math learning, using as the measure of learning the proportion of problems children failed at the beginning of the year and that they passed at the end of the year (see Stipek, Salmon, et al., 1998).

The finding that emphasis on conceptual issues promoted students' enjoyment and interest in learning and understanding is consistent with theory and research in the motivation literature on both intrinsic motivation and goals. High enjoyment and positive emotions are in many respects indices of intrinsic motivation. The results thus provide further evidence for the assumption that challenging, conceptual work is more intrinsically interesting than more traditional basic skills instruction.

The positive motivational effects of pushing students to explain and analyze their answers and problem-solving strategies is consistent with what Turner et al. (1998) found when they examined teacher practices in classrooms in which students reported high levels of engagement and intrinsic motivation. Teachers in these classrooms were more likely to hold students accountable for understanding by making them explain strategies and justify their answers. Teachers in classrooms in which students were less engaged and less intrinsically motivated were more directive and focused more on procedures. The results are also similar to Newmann's (1992) finding: high school students rated their interest highest for the courses they rated as being challenging and forcing them to think.

Because intrinsic motivation is associated with high levels of engagement, our findings are also consistent with Blumenfeld, Puro, and Mergendoller's (1992) description of science teachers whose students were highly engaged. The teachers pressed students to explain and justify their answers, asked students to compare responses and debate the merits of different answers, and required written explanations of results or alternative representations of information. To ensure that students felt "up to the challenge," these teachers also provided considerable support by suggesting strategies, modeling thinking strategies, and scaffolding problem solving.

The effect of conceptually focused instruction on students' mastery orientation—their focus on learning and understanding—is consistent with motivation goal theory and research. It is likely that the conceptually oriented discussions assessed in our math study conveyed to students that their understanding was important to the teacher, which in turn promoted their own desire to understand.

The practical implication of the findings is that students enjoy challenging learning situations that stretch their understanding. Teachers are often fearful of asking students to engage in high-level thinking, especially in public contexts. They are concerned that students will be embarrassed if they are unable to respond or in some other way reveal their misunderstandings. The relatively low level of negative emotions in classrooms in which students were pushed to explain and analyze their mathematical thinking in whole-class discussions suggests that when the focus is on learning and understanding, teachers can challenge students, even publicly, without fear of negative emotional consequences. To be sure, a steady diet of frustration and failure will discourage the most resilient of students. But the findings just discussed above suggest that students enjoy and are motivated by challenging work.

Motivation research also helps us understand why the instructional approaches endorsed by mathematics subject matter specialists promote learning. Many studies have demonstrated that mastery orientation, enjoyment, and positive emotions foster behaviors that enhance learning. For example, compared with a performance orientation, a mastery orientation has been shown to promote greater attention to the task at hand (because of fewer distractions related to concerns about performance), and effective problem-solving strategies (see Stipek, 1998, for a review). Research on intrinsic motivation suggests some of these same benefits. The positive effects on learning found to be associated with instruction endorsed by subject matter specialists, therefore, are most likely achieved partly by promoting a mastery orientation and enjoyment.

I discuss next a study involving younger children, which provides further support for the notion that good instruction is motivating.

SCHOOL TRANSITION STUDY[2]

The second study also involved observations of classroom instruction. In this case, in addition to assessing student motivation in terms of their self-perceptions, as we did in the mathematics study described above, we observed students in their classrooms and coded their level of engagement in academic tasks.

Before describing the study I will make a few comments about the concept of "engagement." Skinner and Belmont (1993) and their colleagues (Connell & Wellborn, 1991) define engagement in both behavioral (e.g., effort, persistence) and affective (e.g., enthusiasm, interest) terms. Newmann (1992), likewise, refers to both behavioral effort and psychological (or emotional) investment in his discussion of schools that promote student engagement. Other researchers, as well, have distinguished between behavior (usually attention and concentration) and positive affect (Turner, Meyer, Cox, Logan, DiCintio, & Thomas, 1998). The inclusion of both behavior and emotional components has important implications for how engagement is operationalized in research.

[2]This work has been supported by a grant from the John D. and Catherine T. MacArthur Foundation Research Network on Successful Pathways through Middle Childhood, with supplementary funding from the W. T. Grant Foundation. The larger study on school transition is directed by Deborah Stipek, Heather Weiss, Penny Hauser-Cram, Walter Secada, and Jennifer Greene.

I think it is also important to distinguish between engagement in academic tasks and engagement in school. A child can be quite engaged in the social or athletic affairs of school, for example, but totally disinterested in intellectual work. Such a student may participate actively and enjoy school, but be inattentive and unengaged when it comes to academic tasks.

Both school engagement and academic engagement involve emotions as well as behaviors, although the behaviors may be somewhat different. For example, school engagement might be seen in attendance rates, participation in extracurricular activities, and non-task-related behavior (talking or passing notes to classmates rather than working on academic tasks). Engagement in academic tasks would be observed, as mentioned earlier, in behaviors like attention, effort, and persistence on schoolwork.

In brief, I have conceptualized a kind of 2 x 2 framework for thinking about engagement—differentiating between academic tasks and school in general, and between behavioral and affective components.

I will apply this framework to the data collected in the study described below, but I confess that I did not articulate these distinctions clearly in my own mind until after the data had been collected. Looking back, we assessed three of the four components in the framework. We assessed children's engagement in academic tasks with a measure that combined behavior (e.g., attention, persistence) and affect (enthusiasm). Thus, for a classroom to get the highest score, students had to show some enthusiasm for academic tasks as well as engage in them actively and attentively. We also assessed children's general affective engagement with school by asking them how they felt about (how much they liked) school and their teacher.

In the future I hope to assess independently the behavioral and the affective components, except inasmuch as affect is inferred from behavior. This strikes me as potentially important because it seems that children could, in the context of serious threats or high pressure, be very attentive, but have little enthusiasm for the learning process. Indeed, they may experience negative emotions such as fear or anxiety in this situation, which undermine rather than support learning. Thus different instructional approaches may be required to promote attention and persistence *and* interest and enthusiasm than are required to promote behavioral engagement alone.

We did not measure behavioral engagement in the school outside of academic tasks in this study primarily because these were very young children whose participation in school activities was decided substantially by parents. I suspect that engagement in school activities outside the classroom becomes much more important to measure in middle school and high school.

The larger study from which these data were drawn was designed to examine how factors in children's school, home, and community contexts affect their pathways through elementary school. The study includes nearly 400 ethnically diverse children—35% Caucasian, 37% African American, 25% Latino, 1% Asian, and 1% American Indian. All children came from families with very low incomes. When the study began, most (76%) household incomes were below $15,000; 21% were below $6000. Parent education was also low: 13% of the parents (usually mothers) had less than the equivalent of ninth grade, and 28% went past the ninth grade but did not complete high school.

The data presented below are from when the children were in second and third grades. At this point, children were spread over 173 classrooms in 126 schools and 43 school districts. The teachers were mostly female (89%) and mostly Caucasian (75%). The schools served primarily low-income children, although they varied considerably in the concentration of poverty, with 0% to 100% of their students eligible for free or reduced lunch, with a mean of 66%. In 25% of the schools, more than 30% of the students were Spanish-speaking, English language learners.

Assessments of Instruction

The classroom observation measure assessed the degree to which practices promoted by mathematics and literacy subject matter specialists were employed.[3] The scale was developed after a thorough review of these subject matter literatures, especially as they were applied to the early elementary grades.

We also assessed two aspects of the classroom climate that were based on the achievement motivation rather than subject matter instruction literature. This allowed us to determine whether children's motivation was predicted by the nature of instruction over and above the effects of the motivational climate. The two motivation-related scales assessed the social climate of the classroom and the degree to which effort and mastery were emphasized.

Trained observers spent a full day in the classroom. At the end of the observation, observers rated 24 items on a 1–5 scale. Detailed descriptions accompany each possible score. A score of 5 is given when the paragraph describing "best practices" represented the kind of instruction that predominated in the classroom; a score of 1 indicated that effective practices were not seen at all. For example, a score of 1 for social climate was given to a classroom for which the following description was the best fit:

> The general classroom environment is unsafe. Most children engage in and/or experience put-downs, taunts, even occasional threats or slurs about themselves or backgrounds. The teacher and other adults do little, if anything, to counteract these problems. By their uneven enforcement of rules of behavior or occasional put downs for children, the adults may even add to the problem.

A 5 was given for a classroom that fit the following description:

> Respect between the teacher and students and among the students themselves is mutual and widespread. People address one another respectfully; they listen politely to each other; children behave as if they respect each other and feel respected by other classmates.

[3]Lisa Adajian played a major role in developing the instructional observation measure. Copies can be obtained by writing to Deborah Stipek.

Scores of 2, 3, or 4 were given depending on how well one versus the other description fit the classroom.

For the analyses reported in this chapter, the items were divided into four categories. Scores used in analyses were the mean of the items in the category. (See Table 1 for a description of the items.)

The seven *math instruction* items assess the degree to which children are engaged in conceptual analysis, mathematics discourse, and have opportunities to practice basic skills in the context of problem solving.

The five *reading instruction* items assess the degree to which there are opportunities for developing inferential and analytic skills and basic skills in the context of meaningful reading activities. The scale also includes items on

TABLE 1
Items in Mathematics and Reading Instruction Assessments

Math ($\alpha = 0.83$)	
Math analysis	Students engage in high-order thinking that goes beyond reporting math facts, rules, and definitions or applying algorithms (e.g., searching for patterns, making and justifying conjectures, organizing, synthesizing, evaluating, speculating, arguing, and inventing original procedures).
Depth of knowledge	Students develop systematic, integrated understanding (e.g., producing new knowledge, discovering mathematical relationships, connecting different mathematical topics).
Problem solving	Basic skills are taught in the context of (as tools for) novel problem solving (rather than as isolated skills).
Math discourse	Students engage in conversation about mathematics that includes high-order thinking skills (e.g., analysis and explanation), not just reporting of facts or procedures.
Locus of authority	Students take responsibility for justifying their own reasoning; students do not rely on the teacher as the only authority.
Reading ($\alpha = 0.75$)	
Reading as meaning making	Reading involves higher order thinking that involves text and trying to understand the substance of what is being read (e.g., using prior knowledge, arguing, hypothesizing, etc.).
Basic skills developed in context of reading	Basic skills are, in part, taught in the context of reading text (e.g., vocabulary words are from text that is understood rather than a list put on a board).
Instructional conversations	Students engage in conversations about substance of reading material which include higher order thinking (e.g., making distinctions, forming generalizations, raising questions).
Both Math and Reading	
Cross-disciplinary connections	Instructions or tasks are explicitly connected to students' personal experiences or contemporary, personally meaningful situations.
Linkages to real life	Topics are connected among different subject areas.

whether children are encouraged to engage in meaningful writing that involves discussion of ideas and revisions, and have opportunities to develop basic writing skills in the context of writing meaningful text.

As mentioned earlier, two remaining observation variables concern the social and learning climate, not instruction per se. The *social climate* variable, shown above, concerns the degree to which the classroom climate is respectful and psychologically safe (e.g., no put-downs). The *focus on effort* variable includes information on the degree to which the teacher emphasizes effort, provides clear and high academic standards, encourages students to assist and support each other's learning, and solicits broad participation.

Student Engagement

At the end of the observation, the degree to which students were engaged in academic activities was rated on a scale of 1–5. Engagement was coded separately for math and reading. Coders were instructed to look at "…attentiveness, doing the assigned work, and showing enthusiasm for the work." A score of 1 was given if students were frequently off-task; a score of 3 was described as "sporadic or episodic engagement; most students, some of the time, are engaged in class activities, but this engagement is uneven, mildly enthusiastic, or dependent on frequent prodding from the teacher." A 5 was given if "…almost all students were deeply involved, almost all of the time, in pursuing the substance of the lesson." Descriptions were also provided for scores of 2 and 4. This measure of engagement was coded at the classroom level.

We also collected teacher ratings of the individual target students' engagement in academic tasks in the classroom. There were usually only one or two target children in a classroom. Four items (works independently, seeks challenges, accepts responsibility, appears to be tuned in) were used from the self-directed learner subscale of the Teacher Rating Scale of School Adjustment (TRSSA) (Birch & Ladd, 1997, 1998; Ladd, Birch, & Buhs, 1999).

Children's affective engagement in school was also assessed at the individual child level. Participating children were asked three questions about their *feelings about their teacher*, using a 1–5 Likert scale (e.g., "How do you feel about your teacher?"). Their general *feelings about school* were assessed with three additional questions (e.g., "How much do you like school?").

Academic Achievement

We assessed children's achievement in the spring of second grade with teacher ratings; in the spring of third grade children completed math and literacy assessments given individually by an experimenter.

Teachers rated second grade children's academic performance in math and reading using a 5-point scale reflecting how well children were performing relative to children their age.

In third grade we gave our own achievement test to participating children. The math test included the calculations and applied subtests from the WJ-R math assessment (Woodcock & Johnson, 1990) and an assessment of children's strategies for solving word problems (Carpenter, Ansell, Franke, & Fennema, 1993; Carpenter, Fennema, & Franke, 1996). The literacy test included the Letter/Word Identification and Passage Recognition subtest of the WJ-R and a test of reading comprehension and verbal fluency (Saunders, 1999). Scores on the mathematics and literacy tests were standardized and combined.

Findings

Does the quality of instruction, defined by subject matter specialists, predict students' engagement? Correlational analyses for both math and literacy revealed significant associations between most of the dimensions of the quality of instruction and the level of children's engagement at the classroom level (see Tables 2 and 3). There are a couple of noteworthy patterns in these correlations.

First, for both math and reading, cross-disciplinary connections and linkages to children's lives outside the classroom were generally more weakly associated with children's engagement than were the other dimensions of the

TABLE 2
Correlations between Quality of Math Instruction and Student Engagement

	Second Grade	Third Grade
Quality of instruction		
Math analysis	.36[a]	.21[b]
Depth of knowledge	.38[a]	.29[b]
Problem solving	.19[b]	.26[b]
Math discourse	.35[a]	.26[c]
Locus of authority	.33[b]	.34[c]
Cross-disciplinary connections	.11[c]	.02
Linkages to real life	.10	.18[d]
Motivational climate		
Effort focus (math)	.56[a]	.51[a]
Social climate (general)	.49[a]	.57[a]

[a] $p < 0.001$
[b] $p < 0.01$
[c] $p < 0.10$
[d] $p < 0.05$

TABLE 3
Correlations between Reading Instruction and Student Engagement

	Second Grade	Third Grade
Quality of instruction		
Focus on meaning	.41[a]	.45[a]
Basic skills in context of meaningful reading	.26[a]	.32[a]
Instructional conversations	.39[b]	.42[a]
Cross-disciplinary connections	.20[b]	.13[d]
Linkage to real life	.15[c]	.22[b]
Motivational climate		
Effort focus (reading)	.56[a]	.58[a]
Social climate (general)	.41[a]	.48[a]

[a] $p < 0.001$
[b] $p < 0.01$
[c] $p < 0.05$
[d] $p < 0.10$

quality of instruction that we assessed. It is possible that these two dimensions are less reliably measured in a one-day observation and that multiple observations would have shown these dimensions to be more predictive.

Although further research would be important to conduct before we conclude that these aspects of instruction do not affect student engagement, it is possible that cross-disciplinary connections and explicit linkages to children's lives outside school, while valuable, are not as critical for promoting intellectual engagement as other qualities of instruction and tasks. Perhaps they make school in general more enjoyable, but when it comes to how intellectually engaged a child is, conceptual problems, meaningful text, and opportunities for analysis and active participation may be more important in capturing children's interest, even if they are not directly related to students' own experiences.

The strength of the predictions based on the motivational climate variables is also noteworthy. Clearly, the climate of the classroom—whether there are predictable and fairly applied rules and routines, a focus on effort and learning, and respectful interactions among peers and the teacher—must also be considered in any attempt to improve children's academic engagement and learning.

One purpose of including both instructional and motivational climate variables was to enable us to assess the predictive value of math and literacy teaching over and above classroom factors that are more traditionally considered contributors to student motivation. Additional partial correlations were computed, therefore, to examine the independent predictive power of the instructional quality and the two motivational climate ratings. The mean of student engagement in reading and math was used as an index of student engagement, and the mean of a composite of the math and reading instructional quality scores was used for an overall index of the quality of instruction. Each partial correlation held constant the other two classroom dimensions.

These partial correlations show that measures of the quality of instruction predicted students' engagement ($r = 0.18$ and 0.15 for second and third grade, respectively; both p's < 0.01, even when the social climate and the focus on learning were partialed out. An effort focus, with both quality of instruction and social climate partialed out, also predicted engagement ($r = 0.32$, $p < 0.01$, and $r = 0.22$, $p < 0.05$, for second- and third grade, respectively). Interestingly, the partial correlation for social climate (with quality of instruction and focus on learning held constant) was significant only in third grade ($r = 0.05$, ns, and 0.36, $p < 0.001$) for second and third grade, respectively.

The next set of analyses was conducted to assess whether the quality of instruction and the motivational climate predicted children's emotional engagement with school in general. Correlation coefficients were computed between the three classroom observation variables used in the above analyses and children's ratings of how much they liked school and how much they liked their teacher. The results indicated that children's feelings about school were not significantly associated with our assessments of their classrooms at all in second grade. And in third grade, classroom assessments were significantly associated only with feelings about the teacher: $r = 0.13$, $p < 0.10$, for quality of instruction; $r = 0.14$, $p < 0.05$, for focus on effort; $r = 0.18$, $p < 0.01$, for social climate.

Presumably our context measures predicted children's feelings about the teacher, not their feelings about school in general, because the context measures were all at the classroom level and described primarily teacher behavior. Young children's feelings about school were generally positive (with means above 4.0 on a 5-point scale). But they did vary, so the question is, on what basis?

We found in analyses reported elsewhere that the feelings about school by kindergartners and first graders, but not third graders, were predicted by the degree to which teachers claimed they had a close relationship with them (Valeski & Stipek, submitted). Perhaps relationships, especially with adults, are more salient to young children's overall feelings about school than is the nature of instruction. It may take children a few years in school to see academics as the central focus, and teachers as teachers rather than as parent surrogates. Taken together, these findings suggest developmental changes in the early elementary grades in what promotes positive connections to school, and perhaps also in how engaged they are in the academic process.

In future research it would be useful to assess the effect on children's school engagement of a broader set of contextual variables, including the quantity and quality of school activity offerings, and the social climate outside the classroom. A developmental perspective is important because different variables may take on greater significance in particular developmental periods. A predictable, easily managed environment and warm, caring adults might be more important for children in the early elementary grades, whereas opportunities for interesting activities and peer interactions might have more weight for older children.

The importance of academic engagement is indicated by the finding that our measure of student engagement did, in fact, predict how much children learned. When we regressed individual students' engagement scores (based on teachers' ratings at the end of the second or third grade) with their previous years' achievement forced out first, the standardized beta was 0.28 ($p < 0.001$) at second grade and 0.18 ($p < 0.05$) at third grade. The second grade findings are stronger, probably because both student engagement and academic achievement were rated by teachers. But they were still significant, even when teachers' ratings of students' engagement were used to predict scores on our independent achievement measure.

Discussion

Consider first the findings that the quality of instruction predicted students' engagement on academic tasks, even when the social–motivational climate was held constant. There are two broad themes worth noting in the ratings of instructional quality used in this study.

We assessed the degree to which teachers engaged students in math analysis and problem solving that required some real conceptual understanding, not just knowledge of calculation rules. Likewise for reading, two of the ratings involved an emphasis on meaning (rather than, e.g., correct pronunciation while reading aloud). The more conceptual instructional approach in this study, as in the study on mathematics instruction, described earlier, presumably promoted intrinsic interest and enjoyment (which unfortunately, we did not assess in this study), which in turn led to the relatively high levels of engagement in academic tasks that we did find.

The second theme in both the mathematics and literacy instruction codes concerns students' active participation and personal construction of knowledge. This theme is reflected in the math item "locus of authority" and in the reading item "instructional conversations." The findings thus support the assumption, discussed above, that active participation and control promote motivation.

The social–motivational climate ratings appeared to have a particularly strong effect on students' engagement. Children in classrooms that scored high on "focus on learning" got a clear and consistent message from teachers: learning is what counts, and I expect you to meet high standards. Many studies suggest that students adopt, to some degree, the expectations for success that their teachers convey (see Stipek, 1998). Previous motivation research also provides evidence for the value of clear expectations, standards, and contingencies for students to develop a sense of control over achievement outcomes (Skinner, 1995). Learning was presumably promoted in classrooms high on our learning focus scale, in part, by giving students a sense of control and high expectations, which translated into more productive engagement in academic tasks.

A positive and respectful social context also appeared to promote students' academic engagement. Connell and Wellborn (1991) claim that "relatedness" is one of three basic human needs, along with feelings of competence and self-determination. They define relatedness as feeling securely connected to individuals in the social context and experiencing oneself as worthy of love and respect. McCombs (1994) likewise emphasizes the importance of a culture of trust, respect, and caring. Moreover, studies in the motivation literature have found positive associations between students' reports of feeling socially connected and supported and their engagement in classroom activities (Skinner & Belmont, 1993; Skinner & Wellborn, 1994).

Why might students be more engaged in classrooms characterized by respect and social support? Perhaps students who feel supported and cared for feel less apprehensive about making mistakes; they do not need to spend their time trying to avoid looking incompetent (e.g., procrastinating, acting out to distract attention from their lack of understanding). Certainly it would be more difficult to become interested in academic activities while feeling anxious, humiliated, or ashamed. Children in such classrooms might also develop more positive relationships with their teachers, and thus have a stronger desire to please them. A positive social environment might also engender a generally positive affective and emotional state that carries over into academic activities. It would be useful in future research to understand better *how* the social context of classrooms affects students' behavior on tasks.

EARLY CHILDHOOD STUDY

In the two studies described above, the findings happily suggest that the same instructional practices promote positive motivational and academic outcomes. A study of younger children which my colleagues and I conducted produced a more complicated picture (Stipek, Feiler, et al., 1998). In brief, instructional approaches promoted by experts produced positive academic and motivation outcomes for preschoolers; for kindergartners, the so-called "best practices" produced positive outcomes on the motivation dimensions measured, but relatively negative outcomes on basic skills tests. The study illustrates the importance of assessing both academic and motivational out-comes in the same study, and of taking a developmental perspective.

Preschool (N = 27) and kindergarten (N = 15) classrooms were rated by observers using a scale that was based substantially on the National Association for Education of Young Children standards for early childhood education (Bredekamp & Copple, 1997; Bredekamp & Rosegrant, 1995). Classrooms that were rated high on the measure were child centered; they had responsive and nurturing teachers who gave clear instructions, embedded learning in children's interests and real-life experiences, provided considerable child choice, and de-emphasized performance comparisons. Teachers who scored low on the classroom measure used didactic, teacher-directed approaches. They were less sensitive and nurturing, and more directive. They provided little child choice and used commercially prepared worksheets and activities with close-ended or single right answers. Scores on our observation measure were strongly correlated with the two most frequently used measures of early childhood education quality—the Early Childhood Environment Rating Scale (ECERS) (Harms & Clifford, 1980) and the Classroom Practices Inventory (CPI), developed by Hyson, Hirsh-Pasek, and Rescorla (1990).

The 228 children in the study were ethnically diverse (29% Latino, 31% African American, 26% Caucasian, and 3% Asian) and represented a broad spectrum of family incomes, from very low (e.g., eligible for Head Start) to very high (e.g., in elite private schools). We assessed children's academic skills using the Woodcock–Johnson Achievement Test, supplemented with items from the Peabody Individual Achievement Test. We also assessed children's motivation both individually, in a laboratory context, and by observing behavior in their regular classroom.

When we examined children's scores on the various motivation assessments at the end of the year we found a number of advantages of the "high-quality instruction" classrooms. Preschoolers and kindergartners in classrooms that scored relatively high on our observation measure expressed less negative affect, exhibited less noncompliant behavior, and were less dependent on others for approval. Thus, what was considered appropriate instruction seemed also to have positive effects on motivation.

The results related to basic academic skills depended on whether children were in preschool or kindergarten. In the preschool classrooms, what we deemed high quality had positive effects on both literacy and math skills as well as some of the motivation dimensions measured. Thus, even though children in the classrooms that scored low on our quality measure spent a fair amount of time doing teacher-directed, basic-skill-oriented academic tasks, they did not perform as well on a basic academic skills assessment as children who spent most of their time engaged in child-initiated, open-ended activities.

The opposite was found for kindergartners. Children made less progress on both literacy and math skills in classrooms that we rated as high quality than they did in classrooms that we rated as low quality. Apparently the time kindergartners spent doing teacher-directed, basic skills tasks did, in fact, promote their basic skills acquisition.

The basic skills test assessed a limited array of cognitive outcomes, and one might reasonably argue that other cognitive outcomes, such as creativity or problem solving, are more important. But practically, the kind of skills assessed by our basic skills tests are highly predictive of children's ultimate success in school. Like them or not, they affect children's academic trajectories.

Our findings suggest that preschool teachers do not have to choose one outcome to emphasize over another in planning their instructional program. In contrast, a kindergarten teacher who wants to base instructional decisions on research findings is faced with a dilemma—to give priority to motivation or basic skill acquisition. A careful look at research on early childhood education should give kindergarten teachers some guidance in developing an instructional program that promotes learning without sacrificing motivation. There is good evidence on early reading, for example, that important skills can be developed using less didactic strategies than were used in most of the classrooms we observed (Committee on the Prevention of Reading Difficulties in Young Children, 1998).

CONCLUSIONS

Researchers need to divide children into components to make individual studies manageable. But too often we forget to put the pieces back together. It is natural for achievement motivation researchers to study the effects of educational practices on children's motivation and for subject matter specialists to study the effects of instructional practices on children's learning.

Teachers, on the other hand, have whole children in their classrooms. They need to promote healthy and productive development in all domains. And they need to be concerned about the effects of development in one domain, such as motivation, on outcomes in others, such as academic achievement.

Researchers could help practitioners who want their practices to be guided by research findings by examining and analyzing the effects of practices across different domains. If an integrative analysis reveals that a particular set of practices has negative effects in one domain of development and positive effects in another, research will be needed to examine the conditions under which the negative and positive effects are most salient. We will need to do studies that can guide practices that minimize negative and maximize positive outcomes. This requires more integrated approaches to research than are usually done.

The analyses described in this chapter represent a very modest attempt to look across two domains of development that are assumed to be related, motivation and learning. Overall, the findings suggest that the same instructional practices promote positive development in both domains. The examination of motivation outcomes for children also helped us understand *why* particular instructional approaches promote children's learning. The findings of the first two studies are consistent with the notion that the positive effects of instructional approaches promoted by subject matter specialists are mediated, at least in part, by their positive effects on children's motivation.

But the third study suggests that instruction endorsed by early childhood education experts may promote kindergartners', and perhaps older children's, social–motivational development at the expense of basic academic skills. The early childhood study, in particular, illustrates the value of simultaneously examining the effects of different practices on different child outcomes to determine whether any trade-offs exist, and, if so, their nature, as well as the value of seeking instructional approaches that maximize outcomes on all important dimensions.

To make matters more complicated, there are also particular qualities of children that need to be considered. Gender and ethnicity are given considerable attention in this volume. There are many other child qualities to consider. For example, students enter a classroom with different skills, levels of self-confidence, learning styles, and so on. Variation in these child qualities, although sometimes found to be associated with demographic variables, vary substantially within groups, however they are defined. Consequently, in addition to knowing which instructional strategies promote positive outcomes on average, good teachers must know their own students well and adapt generally effective instructional approaches to meet the needs of particular children.

References

Ames, C. (1992). Classrooms: Goals, structures, and student motivation. *Journal of Educational Psychology*, 84, 261–271.

Ball, D. (1993). With an eye toward the mathematical horizon: Dilemmas of teaching elementary school mathematics. *Elementary School Journal*, 93, 373–397.

Benware, C., & Deci, E. (1984). Quality of learning with an active versus passive motivational set. *American Educational Research Journal*, 21, 755–765. (Not in text.)

Birch, S., & Ladd, G. (1997). The teacher-child relationship and children's early school adjustment. *Journal of School Psychology*, 35, 61–79.

Birch, S., & Ladd, G. (1998). Children's interpersonal behaviors and the teacher–child relationship. *Developmental Psychology*, 34, 934–946.

Blumenfeld, P. C., Puro, P., & Mergendoller, J. R. (1992). Translating motivation into thoughtfulness. In H. H. Marshall (Ed.), *Redefining student learning: Roots of educational change* (pp. 207–239). Norwood, NJ: Ablex.

Bredekamp, S., & Copple, C. (Eds.). (1997). *Developmentally appropriate practice in early childhood programs* (rev. ed.). Washington, DC: National Association for the Education of Young Children.

Bredekamp, S., & Rosegrant, T. (Eds.) (1995). *Reaching potentials: Transforming early childhood curriculum and assessment, Vol 2*. Washington, DC: National Association for the Education of Young Children.

California State Department of Education (1992). *Mathematics framework for California public schools*. Sacramento: Author.

Carpenter, T., Ansell, E., Franke, M., & Fennema, E. (1993). Models of problem solving: A study of kindergarten children's problem solving processes. *Journal for Research in Mathematics Education*, 24, 428–441.

Carpenter, T., & Fennema, E. (1991). Research and cognitively guided instruction. In E. Fennema, T. Carpenter, & S. Lamon (Eds.), *Integrating research on teaching and learning mathematics* (pp. 1–16). Albany: State University of New York.

Carpenter, T., Fennema, E., & Franke, M. (1996). Cognitively guided instruction: A knowledge base for reform in primary mathematics instruction. *Elementary School Journal*, 97, 3–20.

Cobb, P., Wood, T., & Yackel, E. (1993). Discourse, mathematical thinking, and classroom practice. In E. Forman, N. Minick, & C. Stone (Eds.), *Contexts for learning: Sociocultural dynamics in children's development* (pp. 91–119). New York: Oxford University Press.

Cobb, P., Wood, T., Yackel, E., & McNeal, B. (1993). Mathematics as procedural instructions and mathematics as meaningful activity: The reality of teaching for understanding. In R. Davis & C. Maher (Eds.), *Schools, mathematics, and the world of reality* (pp. 119–134). Boston: Allyn & Bacon.

Committee on the Prevention of Reading Difficulties in Young Children (1998). *Preventing Reading Difficulties in Young Children.* Washington DC: National Academy of Science.

Connell, J., & Wellborn, J. (1991). Competence, autonomy, and relatedness: A motivational analysis of self-system processes. In M. Gunnar & L. Sroufe (Eds.), *Self processes in development: Minnesota Symposium on Child Psychology, Vol. 23* (pp. 43–77). Hillsdale, NJ: Lawrence Erlbaum Associates.

Csikszentmihalyi, M. (1988). The flow experience and its significance for human psychology. In M. Csikszentmihalyi & I. Csikszentmihalyi (Eds.), *Optimal experience* (pp. 15–35). Cambridge, MA: Cambridge University Press.

Deci, E. (1975). *Intrinsic motivation.* New York: Plenum Press.

Deci, E., & Ryan, R. (1985). *Intrinsic motivation and self-determination in human behavior.* New York: Plenum Press.

Deci, E., & Ryan, R. (1987). The support of autonomy and the control of behavior. *Journal of Personality and Social Psychology*, 53, 1024–1037.

Deci, E., Schwartz, A., Sheinman, L., & Ryan, R. (1981). An instrument to assess adults' orientations toward control versus autonomy with children: Reflections on intrinsic motivation and perceived competence. *Journal of Educational Psychology*, 73, 642–650.

Dweck, C. (1986). Motivational processes affecting learning. *American Psychologist*, 41, 1040–1048.

Fennema, E., Carpenter, T., Franke, M., & Carey, D. (1993). Learning to use children's mathematical thinking: A case study. In R. Davis & C. Maher (Eds.), *Schools, mathematics, and the world of reality* (pp. 93–117). Boston: Allyn & Bacon.

Gearhart, M., Saxe, G., Seltzer, M., Schlackman, R., Ching, C., Nasir, N., Fall, R., Bennett, T., Rhine, S., & Sloan, T. (1999). Opportunities to learn fractions in elementary mathematics classrooms. *Journal for Research in Mathematics Education*, 30, 286–315.

Gillet, J., & Temple, C. (2000). *Understanding reading problems: Assessment and instruction* (5th ed.). New York, NY: Longman.

Harms, R. & Clifford, P. (1980). *The Early Childhood Environment Rating Scale.* NY: Teachers College Press.

Hyson, M., Hirsh-Pasek, K., & Rescorla, L. (1990). The classroom practices inventory: An observation instrument based on NAEYC's guidelines for developmentally appropriate practices for 4- and 5-year-old children. *Early Childhood Research Quarterly*, 5U, 475–494.

Krapp, A. (1999). Interest, motivation and learning: An educational psychological perspective. *European Journal of Psychology of Education*, 14, 23–40.

Ladd, G., Birch, S., & Buhs, E. (1999). Children's social lives in kindergarten: Related spheres of influence. *Child Development*, 70, 1373–1400.

Lampert, M. (1991). Connecting mathematical teaching and learning. In E. Fennema, T. P. Carpenter, & S. J. Lamon (Eds.), *Integrating research on teaching and learning mathematics* (pp. 121–152). Albany: State University of New York.

McCombs, B. (1994). Strategies for assessing and enhancing motivation: Keys to promoting self-regulated learning and performance. In H. O'Neil & M. Drillings (Eds.), *Motivation: Theory and research* (pp. 49–69). Hillsdale, NJ: Lawrence Erlbaum Associates.

McLeod, D. B. (1992). Research on affect in mathematics: A reconceptualization. In D. A. Grouws (Ed.), *Handbook of research on mathematics teaching and learning* (pp. 575–596). New York: Macmillan.

Meece, J., Blumenfeld, P., & Puro, P. (1989). A motivational analysis of elementary science learning environments. In M. Matyas, K. Tobin, & B. Fraser (Eds.), *Looking into windows: Qualitative research in science education* (pp. 13–23). Washington DC: American Association for the Advancement of Science.

Middleton, J. A. (1995). A study of intrinsic motivation in the mathematics classroom: A personal constructs approach. *Journal for Research in Mathematics Education, 26,* 254–279.

Mitchell, M. (1993). Situational interest: Its multifaceted structure in the secondary school mathematics classroom. *Journal of Educational Psychology, 85,* 424–436.

National Council of Teachers of English and International Reading Association (1996). *Standards for the English language arts.* Urbana, IL: Author.

National Council of Teachers of Mathematics (1991). *Professional standards for teaching mathematics.* Reston, VA: Author.

National Council of Teachers of Mathematics (1995). *Assessment standards for school mathematics.* Reston, VA: Author.

National Council of Teachers of Mathematics (2000). *Principles and standards for school mathematics.* Reston, VA: Author.

Newmann, F. (Ed.) (1992). *Student engagement and achievement in American secondary schools.* New York: Teachers College Press.

Prawat, R. S., Remillard, J., Putnam, R. T., & Heaton, R. M. (1992). Teaching mathematics for understanding: Case studies of four fifth-grade teachers. *Elementary School Journal, 93,* 145–152.

Renninger, K., Hidi, S., & Krapp, A. (Eds.) (1992). *The role of interest in learning and development.* Hillsdale, NJ: Lawrence Erlbaum Associates.

Resnick, L. B., Bill, V. L., Lesgold, S. B., & Leer, M. N. (1991). Thinking in arithmetic class. In B. Means, C. Chelemer, & M. S. Knapp (Eds.), *Teaching advanced skills to at-risk students: Views from research and practice* (pp. 27–67). San Francisco: Jossey-Bass.

Saunders, W. (1999). Improving literacy achievement for English learners in transitional bilingual programs. *Educational Research and Evaluation, 5,* 345–381.

Schiefele, U., & Krapp, A. (1996) Topic interest and free recall of expository test. *Learning and Individual Differences, 8,* 141–160.

Skinner, E. (1995). *Perceived control, motivation & coping.* Thousand Oaks, CA: Sage Publications.

Skinner, E., & Belmont, M. (1993). Motivation in the classroom: Reciprocal effects of teacher behavior and student engagement across the school year. *Journal of Educational Psychology, 85,* 571–581.

Skinner, E., & Wellborn, J. (1994). Coping during childhood and adolescence: A motivational perspective. In R. Lerner & M. Perlmutter (Eds.), *Life-span development and behavior, Vol 12* (pp. 91–133). Hillsdale, NJ: Lawrence Erlbaum Associates.

Skinner, E., Wellborn, J., & Connell, J. (1990). What it takes to do well in school and whether I've got it: The role of perceived control in children's engagement and school achievement. *Journal of Educational Psychology, 82,* 22–32.

Stipek, D. (1998). *Motivation to learn: From theory to practice* (3rd ed.). Needham Heights, MA: Allyn & Bacon.

Stipek, D., Feiler, R., Byler, P., Ryan, R., Milburn, S. & Salmon, J. (1998). Good Beginnings: What difference does the program make in preparing young children for school? *Journal of Applied Developmental Psychology, 19,* 41–66.

Stipek, D., Salmon, J., Givvin, K., Kazemi, E., Saxe, G., & MacGyvers, V. (1998). The value (and convergence) of practices suggested by motivation researchers and mathematics education reformers. *Journal for Research in Mathematics Education, 29,* 465–488.

Turner, J. M., Meyer Cox, K., Logan, C., DiCintio, D., & Thomas, C. (1998). Creating contexts for involvement in mathematics. *Journal of Educational Psychology, 90,* 730–745.

Valeski, T., & Stipek, D. (submitted). Young children's social competence and relationships with teachers: Pathways to early academic success.

White, R. (1959). Motivation reconsidered: The concept of competence. *Psychological Review, 66,* 297–333.

Woodcock, R.W. & Johnson, M.B. (1990). *Woodcock–Johnson Psycho-educational Battery Revised.* Allen, TX: DLM Teaching Resources.

Zahorik, J. (1996). Elementary and secondary teachers' reports of how they make learning interesting. *Elementary School Journal, 96,* 551–564.

CHAPTER 13

Instructional Practices and Motivation during Middle School (with Special Attention to Science)

DOUGLAS J. MAC IVER, ESTELLE M. YOUNG,
AND BENJAMIN WASHBURN
Johns Hopkins University, Baltimore, Maryland

At the end of the 1980s, the dismal condition of middle grades education in the United States finally began to receive national attention. California was one of the first states to produce a task force report calling for middle grades reform (California State Department of Education, 1987). California's report, *Caught in the Middle*, was followed by a long line of reports from Florida (Florida Department of Education, 1988), Maryland (Maryland Task Force on the Middle Learning Years, 1989), Louisiana (Louisiana Middle Grades Advisory Committee, 1989), and at least 15 other states (Totten, Sills-Briegel, Barta, Digby, & Nielsen, 1996). At about the same time, foundations such as the Lilly Endowment (Clark, Bickel, & Lacey, 1993), the Carnegie Corporation of New York (Carnegie Council on Adolescent Development, 1989), the Edna McConnell Clark Foundation (Lewis, 1991, 1993), and the W. K. Kellogg Foundation (Mertens, Flowers, & Mulhall, 1998) began advocating and funding middle grades reform initiatives.

Meanwhile, researchers began finding and reporting that the transition to middle grades schools was associated with declines in academic motivation and performance (e.g., Anderman & Anderman, 1999; Eccles & Midgley, 1989; Harter, Whitesell, & Kowalski, 1992; Pajares & Valiante, 1999; Simmons & Blyth, 1987; Seidman, Allen, Aber, Mitchell, & Feinman, 1994; Wigfield, Eccles, Mac Iver, Reuman, & Midgley, 1991). In a related finding, middle grades students perceive their middle grades teachers as more remote and impersonal than their elementary teachers and are less certain that their middle school teachers care about them and know them well (e.g., Feldlaufer, Midgley, & Eccles, 1988; Midgley, Feldlaufer, & Eccles, 1989). Furthermore, this research indicated that student work completed in the first year of the middle grades was often less demanding than in the last year of elementary school, that academic expectations in middle grades schools were generally low, and that students had few opportunities to learn important new concepts and apply them to real-world problems (e.g., for a review, see Ames, 1998). These reports, initiatives, and findings—along with the systematic nationwide dissemination of *Turning Points* (Carnegie Corporation Council on Adolescent Development, 1989)—prompted many schools and districts to institute a series of reforms in the middle grades over the last decade.

This ongoing middle grades reform movement is not occurring in a vacuum. It is concurrent with the standards-based reform movement that has also swept the United States since the late 1980s. Professional associations in each of the disciplines have attempted to specify what all students should know and be able to do (e.g., National Center for History in the Schools, 1994: National Council of Teachers of English and the International Reading Association, 1995; National Council of Teachers of Mathematics, 1989; Project 2061 of the American Association for the Advancement of Science, 1993). In turn, state departments of education and local districts have issued written "content standards," "curriculum frameworks," or "standards of learning" that (a) are usually loosely based on the professional associations' standards and (b) are meant to ensure consistency across classrooms and schools in teachers' expectations of what students should learn and how well they should learn it. Furthermore, state departments of education and/or local districts have often implemented assessment programs designed "to hold school systems, schools, administrators, and teachers accountable for students performing at standard" (Mizell, 1998, p. vii).

Both the middle grades reform movement and the standards-based reform movement share the goal of increasing student achievement and resolving student motivational problems by encouraging "research-based" instructional practices that (a) promote students' *understanding* and build *meaning* into their learning opportunities (Knapp, Marder, Adelmen, & Needels, 1995) and (b) assist students in developing and maintaining optimal motivational levels (e.g., high interest, engagement, effort, and valuing of school subjects) and orientations (e.g., being task-focused rather than ego-focused) in the middle grades. This chapter identifies some of these research-based instructional practices, practices that may promote positive changes in middle school students' motivational beliefs and orientations both generally and in science. In identifying changes in practice that can help students flourish in middle school and in science, we will both review the research of others and present data from our own ongoing program of research.

WHAT WORKS IN MIDDLE GRADES REFORM?

Much of the current research linking instructional practices to student motivation in middle school emphasizes the detrimental effects of practices that lead students to adopt a "performance focus," a focus on how their ability or performance compares to others, and the beneficial effects of practices that lead students to adopt a "mastery focus," a focus on improving one's skills, mastering the subject matter, and learning how to do the tasks offered in the classroom. This research suggests that reducing the use of performance-focused instructional practices that emphasize competition, ability grouping, and students' relative ability can prevent some of the negative shifts in students' motivational beliefs that often occur upon transition to a middle grades school. For example, Anderman, Maehr, & Midgley (1999) studied the motivational changes displayed by students after the transition to middle school in one community served by two middle schools. Students who entered a performance-focused middle school came to devalue understanding (e.g., "I don't care whether I understand something or not, as long as I get the right answer") and developed a preference for unchallenging work ("I like my work best when it is easy to get the right answer") more than the students who entered a mastery-focused school that offered all students challenging tasks, eliminated ability grouping, and had an inclusive student recognition program that based awards upon individual growth and development rather than relative performance. Similarly, Roeser, Midgley, and Urdan (1996) report that when middle school students perceive their school to be mastery-focused (e.g., "Teachers in this school want students to really understand their work, not just memorize it") they become more mastery-focused themselves and develop higher academic self-efficacy (e.g., "I am certain I can master the skills taught in school this year") In contrast, when middle school students perceive their school to be performance-focused, they become academically self-conscious (experience more performance-related fear, nervousness, and embarrassment.)

Changes in practice that ensure each student in a middle grades school will have more support from (and more meaningful relationships with) caring adults at the school can also reduce some of the negative shifts in students' motivational beliefs during the middle grades (Ames & Miller, 1994; Mac Iver & Plank, 1997). Schools-within-schools, looping (assigning teachers to the same students for 2 or 3 years), semidepartmentalization (e.g., assigning a teacher to teach two subjects to three class sections rather than one subject to six class sections) and interdisciplinary teaming are examples of structural reforms that have been made in many middle grades schools and that have been found to increase students' perceptions that their teacher cares about them and their learning and to strengthen teacher–student relationships (Arhar, 1997; Arhar and Kromrey, 1995; Felner, et al., 1997; McPartland, 1987; 1990, 1992; Mac Iver, Mac Iver, Balfanz, Plank, & Ruby, 2000; Roeser, Midgley & Urdan,

1996). In turn, when middle grades students perceive their teachers to care about them and their learning, they are more likely to report that they try to do what their teachers ask them to do, give their best effort in class (Wentzel, 1997), and are less likely to engage in risky behaviors (Resnick et al., 1997).

However, changes in school organizational structures "are necessary but not sufficient for major improvement in academic achievement" (Hamburg, 2000, p. xii). That is, research in middle grades schools engaged in reform suggests that major achievement gains are obtained only in schools that have implemented both changes in school organization (e.g., "create smaller learning environments," "form teams of teachers and students," "assign an adult advisor for every student") and in curriculum and instruction (e.g., "transmit a core of common, substantial knowledge to all students in ways that foster curiosity, problem solving, and critical thinking"). For example, in a study of a group of 31 Illinois middle schools (Felner et al., 1997), schools that had made both structural and instructional changes that were consistent with the *Turning Points'* recommendations showed higher achievement scores and displayed larger achievement gains over a 2-year period than did similar schools that had implemented at least some of the *Turning Points'* key structural changes but not changes in curriculum and instruction. Another study suggesting the critical importance of going beyond just structural changes in improving achievement was conducted in 155 middle grades schools in Michigan (Mertens, Flowers, & Mulhall, 1998). When these researchers analyzed outcomes in schools that had one of the key structural changes in place (interdisciplinary teams that were given high levels of common planning time), they found that achievement gains were much higher among the subset of these schools that had received a grant from the Kellogg Foundation that made it possible for their teachers to engage more regularly in staff development activities focused on curriculum and instruction. In fact, there is even evidence from this study that staff development may be more important than common planning time in facilitating achievement gains. Schools whose teams had inadequate common planning (but had a grant that made frequent professional development possible) showed more achievement gains than did nongrant schools, even those nongrant schools whose teams had high levels of planning time.

In identifying "what works" in middle grades reform, the literature suggests that providing students with more personalized and less-performance-focused learning environments and teachers with ongoing professional development that focuses directly on curriculum and instruction have an important impact on students' outcomes. These foundational practices help create a serious, supportive, and task-focused learning environment for both students and teachers. But, this literature does not provide much guidance regarding the specific kinds of learning opportunities that optimize student motivation in particular subject areas. Suppose that a middle grades school has succeeded in providing its students with a more personalized and less-performance-focused learning environment and its teachers with regular time for professional development. What is the next step in ensuring that students give their best efforts in the major subjects? What specific kinds of learning opportunities must be created for students so that they become fully and productively engaged in every class? Because "the subject" matters, it is impossible to identify a generic answer that applies equally well to each major subject area (Stodolsky, 1998). In this chapter, we focus on science, but draw some lessons from science that may apply to other academic subjects in the middle grades.

MOVING BEYOND THE TEXTBOOK IN SCIENCE CLASS: THE MOTIVATIONAL BENEFITS OF "MINDS-ON" AND "HANDS-ON" LEARNING OPPORTUNITIES

Both the National Science Education Standards (National Research Council, 1996) and the American Association for the Advancement of Science's Benchmarks for Science Literacy (Project 2061, 1993) enthusiastically embrace the goal of helping all middle grades students to become scientifically literate. In their instructional implications, these national standards and benchmarks "rest on the premise that science is an active process" (National Research Council, 1996, p. 4). For example, scientific literacy involves the ability to design and carry out experiments, interpret data from these experiments, and communicate those results to others in meaningful ways (Cheek, 1999). However, the opportunity to conduct hands-on experiments, while essential, is not enough: "Students must have 'minds-on' experiences as well" (National Research Council, 1996, p. 2). For example, students should have frequent chances to provide a hypothesis to explain why something happened, offer opinions on scientific issues, suggest questions or topics for the class to investigate, and write in a personal science journal. Students also need the opportunity to read about and discuss current science-related news and experience authentic science writing that is more engaging, current, and accurate than the poorly written, superficial, and decontextualized prose found in the typical textbook. Textbook reading is no substitute for reading scientific articles and book-length investigations of important scientific topics.

Hands-on opportunities to experiment, minds-on opportunities to reflect, and use of curricular materials other than a textbook are rare in high-poverty middle school science classrooms (Wilson & Corbett, 1999). Students in high-poverty classrooms frequently receive instruction that is solely skills focused, rather than a balanced instructional program that also includes meaning-oriented instruction that is active, reflective, and draws from a range of well-written sources (Knapp, 1995). Although there is remarkable consensus regarding the need to offer all students minds-on, hands-on, and multifaceted learning opportunities in science, there is little empirical research regarding the motivational benefits of such instruction in science, especially middle school science.

A FIELD STUDY IN TWO HIGH-POVERTY
MIDDLE SCHOOLS

In the pages that follow, we report findings from a study we conducted to test the assumption that "minds-on" opportunities to reflect, "hands-on" opportunities to experiment, and movement beyond the textbook make science class more engaging and worthwhile for middle school students. For example, when students frequently experience such opportunities, are they more likely to believe that science class is interesting, useful, and educationally valuable? Do students view the provision of hands-on and minds-on activities as a clear sign that their science teacher really cares about them and is doing his or her best to help them learn? Does the provision of such opportunities lead students to work harder to learn about science?

We report the results of "value-added" longitudinal analyses that provide estimates of the impact of science instructional practices on each outcome after controlling for students' prior status on that outcome, using data collected from 63 classrooms in two high-poverty middle schools attempting to implement standards-based instructional programs in science. These analyses will help us begin to flesh out how science teachers' instructional practices are associated with changes in student motivation. The data come from a larger multidisciplinary study of high-poverty middle schools in Philadelphia. The study draws upon student surveys collected during the 1997–1998 and 1998–1999 school years in two schools that serve grades 5 through 8. The surveys were administered annually to all students and, with a few exceptions, contained the same questions in both school years. The surveys asked them about their exposure to a variety of instructional practices as well as their attitudes about science. Of course, students who were fifth graders in 1998–1999 were excluded from the longitudinal analyses. (We had no prior data from them because they were not yet in middle school during the 1997–1998 school year.)

To study the relation between instructional practices and student motivation, one must have data drawn from classrooms that vary in their practices. In many samples, this presents a problem because it is difficult to find enough examples of classrooms using state-of-the-art instructional practices. However, in this sample, many teachers in both schools had received standards-based professional development and materials as part of the National Science Foundation's Urban Systemic Initiative in Philadelphia or as part of the Talent Development Middle School reform effort. (Mac Iver, et al., 2001). Specifically, teachers in these schools had been given standards-based commercial modules (such as Full Option Science System or Science and Technology for Children kits, which include lessons and hands-on materials) and their use of these modules was supported by curriculum-specific professional development (Ruby, 1999), which allowed them to practice the activities within the modules, to become conversant with the basic science content matter that was directly related to the modules, and to become conversant with the instructional techniques needed to effectively implement the modules (such as techniques for managing student hands-on activities and cooperative groups, identifying students' current knowledge and misconceptions, and fostering student reflection). Because most teachers in both schools had access to these active, meaning-oriented curriculum modules and to curriculum-specific professional development, it is likely that there will be sizable numbers of classrooms in these schools in which students experience regular minds-on learning tasks as well as opportunities to read beyond the textbook and to experiment.

The class-level measures of instructional practices are drawn from survey questions that asked students to indicate the frequency of particular practices during the 1998–1999 school year. A section's score on each class-level measure of instructional practices is the mean student score within that section on items that measure that aspect of instruction. For example, a section's score on the *Minds-On Learning Opportunities Scale* is the mean student score on a composite comprised of six survey items asking students to indicate how often their science teacher asked them to:

- Provide a hypothesis to explain why something happened.
- Offer an opinion on a scientific issue.
- Provide questions or topics for the class to investigate.
- Explain answers to teammates or partners and check to make sure that all teammates or partners understand the material.
- Discuss careers in science.
- Write in a personal science journal.

Similarly, *Hands-On Opportunities to Design, Carry Out, and Interpret Experiments* was measured as the mean student score on a composite comprised of survey items indicating how often students:

- Did an experiment.
- Wrote about the results of an experiment he or she had done.
- Explained the reasons for the results of an experiment.
- Interpreted data from an experiment.
- Watched the teacher do an experiment.
- Designed an experiment or part of an experiment.

Finally, *Going Beyond the Textbook*, constructed in a parallel fashion to the measures above, is comprised of three items asking students to report how often they:

- Read other articles on science.
- Did a written or oral report.
- Discussed a science news event.

The response scale for each item in each scale was: never (0), once or twice a month (1), once or twice a week (2), most days (3), every day (4).

The survey also included a set of questions asking students to describe their attitudes about their science class. These items became the basis for the construction of five student-level measures of motivation. Although there are a wide variety of motivational constructs posited by various theorists, expectancy–value motivation theorists (e.g., Wigfield & Eccles, 2000) argue that students' achievement choices, effort, persistence, and learning in a class can be explained largely by their expectations for success in the class (e.g., "Will I learn a lot in this class, if I choose to try?") and by their perceptions of the value of the class (e.g., "Is this class interesting, exciting, and enjoyable? Is it useful?"). Expectancy–value theory also identifies some of the key influences on these expectations and values (e.g., students' previous achievement-related experiences, students' perceptions of teachers' beliefs and behaviors, students' goals and self-conceptions). We embrace this perspective on achievement motivation and measure five expectancy–value constructs that we believe are key to understanding the impact of instructional practices on motivation and achievement in science class: expectancy for learning, intrinsic value, utility value, pedagogical caring, and effort.

Expectancy for Learning is measured by a single item:

- If I work hard in science class, I can learn a lot. (strongly disagree, strongly agree)

Intrinsic Value is measured by a three-item z-score composite, constructed after standardizing each individual item to have a mean of 0 and a standard deviation of 1. The specific items are:

- Science is exciting. (strongly disagree, strongly agree)
- When I work in science class, it is because I'm really interested in the subject matter. (not at all a reason, a very important reason)
- How much do you enjoy the work you do in your science class? (not much at all, very much)

Utility Value is also measured by a three-item z-score composite: "When I work in science class, it is because:

- The knowledge and skills are useful in my life. (not at all a reason, a very important reason)
- It helps me prepare for high school. (not at all a reason, very important reason)
- It helps me prepare for a career. (not at all a reason, a very important reason)

According to most expectancy–value models of achievement, students' perceptions of teachers' beliefs and behaviors affect students' effort, engagement, goals, and values. In this regard, Wentzel (1997) has presented evidence indicating that perceptions of "pedagogical caring" have an especially important impact on student motivation in middle school. That is, middle school students' engagement in and valuing of learning are increased when the students believe that their teachers care about them and their learning. We measure *Pedagogical Caring* with a two-item *z*-score composite:

- My science teacher cares about how we feel. (almost never, almost always)
- My science teacher does everything she or he can to help us improve our skills and increase our understanding. (almost never, almost always)

Effort is measured by a single item.

- How hard are you working to learn about science? (not hard at all, as hard as I can)

In analyzing our data, we first used the classroom-level measures of instructional practices to examine how frequently the average science class experienced active, meaning-oriented instruction and to see how much variation there was in exposure to this type of instruction. Then, taking both the classroom-level measures of instructional practices and the student-level measures of motivation, we assessed the degree to which between-classroom differences in instruction could account for classroom-level differences in students' outcomes. Specifically, we used hierarchical linear modeling (HLM) to test whether classrooms with a higher degree of implementation of the instructional practices also had higher average levels of student motivation, controlling for students' motivation levels from the prior year. We also used HLM to test for sex differences in motivation in science or for general motivational declines during the middle grades in our sample.

Central Tendency and Between-Classroom Variation in Instructional Practices

The instructional practices we measured were used fairly frequently in the average classroom in our sample, but there was abundant variation between classrooms. For example, as can be seen in Figure 1, there were five classrooms where minds-on activities rarely or never occurred, and over a dozen classrooms where they occurred once or twice a week or more. The grand mean of the Minds-On Learning Opportunities Scale was 1.55 (i.e., across items and classrooms, the average minds-on learning opportunity in this sample occurred "more than twice a month" on a scale ranging from "never" to "every day"). The mean of the Hands-On Opportunities Scale was identical to the Minds-On Scale ($M = 1.55$) and similar to that of the Beyond the Textbook Scale ($M = 1.63$). Each scale had a similar standard deviation ($SD_{MINDS-ON} = 0.48$, $SD_{HANDS-ON} = 0.51$, $SD_{BEYOND} = 0.47$) and range. The regular use of these instructional practices in many of the classes in this sample is a promising finding. High-poverty classrooms are often bereft of hands- and

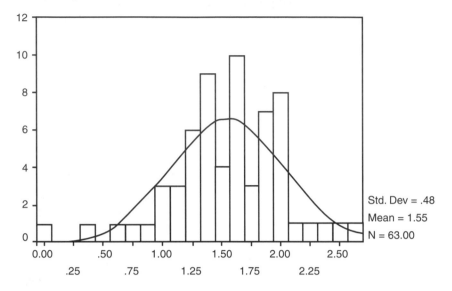

Average Classroom Level Minds-On Activities

Std. Dev = .48
Mean = 1.55
N = 63.00

Minds-On Activities

0=Never, 4=Every Day

FIGURE 1
Number of classrooms (y axis) displaying each level of minds-on activities.

minds-on learning opportunities, but this study shows that that need not be so. The training and materials offered to teachers in this sample was enough to enable many of them to use active, meaning-oriented teaching practices.

Predicting Motivational Outcomes Based Upon Between-Classroom Variation in Instructional Practices

We performed a parallel set of analyses for each of the five motivational outcomes and each of the three instructional practices. The main research question addressed was whether the instructional practices students experienced in their science class during the 1998–1999 school year were predictive of their motivational outcomes in spring 1999, after controlling for students' prior status on these outcomes in spring 1998. Therefore, the main HLM model specified for each motivational outcome and each instructional practice was:

- Level-1 Model: Motivation in $1999_{ij} = \beta_0 + \beta_1$ (prior year's motivation$_{ij}$) + r

- *Level-2 Model:* $\beta_0 = \gamma_{00} + \gamma_{01}$ (seventh grade section) $+ \gamma_{02}$ (eighth grade section) $+ \gamma_{03}$ (multi grade section) $+ \gamma_{04} * $ (*instructional practice score*) $+ u_0$

$\beta_1 = \gamma_{10} + u_1$

The model above specifies the outcome variable as a function of a classroom mean (the intercept), prior status, and a random error term at the student level (level 1). The classroom-level (level 2) model specifies the classroom mean of the outcome variable as a function of an intercept, grade of class (represented as a series of dummy variables with sixth grade as the excluded reference category), a continuous instructional practice measure, and a random error term. The classroom-level model also specifies that the prior status slope varies randomly across classrooms.

In each model, the estimate of greatest interest to us was the effect of the instructional practice (γ_{04}) expressed as a standardized coefficient. A standardized coefficient takes account of the differences in metrics among measures, translating each to standard deviation units. Table 1 lists this coefficient for each model estimated.

As shown in the first two rows of Table 1, both the frequency of minds-on learning opportunities and the frequency of opportunities to go beyond the textbook were related strongly and positively to all five of the motivational outcomes. For example, a 1-standard deviation (SD) increase on the *minds-on* instructional practice scale was associated with a 0.59 SD increase in stu-

TABLE I
Instructional Practices as Predictors of Motivational Outcomes in Science

	Intrinsic Value	Utility Value	Expectancy for Learning	Effort	Pedagogical Caring
Class-Level Predictor:					
Frequency of ...					
"Minds-on" learning opportunities	0.59[a]	0.40[c]	0.40[c]	0.45[c]	0.68[a]
Going beyond the textbook to read about science	0.65[a]	0.54[b]	0.38[c]	0.38[d]	0.69[a]
Opportunities to design, carry out, and interpret experiments	0.43[b]	0.16	0.19	0.31	0.33[c]

Note: Standardized γ coefficients are shown. The coefficient in each cell is from an HLM model that includes prior status on the motivational outcome as a student-level predictor and grade level of class as a class-level predictor.

[a] $p < 0.001$
[b] $p < 0.01$
[c] $p < 0.05$
[d] $p < 0.06$

dents' perceptions of the intrinsic value of science class ($p < 0.001$). All the standardized coefficients in these first two rows are moderately large (around 0.4) or very large (> 0.5).

In contrast, as shown in final row of Table 1, the frequency of opportunities to design, carry out, and interpret experiments (hands-on) was related to only two of the five outcomes. Specifically, students who experienced hands-on opportunities showed significantly greater growth in their ratings of the intrinsic value of science class and of the pedagogical caring displayed by their science teacher.

In summary, the analyses indicate that active, meaning-oriented instructional practices in science are associated with positive responses from students in high-poverty schools. For all three types of instructional practices considered, students receiving more frequent exposure to these practices in their science class were more likely to perceive the class as intrinsically valuable and to perceive their science teachers as caring and dedicated. Both minds-on opportunities and opportunities to read beyond the text—but not hands-on opportunities to experiment—were predictive of students' expectancies for learning, perceptions of utility value, and self-reported effort.

The finding that all three instructional practices increase the students' perception that their teacher cares about them and is doing his or her best to increase their understanding suggests that these practices may be a partial antidote to the ubiquitous decline in pedagogical caring that earlier studies have found after students enter middle grades schools (e.g., Feldlaufer, Midgley, & Eccles, 1988; Midgley, Feldlaufer & Eccles, 1989). Furthermore, although we did not measure the degree to which the students in our sample were mastery focused, we suspect that when students perceive that their teachers care enough to "do all they can to help us increase our understanding," this will help the students to become more mastery focused themselves.

It is interesting that students did not expect to learn more (and learn more that is useful) when they were given frequent hands-on opportunities to experiment. We suspect that students may not fully realize what they are learning as they design, conduct, and interpret experiments. Not only are they learning the answer to a narrow research question (e.g., What does acid rain do to plants?), but they are also learning the scientific method, to recognize and weigh alternative explanations of events, and "to deal sensibly with problems that involve evidence, numbers, patterns, logical arguments and uncertainties" (Project 2061 of the American Association for the Advancement of Science, 1993, p. xi). On the other hand, it is also possible that some of the experiments students designed, conducted, or interpreted were engaging but involved only trivial intellectual work that did not stretch students' understanding. "Without clear academic goals and an understanding of how to reach them, efforts to provide engaging and interesting activities are simply form without substance.... Quality education is not simply about having students busy and happy in the classroom. It's about having them engaged in work that has intellectual teeth" (Berns, et al., 2000, p. 16).

Answers to Additional Key Questions about the Results

Were There Motivational Declines during the Middle Grades?

In some samples, students show systematic declines across the middle grades in their perceptions of the intrinsic and utility value of the tasks they are given in school and also report declines in expectancies, pedagogical caring, and effort (see Mac Iver & Plank, 1996; Wigfield & Eccles, 2000). In this sample, the typical student did not show significant declines in intrinsic value, utility value, pedagogical caring, or expectancy for learning in science during the 1-year period of our study. However, the typical student did display a significant decline in self-reported effort (average change = -0.22, $p < 0.02$). The magnitude of this decline in effort did not vary significantly by grade level [chi-square (1) = 0.13, $p > 0.5$]. Overall, grade level of student was not predictive of change in student outcomes, and there were no significant grade level x instructional practice interactions in predicting change in the outcomes we studied.

How Important Was Prior Motivation as a Predictor of Current Motivation?

Students' scores on a motivational outcome during the prior spring constituted an important predictor of students' current score on that outcome ($p < 0.001$ in every model). The relation between prior motivation and current motivation was strongest for the measures of intrinsic value (standardized $\gamma = 0.37$, $p < 0.001$), utility value (standardized $\gamma = 0.36$, $p < 0.001$), and effort (standardized $\gamma = .34$, $p < 0.001$) and weakest for measures of expectancy for learning (standardized $\gamma = 0.17$, p < 0.001) and pedagogical caring (standardized $\gamma = 0.23$, $p < 0.001$). The relation between prior motivation and current motivation was just as strong in classrooms where active meaning-oriented instructional practices were used frequently as in classrooms where they were used infrequently.

Were There Sex Differences?

We followed up our main analyses with additional analyses to test for sex differences in students' motivational outcomes in science and to examine whether the motivational benefits of active, meaning-oriented instructional practices were similar for boys and girls. Boys and girls did not differ in their ratings of effort, utility value, intrinsic value, or pedagogical caring. However, girls were much more likely than boys to believe that if they worked hard in their science class, they would learn a lot (effect size $= 0.43$, $p = 0.04$). Finally, across all instructional practices considered in the field study, the motivational benefits of the instructional practices were not significantly different for boys and girls.

Why Are the Results of the Field Study Important?

The results provide an evidentiary base—to supplement the existing rhetorical base—supporting the use of active, meaning-oriented instruction in science. All science teachers want their students to find science class engaging and educationally valuable. All science teachers want their students to perceive them as caring and dedicated. The results help inform teachers about the kinds of science instruction that may promote these valued outcomes.

ACTIVE, MEANING-ORIENTED INSTRUCTIONAL PRACTICES IN OTHER SUBJECTS

Although other subject areas are organized differently than science and use somewhat different methods of inquiry and analysis, science education reformers are not the only ones calling for more use of active, meaning-oriented instructional practices. In fact, the value of practices such as these is currently being touted in each of the major subject areas.

One major thrust of current reforms in history education is to move away from traditional poorly written history textbooks that cover so many facts, dates, names, and events so trivially that the material is not intelligible (Tyson, 1999). Reformers are encouraging the use instead of narrative texts that tell history through meaningful stories (the memorable and compelling true tales of people and societies from the past), primary sources (Kohler, 1999), and hands-on and minds-on instructional approaches (Garriott, 1999). The aim is for students to begin to understand the problematic nature of historical interpretation and analysis, to develop "an interpretative acumen that extends beyond 'locate information in the text' skills" (Wineburg, 1996, p. 433), and to appreciate the relevance of history for their everyday lives (Bransford, Brown, & Cocking, 1999).

Similarly, mathematics education reformers are criticizing traditional math classrooms in the United States where students learn terms and practice procedures, where teachers fail to elaborate content with explanations, demonstrations, or examples; where little attention is paid to lesson coherence (Stigler & Hiebert, 1999), and where students are given a large number of arbitrary contextless number problems and "let's pretend" word problems that are not related to each other (Becker, 1993). In contrast, teaching for understanding in mathematics involves developing students' number sense and conceptual understanding. It involves expanding the concept of basic skills to include explicit instruction and practice in estimation, mental math, and in the use of calculators, spreadsheets, and other tools for doing mathematics. It involves giving students hands-on opportunities to use tangible objects to explore number concepts and to apply mathematics to meaningful everyday problems arising from students' interests, real-world data, and measurements that students make. It involves students being given minds-on opportunities to pose problems, to explain their reasoning, and to respond to the reasoning of others as they attempt draw conclusions, to write about mathematics, and to address problems using multiple approaches (Becker, 1993; Bransford, Brown, & Cocking, 1999; National Council of Teachers of Mathematics, 1989; Willis, 1999, Zucker, 1995).

Current reform efforts in English language arts (e.g., Adelman, 1995; Ciardi, Kantrov, & Goldsmith, 2000; Plank & Young, 2000; National Council of Teachers of English and International Reading Association, 1995; Needels, 1995) aim reading instruction at deeper understanding of a wide range of fiction and nonfiction literature from many cultures, periods, and genres and focus writing instruction on meaningful communication with real audiences. These reformers urge the use of minds-on instructional techniques designed to enable students to apply reading strategies and operations while engaged in the reading process, strengthen cognitive elaboration and comprehension skills, and enable students to acquire and benefit from knowledge of the author's craft. These reformers also recommend hands-on opportunities with authentic texts (e.g., reading to obtain guidance in performing a real-world task) and "gateway activities" that provide students with experiences they would otherwise have to *imagine* in order to respond to a writing assignment, and that help them think in ways that will lead them to approach a particular writing task or a particular audience more effectively (e.g., Hillocks, 1995; Jones, 2000).

The jury is still out on whether active, meaning-oriented instructional practices will ever become the norm most days in most subjects in U.S. classrooms and whether these practices will produce consistent motivational benefits and increased achievement for all types of students. Recent evidence, though limited, certainly suggests that these minds-on, understanding-focused instructional practices have both motivational (e.g., Ginsburg-Block & Fantuzzo, 1998; Mac Iver & Plank, 1996; Shields, 1995) and achievement benefits (e.g., Plank & Young, 2000; Mac Iver, Balfanz, & Plank, 1997; Stigler & Hiebert, 1999; Knapp, Marder, Adelman, & Needels, 1995) even in high-poverty classrooms. In our opinion, it is important to follow up these promising findings with detailed practical research that helps us understand more fully the strengths and limits of such approaches and also types of materials, professional development, and in-classroom assistance that the typical teacher may need in order to use these approaches effectively.

Acknowledgment

This research was supported by grant(s) from the Office of Educational Research and Improvement, U.S. Department of Education. The content or opinions expressed herein do not necessarily reflect the views of the Department of Education or any other agency of the U.S. Government.

References

Adelman, N. E. (1995). Aiming reading instruction at deeper understanding. In M. S. Knapp and Associates, *Teaching for meaning in high-poverty classrooms* (pp. 64–83). New York: Teachers College Press.

Ames, N. (1998). *Middle grades curriculum, instruction and assessment.* Newton, MA: Education Development Center.

Ames, N. L., & Miller, E. (1994). *Changing middle schools: How to make schools work for young adolescents.* San Francisco: Jossey-Bass.

Anderman, E. M., Maehr, M. L., & Midgley, C. (1999). Declining motivation after the transition to middle school: Schools can make a difference. *Journal of Research and Development in Education, 32*(3), 131–147.

Anderman, L. H., & Anderman, E. M. (1999). Social predictors of changes in students' achievement goal orientations. *Contemporary Educational Psychology, 25,* 21–37.

Arhar, J. (1997). The effects of interdisciplinary teaming on teachers and students. In J. L. Irvin (Ed.), *What current research says to the middle level practitioner.* Columbus, OH: National Middle School Association.

Arhar, J. M., & Kromrey, J. D. (1995). Interdisciplinary teaming the demographics of membership: A comparison of student belonging in high SES and low SES middle level schools. *Research in Middle Level Education, 18*(2), 71–88.

Becker, H. J. (1993). *Mathematics with meaning.* Baltimore, MD: Johns Hopkins University Center for Research on the Effective Schooling of Disadvantaged Students.

Berns, B. B., Kantrov, I., Pasquale, M., Makang, D. S., Zubrowski, B., & Goldsmith, L. T. (2000). *Guiding curriculum decisions for middle-grades science.* Newton, MA: Education Development Center.

Bransford, J. D., Brown, A. L., & Cocking, R. R. (Eds.) (1999). *How people learn: Brain, mind, experience, & school.* Washington, DC: National Academy Press.

California State Department of Education. (1987). *Caught in the middle: Educational reform for young adolescents in California public schools.* Sacramento, CA: Author.

Carnegie Council on Adolescent Development. (1989). *Turning points: Preparing American youth for the 21st century.* The report of the Task Force on Education of Young Adolescents. New York: Carnegie Corporation of New York.

Cheek, D. W. (1999). Science. In *Curriculum handbook: A resource for curriculum administrators.* Alexandria, VA: Association for Supervision and Curriculum Development.

Ciardi, M. R., Kantrov, I., & Goldsmith, L. T. (2000). *Guiding curriculum decisions for middle grades language arts.* Newton, MA: Education Development Center.

Clark, T. A., Bickel, W. E., & Lacey, R. A. (1993). *Transforming education for young adolescents: Insights for practitioners from the Lilly Endowment's Middle Grades Improvement Program, 1987–1990.* New York: Education Resources Group.

Eccles, J. S., & Midgley, C. (1989). Stage–environment fit: Developmentally appropriate class-rooms for young adolescents. In R. Ames & C. Ames (Eds.), *Research on motivation in education*: Vol. 3. *Goals and cognitions* (pp. 139–186). Orlando, FL: Academic Press.

Feldlaufer, H., Midgley, C., & Eccles, J. S. (1988). Student, teacher, and observer perceptions of the classroom environment before and after the transition to junior high school. *Journal of Early Adolescence*, 8, 133–156.

Felner, R. D., Jackson, A. W., Kasak, D., Mulhall, P., Brand, S., & Flowers, N. (1997). The impact of school reform for the middle years: Longitudinal study of a network engaged in *Turning Points*–based comprehensive school transformation. *Phi Delta Kappan*, 78, 528–532, 541–550.

Florida Department of Education. (1988). *Florida Progress in Middle Childhood Education Program* (PRIME). Tallahassee: Bureau of Elementary and Secondary Education, Florida Department of Education.

Garriott, M. (1999). Bringing history to life. *Basic Education*, 44(3), 6–10.

Ginsburg-Block, M. D., & Fantuzzo, J. W. (1998). An evaluation of the relative effectiveness of NCTM standards-based interventions for low-achieving urban elementary students. *Journal of Educational Psychology*, 90(3), 560–569.

Hamburg, D. A. (2000). Foreword. In A. W. Jackson & G. A. Davis, *Turning points 2000: Educating adolescents in the 21st century*. New York: Teachers College Press.

Harter, S., Whitesell, N. R., & Kowalski, P. (1992). Individual differences in the effects of educational transitions on young adolescents' perceptions of competence and motivational orientation. *American Educational Research Journal*, 29, 777–808.

Hillocks, G. (1995). *Teaching writing as reflective practice*. New York: Teachers College Press.

Jones, L. (2000). *Talent development writing*. Baltimore: Johns Hopkins University's Center for the Social Organization of Schools.

Knapp, M. S. (1995). The teaching challenge in high-poverty classrooms. In M. S. Knapp & Associates, *Teaching for meaning in high-poverty classroom*. (pp. 1–10) New York: Teachers College Press.

Knapp, M. S., Marder, C., Adelman, N. E., & Needels, M. C. (1995). The outcomes of teaching for meaning in high-poverty classrooms. In M. S. Knapp & Associates, *Teaching for meaning in high-poverty classrooms* (pp. 124–144). New York: Teachers College Press.

Kohler, E. (1999). Connecting students to primary sources. *Basic Education*, 44(3), 11–15.

Lewis, A. C. (1991). *Gaining ground: The highs and lows of urban middle school reform 1989-1991*. New York: Edna McConnell Clark Foundation.

Lewis, A. C. (1993). *Changing the odds: Middle school reform in progress*. New York: Edna McConnell Clark Foundation.

Louisiana Middle Grades Advisory Committee. (1989). *Turning Points for Louisiana: A blueprint for quality middle schools*. Baton Rouge: Louisiana State Department of Education.

Mac Iver, D. J., & Plank, S. B. (1996). *Creating a motivational climate conducive to Talent Development in Middle Schools: Implementation and effects of Student Team Reading*. Baltimore, MD, & Washington, DC: Center for Research on the Education of Students Placed at Risk.

Mac Iver, D. J., & Plank, S. B. (1997). Improving urban schools: Developing the talents of students placed at risk. In J. L. Irvin (Ed.), *What current research says to the middle level practitioner* (pp. 243–256). Columbus, OH: National Middle School Association.

Mac Iver, D. Mac Iver, M., Balfanz, R. Plank, S. B., & Ruby, A. (2000). Talent Development Middle Schools: Blueprint and results for a comprehensive whole-school reform model. In M. G. Sanders (Ed.), *Schooling students placed at risk: Research, policy, and practice in the education of poor and minority adolescents* (pp. 292–319). Mahwah, NJ: Lawrence Erlbaum Associates.

Mac Iver, D. J., Plank, S. B., & Balfanz, R. (1997). *Working together to become proficient readers: Early impact of the Talent Development Middle School's Student Team Literature Program* (Report No. 15). Baltimore, MD, & Washington, DC: Center for Research on the Education of Students Placed at Risk.

Mac Iver, D., Young, E., Balfanz, R., Shaw, A., Garriott, M., & Cohen, A. (2001). High-quality learning opportunities in high poverty middle schools: Moving from rhetoric to reality. In T. S. Dickinson (Ed.), *Reinventing the middle school* (pp. 155–175). New York: Routledge Falmer.

350   Douglas J. Mac Iver, Estelle M. Young, and Benjamin Washburn

Maryland Task Force on the Middle Learning Years. (1989). *What matters in the middle grades: Recommendations for Maryland middle grades education.* Baltimore: Maryland State Department of Education.

McPartland, J. M. (1987). *Balancing high quality subject-matter instruction with positive teacher–student relations in the middle grades: Effects of departmentalization, tracking, and block scheduling on learning environments* (CREMS Report No. 25). Baltimore, MD: Johns Hopkins University, Center for Research on Elementary and Middle Schools (ERIC Document Reproduction Service No. ED 291 704).

McPartland, J. M. (1990). Staffing decisions in the middle grades. *Phi Delta Kappan,* 71(6), 438–444.

McPartland, J. M. (1992). *Staffing patterns and the social organization of schools for young adolescents.* Paper presented at the fourth biennial meeting of the Society for Research on Adolescence, February, Washington, DC.

Mertens, S. B., Flowers, N., & Mulhall, P. F. (1998). *The Middle Start Initiative, Phase I: A longitudinal analysis of Michigan middle-level schools.* University of Illinois, Center for Prevention Research and Development. Champaign, IL.

Midgely, C. Feldlaufer, H., & Eccles, J. S. (1989). Student/teacher relations and attitudes toward mathematics before and after the transition to junior high school. *Child Development,* 60, 981–992.

Mizell, M. H. (1998). Foreword: Standards are all the rage. But why the excitement? In A. Wheelock, *Safe to be smart: Building a culture for standards-based reform in the Middle grades* (pp. vii–ix). Columbus, OH: National Middle School Association.

National Center for History in the Schools. (1994). *National standards for United States history: Exploring the American experience.* Los Angeles: Author

National Council of Teachers of English and the International Reading Association. (1995). *Standards for the language arts.* Urbana, IL: National Council of Teachers of English.

National Council of Teachers of Mathematics. (1989). *Curriculum and evaluation standards for school mathematics.* Reston, VA: Author.

National Research Council. (1996). *National science education standards.* Washington, DC: National Academy Press.

Needels, M.C. (1995). Focusing writing instruction on meaningful communication. In M. S. Knapp and Associates, *Teaching for meaning in high-poverty classrooms* (pp. 84–103). New York: Teachers College Press.

Pajares, F., & Valiante, G. (1999). Grade level and gender differences in the writing self-beliefs of middle school students. *Contemporary Educational Psychology,* 24, 390–405.

Plank, S. B. & Young, E. (2000). *Lessons for scaling up: Evaluations of the Talent Development Middle School's Student Team Literature program.* (Report No. 46). Baltimore, MD, & Washington, DC: Center for Research on the Education of Students Placed at Risk.

Project 2061 of the American Association for the Advancement of Science. (1993). *Benchmarks for science literacy.* New York: Oxford University Press.

Resnick, M. D., Bearman, P. S., Blum, R. W., Bauman, K. E., Harris, K. M., Jones, J., Tabor, J., Beuhring, T., Sieving, R. E., Shew, M., Ireland, M. Bearinger, L. H., & Udry, J. R. (1997). Protecting adolescents from harm: Findings from the National Longitudinal Study on Adolescent Health. *Journal of American Medical Association,* 278, 823–832.

Roeser, R. W., Midgley, C., & Urdan, T. C. (1996). Perceptions of the school psychological environment and early adolescents' psychological and behavioral functioning in school: The mediating role of goals and belonging. *Journal of Educational Psychology,* 88(3), 408–422.

Ruby, A. (1999). *An implementable curriculum approach to improving science instruction in urban Middle schools.* Presented at the annual meeting of the American Educational Research Association, April, Montreal, Canada.

Seidman, E., Allen, L., Aber, J. L., Mitchell, C., & Feinman, J. (1994). *Child Development,* 65, 507–522.

Shields, P. M. (1995). Engaging children of diverse backgrounds. In M. S. Knapp and Associates, *Teaching for meaning in high-poverty classrooms* (pp. 33–46). New York: Teachers College Press.

Simmons, R. G., & Blyth, D. A. (1987). *Moving into adolescence.* Hawthorne, NY: Aldine de Gruyter.

Stigler, J. W., & Hiebert, J. (1999). *The teaching gap: Best ideas from the world's teachers for improving education in the classroom*. New York: Free Press.

Stodolsky, S. (1998). *The subject matters: Classroom activities in math and social studies*. Chicago: University of Chicago Press.

Totten, S., Sills-Briegel, T., Barta, K., Digby, A., & Nielsen, W. (1996). *Middle level education: An annotated bibliography*. Westport, CT: Greenwood Press.

Tyson, H. (1999). Why not try a tale well told? *Basic Education*, 44(3), 3–5.

Wentzel, K. R. (1997). Student motivation in Middle school: The role of perceived pedagogical caring. *Journal of Educational Psychology*, 89(3), 411–419.

Wigfield, A., & Eccles, J. S. (2000). Expectancy–value theory of achievement motivation. *Contemporary Educational Psychology*, 25, 68–81.

Wigfield, A., Eccles, J. S., Mac Iver, D., Reuman, D. A., & Midgley, C. (1991). Transitions during early adolescence: Changes in children's self-esteem across the transition to junior high school. *Developmental Psychology*, 27, 552–565.

Willis, S. (1999). Bringing mathematics to life. In J. A. Dossey & S. S. McCrone (Eds.), *Mathematics curriculum handbook* (pp. 71–77). Alexandria, VA: Association for Supervision and Curriculum Development.

Wilson, B. L., & Corbett, H. D. (1999). *"No excuses": The eighth grade year in six Philadelphia Middle schools*. Philadelphia: Philadelphia Education Fund.

Wineburg, S. (1996). The psychology of learning and teaching history. In D. C. Berliner & R. C. Calfee (Eds.), *Handbook of educational psychology* (423–437). New York: Simon & Schuster, Macmillan.

Zucker, A.A. Emphasizing conceptual understanding and breadth of study in mathematics instruction. In M. S. Knapp & Associates, *Teaching for meaning in high-poverty classrooms* (pp. 47–63). New York: Teachers College Press.

Index